# Critical
## James
# THE TENTH INSIGHT

'A new style of novel addresses an eternal quest . . . This time, however, the quest is in search not of the Holy Grail or the Golden Fleece, but of that eternal puzzle, the meaning of life . . . Book yourself in for some spiritual insight [if] you are one of millions who feels soothed by reading literature for the heart and spirit . . .'
*Daily Express*

'Readers who have enjoyed the bestselling *Celestine Prophecy* will not be disappointed by this new and equally fascinating sequel . . . This is a book full of hope and insight which answers many of the questions we are likely to ask now and within the next few years'
*Science of Thought Review*

'*The Tenth Insight* captures not only the adventures of this life but the true spiritual essence of what we are trying to achieve. Brilliant. A must read'
Dannion Brinkley, author of *Saved by the Light* and *At Peace in the Light*

'James Redfield has the genius of inspiring people . . . *The Tenth Insight* is about compassion, forgiveness, and tenacity – *holding the vision* – and carrying it into one's life and the world'
Larry Dossey, MD, author of *Healing Words*

'James Redfield has distilled the spiritual teachings of the ages into a thrilling, fast-paced adventure . . . to help humanity'
Joan Borysenko, author of *Fire in the Soul*

# THE
# TENTH
# INSIGHT
## *Holding the Vision*

## An Experiential Guide

## James Redfield
### *and*
## Carol Adrienne

**BANTAM BOOKS**
TORONTO · NEW YORK · LONDON · SYDNEY · AUCKLAND

# THE TENTH INSIGHT: AN EXPERIENTIAL GUIDE
## A BANTAM BOOK : 0 553 50440 1

First publication in Great Britain

PRINTING HISTORY
Bantam edition published 1996

Text design by Stanley S. Drate/Folio Graphics Co. Inc.

Set in Berkeley Old Style

Bantam Books are published by Transworld Publishers Ltd,
61–63 Uxbridge Road, London W5 5SA,
in Australia by Transworld Publishers (Australia) Pty Ltd,
15–25 Helles Avenue, Moorebank, NSW 2170,
and in New Zealand by Transworld Publishers (NZ) Ltd,
3 William Pickering Drive, Albany, Auckland.

Printed and bound in Great Britain by
Cox & Wyman Ltd, Reading, Berkshire.

*We dedicate this book to all of you—Holders of the Vision.*

# THE
# TENTH
# INSIGHT
## *Holding the Vision*

## AN EXPERIENTIAL GUIDE

# Contents

*PART THREE*

# REMEMBERING

*Part Four*

# IN THE DARK

**7    REMEMBERING ONE'S BIRTH VISION**                153

**8    AN INNER HELL**                                171

## 9 OVERCOMING THE FEAR 185

*PART FIVE*

# RIGHT ACTION

## 10 TRANSFORMATION IN WORK AND BUSINESS 211

## 11    TENTH INSIGHT GROUP ACTION    242

**12** NEW VISIONS FOR OCCUPATIONAL
GROUPS                                    267

*PART SIX*

# FULL CIRCLE

**13** THE WORLD VISION                        305

**14**   HOLDING THE VISION                               323

# Acknowledgments

This book truly wrote itself with the help of many synchronistic calls at just the right moment. Thanks to all those whose ideas appear in this book! As models of new thinking and community, we especially recognize the Institute of Noetic Sciences for their research support and the Center for Ecoliteracy for many inspirations.

Individually, we would like to acknowledge the spirit and guidance of: Larry Leigon for his reflections on the shadow and the nature of changes in business; Elmer Schettler for sharing his thoughts on the path; Donna Hale, therapist and trance channel, for her help on energy dynamics and past lives; Kevin Ryerson for the initiation journey; Kathryn Leighton for all the years of support that paved the way for the current work; Sherrin Bennett, a consultant to organizations, for helping find the patterns in this book; Ann Buzenberg, editor of *The Celestine Journal,* for her generous cooperation; Dr. Henry Wesselman for his conversation about science and spirituality; Dr. Selma Lewis for in-depth explorations of psychological concepts; Paula Pagano, who provided such great field work; Penney Peirce for her generous contributions; Fadel Behmann for suggesting the work of Professor Kyriacos Markides at the perfect moment; Bonnie Colleen of KEST and David Sersta of the Toronto Learning Annex for helping broadcast transformative ideas; as well as Dr. Marilyn Rossner and Father John Rossner of Montreal; Dr. Patrick Tribble; Johnathan Katz; Gilberto Munguia; Russell E. DiCarlo; Jack Coates; and Elizabeth Kibbey (you know what you did!).

Finally, we again thank our editor, Joann Davis, for opening the way for these books to be written, as well as Harvey-Jane Kowal's work in making the manuscript into a book.

And Candice Fuhrman for everything.

# THE
# TENTH
# INSIGHT
*Holding the Vision*

## An Experiential Guide

# Introduction

This book is intended to provide background information and various complementary ideas that support the basic assumptions of the Tenth Insight. If it is true that the insights as they have been outlined in the *Celestine* books are archetypal in nature, and thus built into our psychological growth, then our mission is merely to spread the word and to facilitate in the best way we can an honest conversation about current spiritual experience.

You will see, as you read this book, that a rich and diverse dialogue on the spiritual life is already occurring in all parts of the world. The conversation itself—as it involves the courageous sharing of experience—is the process through which this awakening is taking place. Here in the last days of the twentieth century and second millennium, we aren't so much discovering new experience (although that occurs) as taking seriously experiences we once dismissed or took for granted. The key phrase, of course, is courageous sharing, for as the Tenth Insight suggests, we are at a very important point in history.

The old Newtonian worldview, based as it was on the idea that the universe is a great machine working in a materialistic way (devoid of miracle), is now evolving slowly toward a new worldview that begins to incorporate experiential proof that the world is much much more. We are beginning to see the universe as an intelligent, spiritual place where humans can grow in awareness, feel guided through intuition and magical coincidence, and remember the individual truth we were born to contribute to society.

Courage is key to this awakening because we must first believe we're going to find and repeat these experiences. If the first nine insights are about getting out of our own way and engaging in the transcendent flow in which our vibrations increase and our lives evolve forward, the Tenth is about understanding the power of sacred intention that amplifies the whole process. We have to hold the vision, engage the power of faith and visualization, which is what prayer really is. In other words, it is not enough to just "let go" to the flow of synchronicity, although that is primary. We also must wake up in the morning and intend, expect, that this synchronicity will occur.

This study guide is designed to stimulate the discussion of these and other issues. Again, we put our faith in the importance of the dialogue itself. We know within that a spiritual transformation is occurring. Yet the picture of this new worldview is only now fully emerging, coming forth as individuals and small groups arrive at their own conclusions, talk to others about what they see, gain new information, and evolve their opinions to a more accurate level. This is the grassroots spiritual conversation that is building a new consensus about reality.

And it won't be complete until it includes you.

JAMES REDFIELD

CAROL ADRIENNE

"Either we have hope within us or we don't; it is a dimension of the soul, and it's not essentially dependent on some particular observation of the world or estimate of the situation. Hope is not prognostication. It is an orientation of the spirit, an orientation of the heart; it transcends the world that is immediately experienced, and is anchored somewhere beyond its horizons . . ."

VÁCLAV HAVEL, *Disturbing the Peace*

## PART ONE

# Threshold

# CHAPTER 1

# The Big Picture

EAGLE
SPIRIT

The Tenth Insight is about understanding this whole awareness—the perception of mysterious coincidences, the growing spiritual consciousness on Earth, the Ninth Insight disappearances—all from the higher perspective of the other dimension, so that we can understand why this transformation is happening and participate more fully.

THE TENTH INSIGHT:
HOLDING THE VISION[1]

## HOLDING *OPEN* THE VISION

For beings such as Jesus Christ, Muhammad, and Gautama Buddha, the capacity for holding the World Vision is already a part of their résumé. Among the best candidates in any interview, they will almost always get the position by virtue of their experience and skills.

This book is written for the rest of us.

Not long ago in a group of people studying the Celestine Insights, a man raised his hand and asked, "I'm very concerned about how I can use this information in the real world. I've gone to other workshops and talked with people, and we're all very enthusiastic, but how can I keep that enthusiasm going in the everyday world? How do I keep that feeling going?" He continued, "I'm tired of talking about myself and want to move on to being more involved in the world. How do I do that?" This man was expressing an idea that each of us is asking. It's very likely you have said virtually the same thing to yourself. Our culture *must* ask this question if we are to open to a new worldview that will take us from where we are now to a viable future. Asking, "What can I do to serve the world in a positive way?" is important because immediate action is necessary to pull us back from the brink of disaster, but the viewpoint inherent in the question is rooted

3

at the same level that caused our problems in the first place. It's still addressing the problem in terms of an *external* action. The real action must be accomplished within each of us—not saving *them out there,* but shifting the way *we* view the world, and lifting the veil to unknown wisdom and resources in other dimensions in "outer reality" and other dimensions in our inner reality. Once we are working at this multidimensional level, we will have at once aligned ourselves with the evolutionary goal of spiritualizing our physical "real" world, and we will have entered into a more fluid process that we can hardly imagine at this point. How do we do that?

## STAGES OF CONSCIOUSNESS

The Tenth Insight, along with the other nine Insights described in *The Celestine Prophecy,* by James Redfield, is a stage of consciousness. If you read *The Celestine Prophecy,* you may have had a surprising sense that you already knew most of those Insights—that somehow you had already learned them, but maybe had forgotten them temporarily. That memory is reminding you that you *did* come into this world with a goal to help make the transition to the next step in consciousness.

At the level of the Tenth Insight, you are also able to recognize some or most of the ancient perennial philosophy that we will review in the following paragraphs. At this level of thinking/feeling/intuiting we can say, "Yes, I feel these concepts working in my life." It's as if they are living *through* you.

This awareness is causing you to make a response, like the man who asked the question above. Now what? We're used to being active, controlling our universe—or trying to—and getting results. But so far, we have been preoccupied with *doing something to the outer world,* not working on our *inner world in which consciousness is king and queen.* In order to make that shift, we have to *deconstruct* our old methods and views. That's what the paradigm shift is all about. Can we deconstruct and decondition our minds, take off our blinders and let the light in fast enough to save ourselves and our planetary habitat? That's the question that makes us wake up at three and four in the morning.

It's up to us now—ordinary people stretching into our future. We can do some of the work by choosing to make changes or to love more. However much we are learning and growing and changing our view of what's possible, we also are being worked on by outer forces. Some of the outside forces that we are already aware of are the ecological disasters that are fueling our fears. These situations are forcing us to pay attention to the consequences of every action we take.

The other forces that are influencing our thinking, collectively and individually, may turn out to be beings in the spiritual dimension who have been watching our progress and who have reached a level of concern for our well-being. Sound ominous? Not really. The spiritual dimension that exists beyond the realm of our five senses is appearing to us individually and collectively to wake us up out of the addiction to complacency, fear, denial, and greed that is keeping us trapped in psychospiritual dysfunction. These other dimensions *want* Earth to flourish as the wonderful, incredibly rich source of love, life, and learning that it has always been. Until now most of us have been unaware of that invisible boundary between these planes of existence. At this point in evolution, with the survival of the planet and all her species at stake, it's time for the veil to be removed. It's time to bring in the cavalry. But let's not get ahead of our story.

## No Rx Except the Process

Most of us in the Western world want a map, a set of instructions, and a money-back guarantee on our life's journey. As we understand that life is an unfolding process, we come to see that there is no prescription for success beyond paying close attention to the pattern of energies that infuses and informs us. The igniting energy of our spirit lights the path, and *we do get help from our friends*. If there is any

> . . . our lives are centered on prayer and action. Our work is an outflow of our contemplation, our union with God in whatever we do, and through our work . . . we feed our union with God so that prayer and action and action and prayer are in continual flow. **Lucinda Vardey, Mother Teresa: A Simple Path**

formula, it is to recognize that desire and will are the focusing mechanisms of intention. Faith, or quiet listening for which doors are going to open, is imperative on this path. Trust is the *confident expectation* that our intentions and desires will be answered. With the law of giving and receiving, we give service and receive an inflow of energy.

In the language of the Insights, we "ask questions and follow our intuition." Even simpler, we could say that our lives follow the flow of our thoughts.

## WHAT IF?

What if someone were to tell you that you were already "on purpose"? That you were already immersed in a continuum of conscious energy that was unfolding purposefully? What if you *knew,* without doubt, that you were not alone—not metaphorically, but literally? What if you knew that there were no accidents and that important pieces of information were available all around you that you might or might not be recognizing? How would you live your life if you knew that you would not cease to exist when your present body slipped away from you at death?

How would you feel if you had discovered through an undeniable personal experience that humans are only one level of consciousness in a multilayered universe of intelligent, conscious beings? Terrified? Humbled? Excited? Deeply connected to a source that you had forgotten was there? People who have had near-death experiences and contacts with deceased loved ones, angelic presences, saints, and beings that seem to be extraterrestrial report all of the above feelings.

The Tenth Insight is the level of awareness that we are not alone; nor are we the center of the universe. It is the level of awareness at which we know, "I came here to do something. I'm remembering now. I have a purpose." The purpose might be elusive to you, like a memory sitting on the tip of your tongue. But at this level of understanding, this vague memory is enough to ignite synchronistic events that move you to meet the next person, get the next message.

Perhaps you may not have yet had an extraordinary experience with the spiritual realm or felt any contact with your soul group. Perhaps you have not had a child rescued in midair as she tumbled over a Grand Canyon cliff, sliding down the face to certain death. Joan Wester Anderson, author of two books on angelic presences and miracles, reported the experience of a mother whose daughter had gone camping with friends. One evening she had a premonition that her daughter was in trouble, and heard herself saying, "Dear God, send help now!" When the girl returned home, the story came out that she had fallen off a cliff and was momentarily stopped on a ledge *smaller than her foot* when she felt arms come around her and pull her to the top of the cliff. Maybe you have read about near-death experiences where a person entered a tunnel of light and saw radiant beings and felt such incredible love that she wanted to stay and leave her Earthly life behind.

Even though you have not had these extradimensional contacts yourself, you are surrounded by hundreds of thousands, if not millions, of fellow humans who have had just such encounters with other planes of existence. That means, because you are a part of what biologist Rupert Sheldrake calls the morphogenetic field, *you are part of the process.*

The time has come to hone our skills for paying attention to the mind-boggling information that is flooding in at this time. It's appropriate that our minds be boggled. Why? Because "mind boggling" is the process of deconstructing what we thought was rock-solid reality. The time has come to make every effort to open up to what this information might mean for the survival and evolution of the human race.

Contemporary theorists such as British physicist David Bohm, who has worked extensively with the implications of Bell's theorem, have had to suppose that there is an "invisible field" that holds all of reality together, a field that possesses the property of knowing what is happening everywhere at once . . . the invisible field sounds very much like the underlying intelligence in DNA, and both behave very much like the mind. The mind has the property of holding all our ideas in place, in a silent reservoir so to speak, where they are precisely organized into concepts and categories. **Deepak Chopra, M.D.,** *Quantum Healing: Exploring the Frontiers of Mind/Body Medicine*

We are the bridge-builders between the old way of thinking with the Fifth, Ninth, and Tenth Insights—which include changes in both the way we see ourselves and deal with others and the way we communicate with the *other dimensions.* The answers we seek to everyday questions are not separate from the search for explanations for events that defy our rational mind. The healing that we need to do for the planet depends on our ability to open up to the realities of the Afterlife or spiritual planes of existence that are already in communication with us *and to understand that these dimensions are interrelated to our own consciousness.* Therefore, the everyday questions about how to live your own life, how to serve the planet, will come out of our attendance to the messages we pick up from our intuition and from coincidences that lead us to new thinking.

You may think this sounds much too impractical and weird! However, you don't have to read on. Throw the book in your Goodwill bag or give it to somebody you think is weird, too. But if you stay with us, we will attempt to take you through an imaginal process that uses simple human stories, which we hope will trigger thoughts and feelings and intuitions within you that make sense. Actually, we are in this process of discovery together, and the Tenth Insight reminds us that from now on, we must work in concert with others to build up our group intelligence/intuition to move the caterpillar of humanity out to the branch where it can turn into a butterfly.

Keep putting your sensitive intuitive feelers out as you encounter teachers, books, and synchronicities that are relevant to where you are in your life. Keep listening at the keyhole of the spiritual dimension with

---

Evolution's pattern is that every development be incorporated into the service of a higher function. . . . The neocortex [of the brain] is so powerful that only a little of it is needed to modulate or change the lower, and the issue is what is the other hypothetical 90 percent for? . . . Nature's agenda for us after adolescence is to discover and become one with process, which pursuit will activate and incorporate the rest of our neural structures, bring us in balance, and lead us where evolution intends. Dr. B. Ramamurthi, president of the International Congress of Neurosurgery, proposes that our unutilized portion of brain is designed for exploration of an "interior universe." **Joseph Chilton Pearce, *Evolution's End***

---

all your heart and mind. Remember, this is not going to be a linear path anymore, and you may just have to let go and experience something impossible before you crack the door to your next level. We certainly encourage you to be discriminating about the information you receive. However, don't get stuck on trying to prove anything to anybody or demanding a "scientific" proof. This part of the human journey doesn't work through the old "laws." Your goal is not to get stuck on the black and white argument of "real or not real" (as opposed to "truth," which always feels somehow *true*), but to ask yourself, Does this happening or idea move me ahead to be more loving, more energized, more generous and open to life? That's the truth behind your experience. Don't give up your mind, but give up your mind-set. This is not a sentimental journey, but it is about love—only love.

## IT's HAPPENING NOW

This book has come into being by exactly the same principles that it is describing. A torrent of synchronicities with unbelievable timing has allowed many people to "write" this book. During the writing of each chapter, inevitably someone would call with a piece of information that fit perfectly into the topic of the chapter. We also found that people on this path are mysteriously connected! For example, one day we interviewed by telephone two people—Cindy Spring about Wisdom Circles and Richard Miles about new health paradigms, having received their names from two completely different referrals. Later that week, we found out that they lived next door to each other in Oakland, California, and each had mentioned their interview to the other!

Information is everywhere. Carol Adrienne gave two talks in Montreal at the Conference for the Restoration of the Heaven and Earth Connection—the same topic as the Tenth Insight, incidentally, which was not known at the time she was asked to speak. During the conference, cospeaker Dr. Myrin Borysenko mentioned two research items that Carol had been looking for in California before she left for the conference. During lunch, in a casual conversation at the conference, Kevin Ryerson, the well-known expert intuitive, provided the material about sacred sites which we will cover in Chapter 3. Carol also made a new friend there who a week later sent her a copy of an article about Kyriacos C. Markides, which prompted her to buy his book *Riding with the Lion* (a must read for all of you). The thesis of Professor Markides' book is startlingly similar to the Tenth Insight. His description of Eastern Orthodox mystical experience is an excellent and exciting resource that takes us right into the heart of the mystery, as well as reminding us of the crucial contributions ascetics make toward holding the World Vision.

In another fruitful serendipitous encounter that seemed meant to be, Carol met Elizabeth Jenkins, founder of the Wiraqocha Foundation for the Preservation of Indigenous Wisdom. During a conversation about the similarities of how they got into the work they are doing, Elizabeth was inspired to tell Carol about a book she had read that elaborated on the idea of world servers and soul groups. In addition, her expertise brought forward the Peruvian prophecies of the Q'ero Indians of Peru, who still practice the traditions of the ancient Incas. The Andean tradition, like another piece of a giant puzzle suddenly locking together, has also predicted a shift in dimensions from the third to the fourth level of consciousness at this precise period.

Coincidences are happening more frequently now to those who have become more aware of them or who are probing for meaning. In every workshop we give, we ask, "How many people have experienced an increase in synchronicities?" and 80 percent or more of the hands go up. When we share experiences with other receptive people, we start to feel, "Hey, maybe I *am* part of the critical mass of energy consciousness described in the First Insight."

Our point here is that the "Celestine" process and the principles are not theoretical. When you become aware of the principles and trust the process of how they work in your own life, something amazing happens. And they *are* working in *your* life. Our purpose here is to talk to you about what to look for. We want to encourage you to open up to this mysterious journey and let it work through you.


## COHORTS AND COINCIDENCES

There is a worldwide community of people who are working in quiet ways for global unity and serving the planetary plan—a plan that none of us will be able to completely imagine. These people instinctively recognize one another in the course of everyday activities—on airplanes, playing fields, in bookstores and cafés, at lectures, musical events, dinner parties, rallies, workshops; even at the dentist's, hairdresser's, acupuncturist's, or the office party. We've all had this kind of experience. There is a kind of spark, an electrical energy, when you touch upon a subject close to your heart, and the other person seems to sense your vision. Suddenly there's a rapport and a willingness to open up with some of your goals, and a sharing of ideas and an intuition that this person may be going in a direction similar to yours. Does this seem to be increasing in your life?

No matter where you are in the world, you will recognize another one of your group. The conversation will seem almost effortless, as if the other had just been thinking about similar issues moments before—as if your conversation had started months ago and had just resumed. You will be able to advise each other, almost immediately, even if your fields are completely different. You may suggest books, articles, or new methods that may help each other in what you are trying to accomplish. You will leave each other energized and excited about the connection you have established. Knowing that another person, maybe a complete stranger, understands your vision and resonates to your ideas will fill you with hope and strength for days or weeks to come.

## ANOTHER PIECE OF THE PUZZLE

Have more fun and adventure in the world? Make an impact? Count me in. But many of us do not have a very clear picture of what to do beyond perhaps winning the lottery or "helping others" or "working for peace." In addition, we may feel that our jobs don't come close to being the meaningful activity we crave, and we feel confused about what else to try.

Many of us already believe that nothing happens by accident. By the same token, we may also feel that we don't understand the synchronicities that occur to us or know how to keep them coming. This is the state of mind of the character in *The Tenth Insight* when he begins to search for his old friend Charlene. He begins to realize that there is another piece of the puzzle, the Tenth Insight, that helps us live the rest of the nine Insights for the long term.

## PITFALLS—FEELING OVERWHELMED

The world is changing at warp speed. Changes that used to take thousands of years now take place in decades or less. This acceleration, which is happening at all levels, in all cultures, and in all disciplines, is causing great shifts, innovations, symptoms, and responses. As systems fall in and out of organization, our human response ranges from excitement and enthusiasm to fear and despair. Jolted by news reports or personal experiences of environmental and social problems, we think about taking some action.

> First, starting at around age eleven, an idealistic image of life grows in intensity throughout the middle teens. Second, somewhere around age fourteen or fifteen a great expectation arises that "something tremendous is supposed to happen." Third, adolescents sense a secret, unique greatness in themselves that seeks expression. They gesture toward the heart when trying to express any of this, a significant clue to the whole affair . . . a need within them for a model of new horizons, a need pushing them like the will that appears in the toddler. **Joseph Chilton Pearce, *Evolution's End***

More often than not, we do nothing. As the pace quickens, we scramble to adjust, worrying that we won't keep up or that our future is out of our control. Overwhelmed by our current pace, our jobs and other responsibilities, we can only hope that "someone" will do something. Obstacles to taking action—such as time, finances, family duties—may also function as *justifications* for staying in our ruts. The real root of paralysis may be despair—hopelessness in the face of the sheer enormity of the task.

## POLARIZATION OF THINKING—TAKING FIXED POSITIONS OR STAYING OPEN

Depending on what's happened to you this week, you probably will have either a pessimistic view or an optimistic view about the future. The pessimistic view is that the world is going downhill fast and that economically, politically, and ecologically we are in great peril with no hope to reverse this path in the near future.

The optimistic view is that the world is in great transition, but that humanity, using common sense and intuitive guidance, has a good chance of coming up with new solutions to seemingly intractable problems. Individually, we may fluctuate between these two views of the future of the world. One day we feel lost, uncertain, afraid, and despairing of making any difference in conditions that seem beyond our control. And then another day, we suddenly have hope again, and feel inspired, passionate, fearless, generous, compassionate, and committed to the spiritual path. These conflicting attitudes and energy states may very well arise from the collective mind as it oscillates between poles, as the transition to a new worldview takes place.

The polarization between optimism and pessimism creates a crossroads—which means that humanity is at a point of choice. When one has choice, one has power.

## CHOOSING BASED ON FEAR OR LOVE

Sometimes we have to fall apart before we come back together. And because this falling apart feels scary, Fear can cloud our perspective. We can find every rationale for why the culture is out of control and going downhill fast, and defend that position to ourselves and each other. The Fear becomes the block (and justification for inaction) that tells us: "What's the point? There's nothing I can do."

Taking a bigger view of our situation shows that we are at the extreme pole of materialistic thinking and living. Western culture *has* been going down the road of intense materialism.

Maybe . . . that was within the range of the world plan.

Ultra-materialism is now catalyzing us, forcing us, to look for spiritual balance. If we can see the purposeful process behind our situation, perhaps we can let go of some of the Fear and get in touch with our original vision.

According to sociologist Paul H. Ray, "Our greatest error could be to take seriously the pessimistic temper of our times, and to give in to the fear and cynicism that pervade the media. For then we will come to believe something truly catastrophic: 'Things are bad and getting worse, and nothing can be done about it.' "[2]

The crucial part of the Tenth Insight is to understand that if thought creates reality, then we must keep our intention focused on the positive outcome that we desire to happen.

## THE GOOD NEWS

We are not alone. According to a new survey by Paul H. Ray, there are 44 million Americans whom he dubs "Cultural Creatives" whose core values and preferences are helping shape a new worldview. Ray describes three current predominant American cultures as:[3]

- *Traditionalists*—29 percent of the population, or 56 million people, who would like to see a return to the small-town, religious lifestyle of an earlier America.
- *Modernists*—47 percent of the population, or 88 million people, with roots in "the urban merchant classes, the modern state and armies, scientists, technologists, and intellectuals." Within this group conservatives "tend to idealize the 1920s or 1950s lifestyle, while liberal-to-moderates tend to idealize 1950s and 1960s philosophies, and are more open to new ideas."[4]
- *Cultural Creatives*—24 percent of the population, or 44 million people, who have affinities with humanistic and transpersonal psychology, the ecology movement, and the women's movement. Ray's research reveals that about 20 million, or 10.6 percent, of this transmodernist population are seriously concerned with spiritual life and self-actualization, and ecological sustainability. This segment is primarily upper-middle-class, and women outnumber men by 67 percent to 33 percent. The other 24 million, or 13 percent, tend to be middle-class, and are very interested in the environment and social concerns from a secular view, having only an average interest in spirituality and personal development. This new integral culture is spread fairly evenly throughout all regions of the country.

Empirical evidence from studies such as Ray's plus other commentators on the transformation of consciousness seems to show an emerging desire by many people to incorporate the personal and spiritual into the social and political. A Maclean's/CBS News poll in 1995 revealed that 82 percent of Canadians consider themselves to be "somewhat or very spiritual." Even more interesting is that almost half of those polled said that their lives had become more spiritual in the past few years. People are reading books about indigenous and esoteric spiritual traditions, forming study groups, and practicing ancient rituals. The mystery of life beckons. We are beginning to *remember* that we came to Earth *by choice to accomplish something.* We are noticing more than ever that seeming coincidences have a deeper meaning and are leading us forward purposefully.

## SYNERGY

Books and teachers are important support systems. Even more compelling is firsthand experience. How is energy flowing in your life? Are power struggles indicating a need to grow? At the level of the Seventh, Eighth, Ninth, and Tenth Insights, you are intuitively moving into alignment with others, through your attractions to certain people who seem to be on your wavelength.

Many of us are also experiencing contact with the *spiritual dimension*—although we may not talk about this to others. We recognize the daily inspirations and intuitions that lead us forward.

### EACH INDIVIDUAL IS A FLOW-THROUGH POINT FOR THE
### EVOLUTIONARY PROCESS

We are the hands, heart, and mind of the evolutionary process. As stewards of the life force energy, it's necessary to be able to hold the original intention of how we wanted our life to go and how we wanted to contribute to the world. Many of us have forgotten that we were born with dreams. When we are "in the void" and nothing seems to be *happening,* we need to remember that plateaus are necessary for integration, reflection, and refinement of our vision.

The Tenth Insight begins by suggesting that we strengthen our faith in a purposeful universe by visualization. But visualize what? Life continually presents a choice of where to place our attention and intention. How do we choose? As energy flows through us, we are attracted to different people and situations. How do we stay on track? Intuitions pop into our mind, a synchronicity opens up a new direction, or we receive the grace of unexpected gifts. What do we do with what we receive?

There is no one recipe, no one answer. However, there are questions. Ask yourself, What do I want to do? What is preventing me from doing that? Remember to set your intention to achieve your ideal and then look for the clues that the universe gives you. If you are busy telling yourself, "This doesn't work for me"; "Life is dumb and boring," you are not helping the universe deliver your goods! Our beliefs are the story we tell ourselves inside, and that story winds up on the front pages on the newsstand of our life.

WHAT'S THE STORY?

Holding the worldview becomes an abstract idea unless we connect meaningfully to everyday life. If we just focus on the *literal* events of the world, we miss the deeper messages. Get into the habit of looking for the lesson, the larger commentary, in the world. For example, if you are bothered by the garbage sticking to the fence around the vacant lot next to your house, what is not happening in your neighborhood? What is happening? What's the bigger picture? To find meaning in everyday activities, we weave together the ordinary world with the deeper, hidden, symbolic world.

Whether it is one child's poem, a mythic epic, or a police report about a murder, it is by story that we come to find our place in the world. Stories illuminate the spiritual principles by which humankind lives and evolves. We encourage you, therefore, to enter into this field of knowing with us. Let this book be a bridge between everyday and the World Vision. You can do this by bringing your own attention, questioning, and perceptions to the stories in this book. Begin to *perceive* stories in your own life and in the lives of those you meet along your path. The stories and concepts contained here are meant to stimulate your own *remembering* of the truth of what it means to be in earthly life. If we are truly *present* in our world, we must respond. When we respond, we are no longer paralyzed — we

> Every action or even thought sets up feedback between our action and the fields from which we draw our experience. . . . Enough participation by enough people over enough time can stabilize any field effect by shifting it from personal to social to species-wide and finally universal—from our physical-subtle interactions into subtle-causal structures, but this takes a tremendous amount of parallel or similar effort on a wide social level. **Joseph Chilton Pearce, *Evolution's End***

can see choices. We can take responsibility. Then we make a difference.

Your journey, the story of your life, is yours to write. In that writing, you are also creating a piece of the world's story.

Elmer Schettler, a soybean farmer who lives in Iowa, describes the new attitude that is developing in his life: "I've always been a type A kind of person. In the last couple of years, though, I've been getting more and more in touch with my spiritual side. I'm really beginning to see the world as mysterious and interesting, rather than just a place to try to make things happen." Elmer's view reflects a shift from efforting to noticing what wants to happen. He says, "To me life is about an unfolding, not about working harder. I'm releasing that old Puritan ethic. I want to be more interactive with the universe and let it tell me what it has in store for me.

"I have to remind myself on days when things may not be coming out like I want them to, when I feel frustrated with people who I'm relying on and they aren't doing their job—I ask myself, Why do I feel I have to solve this? What am I working for in the long run? What is the real meaning of what's happening? Then I do some breathing, relaxing for a moment, and reconnect with my inner center. It lets me step back for a minute. I remind myself that I don't want to get into just working harder, or feeling that I have to know all the answers. I remind myself that my life is unfolding. I look for something to enjoy—a sunset, clouds, a picture of my family, and I nourish that part of myself.

"Sometimes when I need help with a specific problem, I'll write it down, put it in my pocket, and let go of it. I look for little things during the day to validate that I'm on the right track. Like the other day at the gym, I had wanted to make a quick list of things to do. I had a piece of paper, but no

Because you are searching, your path is changing.

pen. I looked over at the treadmill and someone had left a pen there. Just a little thing like that, but it made me happy."

## FEAR ARISES FROM FEELING SEPARATE AND POWERLESS

In the West, most of us have been brought up to see the world as circumstances that exist "out there" happening to us randomly. For example, we see problems in terms of categories—unemployment, crime, pollution, war. We believe that we are completely at the effect of these facts, and without a vision we feel separate and powerless. In order to try to *feel* in control again, either we ignore and deny that problems exist, or we take sides as if we could stop these events by being of the "right" opinion. In order to feel energy coming from like-minded people, and to simplify something that looks chaotic, we adopt a polarized position. Politically, we might say we are liberal or conservative, feeling strongly that the truth lies in *one position*.

In our effort to control our own fear, our tendency is to make someone or something the enemy and put blame there. Stereotyping all prostitutes, all delinquent teenagers, all politicians, has a dehumanizing effect. Once we have dehumanized someone, there is little ground for seeing them as a soul, perhaps in pain, who needs help and love. In politics, this behavior is used to "demonize" issues, taking a central theme as the problem and casting oneself or one's party as the savior.

The root beliefs in this behavior are that the world is a battlefield, life is something to be edited, controlled, and seized, and that someone else will get what we deserve unless we fight for it. What if we spent a Sunday afternoon in a circle of people who were totally outside our normal circle? What if we just talked to each other and listened to the stories of what life was like for each of us?

As sociologist Fred Polak showed in his study of 1,500 years of European history, *The Image of the Future*, if a whole culture holds a very pessimistic image of the future, that image will be a self-fulfilling prophecy. The actual predictions about decline don't have to be right or to come true: The pathological behaviors released may be quite sufficient to bring about decline. It's a disease of belief. And the contrary is also true. When a culture holds positive images of the future, they may not be right, but investment in new opportunities, and willingness to build a good society, are sufficient to make a decent way of life, if not the best of all worlds. **Paul H. Ray,** *The Rise of the Integral Culture*

As our children grow into their future, we will need to teach them about intuition—that they have an inside place that they can trust to make decisions. (Of course, they might be teaching *us* by that time.) We could talk with them about control dramas and let the whole family begin to grow and notice the habits into which they have fallen.

According to psychologist Walter Mischel, who conducted research during the 1960s at a preschool at Stanford University, the ability for delayed gratification is one of the most telling tests for how well a child will achieve as an adult. Daniel Goleman, author of *Emotional Intelligence: Why It Can Matter More Than IQ,* believes that "these are times when the fabric of society seems to unravel at ever-greater speed, when selfishness, violence, and meanness of spirit seem to be rotting the goodness of our communal lives. The ability to control impulse is the base of will and character. By the same token, the root of altruism lies in empathy, the ability to read emotions in others; lacking a sense of another's need or despair, there is no caring. And if there are any two moral stances that our times call for, they are precisely these, self-restraint and compassion."[5] In the next decades, the development of impulse control, compassion, sensitivity, personal responsibility, and spiritual connection will be more important than all the technological advances we have made so far. Without them we stand to be at the mercy of our technology. We have already put automatic weapons in the hands of children.

## ON THE THRESHOLD

Imagine for a moment that you were being "briefed" by loving mentors and wise guides before your descent into the body—your birth. We might imagine the conversation going something like this: "Well, if you're ready to go into a body again, do you see any parents down there that will expose you to the lesson you want to work on?

"Once you're down there in your body, don't forget to pay attention to signposts! You won't be given more than you can deal with, and if any of you want extra duty, just say so now! Remember, you'll need to learn to build as much loving energy around you as possible and stay plugged into the spiritual source. There will be times when you feel lost and in pain, but remember to ask for help, and listen carefully to your inner knowing. You'll have whatever you need to keep waking you up to your spiritual nature, so that you can bring that spirit into everything you do. Remember, you'll be meeting lots of other people who are on the path, and just for the fun of it, they'll look very different from what you expect, but they will give you a chance to show how much love you can bring through. It's going to be rough going every now and then, but you will not be alone. Keep in touch. Write when you can. If you need anything, just ask! Bye for now. Oh, and don't forget. You'll be responsible for every action, no matter how small. You'll understand more when you come back here."

## THE WORLD VISION

You may find that you already resonate with much of what you have read in *The Celestine Prophecy; The Celestine Prophecy: An Experiential Guide;* and *The Tenth Insight.* That's because the emerging worldview shares many common themes with what philosopher and author Aldous Huxley called the "perennial philosophy." Over the past five thousand years or so, in both Eastern and Western philosophy, certain core truths continue to light the way.

The World Vision, built on these essential principles, is *within us.* A version of the World Vision also exists in each culture's beliefs about what's possible. The Vision becomes a reality depending on how we choose to live our lives. Not an *external* goal to be achieved somewhere in the future, it's a defining and informing force which is real to us through the values we feel inside. The World Vision is "what matters" to us. It is not a *rule,* or one behavior, or one recipe for a certain outcome, with definable political, economic, or cultural results. The World Vision might be better thought of as a *process* that *yields* peaceful coexistence, balance, and bounty, and that honors and cherishes the differences in species, peoples, cultures, languages, religions, and philosophies.

Take Heart! Unknown to most of us, we're traveling in the midst of an enormous company of allies: a larger population of creative people, who are the carriers of more positive ideas, values, and trends than any previous renaissance period has ever seen. And they can probably be mobilized to act altruistically on behalf of our future. **Paul H. Ray, *The Rise of the Integral Culture***

Below are key points in the perennial wisdom that has shaped, and continues to shape, our evolutionary path.

### I. *Consciousness is causal.*

The field of energy in which we live and from which we create with our intention is consciousness. It is both the creator and the uncreated, or as Deepak Chopra calls it, the field of pure potentiality. *Your attitudes create the worldview.* Imagine yourself as the drop in the bucket—a very big bucket. As you go inside to connect with your hunches (spiritual direction), your conscious thoughts ripple out. Your being begins to catalyze changes in your family, friends, neighbors, and coworkers. The ripples begin to drift toward your political representatives, building and combining with many other ripples that wash in the direction of those who have world leadership. *Once a critical mass of human consciousness grasps the vision of this wholeness, this larger World Vision, the Vision naturally unfolds.*

## 2. *We are immersed in a field of energy. We swim in God.*

We are made of the same divine creative energy as God. Religions call this spiritual energy our enduring Christ or Buddha nature. The material world springs forth from this sea of energy through our collective beliefs and thoughts. Throughout the ages, teachers have taught that we are interdependent with all life and that each form has an important role to play in making everything work. Founded upon patterns and relationships, the principles of the ancient philosophy form a great vessel of God's plan for the universe.

> I believe deeply that we must find, all of us together, a new spirituality. This new concept ought to be elaborated alongside the religions, in such a way that all people of goodwill could adhere to it. We need a new concept, a lay spirituality. We ought to promote this concept with the help of scientists. It could lead us to set up what we are all looking for—a secular morality.
> **The Dalai Lama in *Violence and Compassion: Conversations with the Dalai Lama*, by Jean-Claude Carrière**

## 3. *The universe is purposeful.*

Almost nothing happens by chance. One woman who was questioning whether she should pursue her avocation of writing described in *The Celestine Journal* a major turning point that she felt was assisted by divine forces. She had read Ray Bradbury's *Zen in the Art of Writing: Releasing the Creative Genius Within You.* "It so moved me that I wrote an impassioned letter to Mr. Bradbury thanking him for his inspiration and encouragement to write. Not long after I mailed the letter, our local bookstore had a book signing by Ray Bradbury and announced that they would draw the names of five patrons to dine with him. As soon as I saw the announcement, I knew that I would be among those chosen. . . . On the day of the drawing, mine was the final name drawn! . . . I had a chance to talk with him at length. Now I know that I must go on writing. The universe has a wonderful way of taking care of us if we just allow it."[6]

#### 4. Love is the highest form of energy.

The ageless wisdom recognizes that the reason humankind is on Earth is to grow spiritually by increasing the capacity to love. One woman said, "I have learned to pay attention to the coincidences that happen in my life and listen to the thoughts that float through my mind and in my dreams. I [have] also learned to appreciate even the smallest, most seemingly inconsequential human interaction."[7] This love is not sentimental feeling pasted upon reality. *It is an outpouring of an individual's state of consciousness when that person is connected to the universal energy—which is the frequency of love.*

#### 5. We have many lives to love.

Integral to the perennial philosophy is the notion of reincarnation and the opportunity to experience many lifetimes and ultimately the full range of human potential. Yes, life is often short. Yes, we have this one life to live—fully. We bring forward certain tendencies and gifts with which to accomplish new goals. When you complete the purpose of this lifetime, you will leave it. And, yes, you will more than likely have another chance to do it differently next time.

#### 6. Choices create consequences, which is the law of cause and effect or karma.

As children we learn not to touch a hot stove. Just as we know that actions create consequences in our daily life, we also learn that the law of cause and effect may create consequences from actions taken in previous lifetimes that *may not be experienced until another lifetime.* This is what the East calls karma and the West calls the Golden Rule and justice. Karma is a natural law of the universe, and we say, "What goes around comes around" and "What you give is what you get."

> A few days later, [the Guides] asked me to begin meditating on "the soul of man and his place in the hereafter." They stressed that this was important, because it would make the crossover period that we call death less tedious, and would permit a more accelerated advancement in the next plane. "The faster that we can convert earth-souls into transfigured spirits," [the Guides] wrote, "the more rapid the progress will be toward a fusion of the whole. This may not be clear to you just now, but as you progress in your meditation we can lead you through a transfiguring series of experiences which will divulge the cause for which we are working." **Ruth Montgomery, A Search for Truth**

### 7. *Other dimensions are valid realities.*

Our job is to wake up to the way we keep ourselves separated and recognize our oneness with the source we call God. The old world-view saw material existence as the only "reality" just because it's in our face every day.

According to Professor Markides, one of the basic assumptions about the universe is the reality of other levels of existence. He says in *Riding with the Lion,* "Other worlds exist that interpenetrate our own. These worlds are layered—that means they relate to each other in a hierarchical manner. The world of the five senses is at the bottom of this spiritual totem pole. These layers are not only out there in nature, objectively speaking, but they are also part of the structure of human consciousness itself."[8]

### 8. *Dual nature.*

In the spiritual dimension there is no duality. There is one source—God—and that source is all good. There is no second, equal source of evil. However, in the Earth plane, we are caught in duality—pairs of opposites like good and evil, light and dark, male and female, new and old. By coming into the Earth plane, we have separated ourselves from the one source. Our goal is to remember that source and reconnect.

The perennial philosophy reminds us that in our dual nature we are individuals, yet part of one humanity. Our bodies live and die in time, but our consciousness lives eternally. To be alive on Earth is to face the opposites and make choices. Life forces us to choose, to express, and to move through the duality. Evil arises in proportion to the extent that an individual's choices are against love, compassion, and service.

## OVERVIEW OF THE TENTH INSIGHT

Like the perennial philosophy, the Tenth Insight is the *context* that provides for the implementation of *all* the Insights.

THE CENTRAL IDEAS OF THE
# First Nine Insights
OF THE CELESTINE PROPHECY

- We are in the midst of an accelerating transformation of how we see our world.
- We see that the purpose of our life is spiritual growth through loving action, not just survival in a materialistic world. *The only way we can truly advance individually and collectively is through opening to the full dimension of who we are, following intuitive guidance, and helping others rather than working to advance our own interests.*
- We understand that we are a divine being, temporarily in a physical body.
- We are in communication with the spiritual dimension in the form of intuitive knowing, synchronicities, metanormal events, and healing miracles.
- Most of us have chosen to be here, and we chose circumstances that would strengthen our soul's character and contribute to holding the World Vision.
- We can learn to stay energized rather than engage in fruitless power struggles.

THE CENTRAL IDEAS OF
# The Tenth Insight

- There are levels of consciousness beyond our own in the spiritual dimension.
- We had a Birth Vision when we came into life.
- Collectively, we are awakening to the World Vision that has been held by our soul groups.
- We are realizing that we receive guidance from the spiritual or angelic realm.
- We are deeply connected to the people we have relationships with and some of the people we meet at turning points in our life.
- We are working to make the physical realm more spiritual.

- Together we're remembering that the worldview is based on the core elements of the ageless wisdom.
- We are learning to hold an intuition and to have faith that it is leading us to the next point on our path.
- What we want exists first in our minds and hearts and becomes a reality through holding that intention.
- After leaving the body at death, we will review every episode of our lives. We will clearly be able to see (and feel) how much love we were able to give to others in every encounter.
- The ultimate goal for humanity is to merge the material and spiritual dimensions.

### WISDOM SCHOOL

Imagine the Tenth Insight as part of a wisdom school whose curriculum is all elective. You may already know much of this material, but reading about the stories of ordinary people may help you remember more fully. Our goal is only to stimulate your inner knowing.

For the left brain, we'll present outlines of principles. For the right brain, we'll tell stories. The themes in our school are: (1) previous lifetimes; (2) soul groups (who hold our memories of previous lifetimes and send us energy); (3) Birth Visions; (4) the Afterlife review (an assessment of how successful we were with remembering and accomplishing our Birth Vision on Earth); (5) the World Vision (to unify the spiritual and physical domains through the consciousness of both realms); and (6) stories of those who are pathfinders.

It's natural to resist change. Some of us are fluctuating wildly between trusting the process for a while, and then doubting ourselves and the spiritual point of view. We go back to wanting control and hang on to what is familiar, even though it isn't working very well. Many of us are still asking: "I know I have a spiritual destiny, but what can I do *today?*"

### FINDING YOUR PLACE

The metaphor mentioned in *The Tenth Insight* of "experiencing the valley alone" captures the idea that each of us must go inside and listen to the intuitions and relevant messages that come to us through others. It's important to remember that finding your place is a continuous process. In life's journey, you are constantly responding to your next situation, working through your next obstacle. There is no stopping point at which you can say, "Now I have it." In choosing life instead of Fear, you are fulfilling one of the most important aspects of your own life purpose.

As we discuss later, we must clear away our addiction to past wounds and past failures. Staying in the present moment, we grow by asking for guidance about where to go and what to do next. We focus our attention on our intention, and let the universe open the way.

> The race advances only as all of us surge upward toward the common goal of enlightenment and perfection. Therefore, if we would advance rapidly ourselves we must make the effort to see that others of like interest are also given every tool for self-advancement. **Ruth Montgomery, *A World Beyond***

## WHAT BUSINESS ARE YOU IN?

According to business guru and author Peter Drucker, the first step on the road to success is to ask yourself, What business am I in? or What exactly is it that I am about? If you can't answer that question, then you're probably spending 90 percent of your time doing things that are not your business.

### Being an Information Booth

One woman who has a medium-size mail-order business specializing in spiritual education said, "I'm like an information booth. I want to be there to provide something that I know has value and will help somebody along their way. I feel that I am a catalyst, and I see that I have done that in my different jobs over the years." She went on to say that "a lot of my empathy and perspective was learned during and after those hard years when I was drinking, had my car accident, and then all the physical rehabilitation. In those days, I was very resistant to new information, but I finally began my recovery after several false starts. Now I sell cassettes, books, and other spiritual tools. What means the most to me is to be able to say, 'Hey, here's something you might really enjoy.' Then I let go of it. I'm clear that I'm just the provider. They are going to do whatever they do with it."

By defining to ourselves what business we are in, we can put ourselves in God's Rolodex, so when he/she needs an information booth, he/she knows whom to call for that job.

### Preserving What's Important

One woman, a director of a foundation, also travels and photographs ethnic ceremonies in other countries. She says, "I see *my* business as preserving what's important. I do this in different ways in both my foundation work and in my photography. It seems to be a dominant drive in my nature."

### Conducting Orchestras

Another person, who runs a manufacturing company, sits on a school-board, and heads two professional organizations, said, "My business is conducting orchestras. I find myself in a lot of leadership roles because I have such a strong sense of how things can run smoothly if the right people are pulling together. I'm committed to helping bring out the best in whatever group I'm in, and I love that challenge even when things get chaotic."

> A renaissance comes about when the doors of the mind open to other worlds and alien ideas, and a turbulent new harmony begins to form.
> Graham Dunstan Martin, *Shadows in the Cave*

### Surprising People with a Dazzling Flourish

A technical writer and Little League coach remarked after some reflection, "I listen and synthesize. I'm always looking for ways to make things easier to do, but I also love to surprise people with a kind of dazzling flourish they didn't expect. My work might seem dull to somebody else, but I like to immerse myself totally in a project and put some order to it all—and then show it to somebody!"

### Creating Bright Moments for People

A man who is an operator of heavy machinery and a superb dancer is a good example of balance between work and play. Several times a week he salsa dances, and is well known in his town as being exceptionally upbeat, philosophical, generous, and humorous. After a little reflection, he and his partner laughed, and she said, "You know what business you are in? It's creating bright moments for people!"

---

## INDIVIDUAL STUDY

### Practice: Intention

In the morning, or when you are facing a particularly important decision or interaction, write your intention on an index card. Go within for a moment.

#### Step One—Clarifying the Image
- *Stop the world.* Take a moment to quiet your mind. Close your eyes and go inward.
- *Slow down and gather energy.* Following the rhythm of your breath for one or two minutes.
- *Clarify the image.* Ask yourself, What expectations do I have around this event, issue, or decision?
- *Charge the image.* Write down whatever *positive* expectations or hopes come to mind.
- *Ask.* Now write out whatever *question* is on your mind. For example, "Should I marry Jo?" or "How can I best present my proposal today?" or "Is this the right house to buy?"

#### Step Two—Creating the Goal and Releasing It
- *Intend.* Next, rewrite your question into a positive statement in which you *already have the desired outcome.* For instance, the questions above could be restated in the present tense, focusing on the desired outcome underlying the question by writing, "I am happily married to the right person!" or "My proposal has created the perfect conditions for my next step in growth," or "I am living in the perfect house for me at this time."
- *Release.* Just for now, feel yourself let go of any feelings of doubt. Let go and trust the universe to handle the details. Feel yourself let go of having any particular outcome at all, trusting that divine wisdom is working for the greater good, of which you may not yet be aware.

#### Step Three—Noticing What the Universe Is Suggesting You Do
- *Receive.* Increase your awareness of subtle signs or messages as to the right direction to go during the day.

- *Recharge.* Bring into focus your statement and an image of yourself having the thing you desire.

### Step Four—Gratitude Keeps You Open

- *Give thanks.* Each time you notice even tiny blessings, such as getting a seat on the subway, finding a penny, or having someone smile at you, say an inward prayer of thanks. Gratitude helps keep your intention charged with energy.

You might want to keep a journal to both record and activate your intention and also to track synchronicities and look for meaning within them. Since synchronicities tend to come in clusters, a journal will be a very helpful tool for working with the Tenth Insight.

## GROUP STUDY

### Guidelines

- Show up on time and leave on time, especially if you are meeting in someone's home.
- No leader is necessary or desirable in the group, although someone may volunteer to write down notes or things to accomplish, or to keep track of time.
- Let each person speak without interruption. Give him or her your full attention.
- Send loving energy to each speaker and see the inner beauty of his/ her soul.
- Speak and listen from your heart.
- Avoid gossiping or making judgments.
- Do not discuss the details of people's lives outside the group.
- Group meditation on any issue may be very fruitful. Let people discuss what messages they received.
- If power struggles arise, be truthful about your feelings, kind, and patient but firm. Avoid blaming.
- Meditate frequently on remembering each other's Birth Vision.

### Dialogues

Start reading books and magazines on subjects that stretch the limits of your worldview, such as reincarnation, extraterrestrial abduction, angels, and the healing power of prayers. Synopsize your reading for the members of the groups, and share thoughts on these ideas.

You can also start a dialogue on one of the topics below. Decide which topic has the "most energy" for people. Select your topic and let everyone write their feelings about it for five minutes. Then people can read what they wrote in turn. After everyone has had a chance to read their thoughts, a general discussion can follow.

## Suggested Topics

If you were to tell a five-year-old your life story, what points would you make?

Who do you know that has been an inspiration to you? Why? How?

When do you feel powerless? What could you change about that?

What are you on the threshold of? What door wants to open?

What has seemed purposeful in your life so far?

What do you think about reincarnation?

What would you love to change in your community?

# CHAPTER 2

# How the Nine Insights Prepare You for the Tenth

CROW
LAW

Each of us, once we work to clear our past dramas, can identify certain questions related to our careers, relationships, where we should live . . . [and] if we remain aware . . . intuitions will provide impressions of where to go, what to do, with whom we should speak, in order to pursue an answer.

THE TENTH INSIGHT:
HOLDING THE VISION[1]

## THE NINE INSIGHTS LEAD TO THE TENTH

To give a foundation for exploring how the Tenth Insight takes us to a new level of awareness, we are providing a brief review of the sequence of the first nine Insights. You may skip this chapter if you already have a firm grasp of the principles.

### 1. The Critical Mass

A new spiritual awakening is occurring in human culture, an awakening brought about by a critical mass of individuals who experience their lives as a spiritual unfolding, a journey in which we are led forward by mysterious coincidences.

### 2. The Longer Now

This awakening represents the creation of a new, more complete worldview, which replaces a five-hundred-year-old preoccupation with secular survival and comfort. While this technological preoccupation was an important step, our awakening to life coincidences is opening us up to the real purpose of human life on this planet and the real nature of our universe.

### 3. A Matter of Energy

We now experience that we live not in a material universe, but in a universe of dynamic energy. Everything is a field of sacred energy that we can sense and intuit. Moreover, we humans can project our energy by focusing our attention in the desired direction ("where attention goes, energy flows"), influencing other energy systems and increasing the pace of coincidences in our lives.

### 4. The Struggle for Power

Too often humans cut themselves off from the greater source of this energy and so feel weak and insecure. To gain energy, we tend to manipulate or force others to give us attention and thus energy. When we successfully dominate others in this way, we feel more powerful, but they are left weakened and often fight back. Competition for scarce human energy is the cause of all conflict between people.

### 5. The Message of the Mystics

Insecurity and violence end when we experience an inner connection with divine energy within, a connection described by the mystics of all traditions. A sense of lightness—buoyancy—and the constant sensation of love are measures of this connection. If these measures are present, the connection is real. If not, it is only pretend.

### 6. Clearing the Past

The more we stay connected, the more we are acutely aware of those times when we lose connection, usually when we are under stress. In these times, we can see our own particular way of stealing energy from others. Once our manipulations are brought to personal awareness, our connection becomes more constant, and then we can discover our own growth path in life, and our spiritual mission, the personal way we can contribute to the world.

### 7. Engaging the Flow

Knowing our personal mission further enhances the flow of mysterious coincidences as we are guided toward our destinies. First we have a question, then dreams, daydreams, and intuitions lead us toward the answers, which usually are synchronistically provided by the wisdom of another human being.

### 8. *The Interpersonal Ethic*

We can increase the frequency of guiding coincidences by uplifting every person that comes into our lives. Care must be taken not to lose our inner connection in romantic relationships. Uplifting others is especially effective in groups where each member can feel the energy of all the others. With children it is extremely important to their early security and growth. By seeing the beauty in every face we lift others into their wisest self and increase the chances of hearing a synchronistic message.

### 9. *The Emerging Culture*

As we all evolve toward the best completion of our spiritual missions, the technological means of survival will be fully automated as humans focus instead on synchronistic energy states, ultimately transforming our bodies into spiritual form and uniting this dimension of existence with the Afterlife dimension, ending the cycle of birth and death.

## QUESTIONS ABOUT THE NINE INSIGHTS

If we are to hold the World Vision, we must, of course, be grounded in our ability to follow the guidance we receive. You may find that you have had some of the following common questions and concerns.

*"I have been having more coincidences, but how do I know what they mean? I'm not always sure what to do with them."*
As the character himself says in the Tenth Insight, "The truth, of course, was that parts of the prophecy still eluded me. Certainly I had retained the ability to connect with a spiritual energy within . . . and I was more aware than ever of intuitive thoughts and dreams and the luminosity of a room or landscape. Yet, at the same time, the sporadic nature of the coincidences had become a problem. . . . I would fill up with energy . . . and would usually perceive a clear hunch about what to do . . . yet, after acting accordingly, too often nothing of importance would occur. I would find no message, no coincidence . . . frequently, my initiative, in spite of my best efforts to send energy, would be

completely rebuked, or worse, would begin with excitement only to warp out of control and finally die in a flurry of unexpected irritations and emotions. . . . I had realized something was missing when it came to living the Insight long-term . . . apparently there was some vital part of the knowledge I had forgotten . . . or perhaps not yet discovered."[2]

## Coincidence or Flash of Memory?

Coincidences usually feel exciting or mysterious. Why? Perhaps they feel that way because they connect us to our memory of what we wanted to do with our life. From a spiritual point of view, everything happens for a reason. Therefore, that heightened state of awareness you feel caused by two or more events coming together in an unexpected way means that there is an unconscious significance in the events. Even if you cannot see any immediate purpose for this event, it doesn't mean that there is none. Someday you may look back to this event and see that it signaled a turning point in your life, or shifted your beliefs. For example, a musician in Louisiana had decided that he wanted to become less aloof after having read about control dramas in *The Celestine Prophecy*. He called a metaphysical bookstore to inquire about study groups in the area. The owner told him there were none at present and suggested he might want to take a yoga class instead. The musician decided to follow this up and told us, "Yoga has been exactly what I needed to get in touch with my body. It's even better than a study group for me right now, because that would probably have been more mental, and that's always kind of been my problem. I'm amazed at how my life has opened up since I took this new step." His intention to work on what he felt was a blocked area has led him to experience life in tremendously different ways.

## Synchronicity as Reinforcement

Sometimes a synchronous event happens to let you know that you are on the right track. For example, a mother and daughter from California traveled to Vancouver to take a workshop in neurolinguistic programming. At the first evening lecture they sat immediately behind two other women and started talking. It turned out these women were also mother and daughter. Furthermore, the mothers had the same first name, and the Vancouver mother had just returned from living in the same apartment building as the California daughter. Since no further contact happened between them, the California mother and daughter took this synchronicity to mean that they had made the right choice in taking the workshop, since the synchronicity involved *location* (both women living in the same location).

## Synchronicity Reveals Inner Process

When you begin to ask clearly for information, your level of synchronous events will go up. Alvin Stenzel of Bethesda, Maryland, reports, "When the student is ready, the teacher will appear . . . while working on my latest book, a guide for high school students about choosing a college and preparing for 'life after,' I'd reached a point where I was having trouble finding a good focus, a concept to frame my own beliefs. Taking a week off from writing, I read one of my Christmas presents, *Care of the Soul* by Thomas Moore. . . . There I found just what I needed! Once I acknowledged my need and opened myself to answers, the teacher appeared!"[3]

Coincidences come from a spiritual force that pulls us along, and they always pertain to one of the Insights that we are working on. For example, if we are at the First Insight, then the coincidences are going to give us proof that the transformation is happening. If we are at the Second Insight, then we will get examples of how we are waking up from the old preoccupations. If we are at the Third, then we get insights about how energy flows.

> So we can . . . say the collective unconscious is a field of psychic energy, the excited points of which are the archetypes, and that field has an ordered aspect which is dominated by the number rhythms of the Self . . . the Self is in an eternal process of constant rejuvenation . . . we can look at psychological processes as being energic processes which even follow certain laws.
> **Marie-Louise Von Franz, *On Divination and Synchronicity***

People will come into our lives that know about the issues that are currently up for us. So through synchronous events, we gain insight. As we approach the Sixth Insight, which allows us to identify our own lineage from our ancestors, we get clearer about the synchronicities. They show us the direction we are personally moving toward and highlight the question that is most important to us. When we are more clearly aware of what we came to contribute, synchronous events amplify greatly. Keep in mind, too, that we cycle back through the Insights as we integrate information.

## "How can I probe the coincidences for further information?"

As the event is happening, try to remember to give some energy to the person(s) involved in order to help him/her give you any messages. You may even take the direct approach, and when appropriate say, "I'm really interested in why we have met right now. Maybe you have a message for me!"

You can say this with humor and allow the person to see that you have a sincere intention to connect with him or her.

After your coincidence, take a few minutes to notice the most outstanding elements of the event. Ask yourself questions such as, What have I been wanting to know about lately? What has been my preoccupying thought recently? Why did I meet this person right now in terms of that question? Write down the event and any meaning you attribute to it (even if it may seem rather fantastic) in your journal and date it. Open up to intuitive messages by letting random thoughts come out in free-association writing, while the energy of the event is still strong. The information may be more meaningful to you a few days or months from now.

Another way to probe a coincidence is to pretend that it was a dream. What meaning would you give it if it were a dream?

> Chinese do not ask what caused something to happen . . . they do not have a linear idea of time. [They] ask "what likes to happen together?" . . . then they explore such bunches of inner and outer events . . . there is a tendency of certain events to cluster together . . . Westerners are slowly realizing that in fact there is a tendency for things to happen together, it is not just fantasy, there is a noticeable tendency of events to cluster. So far as we can see, that has to do with the archetypes; namely, if a certain archetype is constellated in the collective unconscious then certain events tend to happen together.
> **Marie-Louise Von Franz, *On Divination and Synchronicity***

### "How might I use my new awareness of the Insights in my work? In my family?"

Obviously, there is no recipe for using the Insights that will fit everyone and every situation. However, you can start looking for the deeper purpose in your relationships with coworkers and family. Many people have found that simply becoming aware of the control dramas shifted them from unconscious *reaction* to conscious freedom to make new choices.

### "How come my wife (husband) doesn't get excited about these ideas? Should I try to explain this, or am I just outgrowing this relationship?"

How many times do we feel frustrated because someone we care about doesn't share our new interests? What tends to happen is that the changes in consciousness bring change into relationships that were based on former assumptions. For example, if your spouse realizes that you are moving in new directions, he or she may have several reactions. She may not care, may be interested, or may be threatened that you won't love her anymore if she doesn't go along with the new ideas. Fear of being rejected or left behind might activate a need to get attention or to control your actions out of fear.

Even if you don't have a partner, new levels of awareness often bring an immediate test. For example, someone who is close to us will verbally or nonverbally express *our own inner doubts* about our new step or perception. So notice if a friend, parent, or partner raises a criticism of your new decision or idea. Do their words reflect some tiny seeds of doubts that you still have not resolved within your *own* understanding? Notice if you have been unusually withdrawn or distant, assuming that your partner is not interested in what you are pursuing. Be willing to share honestly how important your spiritual work, reading, writing, or activities are to you. Be committed to your path, and let your actions, your increased compassion, and your loving energy be a model to others without trying to convince them to follow your way. Each person has his or her own time schedule for development, and as much as you want others to come along with you, they must do so at their own pace and inclination. Don't rush to make judgments about the fate of your relationship until you've explored your feelings with a trusted mentor or professional counselor. Don't forget your sense of humor in your rush for enlightenment!

> You plant a seed in people and it settles down into some deep substratum of the mind. Over time, it starts to grow and suddenly it becomes conscious and they're interested in these things many years later as they themselves have changed in response to these new ideas.
>
> The thing about a paradigm shift—and Thomas Kuhn talked about it at length—is that it's not something that's just an intellectual change of mind. It's a deep conversion experience. . . . So this work of mediating between paradigms and bringing data to the attention of others and hoping that they will change their minds is very slow work. It doesn't happen overnight.
> **Dr. Beverly Rubik** in *Towards a New World View,* by Russell E. DiCarlo

*"My boss is an Intimidator! How might I handle him without losing my job?"*

All of us, at some time or other, encounter difficult people who have angry or threatening personalities. One woman, Frances, worked with an erratic, domineering type of boss who expected her to jump every time he yelled. While there were things she liked about her job otherwise, she felt always on the edge of chaos because she could rarely finish one assignment before he asked her to do something else. When Frances did a review of her parental influences, she quickly made the connection of having had a father much like her current boss. She had always been in awe of her father and had cringed when he was loud and demanding. She began to see that she had re-created a similar atmosphere in her choice of work. "I guess I felt like it was normal to be dominated and verbally abused," she said, "because it felt like what I knew." Frances asked herself, "Why do I have this situation in my life right now?" Although complete awareness happened sometime later for Frances, she did begin to consider that perhaps the purpose of having a domineering boss was to show her where her inner growth needed to occur. In order to move into more creative work, she would have to learn to be a little more assertive and confident. But first she had to take some new steps.

Even though her status in the office was at the junior level of administration, she began to slowly set some boundaries on what she would accept from her boss. One afternoon when the office was slower than usual, she asked to speak to him for a few minutes. With her heart in her throat, she let him know that she felt she was not working at her best. He asked her why she thought that, and she said, "I'm scared of you." She said he sat quietly for a minute or so appraising her, and then she continued, "I can't do my best work when people are yelling at me. I like working here, and I want to be flexible enough to help you out in the best possible way. But I need for you to give me some lead time before I switch assignments. I'd like to work here and not be so afraid that I'm going to catch hell from you every time I turn around!"

Her sincerity opened the way for a brief but congenial conversation between them. She said she left the office with an immense surge of energy for having spoken up for herself in a quiet yet determined way. She worked there a few more months, and then, effortlessly, a new job opened up that was even more to her liking, with a very easygoing boss. Frances learned that she did not need to settle for a painful situation just because it felt so familiar. She realized that the incident gave her the perfect opportunity to confront this inner unresolved issue with her dad. Sometime later she realized that the incident with her boss highlighted a tendency to focus on the needs of others as *more important* than her own. "Just noticing this one tendency—to fixate on trying to please other people because I was afraid of their disapproval—has changed my life! I feel so much lighter." Later, with the aid of a therapist, she was able to recognize that she had projected her own inner need for attention on to her boss.

Generally, a difficult situation gives us an opportunity to see where we are stuck or fearful so we can take appropriate new steps. It could be an opportunity to heal an old wound, to discover an unconscious behavior pattern, to stand up for ourselves, to accomplish a dream, or to learn a crucial piece of information that we will need for our evolving journey. Once our learning is accomplished, life makes sure we move along.

### *"If I believe that I create my reality, how come things aren't changing?"*

Energy follows thought. If you are not achieving the goal you want, you might ask yourself four questions to help get to the root of your "stuckness."

First, do you really believe that you can have, or that you deserve to have, the new goal? Do you have an unexamined belief that no matter what you do, you never get what you want? Ask yourself, How do I tell myself inwardly that I don't deserve my goal? For example, if you want something that costs a lot of money, do you go around talking about how you can't afford it? Do you keep referring to how much debt you already have? Your root *disbelief* could neutralize your intention to attract your new goal.

Second, are you trusting and following intuitive messages that suggest new steps or risks that might put you on the path toward your goal?

Third, is the timing right in order for this goal to be realized? Are you impatient for results, unwilling to wait or follow through with all the steps needed to manifest the goal?

Finally, intuitively, do you think this desired goal is in your best interest? If the result you want is not happening, what message might there be for you?

---

Ask for blessings as if you took it for granted that they would be bestowed, for that is the part which means faith.

Seek to know His will for you. Feel His presence, and then be sure that whatever you ask is for the best possible purpose and not a selfish whim. Remember that the prayer is useless if it would harm another or put you above rivals and friends. Ask that God's will, not your own, be done, and then pray as if you expected to see the prayer granted in an instant.

**Ruth Montgomery, *A World Beyond***

---

Some people have found they get results when they write out their desired goal fifteen times on a piece of paper each day for a couple of weeks, and then forget about it for the rest of the day—letting God take care of it.

Most important, to create our reality we must have most of our psychic energy present and available to direct in positive intention. If our energy is going backward into feeding old wounds and failures, we do not have enough psychic energy available to create the future we desire. Stuck in rehashing each and every negative thing that has befallen us, our minds are feeding negative creations. We continue to feel a victim of our past. Obviously, we are not suggesting that you deny these events or not give yourself time for appropriate and necessary healing. However, when we identify ourselves mostly by what we have survived or suffered, then we have limited our capacity to move beyond them. An excellent description of this process is given by medical intuitive and author Caroline Myss in her audiocassette tape entitled *Why People Don't Heal*.[4]

### *"How can I actualize my present situation so that I can move forward?"*

Since we know everything has a purpose, it is helpful to look for the positive intention behind your current situation. What are you getting out of "not moving forward"? What is the payoff? One man told us, "I had taken a job that I really didn't like at all, but I needed the money. I kept thinking, 'Why in the world am I in this job? I don't even like most of the people here.'" After reflecting on the First Insight, which tells us that life is a mystery, he said, "I decided to approach my current situation as if it were a mystery that I wanted to understand. It gave me a really different view of why I was showing up there every day (apart from my paycheck, of course). I began to talk to people and subtly look for the message they might have for me. This approach totally changed my experience at this job while I was there and made it much more bearable. I started to realize that many of the people there had given up a dream of some kind. By staying in this job I hated, the payoff was that it kept me from looking at the fact that I really didn't want to be an actor with a 'day job' anymore. It kept me from reassessing what I wanted to do with myself, because then it felt like I had no moorings whatsoever." Eventually, he moved back to Indiana and went to college to finish a degree in education, which he hoped would lead to a position as a drama teacher.

In order to move forward, first fully embrace your current situation, being alert for the positive intention behind it. Notice any synchronicities that suggest new options (or even *hints* of options).

Radiate loving energy, and trust that the universe is giving you exactly what you need at this moment. You might also remember the old adage "What you resist, persists."

### "How can I use these concepts so as to be more involved with healing the planet?"

You are already part of the critical mass of individuals who are tuned into the possibilities of healing the planet. Bring a passionate intention to your time on Earth, and a commitment to know who you truly are and use your gifts. When you feel out of the flow, surrender to the higher order of universal intelligence. It is up to you to see where you have been stationed and to take action where it is needed. For example, a recent news story in California showed how the determination of some low-income parents created not only a better future for their own children but a new model of desegregating schools. Ten years ago a freeway on the San Francisco peninsula separated two school districts—one all black and one all white. Margaret Tinsley, an African American, was not willing to settle for having her children go to a school that was academically rated at the bottom. "I also did not believe," she said, "that attending an almost all-black school was going to prepare my children for the future."[5] Her efforts and those of other parents created a landmark suit which led to a unique, voluntary program in which schoolchildren can transfer across district lines. Enrolling between kindergarten and second grade, they are exposed to different races and cultures before they have learned to be distrustful of others who look different. "The Tinsley decision made it possible for our young people of varied cultural backgrounds to get to know one another at a relatively early age," said Jack Robertson, one of the attorneys who argued the case for the plaintiffs. "Kids are not born prejudiced. They learn it."

Notice where life has placed you. What needs to be done there? What are you passionate about? How can you serve a greater need than just your own? The Tinsley decision came about, not from a government initiative, but by one farsighted and courageous mother.

### "Are there methods I could learn that would increase the effectiveness of my prayerful intention?"

Yes. Let go of your past as the basis for thinking about your future!

Before getting out of bed in the morning ask yourself, What is my most pressing question today? Let's say you are making a decision about a medical procedure and you don't know what to do. If you are fearful of making a mistake, confused or uncertain about your choices, try restating your question as a *positive statement about the outcome you desire*. State your question positively: "Each choice I make brings me to complete health and peace of mind."

Get into the habit of imaging how you would like the day to go before leaving the house. Expressing gratitude opens up channels for more good things to come. Whenever you have a realization or success, acknowledge it. You will be positively energizing your own and the collective field.

Abundance flows from an open, trusting attitude. The belief systems of others also impact you. As simple as it sounds, it's very helpful to develop friendships with people who are positive and optimistic. Spend little time with those with a doom-and-gloom attitude.

Release clutter. Look at your home and work environment. What can you let go of? What have you outgrown? Clear your physical, emotional, and financial energy fields of old stuff. Give away what you do not need or that which has no meaning for you anymore. Create a small sacred corner in your home to remind you of your desire to evolve and contribute. Put pictures of role models or teachers there with something from the earth—flowers, rocks, shells, fruit.

Hundreds of studies and personal anecdotes demonstrate that prayer works beyond time or distance. Sometimes, however, we don't always know what we should pray for. When someone we care about is sick, we want him/her to fully recover. According to studies reported by Dr. Larry Dossey, praying for the most positive outcome for a person is very effective.

---

I'm placing my hope in those people who are awake and who have the courage and conviction to see how many other people they can wake up. If that happens, then we will have a renaissance. Listen to those leaders who encourage us to be better people, not those playing to our fears. As I see it, either we are going to have a very rapid decline into a "worst-case" scenario, or else the dream of a new renaissance will be made a reality. The choice is ours.
**Larry Dossey, M.D., in *Towards a New World View*, by Russell E. DiCarlo**

---

Sending loving energy to assist the perfect outcome is helpful for all concerned. In this way, you pray that a higher spiritual wisdom will provide the greatest good.

In *Healing Words*, a book on the practice of prayerful intention, Dr. Larry Dossey writes, "The more we try to push and control these events, the more they seem to elude us. The secret seems to consist in *not* trying and *not* doing, allowing the world to manifest telesomatically *its* wisdom, not ours. . . . Although prayer is effective nonlocally at a distance, we cannot always 'make it happen' by willful intent or by praying for specific outcomes. . . . We can also see prayer as an invitation, a respectful request for the world to manifest in benevolent ways."[6]

*"I know I have a mission, but how can I become more aware of it?"*

As a growing soul, your mission is to perfect your ability to love, although we try to make it more complicated than that. There are four common ideas that we tend to have about a "life mission." The first is that this mission or life purpose exists somewhere "out there" waiting to be discovered. Second, that our life purpose is a specific, namable occupation or activity. Third, that once we have it, our real life will begin. And fourth, that we probably need to do something to change ourselves in order to find or deserve it. Without the certainty of this named occupation, we tend to say, "I'm so confused. I don't know what my mission is. I don't know what I'm good at."

This searching is our desire to remember our original intention or Birth Vision. We will talk more about this process of finding purpose in Chapter 7. But let's take the common views we just mentioned and turn them into practical steps for connecting with your Birth Vision now.

## 1. Internal Motivation

First, your mission exists within you in the form of your natural inclinations, desires, and motivations. Look at what you love to do. What activities bring you joy and satisfaction? What did you do for hours on end when you were a child?

Just for fun write down on a piece of paper all the activities that you did as a child or that now bring you pleasure. Let's say you write down that you enjoy working crossword puzzles. Now take it one more step. Ask yourself, What is it about working crossword puzzles that makes it so delicious that I will spend hours doing it? Perhaps you like doing them because you work alone in a quiet environment, and you have plenty of time to think, and look up words in the dictionary. Maybe you have an exceptional memory, or an uncanny way of pulling out the right word. Maybe you enjoy the tangible sense of closure when you finish a puzzle. All of these "little pleasures" are motivating factors that make this activity *intrinsically* worthwhile to you.

List each interest and talent you have and *look at why you like it so much*. The reasons why you do something are the motivating forces of your unique personality. If you work in alignment with these *motivations*, you will be living part of your life purpose. You may not want to make a living doing crossword puzzles, but the nature of that activity shows what you are inherently attracted to. Therefore, your purpose is *within* you. Watch carefully to what and where your attention is drawn.

## 2. Finding and Living Your Purpose Is a Process, Not an End Result

The second idea is that purpose is a namable occupation. Generally, most of us think that our purpose comes packaged as a career, like airline pilot, real estate broker, dental hygienist, vice-president of marketing, social worker, or interior designer. Consider the idea that your purpose may be to learn to be more compassionate in your response to all beings. Your purpose may be to mentor one special child, create an industry, or be the Rock of Gibraltar in your family. Realizing that your life purpose is revealed over the course of your entire life journey opens your heart to accepting all that comes to you as part of your purpose, not just that which you do to earn a living.

## 3. No Waiting

It is not helpful to assume that until you find your purpose, your life is on hold or is insignificant. The present moment is the only moment you have to fully touch and be touched by life. No abstract idea of success and attainment can substitute for the incredible range of experience that each day brings to you. Look for the purpose of each day's events, and trust that you are in exactly the place that you need to be. Let go of the struggle and confusion to find your purpose, but hold the intention that it will be revealed to you. Surrendering to life's timetable and fully enjoying the present can be the most liberating thing you ever do.

## 4. You Are a Self-Organizing System

Your purpose *is* unfolding. It's not helpful to hold the attitude that something is wrong or that you have to change yourself in order to find your destiny. Your guidance lies within you and is working at this very moment. Your soul's desire to be a part of the world will attract to you the right opportunities for the purpose to unfold. Your job is to (1) stay alert to your internal energy flow; (2) pay attention to what comes naturally; (3) do the work that is yours to do; (4) trust that you will be provided with what is necessary for you to perform your "business." A rose does not question whether or not it can perform the functions of a rose. A beaver does not try to be an owl.

As Buddhist teacher Jack Kornfield says in *A Path with Heart,* "In many spiritual traditions there is only one important question to answer, and that question is: Who am I? When we begin to answer it, we are filled with images and ideals—the negative images of ourselves that we wish to change and perfect and the positive images of some great spiritual potential—yet the spiritual path is not so much changing ourselves as it is about listening to the fundamentals of our being."[7]

Pat Brady Waslenko's letter from Seattle, Washington, to *The Celestine Journal* reports, "Sometimes the results of spiritual growth are subtle, without concrete highly visible changes that affirm we are on the right path. For those of us with damaged self-esteem it is easy to believe that we're doing something wrong or that we don't deserve to have good things happen easily in our lives. I am one in whose life promises are fulfilled slowly and at subtle levels. Two techniques are most helpful to keep me moving forward in my evolutionary process: (1) reminding myself that as long as I am completely willing to do God's will, my every action is holy. This, rather than outcomes, is the part I am responsible for; (2) reviewing my week and listing, on Friday evenings, all the synchronicities I have experienced. Without this conscious effort, many gifts would go unnoticed."[8]

## INDIVIDUAL AND GROUP STUDY

### Progress or Problems with the Nine Insights

Take a moment to reflect on changes in your life since reading *The Celestine Prophecy; The Celestine Prophecy: An Experiential Guide; The Tenth Insight;* or any other impactful book. If you are working in a group, select one of the topic questions below. Let everyone write their thoughts for five minutes or so and then take turns sharing them aloud *without comment.* Give your complete attention to each speaker and send him/her loving energy as you listen carefully for any thoughts that trigger off intuitions in you. After everyone has had a chance to talk, open up the discussion in general.

How the Nine Insights Prepare You for the Tenth

### Progress

- What Insights made the biggest change in your life? What happened?
- How are you different in your relationships with spouse, children, friends, family, or coworkers? Be specific.
- On an index card, write one of the following qualities per card (or any others you wish to explore), until you have a stack of cards with words on them. (Someone might want to prepare the cards ahead of your meeting.)

| | | |
|---|---|---|
| empathy | forgiveness | love |
| determination | surrender | play |
| leadership | adventure | release |
| cooperation | balance | success |
| vision | crossroads | joy |
| kindness | control | imagination |
| fairness | trust | responsibility |
| advocacy | abundance | focus |
| creativity | transformation | harmony |
| beauty | inspiration | wisdom |
| commitment | | |

Pass them around with the blank side up so people cannot see the words. Select one or two words per person, and then use that word to write about how you have demonstrated or experienced that quality lately.
- Write about three activities that you really enjoyed as a child. What are you doing like that today?
- Write out your ideal life: Where would you like to live? What kind of work do you see yourself doing? What kind of people are you with? On a scale of 1 to 10, with 10 representing that you are living this ideal completely, how close are you to your ideal? Brainstorm (take one person at a time) with each other about what one or two steps you could take to move in the direction of your ideal life.
- Write about the three things you can unabashedly brag about! Don't hold back talking about how great you are.

### Puzzles

- What Insights do you understand the least? Why? Discuss these questions as a group.
- Take one of your most pressing questions about the Insights and write it on a 3 by 5 card. Close your eyes and meditate on having a clear message come through in the next few days that will expand your understanding.

## PART TWO

# Mystery

# CHAPTER 3

# Intuition—Imaging the Path

LYNX
SECRETS

I would fill up with energy, for instance, discerning the question foremost in my life, and would usually perceive a clear hunch about what to do or where to go to pursue the answer—yet, after acting accordingly, too often nothing of importance would occur. . . . Apparently there was some vital part of the knowledge I had forgotten . . . or perhaps not yet discovered.

THE TENTH INSIGHT:
HOLDING THE VISION[1]

## LEARNING TO TAKE INTUITIONS SERIOUSLY

When the phone rings, we answer it and receive a message. When intuition calls, we "answer" it by taking it seriously. A major principle of *The Tenth Insight* is that in order to bring forth our Birth Vision, we must *maintain the intuitions* that arise in our minds.

The character in *The Tenth Insight* recalls from the Nine Insights that "one experiences intuitions as fleeting gut feelings or vague hunches. But as we gain familiarity with this phenomenon, we can now grasp the nature of these intuitions more clearly. . . ." Wil adds, "Here in the valley the same thing has been happening. You received a mental image of a potential event—finding the falls and meeting someone—and you were able to live it out, bringing on the coincidence of actually discovering the location and encountering me. If you had shrugged off the image, or lost faith in looking for the falls, you would have missed the synchronicity, and your life would have stayed flat. But you took the image seriously; you *kept* it in your mind."[2]

As we develop our destiny, and are developed *by* our destiny, we must not only recognize fleeting intuitions but maintain them and hold them with faith. Intuitions are *guides* that give us clues about

49

how to handle difficult or new situations. They give us a glimpse of an exciting possibility to spur us on our own path. An intuition might come as a full-blown image, a recurring daydream or night dream, or a simple knowing. One woman said, "One day I knew I had to leave Santa Fe, New Mexico, and return to California. Somehow an inner voice said, 'It's time you went back to school.' But I didn't have the faintest idea what I was supposed to study." By acting on her intuition, she moved back to California. One synchronicity after another led her to a school that had just opened a new transpersonal psychology program. "As soon as I heard about it, I knew it was just what I had been looking for, but didn't know it!"

Similarly, Sandra Fry from Wayne, Pennsylvania, wrote to *The Celestine Journal* about how following a vision also led her to a gift. "I first came into the experience of having an image appear while I was getting a massage. . . . I have learned to trust this process. I was in the heart of exploring my past and at the same time, asking Spirit for a mystical experience to help find the new being inside myself. It was then that I started seeing this chapel and a bell, and knew them to be in the Southwest. . . . about this time, I learned that the American Massage Therapy Association was holding an autumn convention in Albuquerque . . . [which I] attended. The mountains visible from my hotel window, however, created a sense of urgency to get in a car and go explore them. I waited for the right moment . . . I toured museums of Native American culture and history along the way and then a man told me to follow the Turquoise Trail into the mountains. The dirt road he indicated brought me to Cerrillos, an old mining village nestled in the mountains. It was there that I saw it—the southwestern chapel of my vision." Inside she received an inner message that said, "Become your future self." Sandra continues, "I feel like Insight Seven is really where I am right now in gauging the flow, working hard on being present and letting things happen . . . my experience in the chapel felt like I was coming full circle, that a lot of my work is complete. It allowed me to see the past as my teacher. . . . Before going to New Mexico, I had been caught up in a process of release/transform, release/transform. In the chapel for an instant in time, Spirit allowed me to stop, to feel-at-onement with God, to really know that . . . the inner becomes the outer. I felt at one with my Source. That moment was a gift I can always tap back into."[3]

Feelings, daydreams, and imagination are often equated with wasting time or unreality. Nothing could be further from the truth. Imagination is the key to working with the mind, allowing us to enter the spiritual realm to recover ancient knowledge. Imagination is the power of higher vision and prophecy.

If our feelings and hunches are as valid information sources as our physical senses, are they always right? At the moment we were writing this question, the phone rang. It was Blair Steelman, who had called on some other business, but it seemed he had a message for us about the validity of intuitions. Blair, a former air force pilot and businessman who now teaches workshops on mythology and personal performance in Miami, said someone once told him the following story which he now uses to describe intuition. "At the end of the movie *Doctor Zhivago*, Comrade General was talking to a little girl. He asked her how she became separated from her father in the middle of the revolution. She told him, 'Oh, there was a big crowd and lots of commotion, and I got lost.' He asked her again, 'How did you really become separated from your father?' She didn't want to answer the question, but he asked her once more, and finally she said, 'My father let go of my hand.' Comrade General said, 'But that's what I'm trying to tell you. That was not your real father. Dr. Zhivago is your real father, and he would have never let go of your hand.'" Blair said he tells his students, "Each one of us has a 'father' or 'parent' within us who will never let go of our hand no matter what the situation is. The father or parent is the still small voice of our intuition. That voice will never abandon us no matter what is happening in our lives." And if we do get off track? "It's because we grab hold of our false father, the father of our senses, our ego," says Blair. "We grab hold of the positions and forms and roles that we play in our life that are all less than the real us."

How do you test an intuition? "For me it's in the results," says Blair. "If I get an idea and act upon it, and all I get is resistance, that tells me I'm probably off doing something that I *think* I need. It's not

For years, Ernest Hilgard of Stanford University has investigated an enigmatic aspect of personality that he calls the "hidden observer." No matter what our conscious state is, whether we are sleeping, anesthetized, under hypnosis, or drugged, we have another aspect of self that is always alert and aware of everything going on, and that responds intelligently. . . . The hidden observer displays an unemotional, detached intelligence, more powerful and cohesive than our ego-self. . . . It seems to me that we are one with this hidden observer until about age seven, at which point our intellect begins to form and a split takes place. **Joseph Chilton Pearce, *Evolution's End***

what I really need to be doing. For example, every time I just go after something for the money, things get difficult. When I stay within my own being and do things that are in concert with myself, money always happens naturally. I remind myself to be who I am. Then I trust that whatever I need to facilitate that will appear." Blair reminds us that the natural sequence of manifesting a vision is (1) being; (2) doing; and (3) having. "Usually, we are taught the opposite of that sequence: having, doing, being," he says. "We want to have a car, a career, a relationship, whatever it is. Then we try to figure out what we can do to get it. We look to the hot jobs, and then try to make that who we are." Sooner or later, things begin to unravel. If you find the real you and stick with that, you can't go wrong.

## FAITH

When we experience coincidences as *purposeful*, we have an *inner knowing* that is greater than simply understanding a theory. Having had this direct personal experience enhances our ability to "have faith." Faith then feels like "alert expectancy." That state of mind tends to increase intuition and opportunity.

In *The Tenth Insight*, Wil says, "Look at what has already occurred. You came here searching for Charlene and met David, who said the Tenth was a greater understanding of the spiritual renaissance happening on this planet,

> Faith is a certainty that comes from knowing how things should be. The ancestors knew, but not enough of us here have reached that knowing. James Redfield, *The Tenth Insight: Holding the Vision*

an understanding attained by grasping our relationship to the Afterlife dimension. He said the Insight has something to do with clarifying the nature of intuitions, of maintaining them in our minds, of seeing our synchronistic path in a fuller way.

"Later, you figured out how to maintain your intuitions in this way and found me at the falls, and I confirmed that maintaining the intuitions, the mental images of ourselves, was the operative mode in the Afterlife as well, and that humans are moving into alignment with this other dimension. Soon after, we found ourselves watching Williams' Life Review, watching him agonize over not remembering something he had wanted to do, which was to come together with a group of people to help deal with this Fear that threatens our spiritual awakening.

"He says we have to understand this Fear in order to do something about it, and then we get separated and you run into a journalist . . . who [enunciates] a fearful vision of the future. . . .

"Then . . . you next run into a woman whose life is all about healing, and the way she facilitates healing is to help people work through fear blocks by prodding their memory, helping them to discern why they're on the planet. This *remembering* has to be the key."[4]

I think the experimental work of Robert Jahn and Brenda Dunn at the Princeton Engineering Anomalies Research Laboratory is certainly important. They have shown that people can skew the numbers on a random number generator towards higher or lower values by simply wishing them to be high or low, respectively.

It's one of those exceptions to the traditional scientific world view about "the way things are" that we simply can't explain using the old framework. Their data is a real challenge to the prevailing paradigm.

They have shown that mental intention can interact with random physical systems whether they are mechanical, electronic, or radioactive.
Dr. Beverly Rubik in *Towards a New World View*, by Russell E. DiCarlo

This passage tells us to focus on the outcome we intuit, and keep the faith in that image. Remembering *why* we are doing something keeps us in touch with the bigger picture of our original vision if or when we become pessimistic or fearful.

A wonderful example of holding a vision is Marjorie Stern, a fourth-generation San Franciscan and library benefactor. In 1966, after already putting in ten years of volunteer work to raise money and consciousness about the need for a new library building, she wrote a letter to possible donors in which she said, "There are no shortcuts to meaningful civic improvement. It takes years of hard work . . . if we are to achieve our dream of a new main library building." Thirty years later, Stern, now eighty, has seen the realization of the dream that she kept alive with her untiring commitment with the opening of the new main library. Stern's efforts helped raise more than $33 million from seventeen thousand donors—all of whom received a personal thank-you from her. "That's the way life is. Things don't happen in a great hurry . . . I have a long-term view. You have to have that," she says in her understated way. "It's a struggle, and you just have to keep struggling. But you don't settle for less than the best."[5]

## DREAMS

Increasing intention to manifest your own vision stimulates the unconscious to bring information through dreams. Remember, the mystery wants to unfold! Dreams always give you a message about your personal growth or how to better interact with the world. They bring you an insight of which you are not yet consciously aware.

According to dream studies, dreams separate into those that are personal and those that reflect the collective unconscious. To the latter group belong the Big Dreams that great leaders receive, indicating patterns coming in for the future of humanity. As a critical mass of people begins to have experiential knowledge of the spiritual realms, we may find that more information surfaces to a greater number of people through numinous light-filled dreams with archetypal symbols. In order to capture this information, we might want to deepen our knowledge of the following points: (1) how to set up the intention for dreaming to occur; (2) how to enhance memory of the dream in the morning; (3) how to review the dream for information; and (4) how to interpret dream symbols based on both the personal and the collective myths.

### PERSONAL DREAMS

In an interview with Joyce Petschek, author of three books concerned with dreaming, *The Silver Bird, Silver Dreams,* and *Bedroom Chocolates,* she told us some of her experience in being a dream practitioner—someone who delves into dreaming to connect with the messages they bring.

"First of all," she said, "there are several different types of dreams. The most common, of course, are the personal dreams which reflect one's own life themes, anxieties, and relationships. These dreams never give you anything you can't handle, and the messages will come when you are ready to hear them. They are there to help clear your negative emotions and transform your personal energies. If you deny them, they become repetitive. Like a snowball, they get bigger and bigger, more and more anxiety-producing. They can also be versions of the same dream shown from different angles. These repetitive dreams are generally rooted in unresolved childhood traumas. As you release the fear and negativity of these childhood traumas, you will open your psychic potential to receive and explore your personal creativity."

Dreams exist in one's auric field and enter into our awareness through the sleep state of consciousness. We integrate the dream energy and message by exploring them in the waking state through writing them down, painting or drawing images from them, or using the spiritual teaching they bring. By working with them, one brings their energy into waking reality, thus merging the boundaries between the spiritual and physical dimensions. Allan Ishac of New York City wrote to *The Celestine Journal*[6]: "Several years ago, while in the half-state between waking and sleeping, a message was typed across the black screen of my closed eyelids. The words read, '25 Places to Find Peace and Quiet in New York.'" He wrote the sentence down on a scrap of paper and forgot about it. It kept resurfacing every now and then in his papers. At that time he was planning to leave New York, feeling overwhelmed by the pace, the noise, and the general tension. It suddenly hit him that the dream was, in effect, saying, "You teach what you most need to learn." He realized the dream was giving him the title for a book, and he began researching and writing on the weekends. Through a series of synchronicities, he finally published his book, *New York's 50 Best Places to Find Peace and Quiet*.

### DREAMS CLARIFY CURRENT SITUATIONS

In *The Tenth Insight,* Wil, while in the spiritual energy of the Afterlife, sees the journalist, Joel, having a dream—a dream that shows one of Joel's past-life mistakes. He explains the meaning of it by saying to our character, "Yes, but [the dream] has meaning. When we dream, we unconsciously travel back to this sleep level, and other souls come and help us. Don't forget what dreams do: they clarify how to handle current situations in our lives. The Seventh Insight says to interpret dreams by superimposing the plot of the dream against the real situation facing us in life."[7]

### COLLECTIVE DREAMS

"As one expands beyond the personal self, into concern for the collective, so atypical dreams appear," says Petschek, "which emerge when one has learned to surrender and positively receive the unexpected. These are dreams which affect other people, rather than our personal selves, and have the feeling of being precognitive yet relevant to present time. They indicate a willingness to receive information from an unknown source, information which will affect the lives of others."

For example, Petschek told us, "I worked with a U.S. Senator who had a dream of a long conference table with a white paper and pencil on it. In the dream, he heard a voice that said 'don't sign.' Some months later, he relived this scene at a conference in Iceland where the same table and white paper and pencil appeared, and because of the dream, he did not sign the agreement." Such a precognitive dream reflects one's connection with collective energy. This information may affect you personally to some extent, but the import of the message is of broader significance. "Generally," Petschek says, "when you begin to receive these collective dreams, you have shifted your psyche into a concern about others as much as yourself."

Collective dreams have been described by many as being filled with golden or brilliant white light. These dreams are clearly remembered and not forgotten even over a lifetime. Affording one an expanded perspective, they communicate a deep spiritual teaching. "When you are willing to live intuitively, or on the edge, as I call it," says Petschek, "these dreams are sometimes the only affirmations you have about your life journey in the largest sense. When you're flowing with the unknown, you have to trust what comes. Then life unfolds its unseen lessons which you cannot control but indeed can learn from."

## NIGHT SCHOOL

Dream practitioners call some dreams night school. Petschek recognizes these dreams by certain characteristics. "In night school dreams, you find yourself beyond this dimension, in a floating circular space with many other beings, some you recognize from this lifetime, some from unknown dimensions and other lifetimes. The atmosphere is always both strange and familiar. Usually an extraordinary individual is giving telepathic teachings, like in a class. I've seen people I knew in such a dream, and in reality would tell them about my dream. The usual reply was, 'Oh, yes. I was there, and saw you, too.'" She has noticed that night school dreams invariably take place in a crystal sphere and are "crystal-clear." They are illuminated by brilliant white light, always with telepathic communication, and are unforgettable. Another type of dream experience is called parallel dreaming where two individuals are separately dreaming the same dream, seeing each other within it, experiencing the same dreamscape from different points of view.

## REPETITIVE DREAMS

Precognitive dreams can also repeat themselves, indicating an un-known direction opening to the dreamer, a potential psychic pattern coming in. One woman dreamed of an Italian landscape, seen in brilliant white light. Traveling for two years in Italy, she constantly sought this landscape. Only when she finally "gave up" did it appear in reality. She purchased the property, and two years later a significant Tibetan center started, ten minutes from her property, a community in which she became very involved.

## PROPHETIC DREAMS

Predictive dreams have fascinated people throughout the ages. For example, many people dreamed of the sinking of the *Titanic,* and others have dreamed of airplane crashes. These catastrophic events exist in the aura of the collective unconscious before they manifest in reality. These dreams come unforeseen to those who might act on such information, but at this stage of our development, most of us are probably not skillful enough to assist in minimizing the extent of these events. One reason for this is that our beliefs in our ability to psychically change events is not yet strong enough in the collective unconscious. The other is that these predictive dreams occur to individuals, and there is no central bureau set up for collecting and tracking such information so that they might be prevented or lessened through group focus.

A catastrophic dream can occur on the personal level as well. These urgent telepathic dreams usually have a sense of desperation about them and involve potential trouble. Someone is seeking help, and like a radio wavelength, the person in need tunes into a receptive person who psychically receives their message and hopefully will help them. By telepathically speaking to the troubled person in the dream, giving clear instructions about what to do, such potential danger may be averted in reality. One woman related, "I dreamed of a woman friend who was on a ship. I saw a man pursuing her with the intent to strangle her, and I sensed her terror as she tried to elude him. I began giving her instructions in the dream, 'There. Go down that hallway. Turn left. Up the stairs.' I telepathically suggested she turn into an empty stateroom and lock the door and remain until daylight. The dream ended. A few weeks later, when she had returned home, I told my friend about this dream. She explained that she had taken a job as a cook on a yacht and had angered one of the shipmates, having several times refused his advances. Indeed he had tried to strangle her and, terrified, she had reached an empty stateroom and locked herself within. We were both astounded by this synchronistic event."

A woman we'll call Anastasia wrote to *The Celestine Journal* from Toronto: "Around 11:00 P.M. on a Friday evening, I dreamt that my close friend Janet and I were having grand fun in what appeared to be a large hotel room . . . our fun was suddenly interrupted by a loud knock at the door. Looking at me in confusion, Janet called, 'Who is it?' In response, she heard the voice of a former boyfriend whom she hadn't seen in a long time. 'Go away,' she said. 'Leave me alone.' He began to kick and pound the door, all the while yelling at the top of his lungs. Frightened, we barricaded the door. I called Security. The dream ended.

"The next morning, I went to pick up Janet's daughter, who told me the same story as in my dream. She and her mother were watching TV that evening about eleven when there was a loud knock at the door. Janet opened it to face the same former boyfriend who appeared in my dream. The very same things happened when she closed the door and told him to go away. After kicking the door a few more times, he left. Both Janet and I were amazed that, while this was happening at her house, I was dreaming about it!"[8] Apparently, our unconscious may telepathically turn to someone we really trust for help in extreme need. This type of dream seems to offer evidence of how intricately interconnected our psychic energies are to each other.

As you release more and more of the negative voices from your mind, so you may begin to experience teachers in the dream state. These guides in dreams can come unexpectedly or by request if your energy is open to receiving their assistance or information. Petschek believes that people who say they don't dream are generally feeling so overloaded that they don't want any more information. They don't want to look very deeply at their life and may be blocking out dreams. Such an attitude may also result in blocking out subtleties, intuitive messages, and the meaning of coincidences as well.

## AN INVITATION TO DREAM

Petschek suggests the following process for dream information recall. Assume the "king's position," that is, lying on your back with toes overlapping. Then place your fingers in a triangular shape over your solar plexus, close your eyes, listen quietly to your breathing. Let your mouth be slightly open. Your mind will automatically calm. Let each thought that comes float away, without holding or judging it. After a few minutes when your mind seems empty, mentally state a short question that you want answered in a dream. Keep your questions simple and short, requesting information that others seem not to be able to offer. Such requests can be about self-healing, a creative project, guidance for leadership, and so forth. Repeat your question three times and then with a silent mind fall asleep.

If you get no answers to your questions, ask again for only three nights in a row. If you still receive nothing, let it go. You're not yet ready to positively receive the answer.

### MORNING RECALL

Upon awakening, remember to keep your eyes closed and roll onto your back. Observe the last dream scene that appears in your mind, then let the previous scene emerge, and the one before that, as a movie seen backward. Then, on your dream screen, roll the scenes from the end of the dream back to the beginning, imprinting each scene in your mind. When you are fully awake, write down these dream scenes. You will be surprised to find that additional dream fragments still come forward. It's helpful to give your dream a title, and perhaps define each *theme* that occurs in the dream in the margin of your notes.

### SYMBOLS AND FAMOUS PEOPLE

Should the dream be imbued with brilliant white or golden translucency, it indicates you are at a crossroads and suggests the unknown path. The deeper the dream, the more symbolic its contents. Work with each symbol, asking yourself, What is the essence, the teaching, of this symbol? How does it relate to my life? You may want to refer to dream symbol books, but remember that your interpretation of the symbol is twofold: its collective mythic meaning and its personal connotation to you alone. If a famous person comes into your dream, notice what achievements you admire and what you desire to emulate in your personal life. Every person represents an aspect of yourself that is making itself known to you.

### TRANSFORMING THE DREAM

If you received a disturbing dream, one that created anxiety, you are expressing an aspect of a Fear that you are presently ready to confront.

Adult anxiety dreams stem from unsettled childhood issues, often unresolved issues from past lives, that prevent you from emotionally moving forward in your life. Clearing this Fear will increase your self-confidence and greatly expand your potential for new horizons.

In the morning, run through the dream to recall all the elements. Are you receptive to the message or resistant? If you would have desired a different outcome, take the end scene and rewrite it to a more desirable outcome. Let's say you saw yourself failing an exam (a common theme for many of us, by the way). Say to yourself mentally in an empathic voice, "I just passed that exam with flying colors! In fact, my exam paper was so brilliant that I got the top grade in the class, and everyone including the teacher gave me a round of applause. I feel like a million dollars." Make up your own grand finale for your dreams! Notice how your day goes when you do this. This kind of self-talk often increases your energy and reduces stress (especially if you maintain your sense of humor about it!), and you may find that the whole day proceeds much more smoothly than it might have otherwise. Remember your interior work *precedes* outer reality. The dreams are already showing you the quality of your interior reality which precedes the development of your external reality. These simple techniques help to clear your negative mind and open unknown multidimensional levels to you.

## THE MECHANICS OF DREAMS

As you review your dream, begin to notice the choices you made in a dream. One woman recalled, "I dreamed I awoke in an unfamiliar house and I was frightened. I got up to investigate, and found the front door open. A man was in the front hall. I was outside looking in, and he exited unseen to my left from a door inside the house. I went back in and was not so scared now. I wandered around and found myself kind of liking this one-story tract house (normally I don't like this style). In the very back room of this house was a young woman . . . I saw her and we chatted a few minutes . . . then I saw the cat had brought in a half-chewed, barely alive animal like an iguana or caricaturized dinosaur. The young woman was not disgusted by it and was going to clean up the mess. Instead, she began to tell me about this fabulous new archaeological discovery of an ancient culture only a few yards from our backyard. Some other people came over and I heard more details about the ancient culture, their living arrangements. The type of dwellings seemed to indicate that the inhabitants had 'engineering minds.' " While taking in the scene of the discovery and looking at the dwellings, the dreamer realizes that the people who lived thousands of years ago were the same people who were discovering the ruins—in their present lifetimes. She says in the dream, "But those people were us!"

What is the underlying structure of this dream? First of all, we know it is a *collective* dream because its surroundings are decidedly unfamiliar and unforgettable, and it is vivid and intense, filled with white light. There are no personal references to the dreamer's life. Supporting the idea of the collective nature of the dream is the phrase "other people came over," which reveals that others besides the dreamer will be interested in the discoveries in the dream.

The *subject* of the dream is announced in two ways. First, the cat (a symbol for ancient, psychic energy) brings into the dining room something ancient which has been distorted (half eaten) over time. The dining room is a symbol for a place where eating, digestion, and interchange of ideas through mealtime conversation take place. Secondly, the dreamer states that the house was a "one-story tract house," indicating that this dream has one story, and is an informational dream.

The other woman in the dream offers to clean up the mess, but, instead, the dreamer wants to know about the ancient discoveries. This shift in the action from cleaning up the mess that the cat brought in to talking about the archaeological discovery shows the dreamer is making a choice to pursue the informational content of the dream.

The dream begins in the front of the house, moves to the back and then to the middle of the house, and then finally to the backyard. The male intruder represents the dreamer's male shadow side, the male point of view, which is logical and rational. His shadow quality suggests a linear, rational approach to finding the meaning of the dream is of lesser importance than a symbolic, intuitive approach. The dreamer must care for both her male and her female sides and attend to what is going on in both present and past time (the front and back of the house). The discoveries are taking place in the backyard, the place of privacy and ritual. The sequence goes from the front, which represents the known, to the back, which stands for the unknown.

According to Petschek, the first sequence in a dream sets the stage, the middle part is where the creative action takes place and new information is introduced. The end of the dream tells what the outcome of this energy stream is likely to be. This dream went on to present images of finely articulated artifacts made of an unknown, amberlike substance that the dreamer could not identify. She was given in the dream a set of toy figures from this ancient culture and a topographical map. One might interpret the toy figures as an injunction to "play" with this amberlike material.

A collective dream of this type, which offers so much detailed information, will no doubt be followed by similar themes of discovery. In the last scene of this dream, the dreamer sees a man kissing an influential elderly lady for the benefit of reporters and photographers. She sees the flashes of the cameras. This scene indicates that if the dreamer cultivates her understanding of these new discoveries, over time, she will be recognized and validated. This last scene also shows where the potential of the dream is going to go in the future.

The dreamer had been writing a paper on reincarnation before she had this dream. Perhaps the dream's message that the people of the ancient civilization were also the people in the present reflects, through this individual dreamer, humanity's growing acceptance of the idea of reincarnation.

## DREAMS AND SOUL GROUPS

*The Tenth Insight* suggests that there seem to be groups of souls in the spiritual dimension who are other aspects of us. We are told that these soul groups are always near us. They are there waiting to give us energy as our awareness increases and *as we request assistance to accomplish a higher purpose*. In the novel the souls in a group tend to resemble each other *and their member who is living an Earthly life*. Wil explains: "When we dream, we reunite with our soul group, and that jogs our memory of what we really wanted to do in our current life situation. We get glimpses of our original intention. Then when we return to the physical, we retain that memory, although it is sometimes expressed in archetypal symbols."[9]

Although most of us may not remember encounters such as these, we may want to keep an open mind to the idea of receiving nonphysical support during our dream time. Perhaps the soul groups are another way of describing psychic energy. Swiss psychologist Carl Jung looked at dreams as a flow of events, a sequence of images, which represent a certain flow of energy. Analyst Marie-Louise Von Franz says, "That is why in looking at dreams, [the end] is so important, because that shows where the flow of energy is aiming . . . I keep the end sentence of a dream in mind . . . and then I know that that is as far as the flow of psychic energy went. We know then where the life stream underneath consciousness is flowing and what it is aiming at, the direction in which it is going. The opening sentence of the dream is important because it shows the present situation, it shows where the dreamer is now in this world of confusion. Then comes a sequence of events, and the end sentence gives the direction in which energy is flowing."[10]

## ANIMALS, OMENS, AND SIGNS

An ability to read signs and omens is immensely helpful as we work on holding a positive World Vision. When we are confused, a sign helps stop the chatter. It helps us align our thinking with the meaning we give to the sign. Once we think we understand the meaning, we seem to grow in energy. We regain a sense of purpose and go forward.

### *The Animal That Appears at the Beginning of a Journey or Dream Sets the Whole Tone*

In *The Tenth Insight,* the character begins to pay attention to animals that appear at moments when he needs direction or encouragement. When it was important for him to take a higher perspective or get a bigger picture, an eagle came to him. Traditionally, eagles represent farsighted vision, courage, independence, and spiritual tests. He also saw dozens of crows sitting in and circling a tree. Crows, being the holders of the laws of spirit, were a message to open up, to remember the spiritual laws that were presenting themselves to the character. How many times have you been slightly jolted awake by the loud cawing of crows? Carlos Castaneda, the shaman anthropologist, often described the appearance of his teacher Don Juan in the body of a crow.

A hawk was also a significant animal in *The Tenth Insight.* As David remarks, "Hawks are alert, and observant, ever vigilant for the next bit of information, the next message. Their presence means that it is important at that time to increase our alertness. Often they signal that a messenger is close."[11]

In indigenous cultures and shamanistic tradition, animals are allies who signal changes, provide directions, and offer gifts. When the character was looking for direction and was feeling anxious and doubtful about the Insights, a hare appeared in the underbrush. Later in the novel, with the help of David, he was able to understand what this sign meant. By remembering that a rabbit exemplifies abundance (fertility) and also fear (prey for many carnivores), the character could then face his fear openly (rather than being paralyzed) and move beyond it, knowing that abundance would come when needed.

### The Animals Are Aspects of Ourselves We Need to Get in Touch With

In traditional initiatory rites, the appearance of animals often symbolizes the life purpose of the initiate. The appearance of animals is a coincidence of the highest order. Von Franz says, "In all myths and fairytales I have studied, I have never seen a case where a hero with helpful animals does not win out."[12] Ted Andrews, author of *Animal-Speak: The Spiritual & Magical Powers of Creatures Great & Small,* writes, "I have found within most scriptures and mythologies of the world a vein of lore surrounding the spirit of animals and the belief that the divine forces speak to humans through the natural world. . . . All peoples are touched by them."[13] He makes the point that with our scientific approach to everything, we tend to think of nature only in terms of taking it apart and studying its elements. We have lost the mystery and have dismissed our interdependent relationship to our animal colleagues.

The Tenth Insight reminds us of the spiritual dimension in our physical habitat and the rich source of guidance if we choose to open our eyes to it. Andrews writes, "The animal world has much to teach us. Some animals are experts at survival and adaptation. There are times when we can use those same skills. Some animals never get cancerous conditions. Wouldn't it be wonderful to learn their secrets? Some are great nurturers and protectors. Some have great fertility and others have great gentleness. . . . The animal world shows us the potentials we can unfold. . . . Every animal is a gateway to the phenomenal world of the human spirit. What most fail to realize though is that what they think of animals reflects the way they think of themselves."[14]

Andrews encourages us to open up to the natural world by studying the animals, trees, and flowers whose energy we feel closely associated to. By attuning to this wealth of life we connect directly to living archetypes—essential qualities that live through us. He says, "The animal becomes a symbol of a specific force of the invisible, spiritual realm manifesting within our own life."[15] Every animal has a speciality and a powerful spirit. Andrews and his wife have a close kinship with the wolf. In traditional societies, this affinity with an animal is called one's totem. The totem becomes a guide throughout life and helps the individual through crises and life passages and assists in healing. In his book, Andrews recalls a birthday on which he camped in the woods of Ontario and heard the howling of wolves coming from different directions all through the night, even though it was unusual to hear wolves during that time of year. In another trip to the woods, he and his wife had been camping for several days and had felt that a wolf would surely appear. "People visit Superior year after year with no wolf contact, but we felt if the wolf were truly our totem we should have faith and try. As we prepared to leave the area, disappointed, a beautiful wolf stepped out from the trees and stood about thirty feet in front of us. It turned and stared, its eyes locked on ours for what seemed an eternity. Then it crossed and followed us in the shadows of the trees before disappearing once more into the woods, leaving us thrilled and blessed."[16]

Elmer Schettler, the soybean farmer we quoted in Chapter 1, shared his experience with watching for omens and becoming aware of the gifts that animals bring us. "I've found that when I don't force issues and let them kind of ferment, I get my answers," he said. "I have two great friends, Tom and Judy Crowley. Tom and I talk weekly, and one day he called to invite me down for Easter. I was flying down there in my plane, and I suddenly notice that I have a triple 119 on my navigation system. Heading is 119, bearing is 119, and airspeed is 119. I was instantly reminded of a time in 1983 when I had read Kushner's book *When Bad Things Happen to Good People*. I distinctly remembered that on page 119, he said that when you pray God sends you people. When I read that, I was on a United flight 119, and it was 1:19 in the afternoon. So as I'm flying I get chills, and I think this has got to be a significant day.

"Tom and Judy and I went to the Easter service at Unity church, and the sermon was right on target about some things I was thinking about. Afterwards, we drove out of the parking lot, and Tom 'mistakenly' took a right turn instead of a left. As we were turning around, a badger ran across our path. Now, you never see a badger in the daytime! Judy immediately said, 'We have to look up badger in the *Animal Medicine* book!' We looked up badger, and it was perfect because the message was about being more assertive.

"The bottom line is yes, you pray and God sends you messages if you just have the presence of mind to pay attention to them. The universe is talking to us all the time. When I got home I consciously began calling on 'badger energy' to help make me assertive—not obnoxious—but assertive in those areas of my life where I need to speak out.

"Another time Tom and I were talking on the phone on a Saturday morning and a crow comes and sits on my window. I mentioned it to him, but we didn't think to look up the message of the crow. Judy did, though, and the message was reminding us that there is a higher order of right and wrong than what human culture says. It was about personal integrity and speaking out the Truth. All these things make me wonder how many things go by me during the day!"

It may be that if our level of vibration is low, an animal will merely be there with us, performing its usual ecological functions. As David, the Native American character in *The Tenth Insight,* says, "A skeptical biologist reduces animal behavior to mindless instinct, he sees the restriction that he himself has put upon the animal. But as our vibration shifts, the actions of the animals that come to us become ever more synchronistic, mysterious, and instructional."[17]

Dan Miller from Las Vegas wrote to *The Celestine Journal* (November 1995) to tell a story of how he was working at a little garden on a ranch that also had eighty to ninety beehives on the property. Ordinarily, the bees were constantly buzzing near the house and its available water, but never bothered anyone. As he was bending over at the waist pulling weeds, two bees started flying around and between his hands and would not go away. He writes, "I stood up, exclaiming, 'What the hell!' At that instant I heard a rifle report. A second later I heard the slug whistle past where I had been bent over, not a foot in front of me. The bees flew away. I realized later that one of the old ranch hands had gone out to shoot varmints with a .22 rifle. I never did tell the old man how close he came to shooting me."[18]

## We Developed the Animal Traits Ourselves During the Course of Evolution

As a life form whose origins evolved out of the mysterious waters from fish to amphibian, to reptile to mammal, our ancient selves experienced life as those species. A complete spiritual consciousness, therefore, encompasses the vibrations of the animal, mineral, and vegetable kingdoms—not just of humankind.

Paul MacLean, chief of the Laboratory of Brain Evolution and Behavior at the National Institute of Mental Health, developed a three-part model of the brain based on its evolution. Each of these three parts is dedicated to retaining the physiological and behavioral matrices of more primitive life forms. Jean Houston, director of the Foundation for Mind Research in Pomona, New York, writes in her book *The Possible Human,* "One might call it a kind of evolutionary polyphrenia stemming from the fact that we look at reality through the receptors of three quite different mentalities of different ages and functions, with the two older 'brains' lacking the possibility of verbal communication. . . . We find, for instance, that the routine and ritually driven behavior of reptiles and amphibians translates in our human expression into obsessive-compulsive acts. . . . In our midbrain the battlings and nurturings of mammals as well as their elaborate preparations for partnership and procreation provide the emotional momentum for the development of family, clan, and the early basis of civilization . . . [as well as] the neurochemical patterns that make for war, aggression, dominance, and alienation. . . . And finally there is our neomammalian brain . . . part a cold, calculating computer, part the home for paradox and a vehicle for transcendence, it is that aspect of ourselves that apportions our fate and determines whether as a species we will grow or die."[19]

> The discovery of the quantum realm opened a way to follow the influence of the sun, moon, and sea down deeper into ourselves. I am taking you there only in the hope that there is even more healing to be found there. We already know that a human fetus develops by remembering and imitating the shapes of fish, amphibians, and early mammals. Quantum discoveries enable us to go into our very atoms and remember the early universe itself. **Deepak Chopra, M.D.,** *Quantum Healing*

When a particular animal shows up in a dream or real life, it means we're ready to integrate this consciousness into our waking awareness again. In realizing our own common origins and links to other species, we cannot help but become aware of the necessity of preserving this rich diversity of form *and consciousness* from which we sprang. As David remarks in the novel, "We want them to endure not just because they are a part of the balanced ecosphere, but because they represent aspects of ourselves that we're still trying to remember."[20]

### OTHER OMENS

When we ask for guidance, we tend to have a heightened sense of awareness. It's important to fill ourselves with buoyant, expectant energy as we go about the day. We may overhear a sentence that suddenly stands out. We might hear a special word that suddenly distinguishes itself from the sounds made in a crowd, or hear a relevant radio announcement. One man told us how he had been on his way to deliver some music tapes to a country club but had forgotten to bring the directions. He had just stopped at some railroad tracks, wondering whether to turn left or right when, at that moment, he heard an advertisement on his car radio for this same country club. The announcer said, "Just remember, turn left at the railroad tracks!" This coincidence went even deeper because after delivering his tapes, he ran into someone that later made it possible for him to realize his dream of playing music with several famous bands.

Oracles have enjoyed a rich tradition for centuries. The *I Ching,* the *Book of Changes,* is an oracle system, and may be the oldest book on the planet. This book of wisdom observes all patterns of life from the movement of the stars to the relationships within families, to the practice of business, the cycles of agriculture, and the outcomes of warfare. It combines mythic themes with practical everyday concerns, and offers accurate advice through the synchronistic fall of coins or yarrow sticks. Jung became fascinated with the *I Ching* because he felt its hexagrams reflected the archetypes of the collective unconscious. R. L. Wing, author of *The I Ching Workbook,* says, "[Jung] saw human nature and cosmic order united in the collective unconscious through symbols that affect people of any time and of any culture. . . . [The] ritual of stopping time (or 'change') with a particular question in mind is a way of aligning your Self and your circumstances within the background of all that is unfolding in the universe."[21]

Numbers are also potent symbols that convey meaning to us if we take the time to learn their characteristics. Ancient spiritual teachers taught that each number describes intrinsic qualities that could help us attune to what is unfolding. Even the numbers of one's address or office might tell a story. For example, a woman, a highly successful saleswoman, told us that one of the reasons she felt good about taking a certain new apartment was that its numbers added up to 3—always a lucky number for her and also the number of abundance, imagination, and sociability. We have also heard numerous stories from people who repeatedly see a particular number, for instance the number 11-11, which may indicate that a person is part of a soul group working to open up a new portal in the spiritual dimension.

Almost anything can become charged with meaning when we are open and alert for intuitive messages. Sometimes you might be following signals that lead you to deliver a message to someone else. Nancy Vittum from Cupertino, California, wrote to *The Celestine Journal,*

"While writing one morning, I got the strongest inner urging to go to the video store and rent a video. There was none I especially wanted to see, so at first I ignored the suggestion. It persisted, urging me to go early before all the good videos were taken." When she arrived at the store, she ran into someone she had worked with ten years before. It turned out the woman was dealing with her ailing eighty-six-year-old mother, and Nancy had just spent five and a half years caring for her parents before they died. Nancy said, "The woman told me she was sure that fate had brought us together that morning because what I shared had helped her so much."[22]

## DIMENSIONAL OPENINGS

Alice in Wonderland did it. So did Indiana Jones, the Druids, and the ancient Greeks. Shamans still do it—that is, enter another dimension through a sacred place in the living earth. Sacred sites. The very idea conjures up windy mountaintops, howling wolves, waterfalls, caves, enchanted valleys, prophetic stones, and portals to the ancestors. God speaks to us in the sighing trees, in warm rocks humming in the sun, in silent ancient handprints on cliff dwellings, in the ocher paths trod years ago by thousands of bare feet, running and walking to meet the spirit—to be reborn into the spirit. Long before Gothic spires drew our hearts upward, men and women found inspiration and connection to the divine in certain power places on the Earth. How many times have you been lucky enough to have your breath taken away with the splendor of a vista of an endless sea of trees, standing on a mesa with a drop of a thousand yards, absorb the quiet *presence* of an old-growth forest, or be silenced by the roar of a torrential cascade of water over granite boulders?

> . . . only a handful of Hopi are alive who know all of these places. Like their brothers and sisters around the world who still feel and sense the power of place, these wise minds say that the power of sacred places lies in more than visible beauty. They acknowledge that history is important, but of much greater importance, they insist, is spirit. This spirit can work with people of all races, but only if one's mind is clear and one's heart is pure. . . . certain special places in nature have the capacity to facilitate people entering altered states of awareness which are called "spiritual" as a result of direct mental and/or physical contact with them.
>
> James A. Swan, *Sacred Places: How the Living Earth Seeks Our Friendship*

Not enough by any count. Not nearly enough. Sacred sites need no explanation, no map. They are. You feel it, and are enlarged.

Kevin Ryerson, an expert intuitive, author, and lecturer best known for his association with actress and activist Shirley MacLaine, has the rare gift of contacting ancient spirits. In the past few years, he has taken people on journeys to sacred sites around the world in the spirit of the time-honored vision quest, making it possible for them to enter into what he calls the personal dreamscape. The purpose behind the quest, he told us, is to resolve the past, empowering the initiate to receive insights about his or her purpose, about the future, and to experience ancestral intelligence as a living force.

In the red rock territory of Sedona, Arizona, there is a sacred canyon that is known as Red Tank Draw. The canyon, forming a natural wall, is the backdrop for a series of petroglyphs (carved images) and pictoglyphs (painted symbols) on both the left and the right sides. Aligned with the sun, the canyon, when walked by the initiate or the vision quester, takes the person on an entire shamanic journey, beginning at dawn and completing at sunset. The canyon, chosen for its alignment with the four directions, according to Ryerson, reflects and *holds* ancestral, archetypal intelligence. Just reading the description below will connect you to this mythic experience.

At the beginning of the journey you will see creation images of birth and innocence. These primal images symbolize the separation of the spirit from the body on the shamanic journey, but could also be interpreted as *you* separating from your first truth or innocence. It is the archetype of being orphaned, says Ryerson, and the indigenous equivalent of the expulsion from the Garden of Eden. You, the orphan, become now the wanderer, shamanically represented by migratory animals. The petroglyphs clearly show animals moving in association with the Celtic cross, which represents the four directions and a sacred destination—what might be called "wandering with intent" or being on a journey. At this stage, you are wandering among the ancestors and living people, seeking a truth that looks and feels like you, so that you may recognize it.

When you, the initiate, discover a truth that is relevant to who you are, it reempowers you, restoring and reinvigorating your sense of destiny. (How like the coincidence bringing us insight that reconnects us to our sense of mission!) At this point, says Ryerson, the initiate becomes the warrior. In this new state of sensitivity, you may feel almost too sensitive. You may try to protect your truth—a truth that does not need protecting. This stage is represented in the form of turtles (an archetypal symbol for being shielded). The turtle's shell also represents the patterns of divination which could be read by the sage, providing you, now a warrior, with the guidance of prophecy.

You are now the warrior, represented by the archer and the drawn bow. You are now at the place of seven arrows, symbolizing the seven chakras, the origins of material and spiritual energy. These are the psychic zones from which we draw our character and let loose our energy into the world. Deep in the canyon now, you are on your mission. Archetypally, you are the hero. Joseph Campbell, Ryerson reminds us, said the perfect hero's myth was *Star Wars*. Imagine for a moment the exhilaration and acceleration you felt when you were flying with Luke Skywalker through the canyonlike bowels of the Death Star! If you remember, he spoke of a canyon back home where he had performed the same feat. In Red Tank Draw, then, you are on the Hero's Journey.

In your warrior phase, you come to realize that the face of the enemy looks like you—the psychological stage of owning back all your rejected parts that you have put into shadow. At that moment or realization, you become empowered, and initiated into the next phase of the journey, which is the healer. You realize that if you can inflict pain, you can heal pain. The healer is represented by the spiral in the palm of the hand.

The most difficult part of the journey comes when, as the healer, you realize that you are really no different from the warrior you were. Healing merely by trying to *eliminate* disease or pain is still a process of fighting the other.

In an ecstatic moment of healing (connection), you suddenly see the *other's* original innocence. Ryerson comments on this stage by saying, "And in seeing that innocence, you must practice a new standard of truth, the truth that can only be spoken of in the presence of a child."

This is the point of rebirth in the journey. This is when all the ancestors come to welcome a new person (you) into the village. "Literally," says Ryerson, "at this point in the canyon, you come around the corner, and see the spiritual, alchemical template which is only comparable to the moment in the movie *2001*. You see the blackness, the void, the obelisk that can absorb everything, all the pain, all the suffering, all the errors, all the perceptions of identity. This moment is like a snake shedding its skin. It's then that you no longer worry about the future. You know what you are becoming. And what you are becoming is an ancestor. The archetype of the ancestor is resolved to history, resolved to himself, and you realize that just like the petroglyphs, your life isn't real until it's been told like a story."

At the end of the canyon walk, you are confronted with a monolithic red rock cliff. This is the place of empowerment, the only place in the canyon where all the images are repeated as one cohesive vision. This is sacred space. What is taught to the journeyer? "You are taught what you need to know," says Ryerson. "People tell me they get vivid dreams after their walk. They feel more alive. They make inner resolutions with parents, relationships, and careers. The intelligence in the canyon is alive, and influences our lives today. The human family is continuous. What is applicable to the ancestors is applicable to us today."

James A. Swan writes in *Sacred Places: How the Living Earth Seeks Our Friendship*, "Around the world, the Earth's surface is sprinkled with places whose names alone stir deep feelings in us: Palenque, Mount Omei, Mount Ararat, Mount Fuji, Lascaux, Iona, Jerusalem, Delphi, Mount Kilimanjaro, Mecca, Mount Sinai, Mount McKinley or 'Denali,' Chartres, the Great Pyramids, Stonehenge, Haleakala Crater, Mount Kailas, the Ganges River, Mount Katahdin, Machu Picchu, Lourdes, Fatima, and the Sun Temple at Mesa Verde are among the most famous. . . ."[23] We might even visit the contemporary phenomenon of the crop circles of the Salisbury Plain which baffles our logical mind, but plucks the chord of mystery in our soul.

## INDIVIDUAL STUDY

### Mindfulness Meditation

Choose a quiet place in your home where you will be able to sit in meditation. If possible, create a sacred feeling in this place. You might have a small table with flowers or special items that remind you of your desire to cultivate the ability to quiet the mind. Select a regular time to sit in meditation, such as in the morning before leaving the house or in the evening before or after dinner.

Seat yourself with erect posture with feet on the floor, hands resting lightly on your thighs, palms upward. If you wish, you may instead sit cross-legged on the floor with a pillow under your bottom so that you are solidly grounded. To signal the beginning of your meditation, close your eyes, put your palms together over the center of your chest, and make a small bow with your head. Hands on thighs again, exhale the breath, with eyes remaining closed or slightly open but downcast.

Simply notice that your breath goes in, and your breath goes out. When thoughts come into your mind, let them flow right on through. Go back to noticing your breath. Even though the mind strays again to a thought, let it flow away. Feel each sensation of the breath as it comes in through the nostrils, raises the chest, and flows out into the room. Let yourself soften with each breath. Let go of muscle tension as you feel it. Continue to follow the breath and soften the mind, the senses, the breathing. When your mind wanders away, mindfully notice that it has gone. As if you were observing the thought as an object, acknowledge the thought with one word such as "worrying," "sadness," "thinking," "coldness," and return to the breath, no matter how long your mind has been wandering away. Be gentle and attentive in your meditation, always returning to the rhythm of the breath. Sit this way for ten minutes a day in the beginning, increasing to thirty minutes to an hour as you wish. End your meditation with another small bow of the head, palms together. The bowing ritual is not only an acknowledgment of your readiness to go within, but a signal to your ego to relax for a while and open to higher energy.

The immediate effect of meditation is to bring you into the present moment, to let you become aware of where your mind is taking you, as well as to allow you to calm the restless striving mind. Over time, even though your mind continues to wander during meditation, you may notice that awareness of feelings, and the frequency and clarity of intuitions, have increased.

## Mindfulness During the Day

To increase energy and clear the mind, even if you are somewhere in public or at work, take five minutes on the subway or at lunch to sit quietly, eyes downcast but not closed, and notice the quality and sensations of your breathing. This simple act will help bring you fully present into the moment.

Another mindfulness activity to do during the day is to take a five-minute break to stare out the window, or simply sit quietly in front of

---

As a novice in a Buddhist monastery, I was taught to be aware of each thing I did throughout the day, and for more than fifty years, I have been practicing this. When I started, I thought this kind of practice was only for beginners, that advanced people did more important things, but now I know that the practice of mindfulness is for everyone. **Thich Nhat Hanh, *Love in Action***

your work area and become aware of each element of your surroundings, breathing loving energy out into the space.

One man in a workshop said, "My mind is too restless to meditate. I can't get quiet enough to meditate." Quieting the mind before meditating is like cleaning the house before the housecleaner comes. The first step in meditation is the *intention* to sit. Then take the unquiet mind and sit with it, observing, softening, and slowing it to the steady rhythm of the breath.

## Mindfulness When Commuting by Car

When you start your car for the trip to work or to do an errand, make a habit of becoming present when you turn the key. Become aware that you are going out to join a stream of other souls doing work in the world in their own way. As you enter traffic, increase your awareness of vehicles, pedestrians, bicycles, or any other pertinent information. Keep your intention on driving in the most skillful, loving way you can, knowing that you are part of this great stream of beings who are connected to you in ways you are as yet unaware of. Send loving energy to this stream of beings of which you are one part.

When traffic is slower than you wish, imagine yourself at your destination feeling happy and seeing that you are almost exactly on time. If you see a license plate or some other seemingly special message, jot it down when you reach your destination. If it stays with you for some time, do some free-association writing to it.

## Active Imagination

You may want to take time once a week or a couple of times a month to use a guided meditation tape to help bring up your intuitive faculty.

If you have had an intuition or image come into your mind, strengthen it by writing it down in your journal. It is sometimes easier to write down thoughts than to keep them in the mind. To free-associate to it, start with your intuition and then begin to tell a story from it. Let your pen write whatever comes into your mind. Don't stop and change anything, just keep writing and fill up two or three pages. You can review what has emerged right then, or look it over two or three days later.

## Animal Totems

Animal totems are your special animal spirit. The animal "chooses you" by appearing to you in dreams or in nature, or by capturing your imagination through stories or pictures to which you are drawn. If you try to choose your own totem, you will pick an animal for its exotic or glamorous "image," which means your ego is involved! Begin to notice any birds or animals that you see on your walks, or near your house, or when you go camping. What were you thinking about when you saw the animal? If you are worried or concerned about something, what would that animal's message be for you?

If you already have a special relationship to an animal, bring its energy closer to you by keeping a picture or small sculpture of it in your house. Learn about its characteristics and imagine speaking to it when you have a difficult decision. Your link to the animal medicine is through your imagination. You might also want to purchase *Medicine Cards*, by Jamie Sams and David Carson, to learn more about the characteristics of each species. Ted Andrews' book *Animal-Speak* has a wealth of information and suggestions for working with our animal brethren.

## GROUP STUDY

### Visualizing

*For Peace on the Planet (can be done individually or in a group)*

If your desire is to contribute to world peace, but you have no idea how to do that, make an intention to do a visualizing meditation for "peace work" every day or every week. Do the mindfulness meditation until you feel soft and calm. Then bring into mind your vision of what peace looks like. It could be a circle of people holding hands around a desert campfire, people holding hands across continents and seas, people smiling and walking around streets, chatting and doing everyday activities with love in their hearts and faces. It could include people of many cultures sitting together and expressing their views in the spirit of genuine, healthy controversy. Once you have established an image that really makes you feel full of love and aliveness, use it frequently during the day outside your meditation time. Expect an opportunity to come to you that leads you further into peace work.

Visualizing the activity or social action you feel most strongly about is a very empowering act. Remember that energy follows thought, and what you focus on expands. Create one strong visual image for what you feel most strongly about, whether it is preserving the rain forests, loving and caring for all the homeless children, building homes and schools, caring for the sick, or helping people irrigate gardens in the desert. Choose one area that most appeals to you and focus on seeing this positive action taking place. Expect an opportunity to come to you that leads you further into that kind of interaction.

## Topics for Group Dialogue

- How do you handle doubt and fear when your intuition seems to suggest a new direction?
- What animals have appeared in your life at special moments?

## Intuition Practice

- Take turns receiving intuitive messages from members of the group. This exercise can take anywhere from five to ten minutes per person and is great fun. One person sits facing the others with eyes closed and *remains silent*. Everyone tunes into the energy of this person and then verbally gives positive information or images that are received about this person. Everyone speaks spontaneously as the images come to mind. Have one person write down all the information received for that person. When the energy feels complete, let the "it" person give feedback about the accuracy of the information received.
- Experiment with the *I Ching* or another intuitive tool.
- Have each member write down a specific question on a piece of paper. Mix them up, draw out one question (do not unfold it and look at the question), and put the piece of paper in the center of the room. Have everyone close their eyes and begin to pick up whatever images or messages come to them *without censoring them*. Call them out loud and have someone write down these messages. When the energy feels complete, open up the question and see how the answers apply!

## Dream Work

- Analyze the contents of a dream. Make sure everyone wants to do this, as dream analysis may become tedious or boring if some people don't want to participate. Look for the message that reveals something that *you are not aware of* in your current life.

# CHAPTER 4

# Clearing

BUTTERFLY
CHANGE

I thought about the many group situations I'd experienced, where some members of the group liked each other immediately, while others seemed to fall into instant discord, for no apparent reason. I wondered: was human culture now ready to perceive the distant source of these unconscious reactions?

THE TENTH INSIGHT:
HOLDING THE VISION[1]

The Insights have told us that the best thing we can do for ourselves is to fill up with positive, loving energy. However, if we want to be in the flow of life, we also have to stop *spending* energy in repetitive and fruitless energy exchanges with people. We cannot accumulate enough positive energy to create the life we want if we are leaking energy. We leak energy when we allow others to drain us and when we lack perception of our control dramas.

We know we worry. We hear ourselves say twenty times a day, "I don't know where the time goes." "I'll never finish this work." "I can't afford that." "That's way too expensive." "You can't count on anybody." Or some variation of these themes. These are all small ways that we spend energy negatively. We know that some people easily push our buttons and make us feel mad or irritable or guilty.

At the perception level of the Tenth Insight, our Birth Vision is guiding us to the people we need to meet and the work we need to do. Our work is in alignment with the World Vision to the extent that we are mindful of the effect of our actions on others and are actively seeking ways to make the world better for everyone. At this level, we have cleared many of our earlier issues and have let go of trying to control other people. Why, then, do we still run into situations where people push our buttons?

You might start by reminding yourself, "I know the external world is a reflection of my internal state." Ask yourself, Am I stuck in my old control drama behavior? Am I filtering my perceptions about myself and the other person through an old belief because I feel threatened or afraid? What intuitions or synchronicities have I failed to listen to lately? If a struggle is going on inside you with someone, increase your quiet time in meditation. Look at your dreams for telltale scenarios that give you another vivid image of your current internal state and apply that message to your conflict with the other person.

At the level of perception of the Tenth Insight, we are willing to consider the possibility that negative reactions to people may be left over from a relationship with them in a previous lifetime. The Tenth Insight suggests that these irrational feelings of guilt, irritation—maybe even fears of betrayal—could be residual memories from unresolved issues from past lives that we have shared with the person. Of course, we might also have irrational *good* feelings toward a person as well, indicating very positive past-life experiences with that soul. Since negative feelings cause us greater turmoil and affect our ability to live our purpose, we will concentrate in this chapter on how to untangle ourselves from these threads or ropes of negative energy.

## CLEARING CONTROL DRAMAS CREATED IN OUR *PRESENT* LIFETIME

The Sixth Insight suggests that as children we began using certain behaviors in order to stay connected to our parents upon whom we depended for survival. These behaviors grew out of how we perceived our parents. If we saw them as scary and overbearing, we reacted one way. If we saw them as critical and invasive, we reacted another way. If we saw them as victims who continually complain, we reacted yet another way. Over time, these behaviors solidified into what we call control dramas. The *control* aspect means that we were trying to keep control of the sometimes uncertain connection to our parents' love and attention—to ensure our very survival. So we learned how to control our environment in the only way we knew at that level of development. The *drama* aspect means that we kept doing this same behavior into adulthood, being limited by these outmoded habitual responses.

According to our natures, some of us may have screamed and thrown tantrums to intimidate our parents into paying attention to us—learning to control others by being an *Intimidator*. Some of us may have pestered our parents with constant questions or blatantly disruptive acts because they were absent or aloof—learning to become an *Interrogator* to get their attention. Some of us may have tried to hide out or get away with surreptitious disruptive acts because our parents were intrusive and critical—learning to stay *Aloof* and distant. And lastly, some of us may have whimpered and sucked our thumbs in passive reaction to a threatening, intimidating parent—learning to survive by getting others to see us as a helpless *Poor Me,* needing their attention.

As adults these control drama tactics are not only largely ineffective and unfulfilling, but are also *very real blocks to the synchronicities that create fresh opportunities to develop our Birth Vision.* In short, unless we wake up to these reactive patterns, we are stuck. We might be trying, for example, to intimidate others into giving us what we want (money, love, attention, recognition, etc.) by aggressive, judgmental, threatening, or self-centered behavior. As Intimidators, we are fearful of not being taken seriously, and so we want to scare off potential threats to our freedom or our self-importance. Actually, the Intimidator type of personality is often completely unaware of what his or her real needs and feelings are.

*Intimidators see the world as a battlefield.* Anytime we operate from a need to control everything, we limit or cut off serendipitous support. If the Intimidator expects life to be a struggle and that others are out to take his power away, then he will attract that kind of situation. Energy follows thought. The battle going on within the person will be manifested outside in the physical world.

This person will not be able to hold a vision for the world if his main mode of interaction is confrontation and aggressiveness. He is too busy fighting internal battles to be able to extend himself to help others. Everyone who plays out the Intimidator role in his own life is contributing that conflict/battlefield mentality to the unified field of consciousness—thus maintaining the old worldview.

*Interrogators see the world as a game of wits.* These people are always watching others to find weak points, and move in to take advantage. They undermine others' ideas with rhetorical questions that divide and distance them from people, rather than creating honest give-and-take. One of their favorite statements is, "I'm going to be the devil's advocate here." Clearly, controversy is healthy. Legitimate debate is not the same as the Interrogator control drama, which is a habituated response for the purpose of stealing energy from the other person and maintaining a feeling of control. For example, announcing frequently that one is going to be the devil's advocate creates distance and sets up an adversarial position. The real motivation of a constant devil's advocate is to be seen as important so as to ensure a flow of attention. If they raise the question, you must answer, and are immediately placed on the defensive. Therefore, their own need to be important creates a divisive and corrosive element, which is not truly helpful in creating a positive vision for a project or for the world. Their interior drive is to tear down ideas, rather than to be open to other people's wisdom. This control drama on a global scale keeps separation—"us" and "them"—suspicion, and hatred fueled.

*Aloof people see the world as threatening or overwhelming.* They prefer to withdraw and not take an active, responsible part in shaping the world. They are afraid of taking a stand or perhaps making a mistake and being criticized or being seen as inadequate, so they do little or nothing to stand up and be counted. This aloof behavior also keeps people separate and subtly creates a drain on others. By remaining distant and closed off, Aloofs feel isolated, distrustful, and then justified when things fall through or turn out badly. They are unable to see that they were unconsciously creating a failure because they were not truly participating in events. Aloof people are often shy, or afraid to let others know what they feel, because they fear (having had an Interrogator or Intimidator parent) that someone will invalidate their needs or feelings. Feeling invalidated is like a negation or death and throws them into survival mode.

Aloofs see others as potential invaders. They may feel strongly about how the world could be a better place, but not take action because they resist committing to taking the first step. Innately cautious and a little suspicious of others' motives, Aloofs tend to resist serendipitous encounters. On a global scale, they become the "innocent" or apathetic bystanders instead of acting from a healthy responsiveness to the world.

*Poor Me people see the world as unfair.* Other people or situations are the problem. For them, the world is demonstrably out of control and to be defended against at all cost. You can recognize the poor-me attitude in such statements as, "You can't change anything." "Rich people make all the rules." "I don't have any time to myself." "If it weren't for the IRS, I'd be in great shape." "You people never did give me what I asked for." "I'll never be able to get ahead." And on and on. Poor Me's see themselves as powerless and put their wounds and problems right out front in all conversation. They define themselves by their past traumas and extract attention and energy from others by continuously focusing on negativities to lure others into giving them energy.

Actually, our entire culture focuses on the idea of victimhood. Via television, we are able to be present at virtually every crime scene and tragedy. The sheer mass of media coverage feeds the perspective that unless we are very, very careful, we, too, will wind up shot dead, dismembered, homeless, or bankrupt. The poor-me attitude focuses on the fearful and negative aspects of a World Vision. If everything is going downhill anyway, then this is a good excuse to stay mired in inaction.

Caroline Myss, a writer, researcher, and medical intuitive, speaks eloquently on our addiction to a victim mentality in a taped lecture called *Why People Don't Heal.* Myss contends that we turn our wounds into power and become addicted to the identity and privilege our wounds give us. For example, we inevitably share tidbits of our past history with people in general conversation. We let people know the suffering we have endured, whether it be childhood abuse, incest, alcoholism, the death of a child, or some other deprivation or failure.

> The really major disaster of history is the separation of mother and infant at birth. This experience of abandonment is the most devastating event of life, which leaves us emotionally and psychologically crippled. The mother often experiences . . . "postpartum blues," cut off from the bonding that was supposed to happen. For a while she will weep, but the weeping gives way to anger, hardness, an armor covering a gaping wound that is never healed, that most women aren't even aware of, since it is projected onto the general environment and too often taken out on the hapless infant-child." **Joseph Chilton Pearce,** *Evolution's End*

Obviously, when something negative happens, you need support and time to deal with the consequences. With time, you heal and move on. But if you keep the wound fresh and use it as a way to filter everything else in your life, the wound serves as an excuse for why you cannot succeed.

Myss believes that, essentially, we have left part of our soul in these early traumas, and we are continuing to feed them because they still seem unfair. The energy that we get from others who listen to our tales gives us power. Therefore, we cannot or will not let these past wounds go. Naturally, we all have a past and legitimate hardships that have strengthened us. But keeping these negative events alive in the present *saps our psychic energy for creating a new path,* for fulfilling our Birth Vision.

Once we change our perception and realize that those occurrences may have happened for a reason, we can let go of the idea that we were really harmed by anything. Myss says, "You [will] have freed yourself from a disempowering perception . . . the consequence [of that] is an ascension to a higher order of perception. . . . Forgiveness is so powerful because you are calling your spirit back from perceptions of blame, excuse, weakness, all of which are attached to the idea of an eye-for-an-eye justice."[2]

Life changes dramatically when you make inner shifts of perception. When you no longer desire to stay fixated on how others have harmed you, your relationships will shift. Myss says, "The moment you stop being the victim, you are going to have to stop hanging out with victims . . . because they are going to say, 'My, haven't you changed!' They won't be happy, they will see it as betrayal. You have to be strong enough to let yourself be seen as having changed . . . because you cannot take all your worlds with you. . . . There will be a fear . . . what will my world look like if I'm healthy? What does it look like to bond out of strength? . . . When you share wounds, you have a private agenda: (1) you want power over the other person; (2) you have an intention to control them; and (3) you're planning for a rainy day when you are going to need their support, which is long-range manipulation planning."[3]

### CASE STUDY OF THE POOR ME/INTIMIDATOR CONTROL DRAMA

A woman we'll call Jane became aware of how many intimidating people she had in her life after reading *The Celestine Prophecy* in 1993. Feeling drained and angry at how she was "being treated," she also felt guilty and insecure that she was not doing enough to please these people. "Since I had three major Intimidators in my life, I had to face the fact that I was attracting them for a reason. My first thought was how much like my mother they were," she told us. "I think it had to get really painful before I could go deep enough to recognize the pattern. I was absolutely determined to break my control dramas."

Jane called recently to report on her progress in the past six months. "I feel noticeably different now," she said. "For example, I've changed my whole attitude about my real estate business. Six months ago I was feeling that it was wrong for me. Now I am attracting very good clients, and I'm excited to work with them. I feel more creative and optimistic, and that makes me a nicer person. I feel more relaxed inside instead of that old panicky feeling. I've started making money again, but it isn't just about money because I've had financially good years before and I still had a lot of those panicky feelings. I've really worked on my poor-me attitude, and I feel like I've lifted some kind of lid. Irritations just don't have the cumulative effect they used to have." What happened? we asked.

> The power others possess is the power I give them. . . . If I have endowed the *Other* with power that the *Other* does not possess, then I face my own power, do I not? My own power has become my opponent, my enemy. On the other hand, if the *Other* possesses power, but I do not perceive the *Other*'s power as effective against me, he has none—none for me. **Gerry Spence, How to Argue and Win Every Time**

"First, I knew these people were there for a reason. I kept being drawn to difficult people. They could hook me easily—it was almost like being mesmerized. I can't explain it but I knew I was working an old pattern," Jane said. "Secondly, I began to see how there was always a blowup when I ignored my own needs until they built up. I'd see these people as being demanding and selfish, but I'd take all the blame and be overaccommodating. Then because my anger had built up, I'd jump to being a bigger Intimidator than they were. I guess I felt I didn't have any power to confront them unless I was full of anger, which made me feel more powerful.

"I gave myself away so much that eventually I had to take a stand. I got to the point of feeling like I was on automatic. I'd lose my energy and then blow up. Afterwards, I'd feel guilty. I was focusing entirely on them and their problems, forgetting my needs completely.

"My first step was to get an intellectual understanding of control dramas. I also worked with a counselor. During each encounter with one of my Intimidators, I paid close attention to how I was feeling. Then I began to ask myself, What choices do I have here? I tried different options, like 'I have to get off the phone now' or 'I don't like how you're talking to me.'

"In the beginning, after I got off the phone with one of these people, I would have a huge pit in my stomach. But as I kept up my intention to break the drama and keep my power, I saw that they were actually treating me nicer. When they screamed or yelled, I let it roll off my back. I learned more detachment. I kept my attention on taking care of myself, instead of focusing on what they were doing. This was my first major shift—to 'think of Jane.'

"I kept a journal, writing down what they said, what I said, how I felt. I'd review it and kept asking myself, How can I be smoother at this? What could I do differently next time? I really practiced because I didn't know what I was doing! It's like I was on automatic pilot and the visors were up and I was completely blind to my choices."

### Getting Hooked

Jane's story has several elements that are found in the dysfunctional control drama behaviors. First, she recognized a recurring pattern of intimidating people. She was drawn to difficult people and was "hooked." The hook serves the function of getting her attention so she can heal this old system.

### Projection of Anger Colored Other Decisions

Next, she saw that she had been denying the extent of her pain, but all the while building anger. She projected the pain and anger onto the job situation. This projection of painful feelings convinced her that real estate was not the right place for her. Third, she ignored her true feelings and focused only on the behavior of the other person, almost as if she were not present in the event. She would experience an energy loss, react by getting angry, and then feel guilty—which, of course, meant she was spending a lot of energy on replay and guilt.

### Getting Back into the Body as a Source of Information

Jane began to turn her control drama around with the increasing awareness of how she hooked into the drama. As she began to reconnect with the physical sensations in her neck and stomach, she was more able to take care of herself *in the moment,* not just afterward in the replay of the encounter. She began to try different responses, letting others know it didn't feel okay to be yelled at or criticized. Most important, she kept her attention on her feelings, and her intention on working through the scary feelings, trusting this would lead her into liberating choices. She grew beyond the reactive, regressed need to defend and control, to feeling that she could take care of herself even when people were trying to take her energy.

## Realization That Other People Are Not Going to Make Your Life Work Better

Once she saw that her internal conflicts were being worked out in these difficult relationships, Jane began to see much more clearly that at a deep level each person represented something that she *unconsciously thought was necessary to her survival*. "I realized that I was hooked into one person because she was a celebrity, and I was afraid of losing that contact because it made me special, too, to have her as a client. My other client was very wealthy, very accomplished, and he had a beautiful house that I loved myself. I really wanted him to like me, and I wanted to sell a five-million-dollar house! The other person was very smart and extremely successful. She was a very good public speaker, and well connected, which I always felt I wasn't, and I envied her status and hoped that she would introduce me to other people like that. It's interesting, too, because following that realization about her, I 'coincidentally' had a chance to participate in a big event at which I was highly recognized for my speaking ability and my ability to attract a huge attendance. Suddenly, I felt like I got connected to my own source of power and energy! It was so clear to me that when I tried to connect to those three people, I lost energy, not gained it."

## Taking Back the Energy She Gave to Others

In psychological terms Jane owned back the qualities she had projected onto these people. She came into her own and no longer needed to attract Intimidators to heal her lack of self-esteem. She also detached from the underlying belief that her survival depended on pleasing difficult people, as she had done with her mother in childhood.

In order to stay connected to her own energy, Jane says, "I go to nature, run on the beach. I meditate. I look for the beauty around me, or I listen to music. I try to eat well. I've really learned not to react to all the ploys my clients pull. I know when to say no, to stay detached about how far I go in accommodating others so I don't set myself up as a victim. No matter how painful it is to say no, I have to hold my boundaries. I put my true needs first, and let others be who they are without trying to figure them out or change them.

"If I start feeling drained, I remember that I have a choice to change my behavior. Sometimes being at peace with myself might mean I do raise my voice, but the difference is that I'm staying centered in my own energy."

Now Jane says, "I am amazed at how things have shifted. I thought

I was going to leave real estate, but I was offered a position in this new firm where the dynamic is so different. Here, we're all working together. It's fun. I love these people. And you know, now that I'm looking at it, I realize I didn't even try to make this happen. Things have just been in a sort of flow." She was recently at lunch with her friend Patti and Patti's sister, Nadine. Nadine was sarcastically making fun of Jane and Patti's discussion about aromatherapy and astrology as "New Age B.S." Patti began to get upset with Nadine, but Jane said she just suddenly saw the whole thing as hilarious. Jane's laughter was contagious and Patti later thanked her for changing the energy from being so serious to one of friendly exchange. Jane said, "People can't continue with their attacks when you keep your own sense of humor."

Jane's determination, or intention, to change a painful pattern took her *into* the control drama in order to work *through* it. She didn't ignore people or change jobs. She began to see that there was a healing purpose behind the recurring pattern of attracting Intimidators. She found this purpose through writing about each episode and watching for messages in her dreams. She stopped feeling guilty for others' problems. She noticed when her energy dropped, and took measures to keep herself buoyant and full. Her intention to be whole within herself attracted new positive opportunities and changed her attitude about the rightness of herself and her work. As painful as it was for a while, the awareness and psychological work she did moved her to her next level of spiritual growth.

Coming into awareness and breaking free of a control drama always feels anxious at first, because the compulsion has to lift before the inward solution to the lostness can be found. That's why a "dark night of the soul" sometimes precedes increased awareness and spiritual euphoria. **James Redfield, *The Tenth Insight: Holding the Vision***

"Now I notice the warning signs or red flags. I can see these balls coming toward me like in soccer, and I just step to the side. A red flag for me is if a person starts approaching me too quickly, and I feel they are going to start blaming me, or being needy, or being overly aggressive. I can feel when they want something from me. I see them as being outside themselves. That's how I used to be—'outside myself.' I see myself as a moving part of my whole organization, and I'm not the center of the universe. When I was so egocentrically oriented, I couldn't see that everyone else was having their own reality going on, too. Even if they're putting me on a pedestal, and it feels good to the ego, eventually it's an out-of-balance relationship."

### HEAVY EQUIPMENT, HEAVY ENERGY

Jan E. from Oklahoma gave us another story about how becoming more aware of how people tend to control energy has opened up new ways of dealing with recalcitrant customers.

"We rent utility trailers for moving heavy equipment," she said, "and I deal with a lot of men. It seems in my work that many men just naturally tend to have an aggressive attitude when dealing with a woman around 'men things.' They come in kind of belligerent. I think that's how they think they will best get what they want or need. It used to get to me more. Since I read *The Celestine Prophecy* and the *Experiential Guide,* instead of feeling like a victim, I can see what people are doing.

"Understanding that control dramas start in childhood has helped me in that I don't feel so threatened. I can see that people are just doing what they learned to do. Some customers pull the Poor Me drama like, 'Oh, do you have to charge me for the full day?' and so forth. I can really see how they try to get sympathy and manipulate the circumstances in their favor. Seeing it so clearly almost makes me laugh sometimes."

Like Jane, Jan has transformed her internal and external experience of work. She has not psychoanalyzed anybody, she has not proselytized about spirituality, she has not pointed out anybody's faults. *She has made a perceptual shift within herself.* She does not automatically assume now that she is the cause of the rude behavior, nor does she struggle to stay in her own power. With new awareness, even her sense of humor flourishes.

### HARMONY INSIDE

A jazz musician from New Orleans, B.F., wrote a letter telling us: "The Celestine ideas have made a tremendous difference in my life. The coincidences are coming so fast that I started a journal to keep track of them. I have always played an Aloof drama, but now I'm realizing that the more I reach out to people, the more coincidences happen to keep me open.

"I formed my Aloof drama in response to my father who was an

Interrogator. He was an immigrant from Ireland and very practical. I wasn't. Music to him was an impractical idea. He actually talked me out of majoring in music, which cost me a lot. He used facts and logic, and I just couldn't explain my feeling to him. I became aloof and quiet. I've always known I was aloof, and that it kept me from taking greater risks and growing. . . . I wore a mask—which kept me from being myself, and I'm sure, affected my creativity. Now I see that the more I reach out to people, the more coincidences I have."

## ATTRACTING INTERROGATORS

Anne, who owns two businesses, told us that she had been in a big power struggle with her business partner, Joanie, when she read about control dramas. "Instantly, a lightbulb went off for me when I read about the Interrogator/Aloof dynamic. I could see how Joanie fit the Interrogator type. She always seemed to be looking over my shoulder and catching me in this or that error or questioning my methods. It was really bugging me, and I was beginning to doubt whether I was cut out to be in the business. But the even bigger piece of information that I got from the control dramas was seeing myself as the Aloof. I immediately realized, 'Hey, I'm creating this Interrogator response from Joanie!' I

---

THE LOCK: How do you get them so they'll at least listen to you? How do you open them?

THE KEY: The key is too simple. Give them all the power. Tell the truth. Be who you are.

If we could but open them up to receive our arguments!—for whenever the Other wants to hear us, the simplest argument will win. On the other hand, we can deliver the most skillful argument yet conceived by man and, until the Other is willing to hear us, we had just as well join the coyotes howling at the moon.

Empowering the Other to accept or reject our arguments removes the Other's fear, the fear that always defeats us. You could, for example, go to your spouse and say, "I've had enough of this work. I am going to go on a vacation next week. You can either get time off from your job and go with me or I'm going alone," in which case you may well go alone.

Or you might say, "Honey, I am really tired and I know you must be too. Whenever you can get time off from your job, the sooner the better, I'd like to take a little vacation." . . . By acknowledging that the decision rests solely with him, we take a no-lose position, since if we do not so empower the Other, he will always remain closed and protected against our arguments and we will always lose. **Gerry Spence, How to Argue and Win Every Time**

knew I had gone Aloof on her. I wasn't returning her phone calls until a few days had gone by. I wasn't telling her everything I was doing with some of our clients. I was withdrawing my energy from her because I basically wished she'd get off my back. I could see then that becoming distant from her triggered off her abandonment issues. I knew her background, and remembered that both her parents had disappeared on her at different times, and she really never learned to trust anybody. As I tended to get silent and secretive out of my own insecurity, I realized that she was probably thinking that I was leaving her out of everything.

"After that realization, I began to look at how my aloof behavior has affected every aspect of my life. For example, there was a time in my life when I should have questioned my doctor's decisions, but I didn't. I let it pass. Being aloof has also kept me from really committing to marketing my business, which affects my finances. Let's not even talk about my personal relationships!"

## CLEARING THE LOWER EMOTIONS

The ingredients common to all control dramas are the lower emotions. What are they? Whether we tend to be an Intimidator or a Poor Me, we all experience such negative emotional states as resentment, distrust, cynicism, insecurity, self-importance, anger, jealousy, or envy. These feelings arise out of fear or pain when we sense we are losing control over our life. Since these negative emotional states drain our energy and interfere with remembering our Birth Vision, it's helpful to notice when we are in their grip. Obviously, a rich, full emotional life encompasses *all* feelings because each feeling has a message. But if we are mired in heavy energy, we look at life with blinders, creating more of the energy that has fixated our mind. To create a positive World Vision requires us to be flexible, adaptable, and teachable. Just notice how heavy you physically feel the next time you get into a conflict or miscommunication.

### FLUSHING THE FIELD

Clearing our energy can be done by (1) noticing control dramas; (2) replacing old reactive choices with creative solutions; and (3) forgiving our past and moving on. Barbara Brennan is a teacher, healer, therapist, author, and scientist who has researched the human energy field for twenty years. Regarded as one of the most adept spiritual healers, she perceives the human energy field as a matrix structure upon which the cells of the physical body grow. According to her, our energy field is in constant flux as it continuously processes an inflow of information. Attitudes and decisions create changes in the energy dynamics. In an interview with Russell E. DiCarlo in *Towards a New World View,* she says, "When you forgive yourself, wonderful things happen. There is a certain tension and stagnated energy that is held in the field whenever there is anything that you won't accept within yourself. It's kind of like a mucus that you get when you have a cold. So you actually create distortions in your own energy pattern that have to do with unforgiveness towards yourself. These distortions will eventually lead to illness. When you forgive yourself, you are actually unblocking the flow of energy in your field so that it can flush itself out. . . . When you have a non-forgiving attitude towards an individual, there will be a definite pattern in your field. The outer edge of your field will become rigid and brittle when interacting with that person. There will be additional ways that you will not let your life energy flow out towards that person. There are great bands of energy or bio-plasmic streamers that normally flow between people when they interact. There's an exchange of life energy that normally goes on between all living things. . . . But if there is a sense of unforgiveness, all that will be stopped. There will be the same type of stoppage in the other individual also. It's usually a two-way street."[4]

## PERSONAL CLEARING IS PART OF THE SPIRITUALIZING OF THE EARTHLY DIMENSION

As the Third Insight pointed out, we are immersed in the field of pure divine consciousness (before it's been shaped by human consciousness). Each thought and decision affects not only our personal energy field but also those to whom we have karmic ties, and *even the universal energy field itself.* As we clear energy personally, we have moved toward uniting the spiritual and physical dimensions within us.

> Things do not produce each other or make each other happen, as in linear causality; they help each other happen by providing occasion or locus or context, and in so doing, they in turn are affected. There is a mutuality here, a reciprocal dynamic. Power inheres not in any entity, but in the relationship between entities. Joanna Macy, *World as Lover, World as Self*

Since each of us is a spark of God, each clearing creates more loving energy for evolutionary purposes. Many teachers have taught, "If you want peace in the world, be peaceful inside yourself."

## GRATITUDE OPENS THE CHANNEL FOR COINCIDENCES

Brennan says, "All fields have different kinds of boundaries, so the boundary of someone who has a lot of love will be soft and more resilient. As a result they can interact with another human being in a much easier way."[5] Feeling grateful energizes the deeper regions of the divine spirit wherein the Birth Vision resides. According to Brennan, "The intense energy from the core essence then radiates out. It's as if a corridor opens from the core essence . . . and the energy is able to flow out and into the entire world. Gratitude also puts the individual in synchronicity with the universal energy field . . . or the morphogenic fields of the whole planet and the solar systems. That is also very important because it puts you in sync with your life. When you can flow in that way and find that place in life then the entire universe becomes very supportive"[6]

Even though many of us are not yet at the stage when we can see these energy flows ourselves, the firsthand experiences of energy fields of pioneers such as Myss and Brennan, to name only two, raise the capacity of our collective abilities. Interestingly, the evidence pouring in from emerging fields such as bioenergetics has the potential for directly contributing to advances in such important areas as global conflict resolution. Imagine if we brought these awarenesses, perceptions, and attitudes into peace negotiations along with other bargaining strategies! Like a drop of red dye in water, our emotions color the world. As we individually practice more loving and honest behavior in our personal relationships, our energies affect the collective. Without any extra effort, we are creating fertile conditions for others to link into. Much like our examples above of Jane and Jan, who found that once their inner perceptions had shifted and they changed their behavior, their outer conditions shifted almost automatically. Instead of looking for a linear recipe (A + B = C) of "how to change the world," we might set about changing the conditions in our own life, and then notice *what shows up next for us to do in service for others*. By having a more fluid perception of evolution as a process dynamically driven by the *relationship* of events, discoveries, and decisions, we would then understand that our Birth Vision and the World Vision will naturally unfold once we have cleared the way.

## RESISTANCE

So here you are, reading about the Insights and getting excited about making changes in your life. You are hopeful of finding your life purpose. You want to be more loving and to raise your level of spiritual understanding. Lately, you've been becoming aware of certain steps you might take to initiate positive changes. You looked at some of the exercises in this book or other books. They made sense to you.

But you haven't moved toward taking any of these new steps.

You feel like you've been asking for guidance to get out of a stuck place, but, to your great frustration, nothing is happening.

Welcome to resistance. Resistance is a dynamic that can appear in our lives in many different disguises. Let's say somebody who knows you very well has pointed out a behavior of yours that is causing a problem in the relationship. If you get upset about it, there may be a good chance that you recognize the truth of what she is saying. However, you probably won't say, "Thanks so much for pointing this out to me. I am going to absolutely work on this, because I want to grow and be the best person I can be." No. You'll probably get just the merest bit self-righteous about her nervy, presumptuous, mistaken remarks. Or perhaps you become entirely resentful of *all* the nervy, presumptuous remarks she has *ever* made in your relationship. In the computer of your mind, you scroll down every inexcusable remark that you have filed away because you never really got to make it clear to her, once and for all, how great you are in spite of her critical, unenlightened eye. This is resistance. When you feel "unduly slighted," and resentment is one of your chosen negative emotions, then you probably have an inner belief that demands "an eye for an eye" justice. This type of response shows an inability to take in feedback or to notice when things are not working, and it rigidifies and saps your creative energy.

### RESISTANCE MIGHT MEAN A SHIFT IS JUST AROUND THE CORNER

One student in a workshop on the Celestine Insights at Interface in Boston said, "I've found that when I'm really resisting something, that means there is definitely truth there. I've also found that resistance actually signals that I'm about to make a big shift. I've always been a scientific type," he said, "and these spiritual ideas are all new to me. But now when I feel resistant to something new, I start to look for the shift [in my life] that always seems to follow."

Even when *you* know there are changes that should be made in your life, you still may not do them. Ask yourself, What will I have to let go of if I take this new step? Beverly, a radiologist, told us that in reading about the Insights, she kept avoiding sitting down and doing the parental review exercise in *The Celestine Prophecy: An Experiential Guide,* even though it seemed like it might yield some information about why she had chosen her particular parents. The question in her life was whether or not she wanted to stay working in the medical field or get more involved in freelance writing. "I realized that my resistance to doing any self-analysis like this was my fear of looking at who I was as a child in those days, and who I am now. It was hard to think about my mother and father in a neutral way. I always thought I had the 'wrong parents.' I have resented being so overly molded by them."

Beverly's resistance to doing the parental review exercise was an indication of a deeper need to remain "in the dark" about her parents because it served her need to see them as the "reason" she was not developing her writing interests. She came to realize that she was afraid she was starting a writing career too late in life. It was easier to think that if her parents had encouraged her talent earlier she would be further along. What she realized was that their strictness gave her self-discipline, and her medical career had provided many material benefits as well as a sense of self-esteem. In talking about this with a friend, the friend suggested that her discipline and ability to accomplish a challenge like medical school could be transferred to writing and marketing her writing. "Actually," she said, "I don't think I would have had all that much to say when I was young. Now I'm very interested in writing about the changes in the medical field, and I needed this experience to be credible."

### FIND THE PAYOFF FOR STAYING WHERE YOU ARE

When you don't follow through on an intuition or a synchronistic opportunity, you are clearly making a choice. At the root of this choice is another, deeper fear or priority that is currently more important than the new life you say you want. Ask yourself, What am I afraid of seeing about myself? What does my resistance to change *allow* me to be, do, or have? What is the payoff for continuing to describe myself in these limiting ways? Why am I arguing for my limitations?

It's helpful to look, then, at any resistance as a beacon signaling a limiting belief. Without judgment, see the resistance as the place where you need to bring light and gentleness. Buddhist teachers suggest breathing in the resistance you feel, and see it moving through your heart. Imagine it being dissolved and cleansed as it passes through your loving, light-filled heart.

## CLEARING RESIDUAL FEELINGS FROM PAST LIFETIMES

Now that we have reviewed how to clear energy blockages rooted in events in the past of *this* lifetime, let's take a look at connections to deeper strata within us. Why? More and more groups of people are incarnating together in order to work on holding a positive World Vision during this time of immense transition. Being able to work harmoniously is not only a huge advantage but a necessity for accomplishing positive changes in the environment and the culture. Because "no group can reach its full creative power until it consciously clears and then amplifies its energy, we must be willing to consider that we may be working on issues that go beyond this lifetime."[7] Perception at the level of the Tenth Insight gives us that broader perspective that includes reincarnation, a view that our culture, historically, has not taught us.

> The Eighth [Insight] is about knowing how to uplift others, knowing how to send energy by focusing on another's beauty and higher-self wisdom. This process can raise the energy level and creativity of the group exponentially. Unfortunately, many groups have trouble uplifting each other in this manner, even though the individuals involved are able to do it at other times. This is especially true if the group is work-oriented, a group of employees, for instance, or people coming together to create a unique project of some kind, because so often these people have been together before, and old, past-life emotions come up and get in the way. **James Redfield, *The Tenth Insight: Holding the Vision***

For example, within the novel's group of seven who are trying to stop the energy experiment in the valley, Curtis and David express seemingly irrational anger toward Maya. In their meditations, they begin to see fragments of a past life together where Maya made a mistake that resulted in the deaths of Curtis and David. The negative emotions from that lifetime had been carried through to the present incarnation which gave them another opportunity to accomplish a goal together.

The Insight reminds us that even though we may have done a lot of work on our control drama tendencies, we may still find ourselves irrationally irritated by someone else. We need to consider the idea that these animosities may be rooted in past-life experiences. This explanation may account for feelings of guilt, shame, envy, anger, or jealousy about someone in a group, even though there doesn't seem to be any good reason for it. Instead of ignoring the feelings, it may be fruitful to try to bring up to consciousness the reason you were together in a past lifetime, what you had wanted to accomplish, and what you could do differently this time. This is the same process you use when clearing present negative feelings and behavior, but it can be applied to the larger view of an incarnation whose life lessons *then* could help you in the life you are living *now*. Be patient! In the novel, these realizations happened rather quickly to make the point. If there is an important conflict that is worth resolving, and you have tried traditional counseling, you may want to try to access these feelings through regression therapy or a psychic reading from a trusted friend or adviser. As with any professional service, be sure you get good referrals.

### RESIDUAL EMOTIONS OR BLASTS FROM THE PAST

In *Exploring Reincarnation,* psychologist Hans TenDam cites a graphic example of residual past-life feelings in the case of Lanfranco Davito, an Italian policeman. He reports a present-life incident: "[Davito] is on duty when a stranger comes towards him in the street. At the same moment he remembers this man clubbing him to death during a tribal quarrel, and he goes white with fear. Later, all kinds of recollections of this primitive life come."[8] These kinds of painful memories are exactly why we are blessed with forgetfulness at birth. Usually, they do not tend to resurface until we are at a point in emotional maturity when we will not be thrown off-balance by the remembrances. However, a spontaneous recall or even a vague feeling may help us to understand more fully a current relationship with someone we have known in another lifetime, perhaps under very different circumstances.

While it is not advisable to try to do past life recall without competent professional assistance, it may be helpful to you merely to consider the possibility that you have come into life to continue working on unresolved issues as well as to fulfill your life purpose (which definitely includes paying off the karmic debts by not repeating the same mistakes). Those you meet have agreed to help you balance that debt.

As you become more aware of your feelings in the moment, your intuition may furnish you with messages about seemingly out-of-context feelings. For example, you might have acquired a relative through marriage to whom you take an instant dislike. Or you may have to work on a project with someone who irritates you unreasonably. If you are going to be able to fulfill your original Birth Vision, it will be helpful to have a larger perspective on where irrational feelings might be coming from.

In a project-oriented group, a troublesome person might be reflecting an important underlying theme that the entire group needs to recognize and deal with. Groups operating from a Tenth Insight perspective must know how to take their energy out of past issues, and come into the present *with love as the ambient feeling.* As the Insight says, "The clearing process cannot begin until we come totally back to love"[9] Edgar Cayce, the great healer and psychic, repeatedly emphasized that unless we clear hostility with others, we link ourselves to them lifetime after lifetime until it is resolved. Enemies as well as friends may decide to share a family unit in order to work out karmic problems.

We always have a quiet time of "attunement" (at-onement) with the Devas in our garden before working there. We attune to the Devas of trees before we cut them and we have successfully attuned to the Devas of insects to have them leave plants. But when we tried to attune to the Deva or Spirit of the deer to ask them to stop eating our garden, we found that it took many days of meditation to get into rapport with that Deva. The deer had been hunted by the former owners of the land and trust needed to be reestablished.

We also found that we could not attune to nature if we were not attuned to each other. So any conflicts had to be cleared up first. We then discovered that we could not think of nature as just the small plot of garden created by humans, but must include the surrounding landscape and forest in our attunement. **Corinne McLaughlin and Gordon Davidson, *Spiritual Politics***

I look to Grey Eagle and ask, What is the key? And with much feeling he replies, GENTLE-NESS. Your world needs GENTLENESS. And I ask Grey Eagle, How can we learn? He answers, With gentleness, only with gentleness. **Rosemary Altea, *The Eagle and the Rose***

Sometimes a person with a very different vibration than our own might come into our life so that he or she may be healed through this interaction. In his book *Many Lives, Many Masters,* Dr. Brian Weiss reports some of the information that came from higher dimensions of consciousness during the regression sessions with his client Catherine. One such message made it clear that if we do not rid ourselves of our flaws and vices, we will carry them over into the next life. Once we decide we are strong enough to master the external problems, we will no longer have them in the next life. Since we incarnate with people who have agreed to help free us from our debts, we must learn to share our knowledge with other people. The message of the higher being was, "We also must learn not to just go to those people whose vibrations are the same as ours. It is normal to feel drawn to somebody who is on the same level that you are. But this is wrong. You must also go to those people whose vibrations are wrong . . . with yours. This is the importance . . . in helping . . . these people.

"We are given intuitive powers we should follow and not try to resist. Those who resist will meet with danger. We are not sent back from each plane with equal powers. Some of us possess powers greater than others, because they have been accrued from other times. Thus people are not all created equal. But eventually we will reach a point where we will all be equal."[10]

As we are beginning to realize, at the deepest level of purpose, our early family was probably chosen to expose us to a tendency within our soul so that we could refine our ability to love. As we shall see in the following chapters, it is very likely that our soul chose the location and particular parental dynamic partly so that we could heal flawed tendencies such as ridiculing others, defiance, elitism, criticism, superiority, inferiority,

> Nature's imperative is, again, that no intelligence unfolds without a stimulus from a developed form of that intelligence. All evidence indicates that the mother's developed heart stimulates the infant's newborn heart, thereby activating a dialogue between the infant's brain-mind and heart. Then the newborn knows all is well and that birth has been successfully completed . . . this heart to heart communication activates corresponding intelligences in the mother as well.
>
> On holding her infant in the left-breast position with its corresponding heart contact, a major block of dormant intelligences is activated in the mother, causing precise shifts of brain function and permanent behavior changes. **Joseph Chilton Pearce, *Evolution's End***

arrogance, greed, stubbornness, impatience, anger, revenge, judg-mentalism, or self-righteousness. In many spiritual teachings, it is be-lieved that another soul to whom you are connected has agreed to live out the part you need to work on. For example, Dr. Weiss wrote about one session with Catherine where she sees, in another lifetime, a lov-ing man on a farm, taking care of horses. She recognizes him as her current grandfather. She tells the doctor, "He was very good to us. He loved us. He never hollered at us. . . . But he died." Weiss responds, "Yes, but you'll be with him again. You know that." And she replies, "Yes. I've been with him before. He was not like my father. They're so different." Weiss asks, "Why does one love you so much and treat you so well, and the other one is so different?" To which she replies, "Be-cause one has learned. He has paid a debt he has owed. My father has not paid his debt. He has come back . . . without understanding. He will have to do it again." She saw her father's task as learning not to treat children like property, instead of like people to love.[11]

## INDIVIDUAL OR GROUP STUDY

The following exercises may be done on your own or used as a basis for discussion in group study. If you are working in a group, you may want to select one or more topics and write about the subject for five or ten minutes, either at home before the meeting or at the beginning of the meeting.

Since these topics tend to be of a personal nature, it is very impor-tant that you create a safe, nonthreatening environment in your group. You may find that much is gained in hearing how other people handle their topics.

Take turns reading or discussing your feelings about the topics without interruption from the group at large. Once everyone has had a turn, then go ahead to a general discussion or give positive feedback to each other. See who has a message for you in their way of handling the topic!

### Check-in on Feeding Old Wounds

Write for three to five minutes in a stream-of-consciousness style. *You do not have to share anything you don't want to if you are working in a group.*

1. Describe any feeling, person, or situation that you might have been obsessing about lately. Can you see yourself sending energy back to this unresolved old wound? How often do you do this? Hourly? Daily? Every once in a while? What percentage of your psychic energy goes toward keeping this issue alive?
2. What early childhood abuses, illnesses, injuries, character flaws, or other negative events do you share with people regularly? Can you see how telling about this is an attempt to feel important? Does it give you a subtle power of some kind?
3. Where are you feeling stuck in your life? Job? Relationship? Home-life? What steps are you afraid of taking? How much time do you focus on being confused? (Just write out your feelings with no attempt to solve anything.)
4. Describe in detail how your current conflict creates the *same level of tension* that existed in your early childhood.

### Living with Zest

1. Describe what you would most like to have happen in your life.
2. Describe a scene in detail that exemplifies this desire.
3. What is the most pleasurable and fulfilling thing you could do with your day tomorrow?
4. Will you do it? If not, why not? What stands in your way?
5. What kind of attitude is revealed by your answer? Whose voice is that? Mother? Father? God?
6. What priority is revealed by your choice of what to do tomorrow?
7. What do you do for fun?

### Check-in on Control Dramas

1. What control drama behavior do you tend to do under stress?
2. Describe your parents' (or other major caregiver's) tendencies to control.
3. What kind of people do you have the most trouble with? How do they make you feel? Think of one or two specific people who are friends or colleagues and describe some of the feelings you have in your body when you are in conflict with them.
4. Have you been able to "name the drama" and begin to talk about your feelings with the other person? What happened? If not, what are you afraid will happen if you talk to him/her?
5. Imagine a conversation with the person with whom you are having

a power struggle. Imagine that you are both relaxed and in a neutral place such as a café or park bench. Write about how you might bring up your feelings in a sincere, *nonblaming* way.

## Relationship Scan to Clear Negative Energy

Before confronting a problem relationship in the external world, it's a good idea to do some introspection in preparation for clearing negative energy.

Take a moment to reflect on the following questions to see where you are holding on to negative feelings about someone. These unresolved feelings could very likely be causing unconscious energy blocks in other areas of your life such as creativity, finances, or decisionmaking. Have a piece of paper ready to jot down your *first impressions* to these questions.

### How You See the Person
- Close your eyes and ask yourself: "Who upsets me the most in my life?" Write his or her name at the top of your page.
- "In what way does this person drain my energy?" Write down one or two sentences.
- Now write down four or five words that describe the emotional feeling you have about this person. Is it irritation, anger, resentment, envy? Circle the most descriptive emotion.
- Close your eyes again and imagine you are in this person's presence. What physical sensations do you notice in your visualization of him or her, or what do you remember from the last time you saw him or her? Do you have a tightening in the chest, stomach, throat, or neck in relation to the person? Write down four or five physical sensations associated with this person. Circle the most descriptive physical sensation.
- Do you get together with others and dwell on the incidents you've had with the problem person? Do you feel sarcastic or cynical about the person?
- Write down four or five words that you may have used about the person, such as dumb, rigid, scary, nuts, abusive, intimidating, victim, or vicious. Circle the most important description you have used about this person. How could you describe yourself with this same word, even in a minor way?
- What kind of project, if any, are you attempting to work on to-

gether? Write down the best outcome you can imagine and why that may not happen because of your relationship with this person.

### Let the Story Unfold

STEP ONE      Write the person's name at the top of a new page.

STEP TWO      Now write the three circled words that most convey your emotional feeling, physical sensations, and description of the person under his or her name.

STEP THREE      Choose one of those words to start your first sentence.

STEP FOUR      Begin writing and use the other two words in your first paragraph. Write without stopping for three minutes and let anything come out on your page as long as you include those three circled words.

STEP FIVE      Reflect on the intuitive messages that came through in your writing. By letting your inner voices talk to you on the page, you may come to a greater understanding of the process you are in with the other person.

---

#### SAMPLE STORY

**JOHN**
**competitive, angry, snide**

**Snide** is a word that rhymes with hide. And when I am around John very often I want to go hide. He is so **competitive** that it makes me feel as if I am not doing enough. That I can never keep up.

He makes me **angry** when I am over at his house and he never even asks me what I'm doing. It's all him, him, him. He is so snide about whatever I have discovered that I feel like a little kid when I am around him. And the funny part is I'm much better at playing racquetball than he is, I am much more fun around our other friends, and I have a better sense of humor. So why am I not using it!

---

### Rewrite the Story

• If you wish, write out two or three sentences about how you would like to be in relationship to this person. *What would you like to have happen in the best of all worlds?* Write your expectations clearly and simply. End this exercise with a one-minute meditation in which you visualize the person joyfully remembering *their original inten-*

*tion or Birth Vision.* Be aware that your thoughts have shifted the energy between the two of you.

---

### SAMPLE REWRITE

I can see that I also have a competitive nature, and that I am hard on myself for not starting the writing project I keep talking about. I am angry that John has built up his own business and I can see how involved he is in it. I would probably be somewhat like that, too. I do get angry over things, but I really never let John know my feelings. I guess he can't read my mind.

If I am going to have a better relationship with John, I'm going to have to be not so aloof, and just sit there judging him like crazy! Next time I'm around him, I will be willing to listen to his stories for a while, but then I'm going to ask him if he would give me some feedback about what I'm doing. That way he'll realize that I value his opinion and want him to listen to me for a while! I'll try it anyway, and let him know that I'm working on some of this stuff so we can have a better friendship. I wonder what he'll say about that!

---

## GROUP STUDY

### Out in the Open

If you are ready to work through an interpersonal obstacle in a group, ask for higher guidance to come through, and remember that your motivation should be to create a loving atmosphere. Gentleness and compassion are always part of a skillful encounter.

If you have already tried to work with a disruptive member in the group and failed to bring about a harmonious resolution, let your intuition guide your next steps. Rather than let the group fall apart, members might meditate to see if there is something else the group needs to become aware of.

### *Helpful Attitudes*
- Be willing to consider that you may have been together in previous lifetimes. Besides the goal you may be trying to accomplish, you may also have come together to resolve residual negative feelings from other lifetimes.
- Remember the other person is just like you and wants to be loved, accepted, and helped toward fulfilling his or her purpose, too.
- Seeing yourself as a victim of someone else is an illusion. Remember that you have choices in most everyday situations.

- Your goal is to feel loving energy when you are in your group. Immerse yourself in the feeling of love that exists behind all the outward irritation.

## Techniques
- Before arriving at meetings, visualize each person in the group remembering what they came here to do.
- Talk about what's happening in the group. Put the issues on the table.
- Honestly share the feelings you have toward a troublesome person, no matter how awkward the attempt, but don't blame or name-call. Say how *their behavior affects you.*
- Name the drama that you think is controlling the group energy. For example, if the disruptive person in your group acts self-centered and dominates the group by incessant talking and relating everything to him or herself, then you might say, "Well, for myself, I get really irritated when we are trying to move forward in a discussion, and then we wind up talking about *your* problems. It makes me feel like we're getting stuck," or perhaps something like "I don't know if you realize the effect you have on this group. For myself, I am beginning to not want to participate" (or "feel drained when I'm around you and don't know why"). Ask the person, "What are you feeling in this group? What do you notice?"
- Stay as open as possible, and give up the need to be defensive, or *make* anything happen.
- See if you can turn the negative feelings into a neutral feeling. Ask the universe to work out the best possible solution, and detach from trying to control the outcome.
- Stay focused in the present.
- Be willing to consider that the person might best serve the group by working outside it for a while.

---

This effect is even greater with groups who interact this way with every member, because as each person sends the others energy, all of the members rise to a new level of wisdom which has more energy at its disposal, and this greater energy is then sent back to everyone else in what becomes an amplification effect. **James Redfield, *The Tenth Insight: Holding the Vision***

---

# PART THREE

# Remembering

# CHAPTER 5

# Healing, Transforming, and Creating

We know now that the inner attitude of the patient is crucial. A key factor is fear and stress and the way we handle it. Sometimes the fear is conscious, but very often we repress it entirely. This is the brave, macho attitude: deny the problem, push it away, conjure up our heroic agenda. If we take this attitude then the fear continues to eat at us unconsciously. Adopting a positive outlook is very important in staying healthy, but we have to engage in this attitude in full awareness, using love, not macho, for this attitude to be completely effective. What I believe is that our unspoken fears create blocks or crimps in the body's energy flow, and it's these blocks that ultimately result in problems.

SNAKE
TRANSFORMATION

THE TENTH INSIGHT:
HOLDING THE VISION[1]

## THE ENERGY FORCE THAT COMES FROM HUMAN EXPECTATIONS

In *The Tenth Insight,* Maya, a doctor, introduces the idea of using visualization techniques to heal physical problems. She teaches the character that healing occurs by the same processes we use to create our life.

She also tells him that "our Birth Vision contains not only what we individually intended to do in the physical dimension but also a larger vision of what humans have been trying to do throughout history, and the details of where we are going from here and how to get there. We just have to amplify our energy and share our birth intentions, and then we can remember."[2]

Maya reminds us that when we remember what we came here to accomplish, it can restore our health. When we are able to remember what all of humanity is supposed to do—which is to live a spiritual life in the physical plane—we will have healed our negative effect on each other and nature. As above, so below.

## PHYSICAL HEALING TECHNIQUES

One of the most rapidly developing occupational areas is the field of bioenergetic healing, which sees the roots of disease and health in the "inner" dynamics of the body/mind complex. Certainly we would encourage the prudent person to explore any complementary therapies with their physician, and there are many alternative therapies from which to choose.

In his book *Healing Words*, Dr. Larry Dossey cites compelling evidence from sound scientific studies that demonstrates the healing power in prayer, or prayerful intention. In what he calls Era III medicine, traditional doctors may no longer ignore such ancient (but new to us) techniques as intuitive diagnosis and noncontact therapeutic touch. Dossey, in fact, recognizes the deep connection between the soul and the body/mind as one of the most important, if not the most important, deciding factor in health. He discusses the ability that we have within us to stimulate healing through our own physical, mental, emotional, and spiritual resources.

> . . . karmic experiences are often associated with meaningful synchronicities. For example, a person has a difficult relationship with another person and has a past life experience that shows the two of them engaged in some sort of violent conflict. One of them is the victim and the other the aggressor. If this person completes reliving that incident and reaches a sense of forgiveness, his or her attitude towards the other protagonist changes in the positive direction. That is in itself impressive and interesting. However, what is quite extraordinary is that at exactly the same time a significant change in the same direction often occurs in the other person, whose attitude is also radically changed. This can happen even if there was not a conventional communication or connection of any kind between these two persons. **Stan Grof, M.D., in *Towards a New World View*, by Russell E. DiCarlo**

He also explores how "the consciousness of one person can affect the physical substrate of another."[3] Although we don't understand how, the prayerful intention to send healing energy does somehow connect to the other person's field, regardless of time or distance. While we may pray for our loved one's complete recovery, we have no real understanding of what is actually in the best interest of the soul of the suffering person. Sometimes a person's healing proceeds slowly, providing deep insights along the way. It may even be that death is the appropriate next step for the suffering soul.

### "MOTHER TERESA EFFECT"

Dossey cites dozens of studies that demonstrate the healing power of love. For example, in one study, David McClelland, Ph.D., at Harvard Medical School, found what he called the "Mother Teresa effect." Dossey writes, "[McClelland] showed a group of Harvard students a documentary of Mother Teresa ministering lovingly to the sick, and measured the levels of immunoglobulin (IgA) in their saliva before and after seeing the film. IgA is an antibody active against viral infections such as colds. IgA levels rose significantly in those who watched the film, even in many of those who considered Mother Teresa 'too religious' or a fake. In order to test for this effect in another way, McClelland later discarded the film and asked his graduate students simply to think about two things: past moments when they felt deeply loved and cared for by someone else, and a time when they loved another person. In his own experience, McClelland had been able to abort colds with this technique."[4]

> If scientists suddenly discovered a drug that was as powerful as love in creating health, it would be heralded as a medical breakthrough and marketed overnight—especially if it has as few side effects and was as inexpensive as love. . . . This is not sentimental exaggeration. One survey of ten thousand men with heart disease found a 50 percent reduction in frequency of chest pain (angina) in men who perceived their wives as supportive and loving. **Larry Dossey, M.D.,** *Healing Words*

Other research shows that when we have pleasurable get-togethers with our loved ones, or pleasant encounters with coworkers, the positive effects on the immune system last for several days. On the other hand, negative interactions lower our immune system, but the effects are usually not as long-lasting as positive ones.

### SPIRITUAL *AND* MATERIAL ENERGY IS THE HEALING BRIDGE

Rosemary Altea is an internationally renowned psychic medium whose work originally focused on bridging the physical and spiritual dimensions for those who had lost a loved one. In her book *The Eagle and the Rose,* she describes hundreds of sessions in which she contacted the spirits and brought through personal information of great healing power for those still living. Out of this work, she founded a healing organization based in England with patients worldwide. One of many stories is the healing of a seven-year-old girl named Caroline, who had not been able to straighten her right leg since she was two years old. A team of healers worked steadily on her for eighteen months. Altea writes, "[We] worked steadily . . . using our energy, connecting with that universal energy, centering ourselves so that we were good channels for that healing energy to pass through . . . then, eventually, after several months, one evening she walked into the healing center, not hopping as she usually did . . . we knew that she had made it."[5]

---

An Ohio University study of heart disease in the 1970s was conducted by feeding quite toxic, high-cholesterol diets to rabbits in order to block their arteries, duplicating the effect that such a diet has on human arteries. Consistent results began to appear in all the rabbit groups except for one, which strangely displayed 60 percent fewer symptoms. Nothing in the rabbits' physiology could account for their high tolerance to the diet, until it was discovered by accident that the student who was in charge of feeding these particular rabbits liked to fondle and pet them.

He would hold each rabbit lovingly for a few minutes before feeding it; astonishingly, this alone seemed to enable the animals to overcome the toxic diet. Repeat experiments . . . came up with similar results. Once again, the mechanism that causes such immunity is quite unknown—it is baffling to think that evolution has built into the rabbit mind an immune response that needs to be triggered by human cuddling. **Deepak Chopra, M.D., *Quantum Healing***

---

## ATTITUDES IN LIFE AND HEALTH

Nowhere is the emerging shift in consciousness more apparent than in new attitudes about health. In the old worldview we turned to authorities to make decisions about our health. Obviously, we still rely on medical authorities, but the relationship we have to our health-care givers is changing. We are less prone to accept their opinion as the only answer. As we become more educated about healthy lifestyles, we learn that our health is our responsibility. We learn that there is a wide variety of healing disciplines available that work with the whole mind/body system rather than "fixing" separate symptoms. As we remember the spiritual nature of our being, understanding that we are made of energy, we can focus more effectively on our *internal attitudes* rather than looking *only* for an external authority or medicine to cure our symptoms.

In this shift of paradigm, we are all feeling stressed-out to some degree. How we handle stress is one of the greatest barometers for future health and will be crucial in holding the World Vision. Stress is most lethal when we believe that we have little or no control over circumstances, for example in an inflexible work environment (or a paradigm shift!).

When we step away from our old control drama perspectives, we usually find that our internal reactions to external situations shift, and life *feels* better, as we have seen in some of our previous stories. Additionally, when we look for the purpose or lesson in what happens to us—whether it's an illness, an injury, or a bankruptcy—we have exchanged the desire to *control* circumstances for a desire to *work with* circumstances, which usually creates more flow. Therefore, all the spiritual work we do in becoming more conscious of the mysterious nature of life, of being present in the moment, and the true nature of synchronicities directly benefits

---

And, just as our physical heart maintains our body, the non-local intelligence governing the heart in turn maintains synchrony with a universal "consciousness at large." So we have both a physical heart and a higher "universal heart," and our access to the latter is, as in all development, dramatically contingent on the development of the former.

Just as the intelligences drawn on by the brain lead to specific abilities, the heart draws on the supra-implicate order and the realm of insight-intelligence. These higher orders don't articulate as specifics, but as a general movement for the well-being and balance of the overall operations of the brain-mind-body. **Joseph Chilton Pearce,** *Evolution's End*

---

Psychologists seem quick to categorize and say, "What is wrong with this person's behavior?" rather than saying, "Oh, is there a difficulty or a wound here, that for this person, has particular relevance to the way that they become whole, and the way that they become creative, and the way that they awaken their inner intuition and capacity to love." **Joan Borysenko in** *Towards a New World View,* **by Russell E. DiCarlo**

our physical and emotional bodies. With more curiosity and less blame, we start to feel we have more possibilities—which is the state of mind that is most beneficial to health. The more we begin to see how we helped create our current situation, the more power we will feel we have in assisting it to move in the direction of our original Birth Vision.

A Tibetan monk explained that health is not simply a function of eating the right food and exercising. Even though we may live an exemplary life, we still may fall seriously ill. Even though some people live a notoriously unhealthy lifestyle, they remain full of vitality. The monk explained that our physical health is a reflection of the karma we are working with in this life. If we fall ill, it may be because the soul has something to learn from the experience that we cannot understand with our conscious mind.

## THE POWER WITHIN

In *The Tenth Insight,* Maya reminds us that participating in our own healing, physically and emotionally, increases our ability to be motivated and productive in other ways. She says, "We can become inspired to shape a higher, more ideal future, and when we do, *miracles happen.* . . . With enough energy there's nothing that can't be healed— hatred . . . war. It's just a matter of coming together with the right vision."[6]

Easy for her to say, right? Being a character in a novel. But how do we, living an ordinary life, tap into this energy, and how can we reenvision our life? We know that books and workshops provide great insights about the unfolding destiny we see happening in the world. But isn't something more needed to keep us on track *daily*?

This was the question that spurred Michael Murphy and George Leonard, two of the founding figures in the Human Potential Movement, to design an experimental practice integrating the body, mind, heart, and soul. They believe, and most people would agree, that we must develop a practice that helps stabilize us, and that helps integrate all the information we are receiving. They strongly advocate committing to a program for the long term, allowing steady application to bring inevitable rewards, as well as enjoying the process itself.

In their book *The Life We Are Given,* Murphy and Leonard describe an evolution of thinking, starting in the 1960s, concerning human development that takes into account both scientific and ancient practices. Their work, as well as that of others of their stature, has greatly turned up the heat in the alchemical processes of higher consciousness and has been a major force in the general awareness of the emerging worldview.

They write, "Every sacred tradition is having a generative influence in the global village, stimulating countless people to embrace once esoteric ways of growth. This worldwide event has helped produce a momentous new stage in the development of transformative practice. For today, more than ever before, long-term human change can be understood and guided with the help of science. There are many reasons for this, among them new advances in the understanding of psychodynamics by modern psychology; demonstrations of our capacity for highly specific change in psychoneuroimmunology, sports medicine, biofeedback training, placebo studies, and hypnosis research; new discoveries about the mind's ability to reshape motivations, emotions, and the flesh; and sociologists' demonstrations that each social group nurtures just some of our attributes while neglecting or suppressing others.

> Because they arise from the same primordial source, transformative practice and the world's evolution have similar patterns. In both there are periods of stasis—long plateaus of the learning curve—followed by bursts of rapid development. In both, things are sacrificed as something new emerges. In both, new levels or dimensions of functioning take into themselves what went before, giving fuller expression to our latent divinity. And in both, there are times when the process of change itself graduates to a higher level. We are, it seems, involved in such a momentous transition. **Michael Murphy and George Leonard, *The Life We Are Given***

"Never before has there been so much scientifically based knowledge about the transformative capacities of human nature. This knowledge, combined with the lore and inspiration of the sacred traditions, gives the human race an unprecedented opportunity to make a great evolutionary advance. It is possible now, we believe, for humanity to pursue its destiny with more clarity than ever before."[7]

The foundation of their program, called Integral Transformative Practice (ITP), lies in the belief that ordinary people, even with busy lives, can develop extraordinary abilities if they (1) practice regularly over time; (2) integrate the functions of the body, mind, emotions, and soul through diet, exercise, reading, and community activities, group process, and meditation; and (3) enjoy the intrinsic benefits of the practice. They started their program in 1992 with a selected group of people in Mill Valley, California, committed to the discipline of long-term practice. They write, "We held a strong belief in the transformative power—and the sacredness—of life's quiet virtues, including intellectual curiosity and integrity, a sense of the spiritual, unconditional love, healthy exercise, and devotion to practice. We were in it for the long run. 'Yes, we're going to have a good time,' Leonard told the group. 'We're going to have fun. But more important is learning to enjoy regular practice, finding satisfaction in the unembellished beauty of the commonplace, and learning to love the plateau, the periods when you seem to be making no progress, just as much as you love the inevitable spurts of learning and change.' "[8]

> Each of us can draw upon the Unseen for transformation beyond the purview of mainstream science. Some members of our classes, for example, have experienced remissions from afflictions that many doctors think are incurable. But although science cannot explain such remissions (and other kinds of extraordinary experience . . .), there is a growing body of research that supports anecdotal reports of such changes produced by transformative practices. **Michael Murphy and George Leonard, *The Life We Are Given***

Group members were asked to make four different kinds of affirmations. The first was an affirmation for a *measurable physical change* that could be accounted for by normal methods. For example, one person might desire to reduce his weight by a few pounds or his waist size by a couple of inches. The second affirmation was for an *exceptional change in the body, mind, spiritual, or emotional nature*—something that could not be accounted for by ordinary methods. The third affirmation was for an *extraordinary result* that exceeded ordinary human capacity, which would be difficult to explain by scientific thinking. The final affirmation was the same for everyone and stated: *"My entire being is balanced, vital, and healthy."*[9] In all cases, the affirmations were about internal process within the person rather than changes in the external world. Rather than affirm that one had won the lottery, for example, the participants were asked to affirm positive changes in their own functioning.

The studies on the first group and the second one that followed are a fascinating testament to the value of sustained intention and disciplined practice. While the statistical analysis showed a marked correlation to adherence to the program and progress in achieving the desired state, the personal statements were even more encouraging. For example, Murphy and Leonard describe a thirty-nine-year-old psychologist who made this affirmation: "My will is in tune with the Divine Will of the universe. There are no obstructions. All things flow to me and through me; love, health, wealth, success, and creativity." She described her condition at the time she made the affirmation by saying, "I am frequently in conflict over finances, writing ability, and my relationships with [a former teacher]." At the end of the year, she wrote, "This has been my most startling result. My financial situation has tripled as a result of my not plotting how it would resolve. My most serious interpersonal conflict has completely resolved from its state. . . . There has been an almost total shift in my attitude. From former attempts to 'make' things happen to an acceptance of whatever is presented and an acceptance of whatever I am feeling. I truly feel more flowing and internally without the former obstacles that caused me sadness. I no longer feel stuck."[10]

> . . . for every circuit [of energy] you distribute outside of yourself, you increase the amount of time required for anything to manifest in your life. For every circuit you contain within yourself, you increase your experience of what you would call synchronicity and at a master level, instantaneous creation. It's as simple as that. **Caroline Myss in *Towards a New World View*, by Russell E. Di-Carlo**

Other members of the group reported improving eyesight, disappearance of cataracts, reduction of body fat, improved ability to handle trauma, increase in bust size, and even an increase in height, as well as overall improvements not so easily measured. The ITP program is well described in *The Life We Are Given* and provides an excellent support for those interested in unleashing the power within.

## WRITING OUT YOUR FEELINGS

Another interesting study, done by James W. Pennebaker, a professor at Southern Methodist University in Dallas and author of "The Healing Power of Confession," gives us insights into the transforming aspects of journal writing about feelings. Pennebaker has repeatedly demonstrated the benefits that come from writing about traumatic events. The people in his studies not only felt better emotionally after letting their feelings spill out on paper, but their physical health greatly improved as well.

Pennebaker studied three groups of people, all of whom had lost their jobs. He asked the first group to write for twenty minutes a day for five days about their plans and time management ideas for securing new employment. He asked the second group to write for twenty minutes for five days on trivial subjects. The last group he asked to write for twenty minutes for five days on their *deepest thoughts and feelings* about losing their jobs.

After four months, 35 percent of those who wrote about their feelings had gotten jobs, as compared to only 5 percent of the control group who wrote about trivial subjects. *None* of the "time management" group had gotten work. Pennebaker believes that the writing helped "[them] present themselves better in interviews, because they had worked through their anger and bitterness and developed a balanced perspective. They were able to get past the trauma and get on with their lives with confidence."[11] On the other hand, the time-management exercises may have been potentially destructive as a "form of obsession." By focusing relentlessly on the day-to-day struggles, the time-management group remained stuck in anger and anxiety. This study seems to support the Third Insight, which reminds us of the paradox of sending out a strong intention and then *letting go of the need to control the results.*

## INDIVIDUAL STUDY

### Write It Out

If you are facing a particularly challenging problem or situation, why not try the Pennebaker exercise? Write out everything you are feeling about any situation in your life, but write about only one situation at a time. Write for twenty minutes a day, for five consecutive days. Then let go of thinking much about your situation, letting the universe work on helping it resolve for you. Notice how things shift during the next few months.

### Injury/Illness Review

Tuning into the message of each circumstance hones our intuitive skills and increases our ability to stay on course in alignment with divine will.

The following practice is taken from Maya's technique in *The Tenth Insight.* You may want to record these questions and suggestions on a cassette tape with spaces of silence to use in meditation, or work with a friend who can ask you the questions.

1. Calm your mind by following your breath for a few minutes.
2. Remember back to the last time you had an illness or injury.
3. When you first got hurt or became aware of your illness, how serious did you think it was? Your answer here may reveal how much fear you carry around in general, or how much you see yourself at the mercy of the world.
4. Why do you think your accident or illness happened? Your attitude about the cause may have had an effect on your recuperation.
5. What were you doing just prior to the accident or illness?
6. What were you thinking about just prior to the health problem?
7. What other memories cluster around your illness or injury? Does this remind you of past problems? Write down the cluster of memories that come in no matter how irrelevant they seem.
8. What does this injury or illness keep you from doing, being, or having?
9. What does it allow you to do, be, or have?
10. What is the gain you receive from having this problem?
11. In what way do you get power or energy from having the problem? (For example: People give me sympathy. I feel special or important. I don't have to work, take care of the kids, etc.)
12. What fear(s) do you have, or did you have, about the problem? Consider that an irrational, deep-rooted fear may stem from something that happened in a past lifetime. Dr. Brian Weiss, the psychologist who has done much past-life regression study, remarked that sometimes the things we fear have already happened in a past lifetime. You may want to seek a professional counselor with experience in this field.

If you are still experiencing pain from this illness or injury, you might want to try the following:

13. Imagine that the fear(s) is a dark block of energy somewhere inside you or your energy field. Put your attention in that spot.
14. Surround yourself with as much light, loving energy as possible and focus it at the exact location of the block.
15. Consciously send divine healing energy into the exact spot identified by the pain, intending that the love will transform the cells at that spot into a state of perfect functioning.

16. Feel the pain with all your being, and imagine loving energy going right into the heart of the pain, lifting the exact point of your body, the atoms themselves, into a higher vibration.

17. See the particles take a quantum jump into the pure energy pattern that is their optimum state. Literally feel a tingling sensation in that spot.

"Real healing takes place when we can envision a new kind of future for ourselves that excites us. *Inspiration* is what keeps us well."[12]

## Intention and Attention Practice

Imagine the things that you still want to see and the feats you'd still like to accomplish. Imagine what you would most like to be your legacy to the world.

Try writing down some of the dreams you would like to achieve as if you were writing an obituary for your best friend. Here's an example of a wonderful life that appeared in the *San Francisco Chronicle,* about Evelyn Wood Glascock Allen, who died on April 10, 1996, at age eighty-two:

> She was a designer of evening gowns for high society women, graduation gowns for college students and breathtaking outfits for herself. A longtime resident of Chicago, in seven years she came to know more about San Francisco than most lifelong residents. From her studio apartment command post high above Market Street in Fox Plaza, she would survey her domain and plan each day, which might include a $1.25 lunch at the Marina Senior Center, free barbecued ribs at a Marriott happy hour, ushering at the Opera or a James Brown concert, and square dancing at the Rawhide.
>
> A strong woman, a single working mother since 1953, an Alpha Phi alum, a lover of honey baked ham, colorful clothing, and champagne, she was unsurpassed at recognizing the value of found objects on The City's streets. She was the Florence Nightingale of many male souls gone astray.[13]

Write out a short paragraph on yourself as if you had won an award for something, like these three courageous and determined people who were honored in May 1995 by the California Wellness Foundation:[14]

- Rebecca "Maggie" Escobedo Steele spent five years as leader of a San Diego girls' gang. She now works on the problems of Native

American women and Chicanas in Humboldt County. A professional mediator, she helps resolve tribal conflicts and ease differences between tribes and environmentalists.

- After the drive-by shooting of her 35-year-old son, Myrtle Faye Rumph devoted herself to giving children in South-Central Los Angeles positive alternatives to drugs and gangs. In 1990, she and 12 associates founded a youth center that now has a library, recreation room, computer lab, and classrooms. Mrs. Rumph wants to create a quilt, patterned after the AIDS quilt, for people who have lost family members to violence, and to provide conflict resolution training to young people.
- Growing up in East San Jose, Sonny Lara was a gang member dealing drugs at 14. While in San Quentin, he dedicated himself to helping young people, and after his release he became an ordained minister and started an inmate outreach program. He created a gang awareness curriculum for young people, educators, and community leaders, and recently opened a youth center.

Your dreams and goals *help you remember who you are.* Read your statement every few days and be alert to any new developments which open the way to achieve your new life!

## Prayer Work

Every day review the people you know who may need a little extra support. Get in the habit of sending loving energy to specific people, to be used for their greatest good. Extend your loving prayer to those in need all over the planet and then extend your loving prayer out to all forms of life in the physical and spiritual dimensions.

We are including the prayer below, since it came to us from a friend while we were writing this chapter. He found this prayer printed in a small English-language newspaper in Mexico and thought he might try it. He decided that what he most wanted was to be invited to play a certain piece of music with an orchestra. After reading the prayer only one time, and thinking about the music he wanted to play, he inadvertently misplaced the prayer. However, within three days, he received a call from his agent, who told him she had received an invitation for him to play with a large midwestern orchestra. The piece of music he had wanted to play (which is not widely known) was exactly the music they were considering for the program. If you use the prayer and receive your wish, you must publish the entire prayer, including the instructions at the bottom.

---

∞

# Prayer of Application to the Holy Spirit

**H**OLY SPIRIT who solves all problems, who lights all roads so that I can attain my goal. You who give me the divine gift to forgive and forget all evil against me and that in all instances of my life you are with me. I want in this short prayer to thank you for all things and to confirm once again that I never want to be separated from you, even and in spite of all material illusion. I want to be with you in eternal glory. Thank you for your mercy toward me and mine.

*The person must say this prayer for three consecutive days. After three days the favor requested will be granted even if it may appear difficult. This prayer, including these instructions, must be published immediately after the favor is granted without mentioning the favor; only your initials should appear at the bottom.*

---

∞

---

## GROUP STUDY

### Healing Circles

Circles create powerful energies when used for the higher good of others. Your group may wish to spend some time at each meeting sending peaceful, loving energy to friends and family who are suffering. You might also wish to send prayerful intention for the healing of a community, country, or specific issue. Try to be consistent in setting aside time for the healing work. You may wish to say a particular person's name aloud as everyone is meditating and beaming out loving energy.

### Integral Transformative Practice

If your group is interested in long-term practice, you may want to follow the program outlined in *The Life We Were Given*, by George Leonard and Michael Murphy. Working with the support of a like-minded community is very powerful.

## Topics for Discussion

- Who or what most needs assistance or healing in your community? How could you work together as a group to provide a new service or augment what is already in place?
- What seeming difficulty in your individual backgrounds has prepared you to understand a community problem (teen violence, drugs, early pregnancy, learning disability, etc.)?
- Are there children in the community who have never been to a forest? A zoo? How could your group help them visit nature?
- Is your group interested in starting a community garden? Can you involve teens who want to participate *willingly*?
- Pose the question "What special healing service could our group provide the community?" Let everyone meditate in silence for five to ten minutes, and then write down all the ideas that came to the individual members. Was there any coincidence?
- Write about one goal that you would like to achieve that is just a little bit beyond your comfort zone. Work with two other people (groups of three) to brainstorm how you could each take steps toward this goal. This kind of work needs follow-through over time, so set your goals, but be prepared to have the work unfold over time. Some good books on helping you make an adventure of life are:

> *Wishcraft: How to Get What You Really Want,* by Barbara Sher
> *Live the Life You Love,* by Barbara Sher
> *Teamworks!: Building Support Groups That Guarantee Success,* by Barbara Sher and Annie Gottlieb
> *The Artist's Way,* by Julia Cameron and Mark Bryan
> *The Seven Spiritual Laws of Success,* by Deepak Chopra, M.D.
> *Growing Season: A Healing Journey into the Heart of Nature,* by Arlene Bernstein

# CHAPTER 6

# Afterlife Activity and Influence

RAVEN
MAGIC

First, let me tell you about my experience in the other dimension, what I call the *Afterlife* dimension. When I was able to maintain my energy level in Peru, even when the rest of you grew fearful and lost your vibration, I found myself in an incredible world of beauty and clear form. I was right there in the same place, but everything was different. The world was luminous and awing. . . . I could will myself anywhere. . . . I could create anything I wanted just by imagining it.

THE TENTH INSIGHT:
HOLDING THE VISION[1]

## WHAT IS THE AFTERLIFE?

The Afterlife is home. It's where we come from and where we return to. According to ancient wisdom, as well as accounts from near-death experiences and regression studies, the Afterlife is the "place" or dimension in which our individual consciousness continues to exist between lives on Earth. We are coming to realize the great truth that our consciousness, our soul, does not die. Following death in the physical body, we make a transition into the realm of the Afterlife. It exists not "up" in the celestial skies, but right here on the planet in a dimension invisible to our five senses. The Afterlife, often referred to in Christian terms as the hereafter, is our soul's home away from the body.

What the Afterlife *is* depends on who you are, what you think about, and what you expect it to be. The *initial* environment that you encounter in the spiritual domain seems to be formed by the belief systems you lived by here in the Earth plane. While we do not take material possessions with us, we do take our consciousness and our beliefs. What you expect is what you get. In the beginning of your spiritual sojourn, you are still entrenched in your fixations of the life

122

you just left. With help from your soul group, and a willingness to "wake up," you then progress to higher levels and take part in the vast amount of learning that is going on in the Afterlife.

According to reports from Robert Monroe's journeys into these realms, there is an initial resting place, complete with trees, streams, flowers, and grass, that matches the physical world experience of the newly deceased soul. People report that much of the Afterlife landscape is vibrantly beautiful and filled with music. However, there are also lightless realms of suffering, created by those whose dark thoughts and darker deeds have relegated them to their own version of Hell.

In *Journeys Out of the Body,* Robert Monroe describes a part of the Afterlife as a vital creative force that produces energy, assembles "matter" into form, and provides channels of perception and communication.

"As you think, so you are."[2] "Your destination [traveling in the Afterlife in an out-of-body experience] seems to be grounded completely within the framework of your inner-most *constant* motivations, emotions, and desires. You may not consciously want to 'go' there, but you have no choice. Your Supermind (soul?) is stronger and usually makes the decision for you. Like attracts like."[3]

Monroe believes that there are three sources that create the Earthlike conditions in the Afterlife. "First, they [the simulated natural environment] are the product of thought of those who once lived in the physical world, the patterns of which still remain. The second source is those who like certain material things in the physical world, which they have re-created apparently to enhance their surrounding in [the Afterlife]. The third source I assume to be a higher order of intelligent beings more aware of the [Afterlife] environment than most inhabitants. Their purpose seems to be that of simulation of the physical environment— temporarily, at least—for the benefit of those just emerging from the physical world, after 'death.' This is done to reduce trauma and shock for the 'newcomers' by introducing familiar shapes and settings in the early conversion stages."[4]

---

Opening to the Afterlife is being willing to see the sacred in small things, *everything.* It's knowing that every choice you make here counts. You may not take material riches with you, but you return to the spiritual plane with your beliefs and past deeds.

---

In this part of the Afterlife, your experience will be composed of your deepest desires and fears. Thought is action, and you can hide nothing from anyone. The sociopsychological conditioning by which we learn to repress our emotions in the physical plane no longer exists in the spiritual!

## THE DEATH TRANSITION

What we know of the death experience comes from many primary sources. One of the most ancient descriptions of the stages of death is *The Tibetan Book of the Dead*. Written by advanced ascetics who claim to have remembered the passage of their souls between death and rebirth, this book contains descriptions of the process of reincarnation, several distinct nonphysical worlds, and the Life Review. The book was meant to help one die more skillfully and was read to the dying person as a sort of road map of the journey he was about to take. It was also written to help those still living "think positive thoughts and not hold the dying one back with their love and emotional concern, so that she could enter into the Afterdeath planes in a proper frame of mind, released from all bodily concerns."[5]

## GOING HOME

New arrivals who have been developing a spiritual viewpoint on Earth may be alert and ready to enter again into the limitless activities available in the spiritual dimension. Or, if people are not quite ready to accept their newly acquired spiritual existence, they may take as much time as they need to rest and awaken. Apparently, the loving prayers of those left behind on Earth greatly aid our transition from material to spiritual life.

In the Afterlife, we have plenty of time to contemplate our soul's gains and losses, our mistakes and our achievements, in preparation for planning the next lifetime. According to our level of maturity, which is based on how we learned and integrated and became aware of our real purpose on Earth, we are allowed to traverse the levels and work with Guides and Masters.

In the past few hundred years under the dominant scientific paradigm, life has often been reduced to that which happens solely in the physical world. Death is seen as the end of life and is often viewed as a tragedy when it finally happens. This materialistic view of the world offers little sense that we are anything but a small dab of chemicals with a sort of spiritual hankering that helps make life endurable while we're here. Any spiritual phenomena, such as spontaneous healings, communication with dead people, or other miracles, which science was unable to explain, are dismissed as hallucinations or fakes. Even if they did happen to one person, the event is considered too idiosyncratic to be studied, best laid to rest as we moved on to the "more important" heroic advances of prolonging life and battling disease. Most of us have had precious little insight into the transition of the spirit as it leaves the physical shell and enters into the other dimension—the Afterlife. Our culture's worldview has mostly kept a firm boundary between the visible and invisible worlds. Capitalization on people's fear of death has proved lucrative for many industries.

---

The psychic Arthur Ford, who reported from the Afterlife dimension through communications with his Earthly friend, journalist Ruth Montgomery, gave some interesting commentary of some of the special souls he was aware of: "The Kennedy brothers are a striking example of the power of prayer. Such a tumultuous, spontaneous wave of prayers poured forth when the President was slain that he never really lost consciousness. Almost instantly he was attuned to what was going on, and because these prayers swept him onward and upward, he did not for even a little while have to encounter what the priests of his church would call purgatory: a state of souls wandering aimlessly and lost until something awakens them to the potential of their new state of being." **Ruth Montgomery, *A World Beyond***

---

## KNOWING, NOT BELIEVING

The Tenth Insight or level of awareness is being demonstrated now with the growing body of experiential information about the spiritual dimension that is entering the mainstream belief system. Such spiritual events as near-death and out-of-body experiences are rapidly shaping and expanding "common knowledge." This marriage of the sacred with the mundane is the first step in unifying the material and spiritual realms. Through altered states of consciousness such as extrasensory perception (ESP) and out-of-body travels, transcendent meditation, and parapsychological events (seeing "ghosts" or communicating with the dead), we bring the spiritual dimension into the physical, and it *becomes a part of this life*. Bringing in the Afterlife dimension to life in the physical plane gives us a fuller vocabulary of capacities and is bound to create quantum changes in our evolution.

### WE ARE ETERNAL

What could be more life-changing than *knowing*—not just believing—that our consciousness survives intact after our physical death? Like a butterfly, in dying we emerge from the cocoon of the body with wings and iridescent beauty—if we have not made serious errors here that send us into a long and painful personal recapitulation of the suffering we have caused others. Death as we have defined

> I thought of Huston Smith, the MIT philosopher of science and comparative religions. He put forth the argument that we as human beings can study scientifically only that which is below ourselves in consciousness, never whatever or whoever may be above us. **Kyriacos C. Markides,** *Riding with the Lion*

it is not the great void. In this new awareness, life and death are seen as two states of an eternal, mysterious process.

Communication from souls in the Afterlife can be found from many reputable sources. One of the most fascinating is Washington journalist Ruth Montgomery, a leading psychic authority. Although a skeptic in the initial stages of contact with her unseen Guides, Montgomery wrote several books, dictated by automatic writing from the Guides, over the last thirty years. In addition to the wisdom of the Guides, she also communicated with her old friend, noted psychic Arthur Ford, after he died. He, along with the Guides, brought through an amazing amount of information about the spiritual realm.

If we are to have a fuller understanding of the totality of the life experience, then the next step for humanity may be not only to acknowledge the reality of the Afterlife dimension but to begin to consciously tap into it so that it may help us hold the positive World Vision. Our intuitive knowing that we came here with a purpose then becomes part of our reality.

## WHY NOT STAY THERE?

In the Afterlife, or spiritual dimension, we may be able to image anything and create it, but this type of nonphysical creation is not as fulfilling as creation in the physical world is. We choose to be born into the denser vibration of the Earth plane so that we can delight in the physical world and experience the consequences of our actions.

Earth life is necessary for the soul to develop. The Tenth Insight opens our memory as to *why* we came here.

In *The Tenth Insight,* Wil says, "We are learning to use our visualization in the same way it is used in the Afterlife, and when we do, we fall into alignment with the spiritual dimension, and that helps unite Heaven and Earth." Each of us is the alchemical vessel that transmutes energy into actions, uniting these dimensions.

## UNIFICATION OF THE REALMS

In doing the research for this chapter, we were struck by the resemblance of some of the points in the Tenth Insight to the messages that the Guides were giving Ruth Montgomery over twenty years ago. The Guides were very clear with Ruth that the messages they brought were as important for their advancement as for our own—a point also made by the Tenth Insight. They wanted Ruth to communicate the importance of developing our psychic abilities, while in a physical body, in order to better our lives and enrich the souls of others.

Speaking about the Afterlife as the Unknown, the Guides tell her, "The first step for [people] is to try to make contact with what they call The Unknown, so that this power can begin working in their behalf. This power is one of the strongest forces in the universe. With the souls on the unseen side of this imaginary barrier joining with those there who truly seek to advance the cause of others, the powers are almost limitless."[6] This is exactly the point about the unification of the dimensions that comes to us through the Tenth Insight!

They explained to her that this ability to communicate between dimensions would not be possible if it were not for the good of humanity, and not to use it would be a tremendous waste. ". . . God wishes that it be utilized and developed to the fullest extent, so that at last—as in the Scriptures it was foretold—the veil will drop between the two worlds, and all will be as one. Although some may still be living in the flesh in that day, they will be able to converse at will with those who have passed into the next stage. The time can come as rapidly or as slowly as man views the problem with open or closed mind."[7]

The Guides also made the point that each moment of our Earthly life is important not only because it gives us a chance to experience the richness of this plane but also because it is our opportunity to love. It is our opportunity to serve the world plan, as well as attune ourselves to a more spiritual vibration. Many times they admonished Ruth not to waste her life in fruitless pursuits! "[Life on earth] is merely preparation for this phase of life; and we, of course, are preparing for the next phase of ours. That is why we are so anxious to help others through on that plane. It is part of our spiritual development here, and you are retarding us when you refuse to make yourself available."[8] Even though the spirit souls hold our Birth Vision, the unification of the planes cannot happen without our conscious intention in the physical plane. It is up to us on Earth to fulfill this historical purpose. Perhaps this archetypal concept of unity, this thrust toward spiritualizing the physical world, may even be the driving force behind our new awareness and concern for systems thinking and the concepts of "holism" and "holistic." When the culture has fully integrated this understanding of physical/spiritual unity, the eventual realization of the World Vision would be assured.

## COMMON EXPERIENCES IN THE NEWLY DECEASED

Kenneth Ring, Ph.D., is one of the foremost researchers of the near-death experience. In *Heading Toward Omega: In Search of the Meaning of the Near-Death Experience,* Ring gives the testimony of a man who suffered a nearly fatal accident. His description of his death typifies the common sequence of experiences that many thousands of people have also related.

> ". . . the first thing that I noticed was that I was dead . . . I was floating in the air above the body . . . this didn't seem to cause any consternation to me at all. I really was completely dead but that didn't cause emotional difficulties [for me] . . . I realized that I was able to float quite easily . . . I could also fly at a terrific rate of speed . . . and it seemed to produce a feeling of great joy . . . Then I noticed that there was a dark area ahead of me and as I approached it, I thought that it was some sort of a tunnel and, without further thought, I entered into it and then flew with an even greater sensation of the joy of flight . . . I noticed a sort of circular light at a great distance which I assumed to be the end of the tunnel as I was roaring through it . . . this seemed like an incredibly illuminating sort of a place, in every sense of the word, so that not only was it an awesome brightness . . . but it also seemed a marvelous place to be. I was in different surroundings where everything seemed to be similarly illuminated by the same light, and uh, I saw other things in it too . . . [a] number of people . . . I saw my father there, who had been dead for some twenty-

five years . . . I also felt and saw, of course, that everyone was in a state of absolute compassion to everything else . . . It seemed, too, that love was the major axiom that everyone automatically followed. This produced a phenomenal feeling of emotion to me . . . because it made me feel that . . . there was nothing but love."[9]

Common elements of the death transition are also found in both *The Tibetan Book of the Dead* and the recollections of subjects who have experienced past lives under hypnotic regression. According to the ancient text, young souls in their early incarnations are apparently not yet completely aware of the process of reincarnation. Mature souls with more lifetime experience begin to become more aware of their passage through the nonphysical worlds and are consciously trying to learn and grow. Older souls progress into teachers, helping younger souls to become more conscious of their spiritual nature.

### NOT REALIZING WE HAVE DIED

Many people report that immediately upon dying, a person may not realize that he or she is dead, particularly if the death is sudden. This is illustrated graphically in the movie *Ghost*, when Patrick Swayze is so involved in the fight in which he is killed that he does not realize he has left his body for good. When we have died, apparently we still feel that we are in some kind of body through the force of our thought habits.

### HANGING OUT

People may also hang around the Earth plane in their old "haunts" for several days, or linger to observe their family and friends at their funeral. Because of an exaggerated sense of loss or attachment, some souls don't completely separate from the physical plane. They get stuck in wandering, haunting, and hanging about—which retards and delays the process of assessing their last life in the past-life review. In past-life regressions, people sometimes report scenes of chaos—the twilight world of those people who are still attached to the physical world and have not moved on.

### HOW DO WE LOOK IN THE AFTERLIFE?

According to most reports, initially in the Afterlife we usually look like we did just before death. Later on we may take on the form of our body when it was at its strongest and best. Our psychic body is plastic, malleable to our experience, emotions, and thoughts.

## PHASES AND LEVELS

After some time, the soul feels a pull to begin its journey through the different spiritual planes of experience.

From many accounts that describe amazingly similar details, we have learned about the stages of progression that a soul makes through the nonphysical realms. Our level of soul development determines what planes we go to or stay in for a while.

In the lower realms, people have described zones of chaos and darkness, accompanied by terrible sounds such as a sort of thundering, booming, whistling, and unhuman cries and howlings. Others have reported being frightened by terrible-looking or deformed people—people locked in struggles, pain, or grief. Often, the person would move through this zone by ignoring the tormented souls. These areas are the place we reenact our obsessions time after time.

Another plane that people encountered was a conceptual realm of ideas that was calm and pleasant—perhaps even filled with singing and celestial music. Some people report that as they move "upward" in the planes of existence, their body changes to become lighter and clearer.

Other realms are even more beautiful than the realm of ideas—filled with a wide spectrum of unearthly colored lights. Often these higher realms are where our loved ones who have already made their transition to spirit greet us. One might choose to rest for a period of time in these calmer planes. Apparently, as one goes higher in frequency, there is a sense of endless levels stretching beyond the imagination. As the spirit body becomes lighter and more luminous, people have spoken of feeling flooded with joy and boundless love—a bursting joyfulness for being "home" and an eagerness to participate in new learning and expansion.

## LIFE REVIEW IS ESSENTIAL TO DIGEST OUR RECENT LIFE EXPERIENCE

According to hundreds of near-death experiences, people report seeing their life zip before their eyes. They see with great clarity every significant event of the life they are on the brink of leaving. In seemingly the space of a few Earth seconds or minutes, they review decades of meaningful moments in their life. This instant replay communicates one thing—how well the person has learned to love and acquire knowledge. More often than not, people report that they yearn to stay in the spiritual realm, but because of a young child to raise, a desire to give more love, or the realization that they have not completed their purpose, they decide to resume their life on earth.

### THE REVIEW CHANGES EVERYTHING BACK ON EARTH

In nearly all accounts of near-death experiences, the person is dramatically transformed. In *Life After Life*, Raymond A. Moody, Jr., M.D., describes how even a brief review of significant events changed people's values and behavior for the rest of their life. The Life Review is usually, but not always, accompanied by a "being of light." Moody says, "As a rule, in experiences in which the being apparently 'directs' the review, the review is an even more overwhelming experience. Nonetheless, it is usually characterized as quite vivid, rapid, and accurate, regardless of whether it occurs in the course of the actual 'death' (in the case of a re-lived past life regression) or only during a close brush with death."[10]

> It was not exactly in terms of pictures, more in the form of thought, I guess. I can't exactly describe it to you, but it was just all there. It was just . . . everything at one time. I thought about my mother, about things that I had done wrong. After I could see the mean little things I did as a child . . . I wished that I hadn't done these things, and I wished I could go back and undo them. **Raymond Moody, M.D., *Life After Life***

The people (called remigrants) who experience a past-life review during a hypnotic regression often find that the lesson of that lifetime is quite clear. In one of the most exhaustive and thorough books on the subject, *Exploring Reincarnation*, Dutch psychologist Hans Ten-Dam reviews a wealth of information taken from a variety of clinical studies. He says that people report life aims that are "fantastically divergent." For example, one remigrant said that "the main purpose of his life was to learn to laugh, because he had been too serious in previous lifetimes. Another remigrant had been enormously rich during his life, but died poor as a church mouse . . . he had to learn that wealth or poverty does not determine humanity."[11]

## DIRECT KNOWING

In almost all cases of contact with the spiritual dimension, it seems as if the realizations made by people are felt as a *direct, inner knowing* such as, "I felt my mother's presence. I just knew it was her." "Even though I wanted to stay, I knew that it was not yet my time [to die]." "I had an immediate sense that it was my father." Or "I knew that I had to learn how to be more loving." Even though the spiritual dimension is a love-filled home for us, we keep being reborn to experience the wild uncertainty of life in the physical plane! In the Afterlife, most souls who have progressed along in numbers of lifetimes say that they intuitively know that they are eternal. They became conscious that they have a soul and that their soul wants them to have specific experiences and achieve different goals.

---

Sometimes we lose our soul's vision altogether, and become stuck through a trauma or refusal to move on, as did a clerk in an old-fashioned business office reported in TenDam's book. He was "fused with his desk for over thirty-five years, and refuses a promotion because he prefers to stick to his current work.

"In the retrospect on his life he sees his lifeline in front of him as a thin, glowing thread snapping at some point and become dark grey. When the therapist asks him which situation caused this, the remigrant immediately sees the refusal of the promotion. He renounced a chance to develop and so renounced himself."
**Hans TenDam, *Exploring Reincarnation***

---

### THERE IS ALWAYS COMPENSATION

Dr. Brian Weiss gives an account of Pedro, one of his patients, in his book *Only Love Is Real*. Pedro came for counseling because he was unable to shake a feeling of despair that had deepened since his brother's death. Pedro's past-life remembrances in several lifetimes showed interesting choices that brought greater learning. In one, he saw himself forced into the priesthood by his family. He did not want to leave the woman he loved, and thought he would rather die. But, resigned to the inevitable, he entered the monastery. In his regression, he comes to know that the abbot in the monastery was the brother for whose death in his *current* lifetime he is deeply grieving.

When asked what he learned from this lifetime, Pedro said, "I learned that anger is foolish. It eats at the soul. My parents [in that lifetime] did what they thought best for me and for them. They did not understand the intensity of my passions or that I had the right to determine the direction of my life . . . they were ignorant . . . but I have been ignorant also. I have commandeered the lives of others. So how can I judge them or be angry with them when I have done the same? . . . This is why forgiveness is so important. We have all done those things for which we condemn others. . . . I would not have met the abbot [his brother] if I had my way. There is always compensation, always grace, always goodness, if we just look for it. If I had remained angry and bitter, if I had resented my life, I would have missed the love and the goodness that I found in the monastery." After having seen his brother in this past-life recall, he realized that the soul is immortal, and if he had loved his brother and been with him before this life, then he would be with him again. Thus his grief began to heal.

In another recalled lifetime, Pedro saw himself as a female prostitute to rich and powerful men. In that life, she enjoyed manipulating these men and became addicted to that life. There was a young man whom she loved, but she left him for "an older, more powerful and wealthy man. . . . I didn't follow my heart. I made a terrible mistake."[12] In the end she died alone, under the disapproving eyes of nurses in a cheap hospital surrounded by the poorest of the poor.

## REVIEWING OUR CURRENT LIFE EVEN BEFORE WE GO BACK TO SPIRIT

The message of the Tenth Insight is that more and more of us will begin to review the progress of our soul *while still in our physical bodies* rather than waiting till we pass over to the other side. Through silent meditations, journal writing, a numinous dream, or a spontaneous illumination, we may begin to see ourselves from this larger perspective of the soul's development. For deep-seated issues, we may want to seek an enlightened therapist who brings the spiritual dimension into his or her psychological work.

Many of us are already asking ourselves, What have I learned so far, how am I actualizing my original Vision? In what direction do I seem to be growing? As we grow in consciousness individually, we increase our understanding of what is *really* possible, who we *really* are. Then our *being* is the foundation from which our *doing* springs.

We chose to leave the spiritual plane and take on this life so that we could experience the glorious range of choices that will develop our soul to the next level. Your Birth Vision is one facet, one note, of the World Vision. Without the fear of death and the void of oblivion, we can live more joyously, and yet more deliberately, than ever before. That curiosity and sense of playful adventure that was as natural as breathing to us when we were young will continue to encourage us to pursue intuitive images with even more delight, or enter the realms of suffering with a greater perspective of the whole. The World Vision is made manifest each day according to the collective vibrations of your existence and your actions.

## RECOGNITION OF THE AFTERLIFE BY A CRITICAL MASS

In Western, scientific cultures, when people try to describe a near-death experience or an after-death communication from a loved one to family, friends, nurses, or doctors, the responses are often disinterest, thinly veiled disbelief, or comments that the person is simply under duress from grief. For example, "I tried to tell my nurses what had happened when I woke up, but they told me not to talk about it, that I was just imagining things." Or "I don't like telling people about it. People just kind of look at you like you're crazy."[13] Although existence of the spiritual world is integral to almost every other culture's worldview, our Western minds have largely marginalized the spiritual plane to Sundays and superstitions.

The Tenth Insight suggests that remembering the existence of the spiritual dimension while in physical form is the ultimate goal of the evolutionary spiral. Bill Guggenheim and Judy Guggenheim, authors of Hello from Heaven!, estimate "that 50 million Americans, or 20% of the population of the United States, have had one or more after-death communications"—five times the amount of people who have had near-death experiences.[14] Dr. Raymond Moody notes that it is not surprising that those who died and came back think they are unique and that no one else has had such an experience. They are relieved to hear that it is not an uncommon phenomenon.

The First Insight revealed that a critical mass of awakened individuals has to be achieved in order for the transformation to shift *all* consciousness. Enough people have to sense the reality and existence of the Afterlife before this information can be brought through. The reality of the spiritual dimension will have to become a household idea. If we look at the belief systems of our culture, we know that certain other assumptions must necessarily arise together to let new ideas become acceptable. Dr. Moody says that "the temper of our times is, in general, decidedly against discussion of the possibility of survival of bodily death. We live in an age in which science and technology 'have made enormous strides in understanding and conquering nature. To talk about life after death seems somehow atavistic to many who perhaps feel that the idea belongs more to our 'superstitious' past than to our 'scientific' present.

"In addition, the general public obscurity of the topic of near-death encounters seems to stem in part from a common psychological phenomenon involving attention. A lot of what we hear and see every day goes unregistered in our conscious minds." Moody uses the example of what happens when we learn a new word. Suddenly, we hear the word everywhere. The word has been there all along, but we have not been aware of its meaning and skipped over it without being consciously aware of it. The same thing happens when we decide to buy a new car of a certain color. All of a sudden, we see these same cars everywhere.

One example of such selective attention is a physician in the audience of one of Moody's lectures who noted, "I have been in medicine for a long time. If these experiences are as common as you say they are, why haven't I heard of them?" It turned out that the doctor's own wife related to the group a near-death experience of a very close friend of theirs. Her husband had either not paid attention to it or had forgotten it since it did not fit his current beliefs. In another synchronistic example, a physician had read an old newspaper story about Moody's work. The next day a patient came in with his own account of his near-death experience during surgery. According to Moody, "It may very well have been that in both instances, the doctors involved had heard of some cases of this before, but had thought of them as individual quirks rather than as a widespread phenomenon."[15]

The last point that Moody makes is that doctors, who should have heard about near-death phenomena more than the general populace, are trained to take seriously only the physical "objective" signs of disease. "It is constantly pounded into M.D.'s-to-be that they must beware of what the patient says about the way he feels."[16]

We know the power of an "idea whose time has come." Marie-Louise Von Franz, one of the great Jungian analysts, uses the example of how often scientists and Nobel Prize winners intuit the same solutions and innovations virtually simultaneously. The Tenth Insight suggests that the Afterlife will provide us with a wealth of information when enough people are ready to sense it and someone writes it down.

However, if the Fear quotient in the worldview is too high, it will create an obstacle to sensing the divine wisdom. If you are feeling a bit skeptical as you read these lines that any spiritual progress is happening in the face of global conflicts, remember that development of consciousness happens in waves. We are both a particle in the waves and the waves themselves. We will accomplish whatever we can in our days here.

## About Reincarnation

Reincarnation is the idea that our soul, our eternal consciousness, is reborn time after time into many lives in order to learn, grow, and evolve. Knowledge about reincarnation comes to us via such avenues as religious and esoteric doctrines, spontaneous past-life memories of adults and children, induced regression to past lives, and through people who have an enhanced sensitivity to psychic information.

### SPONTANEOUS RECALL OF OTHER LIFETIMES

In spontaneous recall, the person may have a recollection following the recognition of a place or person at first sight. However, past-life researchers such as Hans TenDam believe that déjà vu experiences, the feeling that one has already lived through the moment, are not evidence enough to assume a past-life memory. Such uncommon immediate bonds as love at first sight, if it's true love, however, probably do indicate a past-life relationship.

A recollection may also be triggered by an object, picture, book, or a similar situation. It can also happen under duress, in exceptional physical or emotional circumstances. No previous belief in reincarnation is necessary.

### PHYSICAL MARKS, HABITS, AND TENDENCIES

Evidence seems to show that past lives can leave their mark on the current life in a variety of ways. One may have a significant mark on the body, a peculiar habit, exceptional abilities or talents, or fixed attitudes about life (assumptions) that don't seem to come from the present family system. Sometimes a person remembers a fatal wound in a previous lifetime that matches a current birthmark.

Our preferences may give us clues to our past lives. If you have a penchant for Early American furnishings or Chinese porcelain, or gaze longingly at pictures of the coastline of Greece, such predilections could indicate a positive past life in that era or country. In *Exploring Reincarnation,* TenDam mentions that with young children peculiar behavior may directly indicate a past life. Many past-life recollections have been verified through historical records.

> A charming example is the little girl who slams her milk mug down on the table and wipes her mouth as if she had just put down a pint of beer with great satisfaction. When her parents reprimand her, she bursts into tears and says it is a tribute to her comrades who she does not want to forget. When the family inquires further, she makes remarks about a past life. The girl also looked markedly different from the rest of her family. **Hans TenDam, *Exploring Reincarnation***

## TIME BETWEEN LIVES (INTERMISSION)

Researchers report that the intermission between physical lives may vary from a few years in Earth time to hundreds or thousands. Possibly the less Earthly life experience we have under our soul belt, the more frequently we are reborn in order to learn. According to specific studies cited by TenDam, average intermissions appear to be roughly sixty to eighty Earth years. Older souls may carefully pick their incarnation for a specific purpose to unfold during a specific time in Earth's development.

Based on regression literature and his own research with regressed people who are fairly aware after their death transition, Hans TenDam suggests three patterns of reincarnation and different levels of reasons why people are reborn. These levels may intermix in a life.

### POPULATION I: NATURAL—OR "WOW! I'M BACK ALREADY?"

According to reports from past-life regressers, the people in this group of souls return to life with little remembrance of their intermission in the spiritual dimension. They seemingly have no guidance about what the new life is to be about. According to past-life regression accounts, these lifetimes start by being kind of sucked back into life ("a vacuum cleaner sensation at entering the fetus") without much thought about it, especially if the previous life had been cut short. Eager for life experience, these people are probably engaged in learning basic lessons about life on Earth, without much awareness of the deeper purpose of their soul. Lacking an individual life plan, their new life is largely undirected by deep-seated motivations to accomplish a purpose. With short intermissions (thought to average eight Earth years in between), each life is often close to the old one in time and distance.

### POPULATION II: VOLITIONAL AND EDUCATIONAL— OR "LIFE 101 TO 999"

In contrast to the natural, involuntary return to life of Population I, the people in II voluntarily choose to return to life on Earth, and give much thought to the kind of parents and situation that will give them the best conditions to learn and grow. As the soul progresses in maturity, some teachers suggest we earn the right to design a life plan during intermission in the Afterlife. This plan or Birth Vision sets goals for personal development and settlement of personal karmic relationships. TenDam's regression cases report that there is a retrospect of the previous life (past-life review), consultation with guides and soul groups, a preview of some of the life experiences and people one will meet (like Maya's preview in the novel), as well as an awareness of the intermission itself. The intermission for this population appears to average roughly sixty Earth years.

### POPULATION III: MISSION—OR "THE BIG ONE"

Like the people in Population II, IIIs consciously deliberate in the intermission. However, at this level of soul development, the person has most likely cleaned up much personal karmic debt. With more freedom to express a wealth of developed tendencies and abilities from hundreds or thousands of lifetimes, the people in Population III return to life to make a major contribution to the development of humanity. These people have working objectives for a more far-reaching plan. Driven by an inner knowing that life on Earth is purposeful and that there is a divine connection, they attract many opportunities as well as challenges. Extreme conditions may force them to go deep within. Through pain, suffering, and ecstasy as well as the boredom of mundane perseverance, they receive much guidance from their soul group, higher self, and God. These people may be ordinary, active, and well-meaning people who keep a low profile, or they may eventually become charismatic teachers and world leaders. The Buddhist philosophy is that the bodhisattvas, the lords of compassion, "appear as world teachers according to a fixed schedule . . . the periodic return of the perfected."[17] Average years between lives in Population III are thought to be roughly 230.

## THE INFLUENCE OF SOUL GROUPS

The seven characters in *The Tenth Insight* are involved in a project to stop the experiment in the valley. Their need to stop the experiment serves as a catalyst for them to start remembering their past connections and unresolved issues. Following their understanding of the Ninth Insight, they attune themselves to a higher vibration, to tap into the guidance from those souls in the other dimension that are holding their Birth Visions, hoping they will awaken to them. Wil says about these discarnate soul groups, "We're connected with them. They know us. They share our Birth Visions, follow us through life, and afterward stay with us while we review what happened. They act as a reservoir for our memories, maintaining the knowledge of who we are as we evolve . . . when we're in the Afterlife, and one of them is born into the physical dimension, we act in the same capacity toward them. We become part of the soul group that supports them."[18]

The Insight tells us that while our soul groups do not send us intuitions—those come from a divine source—they do send us extra energy and uplift us in a particular manner so that we can more readily remember what we already knew. They are always sending us energy and hoping we will remember our Birth Vision, and seem to expand and "be happier" when we begin to remember. Guggenheim and Guggenheim write, "The inhabitants [of the spiritual dimension] value knowledge greatly and are encouraged to pursue subjects of their own choosing. These cover virtually all topics, but the favorite ones reportedly are the arts, music, nature, the sciences, medicine, and all manner of spiritual studies, which they in turn try to pass along in the form of inspiration to those still living on earth."[19] According to TenDam and other researchers, "Of the people [who reported counseling with others before birth], more than 60 per cent had more than one adviser, some even had a *circle of advisers*" (emphasis added).[20]

## LOST SOULS OR SOULMATES?

Some people may ask, "How would I distinguish between lost souls who are hanging around the Earth plane and soul groups?" The difference is that lost souls lack enough energy to either leave the Earth plane or go to the spiritual plane. They are stuck somehow in a thought pattern of fear and will be looking to drain your energy.

In a moment of crisis or clarity, your guide or soul group may make itself known with an intervention or inspiration. Your intuition will tell you whether the guide or group is helping you by giving energy or is trying to steal your energy and decrease your confidence and self-direction.

## CRISIS INTERVENTION

In his book *Reflections on Life After Life,* Dr. Raymond Moody cites some of the accounts he collected from people who were rescued from imminent death through the intervention of some spiritual agent or being.

Moody cites an example of a man who was trapped in a vat into which was being pumped a stream of high-pressured, very hot acid. "I had gotten as far as I could into a corner, and put my face into the corner, but the stuff was so hot that it was burning me through my clothing. . . . I realized that in just a matter of minutes I would be scalded to death . . . to myself, I just said, 'This is it. I'm a goner.' . . . it seemed that the whole area lit up with a glow.

"And a verse of Scripture that I had heard all my life, that had never meant too much to me, 'Lo, I am with thee always,' came from a direction which later turned out to be the only way out. I couldn't stand to open my eyes, but I could still see that light, so I followed it. I know that my eyes were closed the whole time, though. The doctor didn't even treat my eyes later. No acid got in them."[21] In this case, the man interpreted this divine helper as Christ. Moody says, "Persons undergoing this [intervention] relate that afterward their lives were changed, that they came to feel they were saved from death for a purpose."[22]

Another man reports that during World War II, he saw an enemy plane diving toward the building he was in. It was firing on the building, and the dust of the bullets was headed in a path right toward him. "I thought we would all be killed . . . I didn't see a thing, but I felt a wonderful, comforting presence there with me, and a kind, gentle voice said, 'I'm here with you, Reid. Your time has not come yet.' "[23]

### ASSUMPTIONS, EXTRAORDINARY ADVICE, AND SYNCHRONICITY

Kenneth Ring tells a story of a woman, Stella, who made significant internal changes during the course of following a vision. Adopted as a baby, Stella grew up in a fundamentalist background. As she grew into an adult and married with family responsibilities, she described herself as extremely shy, retiring, and obsequious. "Not long before her near-death experience in June 1977, she had what seems best understood as a waking vision . . . she was in bed but before she had gone to sleep . . . she saw a series of written characters . . . much later after her NDE, she discovered that the characters were Hebrew . . . and translated into 'Beyond the Vanishing Point.' "[24]

During her NDE, she encountered a being of light: "Almost as though two faces in one. One with the beauty and the peace and the light that was in that place in the face and yet, somehow contained in the same face the form had been beaten. It almost looks like one side [was] out of shape. One totally peaceful and yet one with the pain of the other. [Ring asks if this being communicated anything.] Yes . . . [that] there was a purpose to my being sent back here and the purpose had to do with bringing knowledge, particular knowledge . . . and that there is life after this on a much greater level. . . . We're so much more. That we have the ability and capacity to know. [Did you have any sense of the identity of this being?] I don't attempt to make any identification for anyone else. [Inwardly, what do you think?] I feel very strongly that he, too, had a purpose. Whatever his purpose was is not totally clear to me, but it also was to bring a knowledge, an understanding to mankind. . . ."[25]

The being went on to tell her that she was Jewish and that there was something that was a blockage that she didn't know anything about. It was a key to understanding. Following this episode, Stella began a search for her biological family. At one point she had come to a dead end in her search for clues. "I said, OK, I'm trying to do what you said, but the paperwork's not there, so if this is what you want done, you're going to have to help. And I went back to town and sat down in the restaurant there that night and was trying to think of another way I could go about this, and two policemen walked by the table and I thought, 'I bet there's a clue.' " One of them had returned to the table where he had been sitting because he had forgotten something. She seized the chance to tell him that there was somebody she was trying to find.

He put her in touch with a couple who had run a local newspaper for many years. They, in turn, directed her to a retired judge who had been a resident of the town for a long time. "When Stella met him [the judge] was taken aback. 'It was like turning back the clock when he saw my face. . . . [He] took one look at me and, after, he put me in touch with my grandfather, who had retired and moved down to Florida."[26]

Stella's life dramatically changed after connecting up to her family heritage. She converted to Judaism, divorced her husband, and became a successful businesswoman. She served on the White House Council on Children and Youth and became active in the problems of adopted children. In this instance, the assistance she received from the Afterlife—for example, realization of her lost heritage, and the blockage it was causing, and experience of the spiritual dimension—revealed how restricted her earlier life had been. Similar to the Afterlife retrospect, Stella saw that she didn't do her own thinking. ". . . somehow implanted in that nine-month-old child was the knowledge that my biological mother had rejected me and that if I didn't adhere to all these rules, regulations, requirements—somehow it had been my doing. It set up a barrier, and kept me from going past anything that was required of me in order to not be rejected."[27] In fact, as we have seen with TenDam's research, this *assumption,* "I've done something wrong, therefore, I'd better follow the rules so I won't be rejected," could even be *the* karmic pattern waiting to be healed in Stella's Birth Vision. Thus, she received extraordinary guidance from her higher self or soul group, which was holding the memory of this goal.

## GREAT SOULS STILL WORKING FOR HUMANITY

Ruth Montgomery's book *A World Beyond* is written as an eye-witness account of the Afterlife from the world-famous psychic Arthur Ford. Montgomery and Ford had been close associates until his death from a heart condition. After his transition to the spiritual dimension, he began contacting Montgomery in the early 1970s through the medium of automatic writing.

She queried him about famous people who had died and wanted to know what they were doing in the Afterlife, apparently a place of abundant projects and learning. President John F. Kennedy made an unusually swift transition to the spiritual realm. In one of his communications to Montgomery, Ford reports, "Jack [Kennedy] is at work on international problems and is trying to bring some kind of settlement between the Israelis and Arabs as his primary interest. Bobby [Kennedy] left his heart in the civil rights movement [and is working in that field]. . . . The brothers have strong karmic ties and have been so close in many previous lifetimes that without the one the other seems less than whole. The close-knit family group was by prenatal choice, each wanting to share again his life with the others."[28] He went on to mention how other world leaders such as Eleanor Roosevelt, Franklin Roosevelt, Winston Churchill, and Dwight Eisenhower are still working with groups of souls in the Afterlife as well as inspiring the consciousness of Earthly humans involved in peace work. According to Ford, "The telephone, electricity, the steamship, and many others of like caliber . . . were joint efforts of talented souls on this side and the physical side, working together to bring about betterment of conditions in the physical plane. Einstein, who would nap for a few minutes at various times of the day, was actually tuning in here to the forces which renewed his objective and suggested the next step in his experiments. The moral for all is those nap times [are important], when you as physical beings are able to commune with the spirit beings on this side to replenish energy, direction, and goals."[29]

Another point Ford makes is that souls who have made significant strides for humanity in compassion, dignity, service, and love are not always required to live into the infirmities of old age. As Robert Monroe says in *The Ultimate Journey*, "When you have satisfied your purpose in learning, you may leave!"

## RELEVANT INFORMATION COMES THROUGH ANOTHER LIFETIME

In *The Tenth Insight,* our character sees himself in another lifetime as a monk in thirteenth-century France. He understands that in that lifetime, he came into possession of the Insights and copied them in order to preserve them. He had wanted to make them public, but his ascetic brothers refused to go up against the church.

The value of any past-life information is to help free us to live and love and develop more fully in the present. Compulsions, overwhelming grief, and debilitating fear block good health and well-being. Regression therapy may offer an avenue of healing when other traditional explorations have failed.

Brian Weiss writes about a woman who came to one of his past-life workshops in Mexico City. "She had just experienced a past-life memory in which her current husband was her son. She had been a male in a medieval lifetime, and she, the father, had abandoned him. In this present life, her husband has always feared that she would leave him. This fear had no rational basis in the current life. She had never even threatened to leave him. She reassured him constantly, but his overwhelming insecurity devastated his life and was poisoning the relationship. Now she understood the real source of her husband's dread. She rushed to telephone him with the answer and with her reassurance that she could never leave him again."[30]

Unhealed past-life traumas may manifest as hypersensitivities in a current lifetime. According to TenDam, "Traumas are like hidden manholes, postulates (permanent assumptions made after a traumatic event) are like treadmills, whirlpools, knots, or vicious circles in the paths of your psychic garden. They are ingrained in you as fixed programs: 'If I lose control, I'm lost.' 'If I escape, I will be free.' 'I cannot think because I am a woman.' "[31] If you had a lifetime that was nothing but work, you might come out of that lifetime with a postulate, "Life is exhausting." If you had died in the trauma of falling off a train or drowning, you might have an irrational fear of trains or deep water.

## REPEATED PATTERNS THROUGHOUT LIFETIMES

The character in *The Tenth Insight* views another lifetime in the nineteenth century. In this life, he understands how the negative outcome of the thirteenth-century lifetime created his fear and unwillingness to support Charlene's stand for peace. These two lifetimes created the character's tendency to stay aloof from confrontation. He begins to see how his choice of mother and father was made in order to work through this fear of confrontation.

He also realizes that his previous exposure to the spiritual truths of the Insights in the thirteenth century engendered a curiosity and passion in *this* lifetime. This part of the story shows us that an individual might have a Birth Vision that directly affects the collective Vision—that is, he is on the trail of the Insights as part of his personal karma but is also helping the evolution of consciousness as well. Obviously, part of his Birth Vision involves *his* quest for the Insights just as they are surfacing into mass awareness. Timing is everything. The character in *The Tenth Insight* has a chance now to resolve this test of standing up for his beliefs which he failed before. If not, he will likely face another similar situation in the next lifetime.

## PSYCHIC SCARS

Experiences remain unresolved because either there is too much pain to handle at the time or the person dies before having a chance to complete his lesson. Traumatic deaths may leave a permanent fear—for example, of water, the dark, caves, or heights, whatever the association is to the *pain* around the death. Sometimes the reaction is so deeply scarring that the person unconsciously makes a declaration about it, such as, "I'll never be in that position again." "I'll never be publicly humiliated again." "It's impossible to stand up to authority." "It's hopeless."

One woman who was having difficulty balancing her involvement with her lover with attention to her business described the feeling of uneasiness that she carried around: "I feel kind of like a samurai. I feel like I'm very finely tuned and I have to be ultrasensitive to any change in the air, so I can take measures quickly in case I have to." This is certainly a unique way to draw an analogy! It could be that this is a postulate arising from just such a situation in another life. These statements become fixed in the nature and are carried from lifetime to lifetime. The character in the book, for example, had to learn to trust his intuition, heal his tendency to remain distant, and continue in his quest for spiritual knowledge in the shadow of his past traumas around spiritual matters. According to TenDam, this kind of holdover from lifetime to lifetime is one of three dynamics that help shape the quality of life: retention, repercussion, and fruition.

### Retention of Traits

Retention is the persistence throughout lifetimes of some personality characteristic or physical feature. Abilities such as musical talent and intellectual prowess may be developed over several lifetimes and be brought into the present life, as in the case of child prodigies or geniuses. TenDam believes that paranormal abilities are the result of temple training in past lives. "Meditation . . . out of body experiences, clairvoyance . . . any other paranormal gift, can be traced back in regression to one or more lives with lengthy training."[32] Tendencies, flaws, and even addictions may be traced back to lifetimes where these ideas were deeply ingrained.

### Repercussions from Events in Past Lifetimes

The repercussions of traumatic events, as in the examples above, may continue to plague the lifetimes until they are identified and released.

These unconscious heavy energies may result in phobias, compulsions, and physical problems which defy current diagnosis.

In *The Tenth Insight,* Maya experiences resistance, even though she feels that she is doing what she came to do. She resists the idea that she is part of the group who is destined to come together and work through the Fear in order to stop the experiment. This is a result (repercussion) of the negative experiences she had in the lifetime when she tried to stop the war between the Indians and the white people. She has not yet really tapped into that lifetime, and so has *unconscious memories* that create fear and resistance.

## Reaping

Fruition is the dynamic of reaping from past actions—good or bad. For example, if you had a really wonderful life in Spain in a previous life, you might have a preference for that country in this lifetime without knowing why. By the same token, if you had lived one or more lives in desperation as the father of a huge family that you could not support, you may be very wary of family commitments in this life. Fruition also implies that by developing good qualities or relationships in this lifetime, you may be preparing for even more harmony and loving connection in the next lifetime.

### DOWN THE RABBIT HOLE

Some dimensional openings may literally draw us into a metanormal encounter. Such occurrences are widely accepted in traditional cultures. Malidoma Somé, African shaman and author of *Of Water and the Spirit,* describes an experience he had as a three-year-old. He was out with his mother gathering firewood when he stepped on a rabbit. "It dashed out of its hiding place and a wild race ensued." Diving into the brush after the rabbit, he checked a part of the bush where he knew there was an animal nest. "This nest was an earthen hole dug in a little hill, its opening covered with grass and its inside filled with soft straw. I removed the grass and was ready to leap headlong onto the miserable rabbit, but I never completed the action. All my movements were suspended as if by an electric shock.

"Where I had thought there would be a rabbit there was instead a tiny old man as small as the rabbit itself. He sat on an almost invisible chair and held a minuscule cane in his right hand. . . . All around him there was a glow, a shiny rainbow ring, like a round window or portal into another reality. Although his body filled most of that portal, I could still see that there was an immense world inside it.

"But what surprised me most was that the laws of nature in that world did not seem to operate like anything I had seen before. The little man's chair was sitting on a steep slope, yet he did not fall over backwards. I noted that something like a thin wall sustained him." Petrified, Somé heard the little man say, " 'I have been watching you for a long time, ever since your mother started bringing you here. Why do you want to hurt the rabbit, your little brother? What did he do to you, little one?' His tiny mouth was barely moving as he spoke, and his voice was very thin . . . 'Be friendly to him from now on. He too likes the freshness of this place, he too has a mother who cares for him . . .' While the little man was speaking, I spotted the rabbit, which had been hidden behind him in the magic circle all that time. Meanwhile, I heard a cracking sound, as if the earth itself were splitting open. No sooner had I heard this than the old man stood up, slung his chair over his shoulder, and walked into the opening as if he had commanded it. The earth closed upon him, leaving a gust of fresh breeze in his place."

At that moment he heard his mother's voice calling him. Apparently hours had passed since she had been looking for him, although he felt he had only been talking to the little man a few minutes. When he told his mother the story, she was alarmed because she knew he had seen a Kontomble, a spirit. The people of his tribe, the Dagara, believe that contact with the otherworld is always deeply transformational. Mothers fear their children opening up to the otherworld too soon, because when this happens, they lose them. "A child who is continually exposed to the otherworld will begin to remember his or her life mission too early. In such cases, a child must be initiated prematurely. Once initiated, the child is considered an adult and must change his/her relationship with the parents."[33]

> Traditional education consists of three parts: enlargement of one's ability to see, destabilization of the body's habit of being bound to one plane of being, and the ability to voyage transdimensionally and return. Enlarging one's vision and abilities has nothing supernatural about it, rather it is "natural" to be a part of nature and to participate in a wider understanding of reality. **Malidoma Patrice Somé,** *Of Water and the Spirit*

### ANOTHER TYPE OF DIMENSIONAL OPENING

Part of the attraction that Westerners may have for shamanic and neo-shamanic practices no doubt is rooted in the desire to have personal experience of other dimensions, which was the central idea of the Fifth Insight, the Message of the Mystics. The whole idea of this Insight is that more and more of us will be able to travel into other dimensions by learning how to raise our vibratory level. Dr. Henry Wesselman, a paleoenvironmentalist by training, wrote *Spirit Walker,* a book describing his own experiences traveling into the future. While a graduate student in the 1980s, Wesselman began to have involuntary out-of-body experiences. After months of fearing he was ill or crazy, he began to make sense of what was happening. He found himself some five thousand years in the future on the new coast of the western United States. He came to realize that he was seeing the world through the physical presence of his future ancestor, a man named Nainoa who originally came from the Hawaiian islands after great planetary changes had taken place. Wesselman now believes that all humans have the capacity to enter these other realms of time and space. He believes that we have a "program" in our energetic field that lies dormant until we spontaneously, or through intentional practices, learn to activate it.

---

## INDIVIDUAL STUDY

### Love Grades

Reflect back on your life. If you were grading yourself on your ability to love *everyone* and your openness to acquire knowledge, how would you score yourself on a scale where 100 was the highest, 1 was lowest?

---

And the creation of this new consensus may, in turn, have implications for evolution. For if a need coalesces into a group dynamic, if a new "morphogenetic field" of intentions solidifies, it is possible that some of the habits or laws of nature could get "broken," or changed, thus making new forms of life possible.

Every life saved, liberated, enhanced adds to the building of the new earth and the new heaven. It is here in the liberation and transformation of earthly existence that the "afterlife" is *proven*—but *"proven"* in the Italian sense of *pro-vare*—"to experience." **Michael Grosso, What Survives? Contemporary Explorations of Life After Death**

---

## Life Review

Knowing that every thought and action, no matter how seemingly insignificant, was going to appear in your review, what would you do differently tomorrow?

### *Obstacles*

What areas have you struggled with the most? Choose the most important one or two ideas from the table below, or select some other problem that may not appear on this list. Write for five minutes about how you have experienced this obstacle in the past.

| *Physical* | *Mental* | *Emotional* | *Spiritual* |
|---|---|---|---|
| height | self-confidence | romantic love | racism |
| weight | learning disability | family dysfunction | ostracism |
| too much money | language barrier | depression | betrayal |
| lack of money | mental illness | fear | alienation |
| lack of beauty/ | | loss | distrust |
| handsomeness | | grief | |
| too beautiful/ | | | |
| handsome | | | |
| addictions | | | |
| sexuality | | | |

How have you benefited, if at all, from these seeming obstacles? In what way have the obstacles increased your ability to love? If a friend had the same problem, what advice or suggestion would you give him or her?

### *Achievements*

Without worrying about being properly modest, what are you proudest of about your accomplishments? Write for five minutes on how you came to do that, what helped you the most, and what you wish you had known in retrospect.

## Nice, Little Moments

- In the next day or two, notice the opportunities that come to you to be quietly helpful or kind to someone, *without telling anyone else about it . . .* ever.
- Over the next week, notice how nice people are in stores, at the gas station, at street corners, in your family, wherever your path takes you. Silently notice their kindness, and feel the loving energy between the two of you.

- Practice imagining people as a soul—using whatever image makes sense to you. We can never really know what another person's destiny is, so avoid trying to analyze people to find out what their Birth Vision is, but do send them loving energy (silently) to help them remember it!
- How have you experienced any unexplainable intervention in a crisis?
- If someone who was a friend or family in this life was looking out for you on the other side, who would that be?
- What three or four famous people from other eras are you drawn to? How have their lives or philosophies influenced your life?

## GROUP STUDY

- Study some of the books we have referenced here, or bring in others that you have discovered on reincarnation, past-life therapy, out-of-body or near-death experiences, or after-death communication. Take turns reading some passages that you found interesting and use these as a basis for group discussion.
- Suggest people share any experiences they have personally had if this feels comfortable to everyone.
- Use one of the above suggestions in Individual Study as a basis for writing and sharing ideas. Remember, keep the energy clear and gently remind people not to linger in poor-me energy. However, be sensitive to immediately labeling someone a Poor Me if he or she is genuinely relating an important challenge or loss. Labeling is not helpful.
- Discuss the famous people or teachers from other eras that have most influenced your life or personal philosophy.

## PART FOUR

# In the Dark

# CHAPTER 7

# Remembering One's Birth Vision

HORSE
POWER

When we have an intuition or a dream to pursue a particular course in our lives and we follow this guidance, certain events transpire that feel like magic coincidences. We feel more alive and excited. . . . When we have an intuition, a mental image of a possible future, we're actually getting flashes of memory of our Birth Vision, what we wanted to be doing with our lives at that particular point on our journey. It may not be exact, because people have free will, but when something happens that is close to our original vision, we feel inspired because we recognize that we are on a path of destiny that we intended all along.

THE TENTH INSIGHT:
HOLDING THE VISION[1]

## AWAKENING TO OURSELVES

Written words are no substitute for the personal experience of the mysteries of life. Having traveled this far on your journey, you know the excitement of *experiencing* a piece of the truth you seek. There is no principle or theory that will open the doors you wish to go through before you are ready to do so.

Your question may be "Who am I? What is my Birth Vision?" The only answer may be the inner "Yes!" that resounds from the connection you make when an idea feels right, when a relationship blossoms, or when you've helped someone with little or no fanfare.

Thomas Moore writes in *Soul Mates: Honoring the Mysteries of Love and Relationship,* "It's my conviction that slight shifts in imagination have more impact on living than major efforts at change . . . that deep changes in life follow movements in imagination . . . [the point] is to free ourselves of longstanding and rigid ideas and images of what it means to love, to be married, to be a friend, or to live in community."[2]

153

The Tenth Insight suggests that "we're finally becoming aware of a process that has been unconscious since human experience began. From the start, humans have perceived a Birth Vision, and then . . . have gone unconscious, aware of only the vaguest of intuitions. . . . Now we're on the verge of remembering everything."[3]

### AWAKENING INCREASES ENERGY AND INCREASES INSIGHTS

History is the story we tell ourselves about what we think happened. History is the story of our beliefs, the spiral record of our choices, but not the only basis for the future. The character in *The Tenth Insight,* for example, comes to the realization that "finally, we could look at history not as the bloody struggle of the human animal, who selfishly learned to dominate nature and to survive in greater style, pulling himself from life in the jungle to create a vast and complex civilization. Rather, we could look at human history as a spiritual process, as the deeper, systematic effort of souls, generation after generation, life after life, struggling through the millennia toward one solitary goal: to remember what we already knew in the Afterlife and to make this knowledge conscious on Earth."[4] Birth Visions, while specific to each soul's need to develop certain characteristics, also include the collective goal of becoming conscious. *Birth Visions are the driving evolutionary force within each of us.*

## CHOOSING ONE'S PARENTS AND BIRTH ENVIRONMENT

According to some spiritual teaching, at a certain level of soul development we earn the right to choose the vehicles (parents) for our return to Earth. In *The Tenth Insight,* we see Maya, the doctor and healer, deeply contemplating, in the Afterlife dimension with her soul group, the parents she would select for this lifetime. She considers the advantages of exposing herself, and the negative or undeveloped tendencies that have followed her from lifetime to lifetime, to particular kinds of parents. In this vision, she also becomes aware of the way her purpose fits into the World Vision and how her soul group helps her retain the memory of her life plan.

During her "pre-life" vision for the way her life would evolve, Maya also sees all the people who will enter her life to help her learn her lessons and stimulate growth. She sees that at some point in her life the discovery of the Insights will lead her to a reunion with a particular group of people. From the Afterlife perspective, she clearly understands that her group, and other independent groups, would come together to "remember who they were at a higher level and be instrumental in overcoming the polarization of Fear."[5] This knowledge of her original Birth Vision accelerates her enthusiasm for her life and

> Maya had experienced a full Sixth Insight review and was on the verge of remembering why she had been born. **James Redfield, The Tenth Insight: Holding the Vision**

helps validate the choices she has made. She realizes that her life so far, though not predetermined, has been in accordance with the deep design of her original intention. In the book, the characters see Maya go into the portal, the opening between dimensions, at the point of orgasmic release in her parents' lovemaking.

## APPOINTMENTS, PLANS, AND PURPOSES

Not all of us think ahead in life. We plunge into new ideas with only the vaguest idea of where it might take us. And so it is for some of us in choosing a new lifetime. As we saw in the last chapter, there seem to be three distinct populations of souls—ones who are reborn with little or no plan; those, like Maya, who have a plan; and those who have an epochal mission. Reports from regressions conducted in 1979 by Helen Wambach, a psychologist and past-life researcher, revealed some interesting statistics about the motivations for different lifetimes. Eleven percent said they were resistant and more or less afraid to take on another lifetime, and 55 percent had at least some hesitation. Eight percent of the people regressed said they felt nothing about their birth in terms of a plan. Twenty-three percent said they had had a plan and saw themselves consulting with their Guides before their descent into life.

Three percent felt they were "too hurried" or that they had acted against advice (from their Guides or soul groups).[6] The variety of these attitudes certainly reflects the range of how a lot of us view our lives once we get here! The inference from this information is that about 20 percent of the group interviewed seemed to have reincarnated whether or not they wanted or planned to. The rest were at least accepting of being reborn.

Apparently, plans are made to accomplish many things, large and small. Souls whom we've known throughout many lifetimes volunteer to play with us in the new drama of life that we have requested. Appointments are made in the spiritual dimension to meet one another later and to do things together. Reflect for a moment on the people who have been special in your life. Can you imagine making plans to meet up with each other here? Do you remember how you met your best friend? Your spouse? Someone who arrived at a turning point? Were you aware of "fate" or synchronicity at the time?

### NEITHER TOO AMBITIOUS NOR TOO HUMBLE

Based on accounts of people who saw their previous lifetimes from the perspective of the Afterlife, TenDam made some observations that we might do well to consider the next time we design a life in the spiritual dimension. Since we cannot escape the consequences of our choices and actions, he suggests: "Be extremely careful about fixing your will or judgement in a particular notion. Apparently, firm intentions and rigid judgements may operate throughout incarnations. Be neither too ambitious nor too humble in your life plan. When making a new life plan, first consider the attitudes and abilities you have been developing, and the obvious further goals of development. Next comes the heritage of traumas and postulates. Often you do not find a combination of parents, sex, and living conditions ideal in every way. Besides what you yourself want and can handle, the actual living conditions [of your life on Earth] usually set limits to competence development and karma settlement. Try to find prenatal and postnatal conditions that stimulate selected traumas, without stimulating the others. Further, look for adequate and instructive circumstances. You can only work at so many problems accumulated in your lives."[7]

### CAN WE HAVE WHATEVER WE WANT?

Our choice of incarnations seems to be limited by the level of our soul development. Perhaps less developed souls (younger souls) who have not yet earned the right to make a life plan must take whatever parents they can get! According to regression reports, young souls seem to spend less time in the spiritual state between reincarnations as their desire for physical experiences sends them quickly back to Earth. Souls who have caused much harm and suffering may spend eons in the lightless realms as they reexperience all the suffering they caused and struggle to awaken to their spiritual nature. While no wrathful, avenging, or judging God banishes or punishes us, neither can we escape the repercussions of our deeds. However, once a request for help is made, spiritual help is granted through the service of souls who volunteer for this task.

The soul, with the advice of its Guide or soul group, will make its selection of birth parents and environment, but then, according to certain philosophies, one has an "interview" with the Holy Spirit to ascertain if the options under consideration are in alignment with the soul's development. The soul apparently makes a kind of reservation on the mother it has selected, and can enter into the growing fetus immediately or at any time before birth, or even within a few days following birth.

### WE HAVE FREE WILL EVEN WITH OUR PLAN

These pre-life visions are the *ideal,* or best-case, scenarios, that would unfold if all of us were following our intuitions perfectly. Even though we apparently set down the type of path we want to pursue, and even though we make agreements to meet certain other souls during the course of our life, there is no evidence to suggest that life is completely predetermined. The whole point of living is to learn, to make choices, and to grow from exercising free will. The idea of the *life plan with free will* is analogous to deciding to go out to dinner and selecting where you will eat. Will it be a diner? A drive-in? A casual or formal place? Chinese? American? French? You finalize your choice for various reasons based on location, type of food, menu, price, but once in a particular restaurant, you don't have complete control over your experience. You make choices based in the moment. First course? Meat or vegetarian? Dessert? Coffee or tea? You might get into a conversation with your wait person, make the acquaintance of other diners by chance, or see an old friend. Perhaps there is a delay, a fly in the soup, or maybe you even have an allergic reaction. If all goes well, you may absolutely enjoy yourself. The plan was to have dinner, but how and where and what you eat depend on choices you made freely in the moment. This is the same of life. You have opportunities, and some you take and some you don't and it changes the course of your life. Even though you have a general goal you want to work on, there is much leeway for you to live your life. The way you learn your lessons is not always predictable.

## BIRTH VISION

In *The Tenth Insight*, the characters come to realize that "apparently, before we are born, [many] of us [experience] a vision of what our life can be, complete with reflections on our parents and on our tendencies to engage in particular control dramas, even how we might work through these dramas with these parents and go on to be prepared for what we want to accomplish."[8]

One person gives an account of his desire to stay conscious of his purpose and Birth Vision: "I felt I was waking from a long dream. I had been resting for so long. I felt it was time to . . . return to the field of life.

> You chose to be born within a particular family because that made your purpose easier to fulfill. While still in your mother's womb, you told the living certain things to remember. But even if they were to tell you these things, would you believe them? Would you trust them enough? You would not, because when we come here and take on human form, we change our opinions like the wind. When you do not know who you are, you follow the knowledge of the wind.
>
> **Malidoma Patrice Somé, *Of Water and the Spirit***

I was aware that I had a lot of things to accomplish in my next life. I could not fail as I had before. It was very important that I strive to be more conscious of everything once I was reborn. . . . I knew when I returned to the world a temporary amnesia would overcome me. I would forget my purpose and my mission. I had done this each time. This time I sensed that I would remember sooner. I resolved then and there to become fully conscious in that lifetime, to overcome my imperfections, to strive for something higher, deeper, and purer than my usual round of experiences. I had lived many times. I had known love, hate, fear, death, disease, hardship and plenitude. But through all of these experiences in all of my lifetimes on earth, I had not found lasting joy and satisfaction. . . . I wanted to be on earth as I was here, totally conscious of my existence. To realize that I was not simply a person, but that I was part of God, an extension of Him. This I would forget on earth. *But I was determined to strive for that higher awareness*" (emphasis added).[9]

Another man, a clerk in a camera store in a small town in Delaware, reflects on his vision of God that occurred shortly before rebirth: "I saw God. . . . No words, no pictures, no language could ever describe him. All forms emanated from Him; I saw all of the universes, all of the persons, all of the worlds contained in Him. I expressed my feelings to Him, my sorrows at having failed before. He seemed undisturbed by my failures. He was encouraging me to try again. With this new inspiration I came back to life, determined this time to help others, to serve the world, and *to become fully conscious of both my inner and my outer existence*" (emphasis added).[10] In these deep movements of these men's souls, we see the undercurrent of the World Vision—the desire to bring spiritual awareness into the material world.

Interestingly, 60 percent of the people with prenatal memories under regression could answer Helen Wambach's question about their aim in life, the reason for coming back. The other 40 percent who reported no particular plan were usually those people who had not themselves chosen to return (part of Population I—the natural return to the physical). TenDam offers this summary of the research on people's remembrance of a life plan.[11]

- 27 percent came to help others and to grow spiritually themselves.
- 26 percent came to acquire new experience as a supplement or correction.
- 18 percent came to become more social.
- 18 percent came to work out personal karmic relationships.
- 11 percent came for miscellaneous reasons.

Of those people who looked at their previous lives it's interesting how clear the reason is for the lifetime. Wambach's study showed such specific reasons as, "I had a lot of work left to do in the relationship with my mother." "I had to tie together and round off all the loose ends from the life just before." "I wanted to expose myself to a weak and indulgent life and to overcome this." "I went back to be able to feel things and to touch them." "I wanted to come back because I just had died young." "I knew that my parents needed me because they had lost a 15-month-old girl in a fire."[12]

## CHOOSING A DIFFICULT PATH

It seems that some souls choose to challenge themselves by being born into abusive, dysfunctional, or constrictive environments. Such lifetimes test the limits of endurance, patience, and forgiveness. Interestingly, these souls may have been the most optimistic about what they wanted to handle in physical life. Before birth, they were sure that they were strong enough to awaken, work through their anger and resentment at their deprived conditions, and help heal the family system—in preparation for their mission.

In the case of traumatic events that befall a person, how much of that is dictated by the soul's desire for experience? If a woman is raped, does that mean that her soul chose that event? If a man loses a son, does that mean he set that up beforehand? According to the reports of remigrants, those who have had a chance to evaluate their life from the Afterlife perspective in regressions, the answer is that specific events are not usually outlined beforehand. A soul might very well intend to expose itself to conditions that would challenge and test it. The soul might wish to accelerate its development by opening itself to the karma waiting to be experienced and resolved, but it might not have selected the specific time, circumstance, or trauma.

When a child is lost, usually there is an agreement from both souls to live out the experience together for each other's higher good. If a soul intentionally caused the death of someone else, the consequences of that action must be balanced. A soul may choose to sacrifice itself in one life as a way to pay off its karmic debt. Sometimes a soul who may not want to stay in a physical body will voluntarily intercede in an action that is unfolding in order to give life to another. Some babies die early because their physical body may not be strong enough to reach maturity, or because they never intended to complete the life in the first place for whatever reason. A child may live long enough to bring joy to the parents, but an early death may give the parents a chance to experience a deeper spiritual awakening than would have been possible any other way. Evidence suggests that there are many deeper purposes behind events than we are usually aware of or prepared to understand.

> There is no magic potion . . . that gives us wisdom. Only our experiences will teach us and then, only if we are truly willing to learn. We can read a million books whose words inspire us, will help to point us in a certain direction. But only the experience can give us true meaning to the written word. **Rosemary Altea, *The Eagle and the Rose***

## LIFE REVIEW *NOW*

None of us accomplishes our Birth Visions perfectly. But the more conscious we can become, the easier it will be to stay open, following our intuitions. Connected to our source, we can give more love. We can work through our control dramas. More self-reflective, we might ease up on ourselves and enjoy the great ride of life. In the novel, Wil says, "Don't you see? This has to be a key part of the Tenth. Not only are we discovering that our intuitions and our sense of destiny in our lives are remembrances of our Birth Visions. As we understand the Sixth Insight more fully, we're analyzing where we have been off track or failed to take advantage of opportunities, so that we can immediately get back on a path more in line with why we came. In other words, we're bringing more of the process into consciousness on a day-to-day basis. In the past we had to die to engage in a review of our lives, but now we can wake up earlier and eventually make death obsolete, as the Ninth Insight predicts."[13]

---

A recent account by a Texas woman indicates a combination of hidden observer and target-cell memory that, while obviously very rare, could play a profound role in our lives if we knew how to open ourselves to it. On the day this woman's husband left her, while she was at her office working, the details of their twenty-year relationship began "passing through" her head. The review is complete, in proper sequence, and centered exclusively on their relationship and the misunderstandings and errors on both sides that had ruined it.

The experience went on for hours, the memories "began and ended as if a tape had started and stopped . . . I felt incredulous, overwhelmed, awed . . . It was fascinating and breathtaking. Yet as I experienced this I was aware . . . of the heat of the noonday, of walking in the bright sun." She was, however, only vaguely aware of where she was as she continued her duties. Again, . . . two parallel realities played to one witness. **Joseph Chilton Pearce,** *Evolution's End*

---

In Ruth Montgomery's book *A Search for Truth*, the Guides tell her, "The time for every [person] to think about his future is while he is living in what will become his past. Regard each day as an unblemished page in the book of life. Let no ink or mud spot or smudge of dirt blemish those pages. Take them with you, spotless, into the next stage and you will have advanced far beyond your wildest dreams. The best thing to remember is this: *Greet each day as the untarnished future, and handle it as carefully as if it were already a published record of your past.*"[14]

## COMMITTING TO ONE'S LIFE PURPOSE IN TERMS OF
## SERVICE AND BEING

Paradoxically, the best way to attract what you want is to focus a strong intention to create that thing and *then release the struggle around "figuring it all out" or controlling the outcome.* The less you struggle, the more your path will begin to unfold.

All too often, we tell ourselves that we must "work hard" to find our purpose. We wind up with a serious, rather grim attitude to "doing good," or we feel that we have fallen short in some grand accomplishment. One regressee said about a past lifetime in Egypt that was filled with much suffering, "Many things come from that kind of a life, many things . . . endurance, patience, many things. It seems mundane, it seems worthless—but the soul learns many things."[15] When asked if everyone on the soul plane has an awareness of what has been learned in a lifetime, she replied, "Yes, in the soul plane." Even people who seem oblivious to life in their incarnation do have an awareness on the soul plane.[16]

### PRACTICE IS PERFECTION

It is helpful to create the harmonious conditions for the arrival of your good fortune by practicing certain vibrational states each day, such as appreciation, gratitude, forgiveness, detachment (from the need to have your desire fulfilled), humor, love, openness, and expectancy. Being your authentic self, and using your talents gratefully and generously, ensure that you are engaged in the flow. In addition, it's important to practice circulating wealth and seeing the

Can a person change their world view simply by reading a book that causes them to change their beliefs about the way things are?

You generally will not convince people, particularly Westerners, about the significance of the spiritual dimension just by giving them books to read. The critical factor in a genuine spiritual opening will probably always be a direct personal experience . . . it can begin by reading some books and hearing some lectures, attending spiritual groups, and undergoing some subtle forms of transformation in meditation and other spiritual practices. **Stan Grof, M.D., in *Towards a New World View*, by Russell E. DiCarlo**

best in others, so that you will be flowing with the law of giving and receiving.

One woman was struggling with trying to resolve a fifty-five-year-old family conflict. She kept devising ways to get what she considered her due share of the heirlooms and was fixated on getting money from them. Slowly, with much inner turmoil, she saw that her true desire was for peace of mind and connection. At the age of eighty-six she finally saw that she had always held a heroic belief that she had to fight for her rights and had felt alone and isolated for many years. She had forgotten her source and strength was in God.

Go into silence and listen for the inner direction *for you.*

### SERVICE IS THE PATH

As we mentioned in the last chapter, Ruth Montgomery's messages from Afterlife Guides kept stressing the importance of service as the path to fulfill one's destiny. They were extremely clear that the most important actions we can possibly take to advance ourselves as souls is to help others when they cross our paths. She writes in *A Search for Truth,* "Constantly the Guides harped on the theme of service to others, 'which must be done not only in a spirit of charity, but as a burning need to fulfill one's own mission.' We must, they said, be more interested in helping others than ourselves. In so doing, we would automatically be advancing our own cause. 'That was the message that was brought to your world eons ago by Christ and other religious leaders,' they wrote. 'The message has not changed one iota. It remains, as it was then, when Christ said "love one another." This is not *one* way to advance spiritually, but the *only* way.' "[17]

The mystery of your life wants to reveal itself. The Mystery is unfolding as you read these words.

---

Know only that when it is your time to leave the earth plane, and to begin your life anew, the wealth that you bring with you will be the wealth of learning that you have gained which is within your heart. Grey Eagle, *The Eagle and the Rose,* by Rosemary Altea

---

## INDIVIDUAL AND GROUP STUDY

The following exercises can be done individually or worked on with friends or in a study group. The information might be completed as a home assignment and then discussed in the group in pairs or in the group at large, if everyone is comfortable sharing their personal stories.

### Thinking About Your Parents from the Spiritual Perspective

Take a moment here to reflect the deeper meaning behind the parents (or other caretakers) that you chose to expose yourself to in this lifetime.

#### Father
- If there were a caption under a photograph of your father describing his life, what would it say?
- What was missing from your father's life? Was there something he wanted to accomplish but didn't do? What characteristics were weakly developed or missing in him?
- What were the most important things you learned from him?
- How are you like him?
- How have you developed in ways that are different?
- What influence did he have on your own path?

#### Mother
- If there were a caption under a photograph of your mother describing her life, what would it say?
- What was missing from your mother's life? What did she not do that she wanted to do? What characteristics were weakly developed or missing in her?
- What were the most important things you learned from her?
- How are you like her?
- How have you developed in ways that are different?
- What influence did she have on your own path?

#### Reflection on Your Spiritual Philosophy
Take a moment to ask yourself:

What did my parents believe about God?
*Father*
*Mother*
What beliefs did my parents have about life after death?
*Father*
*Mother*
What three values were most important to my parents?
*Father*
*Mother*
What idea(s) did my parents most impress upon my mind?
*Father*
*Mother*
What legacy would I say my parents left the world?
*Father*
*Mother*
What did I learn to do or not to do from watching how my parents
lived their lives?
*Father*
*Mother*
What would I say were the most prominent missing features of my
parents' lives (e.g., good health, success, self-esteem, affection,
sense of humor, creative fulfillment)?
*Father*
*Mother*
In what ways am I just like my parents?
*Father*
*Mother*
In what ways have I differed or evolved from the way my parents lived
their lives?
*Father*
*Mother*
Assuming there was some reason that they were the perfect parents
for me in this life, what would that reason be?
*Father*
*Mother*

### Birth Vision Statement

Close your eyes for a moment and take a couple of deep breaths. Relax
your body. Imagine that you are on a hill looking down at a road. On
that road you see yourself walking. What images do you see about

your life at certain points on that road? What kinds of images or messages await you at the end of the road? Fill in the sentences below with the images or intuitions that you received:

> $A$t the beginning of my path I see . . .
> $I$n the middle parts of my path I see . . .
> $N$ear the end of my path I see . . .

How would you describe yourself to someone else in terms of the following areas? Date your responses and read them again in six months, a year, five years.

My strong points are . . .
I have a talent for . . .
The kind of occupation or activity that has been most fulfilling to me
　is . . .
I have contributed to the world by . . .
The three biggest challenges I've had are . . .
My challenges have helped me by . . .
I view life as . . .
What I value most in life is . . .
I get most excited about . . .
I am happiest when . . .
I am proudest of . . .
I am in the business of . . .
The thing that can never be taken away from me is . . .
The one thing I'd like to experience next is . . .
The legacy I would most like to leave is . . .
I have the feeling that my Birth Vision . . .
My World Vision is . . .

## Following the Vision

We know that aspirations and images about an ideal life come to us from our deeper Birth Vision. Accept your daydreams as real desires that in *some way* want to be fulfilled through you. Sure, you may never be an opera star, but you might go for it as long as you have the heart. Or you might have even more fun (isn't that part of what you want?) organizing a singing group at a local school or community function. Persistent rather than obsessive, clear rather than fluctuating, visions should lead to actions. Actions put you on the path to fulfillment.

Humans are not just response mechanisms geared to outwitting given conditions in order to survive. Humans are dream makers.

### Vision Play

- What image keeps coming into your mind? What do you want that you do not have?
- What do you have that you would not want to lose?
- Pretend that tomorrow you will wake up into an ideal living and working situation where you are expressing your best qualities. Write a few sentences about that.
- What *one* word would you choose to describe yourself? In what way is that quality useful to the world in general? How are you using that quality now? Write a few sentences about that. Let whatever wants to come forth reveal itself.
- Start reading the obituaries in your paper, the longer ones about people who have achieved some kind of prominence. Far from depressing, these "life reviews" gift us with a story of someone's high points and ennobling challenges. Even the short death notices may give you the overview of a long life of responsibilities well met, inventions brought forth, talent rewarded, and most of all love given without measure. Some lives leave simple, quiet legacies of patience, selflessness, or oft-repeated quirky episodes that shape the family history for generations. There is poetry in lines such as:

> Social worker, retired parole officer, flamenco guitarist; his wisdom, kindness & music, will dance in our hearts & touch our souls always.[18]

---

> Mr. R. founded drive-through dairies, and bought milk directly from the farmer . . . [and sold] the freshest milk you could buy . . . going back to the original glass bottles for concern about the environment and landfills.[19]

---

> Brownie McGhee, the blues guitarist and singer, preserved and popularized the blues style of the Piedmont area of the Carolinas. Piedmont blues meshes bouncy guitar picking and strumming with rhythmic, hooting harmonica; he sang with earthy conviction.[20]

---

> Eleanor Clark, a master stylist . . . wrote a series of soaring ruminations on everything from ancient history and early Roman poetry to modern social conditions.[21]

She was very active as a member of the Happy Belles and Telephone Pioneers.[22]

E.P., a Mayan Indian who attracted worldwide attention for his ancient healing methods using only herbs and prayer, died at 103 . . . in his humble hilltop hut in the tiny village of San Antonio, in western Belize . . . [he] was generally regarded as the master of them all by other traditional Mayan healers.[23]

Apparently soulmates, a couple in their seventies both died of cancer within hours of each other:

The quirky and humorous couple both left impressive marks on their chosen professions [he an author, professor, historian, she a noted artist and advocate of public art education]. He "deeply believed in the power of the classroom teaching to excite students to challenge accepted societal beliefs." He founded the Penny University, a weekly series of free public academic debates. She created the California Prison Art Program which brings top-notch artists into prisons to teach.[24]

And karma in the making:

B.O. A Manchurian-born immigrant who rose through underworld struggles in New York to become what law enforcement officials called the leader of the most powerful organized crime group in New York's Chinatown . . . went to prison for 17 years . . . experts say he allowed himself to be framed and imprisoned to protect someone higher in the organization.[25]

### Current Progress, Problems, and Pursuits

Take one of these questions per day or per week to reflect upon. *Don't try to work with them all at once.*

Write out a couple of sentences or paragraphs answering the *question that speaks to where you are right now.*

These questions may also be used as a foundation for a discussion group.

#### Checking In

- Is there *any* situation or relationship in which you feel unresolved or anxious?

We know that if we owe someone an explanation, an apology, a phone call, it continually saps small parts of our energy until it is resolved. The same thing is true if you have made a decision to do something, but it doesn't feel right. Burying your feelings or delaying dealing with issues only increases the pressure of this energy drain. Bring these circumstances into conscious awareness. Ask for help from the universe to resolve it. Follow through on your intuitions. Notice how something will take you to your next level.

- Is there anything that is even a *slight* drain on your energy?

  Make a list of *anything* you wish were different (e.g., I wish I didn't have to go to PTA next week. I wish I knew what was wrong with the dog, the computer, the car, etc.). Once you have become aware of and have written down the point causing the energy drain, you may get your answer or experience a shift very soon.

- What obstacles do you see in your path right now?

  Obstacles force you to go deeper into the issue, deeper into your creativity. What are the hidden payoffs for having these obstacles? What do the obstacles prevent you from doing that might be scary? For example, if you feel lack of money is an obstacle to expanding your business, are you unconsciously afraid to go to the next level?

- What parts of your life are working well?

  These are part of your Birth Vision. Think back to the time when these good things appeared in your life. What frame of mind were you in to attract these things? Acknowledge how much you have accomplished. Notice how successful you are. Express gratitude each day for this success.

- In what situations right now do you experience lots of energy?

  Being energized is a good sign that you are connecting to an inner rightness that is keeping you connected to your Birth Vision.

- What budding goals seem to be emerging?

- If you were to make a prediction about what will happen in the next six months, what three things would you predict? Include today's date.

- What is your most important question at this moment?

  After writing down your question, define the outcome that underlies this question. For example, if your question is, "Should I marry Joe?" your underlying desire is for a happy marriage with the perfect partner (whether or not it is Joe). Therefore, rewrite your question as a positive statement of the outcome you desire: "I am now happily married to the most perfect person for me."

# CHAPTER 8

# An Inner Hell

OWL
THE DARK

It's all a reaction to Fear. The people there would be paralyzed with Fear if they didn't find some way to ward it off, to repress it below consciousness. What they're doing is repeating the same dramas, the same coping devices, they practiced in life, and they can't stop.

THE TENTH INSIGHT:
HOLDING THE VISION[1]

## GOD OR GOD *AND* DEVIL?

The question of good and evil has occupied the mind of humanity for thousands of years. The perennial philosophy and the Tenth Insight hold that there is but One Force, a unified field of energy, the force of God—All-That-Is. There is no second force, no Devil, no *embodied* force of evil with the power to wield punishment against us in life or after our death.

God created humans, endowing us with free will, so that he/she could know himself/herself through our endless creativity. Our every facet is a face of God. In order to keep evolving and diversifying our Godness, it is necessary to exercise our free will without becoming separated from God. Our choices create good, not evil, when we stay in alignment with our God qualities of love, compassion, joy, play, service, and creativity, which serve the greater good. The evil that exists in the world is fed by our fears. We endow evil with power when we believe in humanity's "inherent sinfulness" or when we scorn spirituality as a meaningless soporific. The Devil has been used historically to explain evil in a simplistic way. In order to understand evil we must explore the more complicated psychological nature of humans.

171

## An Inner Hell

If there is no separate, second force of evil in the world in opposition to All-That-Is, is there a Hell? In pictures of Hell we see a procession of doomed, naked souls, stripped of any chance of salvation, dejectedly marching into the flaming pits or screaming in terror. While we may smile in our sophistication at this literal image, believing ourselves exempt from such a fate, each of us has lived at least one day or one hour or one lifetime in our own burning hell inside our skulls, trapped, stricken senseless with rage, horror, guilt, envy, jealousy, or terror. Who among us has not been capable of some measure of self-created hell?

Some of us have dwelt in Hell from our first breath or even before that, unwanted and despised within the womb. The inner hell starts here on Earth. From infancy, some souls are pinched and kicked, slapped and scratched, shut in closets, terrified of those who are supposed to care for them. Abused or vilified, invaded in their sexual areas, beaten, ignored and devoured by their parents' drug habits, these souls, in the worst cases, grow into adults with little or no sense of the oneness with and goodness of God. Despite unbelievable adversity, we know that some souls miraculously grow around and through the evil that has wrapped itself around them. In other cases, the trauma has been too severe. As if they have had their humanity burned out, others live to inflict the inner hell they carry onto others, perpetrating despicable acts. The cycle continues. The inner hell is a certainty that there is no love and that power can only be had by causing another to suffer.

Our own inner hell might be an insecurity and rigidity that keeps us isolated from love. Hell might be living with boundless lust, greed, envy, paranoia, mental illness, fear, rage, self-loathing, obsession, or pride. We know that these kinds of fixations separate us out of the flow of life, paralyze our creativity, and force us into repetitive self-defeating unfulfillment. Hell is dark and heavy, cold, endless, lonely, and hopeless.

### BRING YOUR OWN BELIEFS

If we complete the mandate of "As above, so below" by equally acknowledging, "As below, so above," we can begin to see that whatever consciousness we take to our death transition is that consciousness with which we enter our Afterlife existence—*and that consciousness with which we create our reality there.* You *can* take it with you. You take your ability to create your world with you. Just like being born with certain abilities and tendencies from experiences in previous lifetimes, we are "born" into the Afterlife at death with the recently developed abilities and mind-sets. Therefore, as there is no personified external force of evil, no Devil, there is no other Hell than the one we bring with us in the form of our negative energy into the spiritual dimension.

Furthermore, if we do not realize right away that we have left the material plane, that we are indeed "dead," we will continue to re-create those mental obsessions endlessly in the spiritual realm. Remember, in the spiritual dimension, thought creates everything instantly. If you think about having sex, you're immediately engaged in that activity. If you want to see someone you know, you are instantly transported to that energy field (if the person is open to being visited). So "hell" is built from the mental constructions set up by souls with little ability for self-reflection, and who cannot wake up to the spiritual dimension after their physical death.

## NO PLACE TO HIDE THE FEAR

Robert Monroe talks about his encounters with the Fear as he traveled in the spiritual realm. Through direct experience he learns that his every thought, including his fear, will be immediately manifested in the spiritual dimension. In that place, one cannot hide one's judgments and feelings behind a social veneer like we do every day on Earth. Everyone is naked. Monroe describes how he learned to work with the emotions that he had managed to keep repressed in physical life during his trips to what he calls Locale II in the Afterlife. "One by one, painfully and laboriously, the exploding uncontrollable emotional patterns had to be harnessed. . . . If it doesn't happen during physical life, [I suspect] it becomes the first order of business upon death."

"[The areas of Locale II] are peopled for the most part with insane or near-insane, emotionally driven beings. . . . They include those alive but asleep or drugged and out in their Second Bod-

> If we choose to live in darkness, while on earth or after "death," if we choose to allow the light to diminish, then we choose a dark place. But always it is our choice. I am saying that there are no fires of hell unless we choose it to be so.
> Rosemary Altea, *The Eagle and the Rose*

ies [the "body" we have in the spiritual dimension], and quite probably those who are 'dead' but still emotionally driven."[2]

## SELF-JUDGMENT DAY

According to Guides in the Afterlife and reports from near-death experiences, whatever suffering we cause others in our Earthly life, we will suffer ourselves in even greater intensity once we return to the spiritual dimension. Even though there is no "Judgment Day" visited upon us from God, we will pay through our own suffering in the Afterlife for *all* the harm we caused another. Guiding souls in the Afterlife help us to see what we learned in our just-completed life and how much we were able to love so that we may progress in our next lifetime.

If we have done even one good thing in our lifetime, this action can cancel many of the negative things we have done. Instead of worrying about the negative things we may have done in the past, it's important now to concentrate on doing only good.

At the level of awareness of the Tenth Insight, we are already taking stock of our beliefs and behaviors and attempting to wake up. Through the "pathology" of our misguided control dramas as well as our achievements, we have a chance to see our inner mythology—our story. If we don't wake up in this physical dimension, we might have trouble waking up in the Afterlife as well.

## HERE AND NOW

To a greater or lesser degree, *in physical life* we build our own version of Hell by staying attached to, and unconscious of, our control drama tendencies. When we forget our connection to our divine source, we have to construct a very narrow set of behaviors in order to reduce the world to a manageable level. Living in a defended zone fenced in by fear, we are not open to the full-blown mystery of life. We have become contracted, defended, fearful, and separate. Our language starts to show our fences in statements like, "I'm a rotten person." "I'll never make anything of myself." "No one loves me."

When we no longer remember that *we* set up these limitations in our mind, we project the unrecognized constriction into the external world. Let's make sure we understand this point because it is an essential part of the crux of our so-called problems in daily life. If we have had certain experiences in life, we are going to see/experience/feel our everyday encounters through this filter of past experience. It's the nature of desire to want what you don't have. For example, young Juanita was short and round. She thought girls who were tall and thin had an advantage. Frank was bookish and frail. Since he had a rich interior life, but withdrew from competitive activities, he cultivated an outsider image. Shantara was the middle child of five sisters and felt like a nobody, lost in the crowd. At some level of consciousness, we are always worrying about losing control, being lost, losing our livelihood, being a loser without love, success, or happiness. How appropriate that Christ positioned himself as the shepherd, since a basic human archetypal fear is lostness. If we define ourselves a certain way, we entrench ourselves down a certain path. We can be the misunderstood artist or the noncreative blob. We can be the helpless failure or the efficient expert. We paint ourselves into a corner and then tell everybody that God did it.

## FILLING THE HOLE WITH GOD

Once these judgments are entrenched in our mind as reality, the level of fear is so great that we cannot give it up without experiencing anxiety. No amount of positive thinking is going to make us tall and thin. No amount of rationalization is going to make us a football hero. No amount of résumé writing is going to make us special. If you've been telling yourself that you are a worthless, shiftless worm, you cannot suddenly shift from that story to nothing. We cannot take out a great big gob of Fear without having a gaping hole that has to be filled in with something else—trust, new wisdom, and connection to God.

## THE SOIL OF FEAR

The roots of dogma and ideology are grown in the soil of fear. Hell is being caught in our own dogma, our own inadequacies, over and over again without the gift of love, compassion, and greater self-understanding of who we really are. A high level of fear over time is like a low-grade fever, permeating our thinking, fettering our perceptions, and hedging our choices. One woman who relived a past lifetime said, "One [of my lifetimes] was a great spiritual growth, but through isolation, and in that lifetime there was death by torture. It was near Jerusalem. [Because of my religious belief] there was much trepidation and holding back. . . . Fear of violence, fear of speaking her own mind resulted. Fear must be removed. It has to be out of the way, so that the being can venture forth to new growth experiences. More could have been gained from the other experiences had fear not gotten in the way. Stumbling blocks that are self-imposed just waste time. There are enough of them without creating any."[3] This woman saw how fear had created losses throughout several lifetimes. Maybe we should think of each lifetime as a painting. What the hey. What colors are you going to paint with this time?

## ALL IS GOD

In our spiritual existence between Earth lives, we dwell in the true vibration of the universe—we dwell in loving energy. But if we cannot perceive this loving energy, because of our addiction to our false perceptions, we are like the goldfish who, transferred from bowl to ocean, keeps swimming in tiny circles the size of her bowl. True liberation comes when we lose our sense of separateness, our need for control, and our fear of physical death. True liberation is using the full range of the palette—ruby red, alizarin crimson, cadmium orange, yellow ocher, hunter green, purple, terra-cotta, Mars black, blue-violet, gold, silver, and aquamarine. True liberation is being able to smell vomit, sulfur, money, honeysuckle, babies' necks, garlic, fresh tomatoes, frankincense, peaches, and semen, and know that all is God.

> There is no evil except that which we create, for I have seen no signs of a devil on this side of the veil. We are our own devils, with our thoughts and subsequent deeds . . . this evil gathers force as each passing generation leaves its own stamp of evildoing on the force that we think of as a devil . . . if [evil] is to be destroyed, it will be done through man's awakening to the fact that even thoughts are deeds and that the "devil" shrinks in size each time we replace an ugly thought or action with a loving kindness. Thus we will approach the so-called millennium when good replaces evil in the hearts of those who inhabit earth, not only in the flesh but in the spirit, as we here are now doing. **Arthur Ford to Ruth Montgomery, A World Beyond**

## NEITHER DEAD NOR ALIVE

An example of someone who doesn't realize he is dead and is still caught up in his obsessive agenda is brought to us by Robert Monroe, in one of his many out-of-body excursions into the nonphysical dimensions. After many years of traveling in the spiritual realm and having received much guidance from discarnate guides, Monroe found that he began to be drawn to souls experiencing difficulty in their death transition. In one instance, he found himself watching a young soldier engaged in a battle where both sides were armed with swords and spears. The young man was struggling to get up, without realizing that a spear had penetrated him and had gone deep into the earth underneath him. Monroe reports, "I saw his head—no, not his physical head—lift out of his body, and I reached over, grabbed it, and pulled. He slid out easily. . . . He reached down and tried to pick up [the sword], but his hand went through it. Puzzled, he tried again . . . I told him to take it easy . . . that he himself was dead." The young man, disbelieving, went back into the battle. "A moment later a short, bearded man attacked him from behind and the two fell to the ground punching and gouging one another. It took me a second or two to realize that they were *both* dead. . . . They might still be rolling on the ground centuries later, trying to kill each other!"[4] Later on he came to realize that this young soldier was himself in a previous lifetime, and this encounter provided him with valuable insight into his own nature.

In another instance, he encounters a physically dead woman. Unable to recognize that she has left the physical dimension, she refuses to leave the house her husband built. This was her life. The house was her symbol of his love for her, and at that point, that was all she had. He helps her to recognize that she is dead and that her husband is waiting for her to join him. Freed from her misperception, she leaves the zone of her illusion and begins her journey of further learning, her journey back to love. At yet another time, Monroe offers assistance to an angry man who is struggling to figure out why there is no Heaven or Hell as he had expected. With the belligerence that was obviously characteristic of the man's Earthly life ("Go on, get out of here! Every time somebody tried to help me, it just meant trouble!"), the man refuses Monroe's help.[5] This is a perfect example of how a perpetually angry viewpoint can solidify into a postulate for the next lifetime. In this case, the postulate is: "Every time somebody tries to help me, it just means trouble."

Again in the gray realm of lesser consciousness, Monroe sees a group of souls caught in a cycle of repetitive sex addiction. Eventually, he begins to understand how a person's fixated belief systems continue through the transition of death into the Afterlife, creating mental constructions of seemingly "real life." For those who cannot accept that they have died, there is the drive to create the same mental constructions they used in physical life. Without a spiritual base, what else do they have to repress the mystery and insecurity of life in reaction to their fear? These illusional realities are severe forms of control dramas, even more intense and nonreflective than on Earth.

By being trapped into one or more of the control dramas to get energy, the soul keeps proving that the world is a threatening place and others are out to get it. Through the law of cause and effect, our beliefs and expectations must attract or create exactly those kinds of situations and people so that the mental vision can be fulfilled. Without awareness of greater freedom and possibilities, we reproduce the same constructions in the Afterlife as we do in this life on Earth. We were safe within these constructions, or so we think, so let's keep doing what we know, even though it isn't giving us what we really want.

With the law of cause and effect building our world for us, there is no need of an externalized, second force of the Devil to do a job that we do ourselves so well!

## SPOOKED

The Tenth Insight suggests that if one encounters a poltergeist or "ghost," it is helpful to understand that they are lost souls, rather than feeling afraid of them or vulnerable to them. The best approach is to send them loving energy to assist them in moving on. They are trying to get energy from those on the Earth plane and need to move on to connect with their spiritual source of energy. We must also not dehumanize those souls who are stuck by thinking they are demons or devils. They are souls in a growth process, just like ourselves. Like Robert Monroe's example, some of us in certain soul groups may even work in our dream time to help wake up those souls who continuously replay old behaviors, hoping someone from Earth will respond.

According to the Tenth Insight, divinely connected souls in the Afterlife never try to pull you into their energy field. If you have contact with Guides in your meditation or spontaneously in an after-death communication, open up and listen to them without giving yourself over to them as if they had all the answers.

## SUICIDE

One of the gravest acts a soul can commit is suicide. Whatever problem prompted the desire to leave the Earth before the life was fully lived will not be solved in the Afterlife either. All the guidance from discarnate teachers is very clear that suicide without very serious mitigating circumstances—such as terminal illness or certain captivity and torture—brings dire consequences in the spiritual dimension. Since the gift of life was thrown away before its time, suicide also seems to incur long setbacks to having the opportunity for another Earthly life.

According to some past-life researchers, suicides must go through a long period of time before they can reincarnate, much longer than persons who have died of natural causes. Having regressed to a less evolved state, the person may have to go through many other difficult lifetimes in order to attain the level of development they had reached before they had taken their own lives. These extra lifetimes may even be rather horrible, but allow them to work off what they describe as their penalty and start to lead normal lives again.

However, divine grace is a forgiving energy if remorse is truly expressed. Apparently, if the person who committed suicide makes an effort in the Afterlife to ask for God's help, old souls will gather around him to help show him his true existence and help him start his spiritual education process. In addition, prayers from those still on earth definitely reach across the threshold of the Afterlife to assist the soul to connect with loving energy in his time of darkness.

If someone you knew or loved has committed suicide, pray daily for him or her to wake up to the loving energy of the spiritual dimension. Pray fervently that your loved one will be seen and heard by souls whose work is to heal and guide. Nothing is impossible in our spiritual existence when we care about each other. The distance between you and your loved one is nil with loving intention.

## THOSE WHO CAUSE HARM

From a spiritual point of view, the true nature of a person is God—a spark of the divine light, inherently good. So why do people commit unimaginably ghastly acts? The statement by Wil in *The Tenth Insight* addresses this age-old question by saying, "They [people] just go crazy in the Fear and make horrible mistakes. . . . and these horrible acts are caused, in part, by our tendency to assume that some people are naturally evil. That's the mistaken view that fuels the polarization. Both sides judge these people, and increasingly dehumanize and alienate each other, which increases the Fear and brings out the worst in everyone. We can't bring in the World Vision, or resolve the polarization, until we understand the real nature of evil and the actual reality of Hell."[6]

## NO BLAME—WORKING FOR GOOD

If our collective desire is to create a world with more love and more harmony than we presently have, then it seems obvious that we must work on loosening our deep-seated belief that evil exists in those with whom we disagree. On a daily basis, we can work on changing the automatic judgmental response that labels people. We know we are in judgment when we want to have a quick closure or an eye-for-an-eye retribution, without taking the extra step of getting into the skin of the other person. Instead of seeing conservatives, liberals, fundamentalists, New Agers, or rednecks, we can look at the soul of the person behind the action.

> "How much easier the task will be to review your past life," he counseled, "if you live each day as if that was the sole recording of your entire lifetime. Keep that page so neat and tidy, so filled with loving care, that if your life ended that evening at midnight the page would be spotless and blameless. If you take the task of living only one day at a time, keeping some such moral as that in mind, it is easier to progress, for surely even the worst of us can live one day in nearly blameless harmony with all about us." **Ruth Montgomery, A Search for Truth**

When we have come to the point in our understanding that we *know* that energy follows thought, we will not even want to form these damaging thoughts about another. Without trying to change the world, we change it naturally through choosing not to damn. Turning the other cheek might then be reinterpreted from the old idea of "hit me again" to "seeing the other side of the question." Whenever we are *automatically* suspicious, whenever we *automatically* keep separate from others who are seemingly different, we lose a little bit of God. Since we are *all* involved in creating a consensus of reality, every thought form you have spices the stew. The Devil then becomes the metaphor that it is, a human ego that is driven by fear and dissociated from its connection to divine love. The Hell that we fear is not someplace to which we will be banished by a wrathful cunning Devil, but a place we need not create at all. If the creation of Hell is the result of our own consciousness, then we are immediately empowered to begin to break our compulsive and negative thought process—now.

---

## INDIVIDUAL STUDY

### Non-Judgment Day

Eliminating judgment of others and of ourselves is one of the highest spiritual accomplishments we can achieve. Every time we make a negative judgment, it stays in our subconscious mind, tainting our supply of energy. Usually, we are our own worst judges of our character . . . and for what reason? Judging ourselves does nothing to change behavior for the better, but only adds another nail in our box of low self-esteem. For one full day, see if you can make not one judging remark about someone else or yourself. If you catch yourself making a judgmental remark, simply acknowledge that you are becoming less and less willing to add negative fertilizer to your inner garden. What kind of remark or awareness could you make about yourself or someone else to neutralize your tendency to be judgmental?

### Getting on the Same Side

If there is someone you disagree with, try listening to him or her *through your heart*. Listen to what the soul is trying to say beyond the words. Your goal here is to find some way to get on the same side as the other person in some aspect, without agreeing to something you don't believe in. Find something about the person that you truly agree with. For example, if Bob is trying to convince you that environmentalists are unrealistic about the needs of business, perhaps you could ask him what kinds of problems his business faces in relation to the environment in a sincerely interested way. He probably has a lot of conflict between his ideals and his ability to find a solution, and, at heart, no doubt wants much of the same things you do.

Imagine what it would be like to be living in Bob's body, with Bob's fears, and his hopes and dreams. When he tries to argue with something you have said, notice your feelings inside your body. Be willing to say that his ideas have made you feel sad, angry, stupid, or afraid. Avoid blaming him by saying, "You make me mad." It's more skillful to say, "When we argue like this, I feel really frustrated and angry. Maybe these problems are bigger than both of us to solve. How do you feel?" Being open with someone is not the same as giving him permission to walk all over you.

Let a person know you are really listening to what his side is by saying something like, "It must be hard to have to work at such a stressful job." Or "It must be hard not having much support from your family." The phrase "it must be hard" immediately puts you on the same side. You don't have to agree to what the person believes in. Practice looking for similarities rather than differences. It's a more healing place to discuss any issue. Remember you both want love and acceptance. If God appeared in front of both of you, you'd both be awed and grateful.

### God Walking

Pretend that you are walking with God or Christ or Buddha or Muhammad, and imagine the kindly response they would have to any situation. Take a moment to ask them to stay close to you before entering a difficult situation.

### Breathing in Suffering

When you read about tragedies or see something negative on the news, practice breathing in the suffering into your heart, and feel the heart cleansing and restoring peaceful energy. Breathe out the peaceful energy and send light to those who are in pain or grief. Remember that there is enough God for everyone.

### Professional Help or Self-Help

Many times we have heard people say, "What a relief! I thought I was the only one." If you have some obsessive behavior that you feel helpless to "control," let somebody know. There is no reason to think you are alone in your problem or that you are too far gone to be healed. Too many miracles have happened through people reaching out to one another to suffer in your self-imposed hell. Don't take it with you! Set an intention to be guided to someone who can help you. If at first you don't resonate with a particular counselor or group, then find one that fits you.

Be honest. What habit would you like to change?

## One Day of Silence

Can you spend one day (or one afternoon) alone with yourself, preferably outside? Try to spend one day every couple of months when you turn off the telephone, turn off the television and radio, and do no reading. While you may wish to not even speak, don't forget that you can communicate worlds with smiles and nods. What happens? This sounds easy, but it could change your life.

---

## GROUP STUDY

---

Groups take time to develop trust in each other. We have repeatedly suggested that your group is best served by a revolving facilitator rather than having just one designated leader. The Eighth Insight groups function at a higher level when all members bring through insights when the energy moves them.

Fadel Behmann, a Montreal physicist, has been participating in a weekly group for four years. While there is a core group that has stayed together for most of the four years, the group is also open to new members. He told us, "Once the group bonds, there seems to be a group entity which functions as the *Other* in our dialogues. Everyone cares about that entity, and participates actively *as it* by listening, talking, thinking, intuiting—everything we do as an individual. When we are each absorbed in the group entity, we have insights—we make new meanings that we wouldn't have had by ourselves." What does it feel like? we asked. "When we are saying goodbye and going home, people will say things like, 'I'm much more energized now than when I came tonight!' or 'I feel refreshed.' People feel like they can take life on more openly. They can perceive others better without judgments and criticisms. They feel connected to something. That's when you know the group entity is strong."

The following exercises might best be undertaken if your group is fairly well bonded.

## Healing Hell

In your group, try writing for a few minutes on how you would describe hell. Would hell be being trapped in a candy store for two weeks? Would hell be being trapped in an elevator with ten of your most critical relatives? Being in a war zone? Living on earth without any trees? Let everyone read aloud or talk about what they see as really scary, dangerous, unthinkable, or unforgivable. *Note:* Let everyone speak without *any discussion* on their contribution. Simply take in what they say, breathe it into your heart, and release the fears into the light of God's love. Watch your feelings as you listen with your heart. The energy may get pretty dense in this exercise, so after you have all shared your descriptions of an inner hell, you may want to shift the energy by playing inspiring music, dancing to some jazz, or getting into a circle and doing neck massages on each other.

### Hell Week

Take turns sharing all the hellish things that happened to you this week, or things you were afraid might happen. Do not have any group discussion after each contribution. Merely listen with your heart, breathe in the other's comments and suffering, send light into what you hear, and let it go to God. Do not offer sympathy or advice, but do send loving energy silently to the person. Let each other have the luxury of being open without having to explain, justify, or be any way at all.

After all have shared the hellish things that have happened, take turns again sharing the good things, the blessings, the fun, the unexpected delights that also befell you this week. Again, no discussion, no comment. Let the energy come through all of you to suggest the best way to end your session on a joyful note. Music? Brownies? Neck rubs? Hugs?

### Community Service

See if your group has any energy to give some time to starting a discussion group in a local institution like a juvenile hall, a hospice, an elder home, or a prison. How about starting a group that meets with families of incarcerated people? Don't do anything unless you feel free enough in your heart to participate without having to "fix" anybody. Do it only if you feel *you* need the contact or an outlet for your love!

# CHAPTER 9

# Overcoming the Fear

RABBIT
FEAR

So why has it taken so long for someone to grasp the Tenth? . . . It has something to do with the Fear that arises in a culture that is moving from a material reality to a transformed, spiritual worldview.

THE TENTH INSIGHT:
HOLDING THE VISION[1]

## How We Scare Ourselves

In *The Tenth Insight*, a character named Joel, a cynical journalist, introduces some of the ideas that are causing Fear on the planet. Joel represents that part of all of us that is afraid that the world is already out of control and will only get worse. From Joel's point of view, positive thinking is equivalent to utopian thinking. In the face of the realities he perceives, positive thinking is naive and useless. This point of view argues that there is compelling factual evidence that all socioeconomic and cultural systems are heading for an eventual explosion.

Have you ever noticed that when you are afraid, you tend to jump to conclusions? You feel afraid, and drive that Fear down a road to some seemingly logical outcome, because at the moment, you are in fear and you are separated from God. Separated from any hope, you feel paralyzed to effect any change. Fear-based forecasts always jump to a conclusion. The dark side of "a leap of faith" is the jump to a conclusion, undertaken in an effort to gain control. Joel, as well as we who fall into this type of thinking, build a pessimistic case on the following points. Let's look at some of the underlying beliefs and fears that blind us to other creative possibilities.

- *The earth's population is exploding.* Fear: "We'll be swallowed up in the faceless mob and all resources will be destroyed." Belief: "Sex and reproduction are out of control."

- *The middle class is shrinking, and we are losing faith in the system we have created.* Fear: "It's us or them." Belief: "Only socioeconomic position and stockpiling money will protect us."
- *Education is failing to keep up with the demands.* Fear: "We'll lose our dominant position." Belief: "We don't have enough money to spend on a quality educational system because there are too many people who don't pay their way. Children won't learn unless coerced."
- *We must work harder and harder just to survive.* Fear: "The Puritan ethic was right, and we are guilty of not keeping up." Belief: "Even though what we are doing is not working, let's work harder at it."
- *Crime and drug use will soar as social norms fail.* Fear: "The boogey man will get you." Belief: Crime is another version of our ancient fear of the dark. Crime is the dark side of our own greed acted out by disempowered people. Drugs are the addiction to wanting to tune out from the abyss of a life lived without purpose. We all tune out in one way or another.
- *Religious fundamentalists will have the power to sanction the death of those they consider heretics.* Fear: "I am powerless." Belief: Fundamentalism is the wrathful aspect of God in his Intimidator mode. Fear of fundamentalism is perhaps akin to the fear that we might not be strong enough to stand up to Daddy and become a self-sufficient person.
- *There is a mob mentality ruled by envy and revenge.* Fear: "I am small and separate and alone." Belief: "My brother wants my toys. All my toys. No one can stop him."
- *Politicians only care about getting reelected.* Fear: "Help, Daddy won't save us." Belief: This is similar to the developmental stage of seeing the human frailties of our parents and realizing that we are on our own.
- *The world is changing too fast; we have to look out for number one.* Fear: Akin to our primordial fear of falling, this fear puts us into survival mode. Belief: "There is no God. There is no Plan. Hang on. Get it while you can."
- *We're maximizing short-term profits instead of planning for the long term because consciously or unconsciously we don't think our success can last.* Fear: "Time is running out." Belief: "The only bottom line is the financial one." This viewpoint also demonstrates the low level of our collective ability for delayed gratification.
- *All the subtle assumptions and agreements that hold civilization together will be totally subverted.* Fear: "Chaos will devour me." Belief:

"Civilization must be controlled by an external source. We cannot trust society to be self-organizing because people are inherently evil."

- *Spirituality is just rhetoric.* Fear: "We're on our own after all. We're going to disappear after death." Belief: "We are just animals, we're going to die, and there is no purpose for being here."
- *Maybe it's just a divine plan to separate the believers from the wicked.* Fear: "I'm on the outside." Belief: "Evil is another force equal to God."

## Scriptural Warnings

- *The Bible says these are the last days that are being set up for the return of the Christ.* Fear: "Our destruction has been preordained." Belief: "The Bible is a literal message about our future, and nothing we have done so far has been able to change the prediction."
- *We have to suffer wars, natural disasters, and other apocalyptic events such as global warmings, riots, and chaos.* Fear: "We are being punished." Belief: "We have sinned." This fear reflects a collective poor-me/victim attitude that stops creative response.
- *War will ensue, and then angels of God intervene and install a spiritual utopia that lasts a thousand years.* Fear: "Our dark side will prevail, and we'll get what's coming to us." Belief: "You can't have the good without the bad." This attitude thinks darkness and evil are inevitable, and abdicates the co-creative aspect of God and wo/man, giving all redemptive power to the angels of God.

## Conspiracy Warnings

- *A politician will emerge and gain supreme power with a centralized electronic economy.* Fear: "Big Brother authoritarianism will prevail over the individual. Loss of self." Belief: "We will be monitored by an electronic implant into our hand." This is a kind of global Interrogator control fantasy, whereby a centralized authority will have complete control over our whereabouts and actions, and we will have lost all freedom.

> That which we do not bring to consciousness appears in our lives as fate. C. G. Jung

## THE INDIVIDUAL SHADOW

At the beginning of the twentieth century, while Western culture was looking to control the forces of nature and busily building a heroic future, depth psychologist Carl Jung peered into the darkest place in the human unconscious, a place he called the shadow. The shadow is the place where we hide away those things about ourselves that our ego has rejected. Stuffing feelings into the shadow starts early. Perhaps your mother said to you, "Shush! You're always so loud," and you learn that part of you is disruptive to others. Or Grandmother says, "Ugh! You peed in your pajamas again. Bad boy!" and you feel shame for your loss of control. Or your brother says, "You're too fat to take dancing lessons," and since he's older and much more cool than you are, you believe him and the dancing becomes a risky place to expose yourself to the eyes of the world. Or Father growls, "Hey, stupid. Quit trying to show off," and you thought your ability to recite a poem from memory was really coming along, but now you see it makes you different from him.

Throughout our upbringing in our family and our educational, religious, and social environment, we are ridiculed, nagged, and scolded for innumerable transgressions: being too loud or lazy, selfish or sexual, smart-alecky, or too picky. We also learn that certain behaviors may be ridiculed or not rewarded, so we repress a desire to write poetry, act, or daydream because we want to fit in. People tell us that we are critical, weak, uncoordinated, too tall, too heavy, slow, or illogical and we naturally try to defend ourselves against the pain of separation from their love. We either deny our unacceptable traits or accept the judgments against us, shoving them into the shadow so we don't have to deal with the pain.

Into the shadow slips our greediness, our anger about the unfairness of the world, our prides and prejudices. In this place are all the things we never want to be—selfish, small, stupid, lustful, ugly, mean, afraid. In here are the decisions we have made about *ourselves* and our *disowned* abilities: "I'm not creative." "I was never good at math." "I'm not good at small talk." "I grew up on the wrong side of the tracks." "God, if only I didn't have this huge (or tiny, sharp, flat, or pug) nose." In this buried storehouse of the shadow lies our undeveloped talents, our infantile attachments, and the roots of our obsessions. All the small fears and judgments begin to cluster into more global assumptions and larger fears of the world. Into the shadow slither our fears of the unknown—the fears and distrust of others whose ideas, behaviors, or looks are different from ours, and who might want to hurt or control us. Into the shadow goes our fear of death and the fear of disappearing forever without a trace.

## STORAGE CLOSET AND PROJECTOR

Behind the scenes of our waking consciousness, the shadow functions in two major capacities. The first function is to be a storage place for our white elephants and refuse—a garbage dump of traits about ourselves that we do not want to own. It's also the place we keep our undeveloped abilities or desires such as "I always wanted to be a photographer, but . . ." or "I was really good at tap dancing when I was three . . . but." Get the picture?

Secondly, the shadow functions as a film projector which transfers our fears and imperfections outside ourselves onto people in the outer world. So the shadow is a place within our psyche that holds energy that we have deemed not usable or desirable. It may be that so much is stuffed into the shadow that it begins to boil and surge, leak, or erupt. Most of us know by now that slips of the tongue and outbursts of unexpected feelings such as rage or grief are leaks from this stored energy. When we empty some of our inner-world dark energy— energy that may be tainted with guilt or grief or self-loathing—into the outer world, we often feel a discharge of tension, producing relief. But if we have not become aware of this transference of energy from our inner world to our outer world, we are unconscious that this process ever took place. Once externalized, our own inner imperfections are then seen as faults, or even evil, *in others.* Now these feelings and judgments are out in the world and look like reality, or so we think. Still unconscious that we are seeing the world through our inner filter, we see the evil we don't see in ourselves in *others,* creating enemies. Galvanized to overcome this now-obvious threat to our survival or way of life, we set about to combat the evil and correct the wrongdoings that we see everywhere. One obvious example of this projected shadow is the politician or religious leader who speaks out against sexual wrongdoing, but who secretly participates in his or her own sexual exploitations. We all know someone who says one thing and does another, or who has been found doing the very thing he/she has campaigned against.

## RED FLAGS

While you will never be able to know all the contents of your uncon- scious, it's important to at least realize that your world is being constructed by some beliefs you can identify, and by some beliefs and judgments that you take for granted without much awareness. What are the red flags of the shadow? How can you start noticing the areas where you might be shut down? How could you start noticing beliefs that might not be so useful to you anymore? Since our purpose is to experience life in its fullest, deepest sense, perhaps working with the shadow will help us to unleash some of the powerful creativity that we have within us. You may be looking at your own shadow when:

- You get really upset about someone else's behavior, such as, "He is the most controlling person I've ever seen!" How much need for control do *you* have?
- People tell you things about yourself that irritate them, such as, "You let people walk all over you. You need to stand up for yourself more." Is there a grain of truth here?
- You make slips of the tongue or make obviously bad choices. "How could I have told that stupid joke about fat people to my mother-in-law when she's always talking about her diet!" Or perhaps you've done something uncharacteristic which doesn't fit your picture of yourself, such as, "I never should have bought that red dress with the slit up the side." The inadvertent comment about your mother-in-law belies perhaps an unrecognized hostility. In the second state-ment, the red-dress part of you is trying to get your attention—maybe you need to express your individuality and earthiness more fully. Maybe you have a need to change some of the rules in your life or release those parts that you have outgrown.
- You think, "Evelyn is so creative. I wish I had her talent." Who told you that you weren't creative? Why did you shut down?
- You make sweeping generalizations about one person or one whole group of people, such as "Short people are arrogant," or "Homeless people don't want to work for a living."

## STUFFING AWAY OUR "DARK" PARTS

The shadow is formed starting in early childhood, when we begin to hide all the stuff we don't like about ourselves and all the criticisms that are made about us. By the first couple of years we learn the *family shadow*, all the unconscious feelings and actions that are not okay to express. We are born with the potential to develop and express a com-plete personality. Energy radiates out from all parts of our body and all parts of our psyche. But it doesn't take long before our parents, siblings, and others in our environment start making judgments about us. They say things like: "Can't you sit still?" Or "It isn't nice to try and kill the cat." Or perhaps we might innocently overhear them tell someone else, "She's too quiet. I hope it doesn't mean she's dumb." All of a sudden, our natural enthusiastic and curious response to the world gets dampened, and we want to rid ourselves of the part that others don't like. To assure our position in the family, neighborhood, and circle of influence (our friends), we try to disown or deny the "unacceptable" parts of our nature. Teachers are also powerful shapers of our self-image. They might say, "Good children don't get angry over such little things." So we take our anger and stuff it away, along with our guilt and resentment at having our feelings invalidated. How many of us have lied in school to try to be more like the popular people? How many times have we lain awake at night rewriting our conversations to show how cool, smart, witty, or indifferent we really are!

## OUTER CONFLICTS ARE A PICTURE OF YOUR INNER SPLIT

As long as we live an unexamined life, and fail to acknowledge our individual shadows, we will continue the same consciousness in our worldview that will create the polarization between a "good" future and a "bad" future. The inner split between what we choose to see as okay and not okay within us will be reflected back to us from the world. Generally, how you see the worldview depends on how you experienced the world so far. Andrew Bard Schmooker writes, "Our inner split makes us attached to the war of good against evil. But if we hold that the *warring mode is itself the evil*, then we are challenged to find a new moral dynamic that embodies the peace for which we strive. The extent that morality takes the form of war, we will be compelled to choose sides, identifying with one part of ourselves and repudiating another. By this warlike path, we raise ourselves above ourselves, perched precariously above a void."[2] When we are threatened, we freeze, we scurry, we run to hide, or we strike out. We take a position to take control.

## WHAT IS LIVING THROUGH ME?

The shadow is probably an inevitable and necessary part of the human psyche, at least at this stage of human development, for otherwise we would be overwhelmed with having to deal with things before we had the maturity or ego strength to do so. Just as we need to turn out the lights and go to sleep for eight hours each night, we need to have a place to safely carry that which we need to put on the back burner. However, as our understanding matures, we naturally begin to develop new facets of ourselves in order to move in the direction of our original Vision. The more awake we are to the shadowy existence of our fears, the less we will be prone to be laid low by them. The more open

> For the unconscious always tries to produce an impossible situation in order to force the individual to bring out his very best. Otherwise one stops short of one's best, one is not complete, one does not realize oneself. What is needed is an impossible situation where one has to renounce one's own will and one's own wit and do nothing but wait and trust to the impersonal power of growth and development. When you are up against a wall, be still and put down roots like a tree, until clarity comes from deeper sources to see over that wall. **C. G. Jung**

we are to acknowledging our undeveloped capacities, usually the more eager we are to play with them.

## JUST THINKING—NOT THINKING/FEELING/INTUITING

We are most prone to the shadow when we are *thinking* about how to control something. When we are only using our thinking function, we are probably not experiencing life as fully as if we were using all our senses and getting feedback from all these angles. Thinking is only one of the four functions of life—feeling, intuiting, and sensing being the other three. These four states together show us that we are alive, and fully *associated* to life—as opposed to being dissociated, or in the shadow. When we hold the attitude "I'm curious what is living through me," we are constantly in awe of everything life brings us. We are open to the possibility then of connecting to our Birth Vision. We are like a radio receiver that can tune in information from our senses, our intuition, our rational mind, and our feelings.

Think of your shadow as a force that distorts your perceptions or limits your sense of your potential. A big shadow with a lot of unexamined energy can cramp the energy flow of synchronicities that are meant to lead us to our Birth Vision.

Like a fish immersed in water, we have no reason to question the elements of our surroundings until they fail to nourish us. Once we open our fishy eyes to the idea that there is more to us than we know, our perseverance, our logical reasoning, our heart, and the fire power of our spirit will take us where we need to go.

## FEELING THE SHADOW AND ITS LIMITING FEARS WITHOUT AWARENESS

What happens when you decide to take on some new project? If you are strong in thinking ability, you might sit down and write up a list of all the things you have to do to get this project under way. That might seem like the logical thing to do. However, anytime we step into unknown waters, we need to be able to swim past our fears!

Marjorie, a high school administrator, decided that part of her Birth Vision was to promote ecological information. A friend of hers knew a popular ecology author and teacher, and Marjorie approached him about doing a public seminar in her town. He agreed. After her initial enthusiasm died down, she began to feel nervous about the commitment she had taken on. She put out a few flyers about her event, but kept procrastinating about other steps she had planned to take. A month before the event, she called the author in a mild panic about the lack of enrollments. What was happening? Marjorie was confronting her shadow.

When Marjorie was a child, her mother emphasized the importance of doing what was right—but also safe. She used to say things like. "Why do you want to rock the boat? Be quiet. See what your smart mouth got you! It's better to be safe than sorry." So far, Marjorie had gotten along without developing much assertiveness. She had also never considered herself much of a leader, nor had she really seen herself as creative. Promoting this event began to require that she look at herself in a different light and use undeveloped traits in order to succeed. Marjorie's rational mind had devised its plan, but her shadow fears and imprecations undermined her practical efforts. As her fears grew, her ego-consciousness tried harder to "figure out" a way for her event to get publicity, but she continued to stall. At this point, she was going around in circles, being extremely hard on herself for not accomplishing more, and imagining no one would show up for her event. By this time she was deep into her shadow thinking, struggling, controlling, and visualizing the negative.

What to do? In working with her, we made a few suggestions to help her become more fully present, engaging all her senses. What feelings did she have about this event? What did she think was the worst that could happen? How did she feel about calling newspapers and radio stations? What intuitions or images was she getting? To get in touch with her body, and ground herself, we even suggested that she go to a place in nature that was nurturing for her, and reconnect with the earth, the trees, water, and air. According to shamanic practice, sometimes in the face of great fear we just have to "press our belly into the earth."

Next we suggested she write out in a stream-of-consciousness manner all her feelings—fears, hopes, any feelings—she had about doing the event, for a period of twenty minutes a day for five days. We also reminded her to jot down any dreams that she had during this period.

And the last suggestion we made was to let go of the need to have the event happen or not happen. This was the step of letting go of trying to control results.

The outcome? After doing some of the work we suggested, Marjorie finally had to admit that she was too far out of her comfort zone, and she canceled the event.

## OWNING BACK THE SHADOW

The step of "owning back the shadow," however powerful, is also not without its challenges. The characteristics or attitudes that we need to pay attention to on our way to developing our Birth Vision may create conflicts. Instead of shaking our fist at the universe, we need to remember that our *attitudes* create a large portion of our world. So often someone says, for example, "I want to start a summer camp for underprivileged children." But somehow the project never gets going because all of a sudden the car breaks down, our son gets dragged off to jail, we break four toes on one foot, or we never follow through on our first phone call to the Parks and Recreation Department to inquire about licensing. Whenever you get mobilized to start something new, notice what gets in the way. That's the thing that's "up" for you, and is probably some long-buried item that you had forgotten about or had never dealt with. Don't worry. It's just the next step, and does not mean you were stupid to have the dream of your summer camp for kids. Each obstacle is part of the process. Perhaps you could think of your obstacles as "fine-tuning" you!

## "I FEEL SELFISH ASKING FOR ANYTHING FOR MYSELF"

The denied parts may come at us through another person whom we perceive as hostile or immature—because *we* are angry about having cut off parts of ourselves to please others. Let's say you think your spouse spends too much time playing golf or hunting or going to workshops. Is your resentment of his or her time a displaced feeling from a part of you that wants more personal time? One man said, "I'm getting a divorce, and I'm really angry that my wife spends so much time on taking classes, and I have to watch the kids all the time on the weekends. She is so selfish, I can't stand it." We commented, "It must be hard being a single dad with so little time to do anything for yourself. Do you wish you had more time to take classes or play tennis?" He stopped for a moment, then quietly said, "That's exactly what I need right now. I guess I feel selfish asking for anything for myself." As simple as this exchange was, it brought some light to the man about how he was projecting his own needs onto his wife, and judging her wrong for taking care of herself when he had not even acknowledged his needs to himself.

> Every minority and every dissenting group carries the shadow projection of the majority, be it Negro, white, Gentile, Jew, Italian, Irish, Chinese or French.
>
> Moreover, since the shadow is the archetype of the enemy, its projection is likely to involve us in the bloodies of wars precisely in times of the greatest complacency about peace and our own righteousness.
>
> The enemy and the conflict with the enemy are archetypal factors, projections of our own inner split, and cannot be legislated or wished away. They can be dealt with—if at all—only in terms of shadow confrontation and in the healing of our individual split.
>
> The most dangerous times, both collectively and individually, are those in which we assume that we have eliminated it. **Edward C. Whitmont** in *Meeting the Shadow*, edited by Connie Zweig and Jeremiah Abrams

Whatever part we have squashed does not grow—our original artist or musician or dancer is tiny and atrophied for lack of exercise. The disowned parts have remained undeveloped like children kept in a closet. Maybe part of our Birth Vision is something we have tossed out when we began to adapt to our physical and emotional environment to please others.

## THE COLLECTIVE SHADOW

The shadow exists not only in our personal psyches but in the collective psyche of humanity. There is a collective energy in your village, town, city, or country. Think about the community you live in. Does it have a particular mind-set? How does your community describe itself? Do the people there think of themselves as "God-fearing people"? "Hardworking farmers"? "Sophisticated intellectuals"? Poet Robert Bly notes, for instance, "I lived for years near a small Minnesota farm town. Everyone in the town was expected to have the same objects in the bag [shadow]; a small Greek town clearly would have different objects in the bag. It's as if the town, by collective psychic decision, puts certain energies in the bag, and tries to prevent anyone from getting them out. . . . There is also a national bag . . . if an American citizen is curious to know what is in the national bag at the moment, he can listen closely when a State Department official criticizes Russia. . . . *Other* nations . . . treat minorities brutally, brainwash their youth, and break treaties."[3]

When we look at the national drama of the O.J. Simpson case, we see part of what's in the bag. Our fascination with this case, as well as with *all* the violence we pay for as entertainment, shows us how deep are our collective feelings of powerlessness and rage. At some level we all feel like a victim of something. At some level we each know that we are contributing to the problems with many of our daily acts such as driving our cars, throwing things away, wearing clothes or cosmetics that exploit humans and animals, and on and on. A collective victim mentality is fed by a continuous diet of news about local and worldwide tragedies, wars, and ecological and economic breakdowns. If we think like victims, we reinforce the idea that someone is the Intimidator, that we are powerless, and we have created an "us and them model" which maintains the struggle for power. Rationally, we might tend to deny the feelings of powerlessness and tell ourselves to have a stiff upper lip, as if it's not okay to feel hopeless, as if it's not okay to witness suffering. But to remain in our humanity

> As the inspired metaphysical teacher Rudolph Steiner noted, nationalistic chauvinists who hate other countries are actually having premonitions that they will be born into that nationality in their next life. The Higher Self knows, but the personality resists. **Corinne McLaughlin and Gordon Davidson**, *Spiritual Politics*

and to be able to work from our hearts, we cannot afford to put despair in the bag of our shadow. That despair will keep us connected to what matters to us. It will keep us connected and alive to our caring. Only then will we be able to engage the flow of creativity and intuition needed for problem solving.

## CONFLICTING URGES MOVE THROUGH US

We can choose to be blocked and paralyzed by our Fear, creating enemies and impossible situations, or we can decide to open to our suffering, trusting that our Birth Vision will show us where we need to go. We all want to be successful. Having fears about something or about ourselves does not mean we are doomed. Feeling the icy tendrils of fear around our throat or chest or feeling the bottom drop out of our stomach does not mean we are not spiritual. It means at the moment, we feel separate and alone and not sure of our ability to cope. If we decide that we can only be successful though our heroic face, our perfect face, we will surely be cut down to our human face—the one with all the pimples, scars, frowns, and smiles. We are most prone to failure when we:

a. Focus on "protecting" ourselves from everything different or unknown
b. Lose sight of our purpose
c. Make choices from an anxious state of mind
d. Feel separate from others and from God
e. Fight for power
f. Steal energy from others
g. Resist change
h. Automatically blind ourselves to new information because it doesn't fit our pattern of belief

The Tenth Insight reminds us that we can move past Fear when we:

a. Attune with God by asking for guidance
b. Trust the purposefulness of our intuitions
c. Hold firm mental images of the ideal we wish to have
d. Align with courageous and wise individuals who inspire us
e. Remember other times when we felt connected and inspired
f. Remember that even though we may feel insecure, we are *not* alone
g. Remember that there is a spiritual purpose underlying the mystery of existence

## The Polarization of Viewpoints Is Our Greatest Threat

What do you think about the future? Are you an optimist? Why? Are you a pessimist? Why? More than any other single element, a divisive polarization of views about which direction the world is headed, up or down, has the potential for creating the very future that we wish to avoid. In *The Tenth Insight*, Wil says, "During a transition in culture, old certainties and views begin to break down and evolve into new traditions, causing anxiety in the short run. At the same time that some people are waking up and sustaining an inner connection of love that sustains them and allows them to evolve more rapidly, others feel as though everything is changing too fast and that we're losing our way. They become more fearful and more controlling to try to raise their energy. This polarization of fear can be very dangerous because fearful people can rationalize extreme measures. . . .

> Our best hope for survival is to change the way we think about enemies and warfare. Instead of being hypnotized by the enemy we need to begin looking at the eyes with which we see the enemy. . . . It seems unlikely that we will have any considerable success in controlling warfare unless we come to understand the logic of political paranoia, and the process of creating propaganda that justifies our hostility. **Sam Keen** in *Meeting the Shadow*, **edited by Connie Zweig and Jeremiah Abrams**

"Any kind of violence . . . just makes it worse. . . . if we fight them with anger, hate, they just see an enemy. It makes them more entrenched. They become more fearful. . . . We're supposed to fully remember our Birth Visions . . . and then we can remember something more, a *World Vision*."[4]

## Remembering Our Purpose Gives Us the Energy to Live Past the Fear

Remember how excited you got about moving to a new town? Going to college? Starting a new job? Getting a degree? When you were in touch with your purpose, you were energized and probably didn't let your fears stop you from moving forward. The same rise in energy (felt as optimism) will happen if we collectively remember our World Vision. Remember, we are all interconnected, and a rise anywhere in the field has to affect the energy level of even those who are in fear.

As our character says in the novel, "They would be touched, awakened from their preoccupation. They would choose to stop. . . . We [can] remember beyond our individual birth intentions to a broader knowledge of human purpose and how we could complete this purpose. Apparently, remembering this knowledge brings in an expanded energy that can end the Fear. . . ."[5]

Wise souls here and in the Afterlife have always known that taking sides is a simplistic and uncreative, destructive path. Fear is a powerful fragmenting energy, and is the reverse of unification. Running scared, we get caught up in the struggle to be right, *forgetting that we all want similar freedoms and joys that can be attained if we work together.* If we succumb to this seduction to be on the winning side, and at the same time secretly feel powerless to do anything to effect a transformation, we are likely to abdicate our responsibility altogether. We might think, "Forget it. Let somebody else deal with it. It's all B.S. Nothing I do can make any difference."

> You have to recognize that what you think not only affects the world—it is the world. Fred Alan Wolf in *Towards a New World View*, by Russell E. Di-Carlo

In his book *Violence and Compassion: Conversations with the Dalai Lama*, screenwriter and author Jean-Claude Carrière asked the great Tibetan spiritual leader which view he would choose—the pessimistic view of the world or the optimistic. "Without hesitation, the second. I say this for at least three reasons. First of all, it seems to me that the concept of war has recently changed. In the twentieth century, up until the years from 1960 to 1970, we still thought that the final and indisputable decision would come from a war. It was a matter of a very ancient law: the

> The most important [belief] is a felt sense that no matter what happens, at some level it's OK. I basically give a "yes" answer to what Einstein once said is the most important question in the world, "Is the universe friendly?"
>
> I think there is a pattern, a process and design in the universe. I think there is place in the universe for enduring human consciousness. . . . This belief has contributed immeasurably to my peace of mind and my serenity. For me, the notion that whatever happens is OK, drives me to even greater activity, not less. Larry Dossey, M.D., in *Towards a New World View*, by Russell E. DiCarlo

winners are right. Victory is the sign that God, or the gods, are on their side. Consequently, the victors impose their law on the vanquished, most often by means of a treaty, which will never be anything but a pretext for revenge. Hence the importance of arms and above all of nuclear arms. The race for the bomb has imposed upon the Earth a real danger of annihilation. [I am convinced that] the danger is lessening.

"As for the second reason for optimism, I believe that despite certain appearances the notion of *ahimsa*, or nonviolence, is scoring some points. In the time of Mahatma Gandhi, a man whom I revere, nonviolence was mostly taken to be a weakness, a refusal to act, almost cowardice. This is no longer true. The choice of nonviolence is nowadays a positive act, which evokes a real force. . . . I think that as a result of the press itself, of all the things we call communications, religious groups are visiting one another more often and are getting to know one another better than they did before."[6]

When asked about the tendency for some Muslim countries to close themselves off from others, keeping foreign influences away, he responded, "Isolation is never good for a country, and it's become impracticable. As for the Muslim countries, even if some of them maintain and reinforce their closed doors, on the whole, if one looks at the whole world, isolation is losing ground. For twenty years now I've been visiting many countries. Everywhere I go people tell me, 'We're getting to know one another better.' . . . For my part, I meet with other religious leaders as often as possible. We walk together, we visit one religious site or another, whatever tradition it may belong to. And there we meditate together, we share a moment of silence. I get a great sense of well-being from that. I continue to believe that in the domain of religion we are making progress by comparison with the beginning of the century."

And the third reason for optimism is, "When I meet young people, especially in Europe, I sense that the concept of humanity as one is much stronger nowadays than it once was. You know, it's a new feeling that seldom existed in the past. The 'other' was the barbarian, the one who was different."[7]

Notice that the Dalai Lama is not only optimistic about the future of humanity, but chooses to look for real-life evidence of positive changes. Read his words above again, and notice any feelings in your body.

Here is a great spiritual world leader, a living example of how to hold the World Vision. He is not exhorting or threatening others with damnation if they fail to awake. Notice that he does simple things like walking, visiting a variety of holy places with respect, listening, and meditating no matter if he is meeting other world leaders or ordinary people. Notice that he responds to the question about countries that adhere to a closed position by saying that isolation is impracticable, rather than *judging* or denouncing the policy. Peacefulness comes through his words and actions at all times. The Dalai Lama shows us how to keep the ideal of what we want foremost, and let that ideal become manifest.

## FOCUS ON FEAR OR THE IDEAL?

Holding a positive World Vision is giving energy to an ideal. Many of the messages of the Edgar Cayce readings remind us to set an ideal in our mind of what we want, and this will keep us on track. Enormous opportunities exist in daily life for offering love, compassion, and patience. An ideal is not some never-to-be-reached perfection, but a navigational energy that both attracts and guides us. Think of the ideal as a beloved wise friend who is a few steps ahead of you. She looks over her shoulder to see if you're keeping up, and smiles and beckons you with her finger.

---

We think we need an enemy. Governments work hard to get us to be afraid and to hate so we will rally behind them. If we do not have a real enemy, they will invent one in order to mobilize us.

It is not correct to believe that the world's situation is in the hands of the government and that if the President would only have the correct policies, there would be peace.

Our daily lives have the most to do with the situation of the world. If we can change our daily lives, we can change our governments and we can change the world.

Our presidents and our governments are us. They reflect our lifestyle and our way of thinking. The way we hold a cup of tea, pick up a newspaper, and even use toilet paper have to do with peace. **Thich Nhat Hanh,** *Love in Action: Writings on Nonviolent Social Change*

---

### LOOKING FOR THE POSITIVE

Like the Dalai Lama, who sees positive change in young people, a big part of holding the World Vision is purposefully acknowledging even small changes. For example, you might begin to increase your awareness of positive events that you read about in the media. Is that possible? Sure it is. A recent story in the *San Francisco Chronicle* noted that a new federal report shows that by the year 2050, the population of the United States is expected to be half "minorities" and half white. The article quoted Cheryl Russell, a demographer who has written extensively on baby boomers, on some of the changes this will bring to various industries. But even more interesting, she was reported as saying that "the effect of long-term changes on the nation's racial composition should not be gauged by the conflicts being experienced now. . . . We're clearly in a time of transition, and when you see battles over things like affirmative action, some people believe we're in for a lot of conflict. But the reality of American life is that the level of tolerance towards each other is much higher than it was. That story never gets told, but every survey shows it," she said. "Young people are already used to living in a pluralistic society, and their kids will be even more attuned to it."[8] As of this writing, scientists are noting that the hole in the ozone layer is starting to get smaller, and if all goes well, it may close in ten or twelve years. In Africa it was reported that people in some countries are choosing to limit their families to two children because they realize they cannot afford to raise more than that. As we write this there is a march on Washington of people concerned over the poverty level of children in the United States. Our culture, our planet, can heal if we set our ideal and follow our intuitive guidance to give service wherever we have been "posted."

## THE HIGH BEAMS OF LOVING ENERGY

In the Eighth Insight we learned how to uplift others by sending divine, loving energy to another person to bring out that person's higher qualities. With the Tenth Insight, we send that same loving energy while *visualizing that the individual will remember what he or she really wants to do with his or her life*. It is an empirical fact that thinking positive thoughts about someone strengthens that person. If we think we can do something, we probably can.

Fran Peavey, a teacher, activist, and comedian, tells how, in 1970, she and a group organized against a napalm factory in Long Beach, California. She begins, "Instead of focusing on the 52 percent 'devil' in my adversary, I choose to look at the other 48 percent, to start from the premise that within each adversary I have an ally. That ally may be silent, faltering, or hidden from my view. It may be only the person's sense of ambivalence about morally questionable parts of his or her job. Such doubts rarely have a chance to flower because of the overwhelming power of the social context to which the person is accountable. *My* ability to be *their* ally also suffers from such pressures."[9]

She discusses her strategies of enlisting support through slide shows in the community, picketing the factory, and learning everything she could about the president of the company. She and her group spent three weeks preparing for a meeting with him, investigating the company's holdings. Before the meeting, they also talked a lot among themselves about how angry they were at the company president for the part he played in killing and maiming children in Vietnam. They decided that venting that anger at him would only make him defensive and lessen their chances to be heard. "Above all, we wanted him to see us as real people, not so different from himself. If we had seemed like flaming radicals, he would have been likely to dismiss our concerns."[10]

The group also "found out as much as we could about his personal life: his family, his church, his country club, his hobbies. We studied his photograph, thinking of the people who loved him and the people he loved, trying to get a sense of his worldview and the context to

---

So the people of the Third World have to be educated. And it has to be done energetically, without any sentimental reticence. It's an immediate necessity, it's an emergency. They have to be told, despite all the misunderstandings it may involve: you're on the wrong track, your demographic growth is much too large, it's leading you to even more terrible poverty. . . .

Other countries . . . have nothing, and tomorrow they will have less than nothing. We have to fight this growing gap. . . . That ought to be our goal. Bringing the two worlds close enough to make them comparable, and if possible equal.

All the problems—famine, unemployment, delinquency, insecurity, psychological deviancy, various epidemics, drugs, madness, despair, terrorism—all that is bound up with the widening gap between the people, which needless to say, can also be found inside the rich countries. . . . Everything is linked together, everything is inseparable. Consequently, the gap has to be reduced. **The Dalai Lama in** *Violence and Compassion*, **by Jean-Claude Carrière**

---

which he was accountable. When the three of us met with him, he was not a stranger to us. We assumed he was already carrying doubts inside himself, and we saw our role as giving voice to those doubts. Our goal was to introduce ourselves and our perspective into his context, so he would remember us and consider our position when making decisions.

"Without blaming him personally or attacking his corporation, we asked him to close the plant, not to bid for the contract when it came up for renewal that year, and to think about the consequences of his company's operations."[11] Peavey describes how the group communicated their quiet commitment to dealing with the whole issue of economic dependence on munitions and war. "When the contract came up for renewal two months later, his company did not bid for it."[12]

### THE PATH BETWEEN CYNICISM AND NAIVETÉ

Peavey is aware that "making friends with the enemy" is no simple solution that works in all cases. She raises such questions as how to deal with the anger we have against our enemies. Can we differentiate between hateful actions and the people behind them? If we empathize with our enemies, do we undermine our determination to create change? Clearly, "treating our adversaries as potential allies need not entail unthinking acceptance of their actions. Our challenge is to call forth the humanity within each adversary, while preparing for the full range of possible responses. Our challenge is to find a path between cynicism and naiveté."[13] Approaches to social change such as Peavey describes helps pave the way for all of us to try something new.

## RELEASING FEARS WHILE IN THE SPIRITUAL DIMENSION

Before we could fly an airplane, we had the desire to fly. Before we could talk on the telephone, we had the ability to communicate telepathically. Who knows what kinds of magic will emerge out of the twin evolutions of technology and our inborn, as-yet-developed human capacities! As we learn to journey into the spiritual dimension, perhaps what we fear today will not even be an issue as we intuit new methods of manifesting and healing or accessing the wisdom stored in the universal intelligence.

Robert Monroe, after years of contact with the spiritual realm, began to realize that he could work on releasing fears—fears he didn't know he had. "I discovered that I was indeed far from fearless. I may not have been consciously aware of these fears, but there they were, large, ugly blasts of raw energy. . . . There were old fears and a constant inflow of new ones. They ranged from little items, such as anxiety over the effect of a rainy day on our construction project, to big worries about the world changes developing."[14] Over the years, however, he noticed these fears were dissipating. "Many more fears were being dissolved than the number of new ones which were being generated by my current activity. With this awareness came a major revelation: [when I was in the spiritual dimension I] had instituted this process and kept the fear-dissolving operation flowing as needed. No outside source was providing any assistance, as I had wrongly assumed. I was helping myself!"[15]

Feeling sad, discouraged, angry, or concerned for the planet are real and important outpourings of energy. Humans tend to resist change! Unless things get painful, we often don't take the action that is called for. Our feelings are the path to wholeness. When we lose our humanity in fear, we get caught in a struggle that may not lead to the result we really want. When we don't feel, when we dehumanize, when we write somebody off, we lose our connection to what really matters, like spending an afternoon in the sunshine with our children, sailing our ship across the sea, or holding hands with our grandmother at sunset.

## INDIVIDUAL STUDY

### Shadow Exercise

The purpose of this exercise is to help put yourself in another's shoes. Developing empathy and compassion *in yourself* is some of the highest spiritual work you can do toward holding the World Vision.

### Step A

Take a moment to jot down the names of three or four people you don't like or with whom you disagree. Beside the names write out the things you don't agree with or don't like about them. For example, Carl, a single father and businessman, wrote that he doesn't like:

1. My brother-in-law George. Because he always rubs it in that his business is really going great because of all the new technologies he's using. He thinks I should get more up to date.

2. Politicians. Because they are phony. You can't trust them. They don't get anything done.
3. Bleeding-heart liberals. Because they aren't realistic.

## Step B

Now go back and describe each of the people as if you could see their higher purpose. Use your imagination to speculate what deeper, *positive* purposes lies behind the outer characteristics that you see and judge. Carl wrote:

1. George seems to be very interested in the effect of technology in the twentieth century. He is a guy who is very driven to achieve. Maybe in another lifetime he didn't have many opportunities to use his abilities. George likes to tell others what he knows about. He's a natural teacher.
2. Politicians are people who have an ideal that they start out thinking they can achieve. They are persevering. They are people who risk being shot down by everyone's criticism. They are people who want to be part of a system. They are people who are learning how to adapt to constantly changing conditions in order to learn about the right use of power and service.
3. Bleeding-heart liberals are people who want to help others. They are people who have strong principles about right and wrong. They spend time from their own lives in trying to make a difference in those areas where they have a special interest. Maybe they have suffered in other lifetimes, and they vowed to try to do some good for others in this lifetime.

In step B you detach from the normal way you perceive others and speculate on the original intention of what these people wanted to do. By taking another position, looking for a positive reason why people are the way they are, *you* have an opportunity to become a bigger person. Holding more than one perception of someone opens you to have a more creative interaction with that person.

## Step C

Now go back to what you have written in step A. Scratch out the name of one of the people you don't like and insert your own name. Now describe something *you* do that is similar to what you don't like about that person. Notice how you feel when you read the sentence aloud to yourself. Carl read aloud to himself, "[Like George does,] I sometimes rub things into other people. Like when I said to my ex-wife, 'I told you that you should have taken care of the insurance premium, and now it's lapsed.' " He said that he felt a little "quietness" in his heart area as he realized that he could be bit like "old George" at times.

What about Carl's feelings about politicians? In the first step, he wrote he didn't like them because they were phony, you couldn't trust them, and they never got anything done. Looking at himself now he wrote, "Sometimes I guess I am kind of phony, too. Like the other day when Bill came over and I said how glad I was to see him. I really don't like this guy, and yet he's one of my clients so I don't want to offend him. I haven't always kept every promise myself. Like that time I told Barbara that I ordered the new materials, but I didn't want to let her know I had forgotten." Carl even began to remember how his father always put down politicians in the same way. When Carl was a teenager, he had wanted to run for student body president, but his father thought it would take too much time away from his after-school job. Like the politicians he disliked because they didn't seem to accomplish their goals, Carl felt about *himself*, "I wish I had accomplished more in my business up to now."

In examining his feelings about liberals, he wrote, "I, Carl, have sure not always been realistic. And nobody ever helped out our family when we were poor, so why should I worry about people now who don't want to work when I can barely keep my business going?" Carl was ready to make some connections about himself and the projections he was placing on those he didn't like or didn't agree with. He was still having difficulty in accepting that he had a very strong need to reach out (like the "bleeding-heart liberals") and help those who were less fortunate than himself. He remained convinced that liberals were deluding themselves about the real world.

In this exercise we see how Carl's dislike of George, politicians, and liberals all reflected some part of his own denied shadow. When we begin to "own back" or recognize ourselves in those things we judge as bad, we begin to open to the wholeness of our soul. The more energy we send to keep our negative qualities in the dark, the less energy we have to create from our *whole self*.

For example, miracles will happen to Carl when he (1) releases the resentments he hangs on to about his early poverty; (2) recognizes that his desire to accomplish something more in business is the voice of his Birth Vision; and (3) allows himself to serve a humanitarian cause that is bigger than himself. Not only will he be doing a big part toward holding the World Vision, but he might just feel more alive, and have more fun, adventure, and fulfillment!

## GROUP STUDY

### Dialoguing with Fear

If your group is well bonded and you have created a safe environment for people to share rather deep issues, you may want to explore people's feelings about some of the fears and beliefs listed at the beginning of this chapter. Let each person speak as the energy moves through the group, but it's a good idea to let people speak without interruption, advice, or response until you're ready for a general discussion of feelings.

### Meditation

Your group may want to end your meeting with a group meditation focusing on one of the fears and beliefs that are most strong in your members. For example, if people have a big fear and belief in overpopulation, try a meditation in which you visualize young people of childbearing years remembering their Vision to live on the Earth in a balanced way.

If you wish to work with the fear of a mob mentality, create a visual image of people hugging one another, holding hands, helping each other over a bridge, dancing in their backyards, or voting together for positive social change. Be creative, but realize that you hold great power in your meditations.

A study of long-term, mass meditations by experienced meditators revealed statistically significant positive effects in the cities where the meditations took place. Dubbed the "Maharishi effect," group meditation has produced a drop in crime rate and hospital deaths corresponding to the meditation periods.

### Projects

If you were going to take on a project and you had every reason to believe that it would be successful, what would you all like to do together as a group? If you decide to take on something, ask everyone to start coming up with fears about how the project might fail and put them on a sheet of paper. How realistic are these fears? What could you actually do to either let that fear teach you something or turn it into a positive force?

## PART FIVE

# Right Action

PART IV

Right Action

## CHAPTER 10

# Transformation in Work and Business

DOLPHIN
LINK

There is a new ethic moving toward enlightened capitalism, oriented not just to profits, but to filling the evolving needs of spiritual beings; making these products available at the lowest possible price; and ultimately toward full automation and liberating humans to engage in spiritual tithing envisioned in the Ninth Insight.

THE TENTH INSIGHT:
HOLDING THE VISION[1]

## BUSINESS AS A SPIRITUAL PATH

"Business people may have a longing for this new way of doing business—this new trend toward spirit in business," said California entrepreneur Mark Bryant, "but they might not have the ability to implement this because of the nature of what is already in place. There's also tremendous pressure for short-term results. If a company has had two bad quarters, the CEO is likely to be removed by the board of directors. So the real power of the company is held by the shareholders."

Mark, who has started five successful businesses, is a good example of someone who is actively balancing his spiritual discoveries with home, family, and (now) three demanding businesses. His question was, "How to be in business and, at the same time, grow spiritually and psychologically, as well as financially?" He gave himself about eighteen months to investigate all kinds of books on paradigm shifts, innovative models and techniques, and metaphysical systems and practitioners, and how they might be used to increase intuition in business. "Twenty years ago I was with a large corporation, and I used all the available psychological tools—personality profiles—in the human resource department to understand myself better. But I felt that I needed other kinds of systems that would give me a bigger picture of myself. My intuition led me to metaphysics. I know this sounds kind of strange for somebody who is a Christian and who comes from a corporate background, but I found many ideas in metaphysics that went deeper than the psychological model. Even though I was interested in an inward look, I did find it helpful to work with other people in assessing myself. This was what started my research into metaphysics. I think people should know that you don't have to go this road alone."

What was the result of Mark's search? "For one thing," he answered, "my sense of purpose and aliveness is much, much stronger. I know myself better now, and therefore I'm much more aware of whether or not a business opportunity is going to work for me in the long run. Now I'll pass on something that in the past I might have done and regretted. I trust my intuition a lot more, and that's made me more efficient. Also there is something else that's kind of hard to put into words—but I feel a greater sense of ease about everything that I do."

What advice would Mark give to other businesspeople? "Well, a lot of people in big business are starting to feel trapped. With rampant downsizing there's a sense that you don't have any control over your destiny no matter how well you perform. People get disenchanted with the corporate world, and they may start to look at franchising or being a consultant or sole proprietor. But I think that just changing your external situation is not the only answer, and may not bring you the feeling of fulfillment unless you change the way you see yourself. I feel that if you don't work on yourself—on creating security in knowing who you really are—you may be disappointed again in whatever small business you get into. Any business can have its own rigidity, hierarchy, and unhealthy conditions. You may want to be your own boss, but you may also have a conflicting desire for somebody to take care of you." Mark emphasized the following points that have worked for him: "First, you have to realize your gifts, and how to work with them instead of wishing you were somebody else. I notice that people tend to see themselves and their skills two or three levels below who they really are. They tend to look at their *external lacks*, like 'I can't start a business because I don't have a degree,' instead of asking what do I really want? They let their judgments about themselves, their shadow, define them. They're not looking at their true self, they're looking at their external image.

"Secondly, I've found that working with your gifts is an evolutionary process. For example, I know that I'm more of a visionary/actualizer, but not as good a producer. Therefore, I have partnered with somebody who is a very good producer. We have a business marriage that works because we're both aware of our strong points. Knowing your strengths and weaknesses, and looking for someone to complement you, to round out the picture, is the most efficient way to work.

"Thirdly, and I know this may sound odd, but I found that what helped me get out of my feeling of being trapped in the predominant business culture was to think of myself as a soul. I think you have to rekindle the soul you were when you were a youth. In your early days, you are a lot more free in your thinking about yourself. Anything is possible. Kids have no limitations because they're still looking at themselves at a soul level without all the dogma of institutions and culture.

"I think metaphysical and spiritual ideas without doubt are changing the way we work and the way we think about our livelihood. But this is a new language for a lot of businesspeople. In the past few years we've been getting a lot of information about being good managers (controllers) and the value of decentralization, and all this is very practical. However, the important shift is really about making shifts inside yourself— not *using* spiritual methods externally to make more money. The real

I distinguish between job and work. A job is something we do to make a living and to pay our bills, but work is the reason why we are here. It has to do with our heart and joy and all the mystics. East and West write about this. The Tao Te Ching, the Chinese Scriptures, say, "in work, do what you enjoy." The idea that there is a connection between joy and work is new to a lot of people because in the machine universe of the Industrial Age, joy was not one of the great values. . . .

We have been defining work in such a narrow fashion during the Industrial Age of factory work that we have missed the other aspects at work like heart work and art and healing and celebration and ritual; all of which are works in healthy communities. Native people spend at least half of their time celebrating and doing rituals. We don't and there is wide spread violence in our culture.

I'm very involved today in working with young people . . . using rap music, house music, techno music and dance—some of the forms that we have available today at the edge of our youth culture and our urban culture to rediscover celebration. That's very good, very needed work. Celebration is one way that people heal—it's the most fun way—and the cheapest too. **Matthew Fox in *Towards a New World View*, by Russell E. DiCarlo**

change is in how you experience life at work and how you work *with* life."

Spirituality in work and business means you are checking *inside* yourself every time you have to make a decision. Instead of looking only at your financial balance sheet, you're looking at the feeling of internal balance to see if what you are doing feels in alignment with your purpose and what you represent as a soul. You're the only one who can ask, "Does this feel right? What's the deeper implication of this action?" There's no way for anyone else to tell you that. Spirituality in business is about paying attention to the spirit within you, with a desire to serve the greatest good.

Obviously, business at present is not set up democratically to give each worker creative autonomy and personal accountability. Business, with its eye turned only to *external* criteria, with its belief in the sanctity of control and predictability, is antithetical to giving people the freedom to produce goods and services based on their own intuitive flow and spiritual guidance about what's right for the situation. Most of us serve an external goal, an extrinsic purpose. At present anyone who has not made a perceptual shift would think the idea of encouraging self-reflection in business is foolish flakiness, nothing short of dangerous anarchy. Even those of us who consider these new ideas intellectually stimulating also carry our secret doubts that "other people" can ever be trusted to move beyond common greed or laziness—if not evil intent. Most of us are well aware of the flabby state of personal integrity and self-governance at this point in human consciousness. We have never been without our role models, though, who have shown that God does work in mysterious ways. We have never been without God. The current pervasive transformation of consciousness is not confined to Sunday morning or church pews. What may not be in place in terms of the structure of the workplace, however, is alive in terms of longing. Our enemies are only fear and inertia.

## LEARNED HELPLESSNESS—
## FREEING THE WORKPLACE MENTALITY

At a recent conference in Montreal sponsored by the International Institute of Integral Human Sciences, Miron Borysenko, Ph.D., talked about the concept of "learned helplessness." Dr. Borysenko, a medical scientist and cellular biologist who studies the mind/body connection and the effect of stress on the immune system explored some fascinating biological findings that help us ground our thinking in all fields, including business. In one amusing example, he showed a slide of a little bird sitting in its cage even though the door was wide open. "If you raise birds in a cage and open the door," he said, "they'll stay in the cage. The same thing is true for humans who may long to make a change, but don't trust themselves to rise to what the change might require of them. The place where you are might be miserable, but at least it's safe."

Borysenko demonstrated the principle of learned helplessness with an experiment in which two rats were exposed to random electric shocks, while a third, control, rat received no shocks. Rat 1 was able to turn a wheel that turned off the shocks to him *and* to rat 2. Although rats 1 and 2 received the same amount of stress for the same duration of time, rat 2 (who received inescapable shock) got a bleeding ulcer, and rat 1 (with escapable shock because he had control of the wheel) was even healthier than rat 3, who received no shock. Borysenko explained that when the rats were put into a maze, rat 1 was the first to find the water. He had already learned to cope. Rat 2 took the longest because he had learned helplessness and had generalized it to a new situation. Findings from similar studies and others done with human subjects indicate that stress by itself is not harmful as long as the individual has some sense that it can make a difference in its world—that is, can have some control over its environment. In fact, challenge, with a positive sense of control, feeds self-esteem and creativity.

Borysenko's images correlate to what we have learned about our conditioned control responses since childhood. The bird free to fly but sitting inside the cage is a good image of the Aloof drama, which in effect says, "I don't need to let people know what's going on with me. Better to stay quiet and hunker down. Don't rock the boat." The rats who learned to think of themselves as helpless show us a graphic example of the Poor Me control drama: "I have no say about what happens at work. I'm one of the peons. I can't make any changes because no one will let me."

Also consider the implications of the rat study in terms of the question "How do I know when I'm in alignment with myself internally?" Rat 2 (to use the poor hapless rodent as the analogue to the conditioned worker) seems to have made some decision about himself based on an external source (inescapable shock) that created a global message such as "I'm weak and not in control of what happens to me" that was transmitted to his cells. The cells, now defining themselves with the message of "I'm weak, and not in control of what happens to me," lose, to a large extent, their ability to maintain health. Our feelings of depression depress our immune system. Negative feelings of frustration, anger, blame, resentment, and hopelessness arise when we have separated from God. If you are experiencing frustration and anger on a daily basis, if you spend lots of time mentally pointing fingers at supervisors, coworkers, or clients as if they were blights on your day—you are not in alignment with yourself. Borysenko gives the example of watching a man in the car next to him stalled in traffic pounding on his steering wheel. "Seeing that man be so upset really showed me that it's not what's going on out there that's important, it's what's going on in *here*."

---

The practical test I give people is this: "What joy do you derive from your work" and "what joy do others derive as a result of your work?" . . . We need jobs, but I think the key is, how can others derive blessings from our work? Because that's what work really is; for human beings—it's a return of blessing from blessing.

It's our thank you to the community for being here and that's why unemployment is so disastrous to the human soul. Unemployment creates despair and when there is despair, you have crime because you have self-hatred and you have violence.

You have all the things that we're building prisons for in this country. I think a much cheaper and simpler solution would be to have a big debate on what work Gaia or the earth is really asking of us today. There's all kinds of work—new kinds of work—that we need to do on the human heart to bring about ecological and social justice in our time. **Matthew Fox in *Towards a World View*, by Russell E. DiCarlo**

---

### YOU SET A STANDARD

Business, making a living, working at right livelihood, like every other part of your life, is a chance to experience God, spirit, universal intelligence, whatever you choose to call your spiritual source. As a holder of the World Vision, you set a standard by your actions, goals, and synergetic process with others.

Larry Leigon, cofounder of the nonalcoholic wine company Ariel, and now partner in Global Insights in Novato, California, is also a certified master practitioner of neurolinguistic programming with an emphasis on healing. Leigon exemplifies the new kind of businessperson who has made a paradigm shift from external values to internal values. In an interview, he discussed his journey from growing up on a large cattle ranch in Texas to consulting and lecturing about spirituality in business. "Most people have not yet realized just what spirituality in business is because they are trying to fit it into the old perceptual categories like 'How can we *use* spirituality to be better in business?' Or equating spirituality with business ethics, which is still an external focus. Or trying to make business more ecological. Those are all fine values, he claims, but they are *externally* focused.

"The real crux of the paradigm shift," Leigon insists, "is the switch from putting all one's attention on controlled, measurable, predictable *external* factors to functioning from an *internally* based attunement to a higher or deeper purpose. I've discovered that exploring and honoring what really matters to me results in a totally different set of external behaviors. The Buddhists call it right livelihood or one's dharma, or one's path. I ask myself is this what God wants me to do? Does this feel aligned with my values? When I check my inner alignment with my values, then I decide which client to work with, which product to develop, which course of action to take. That's exactly opposite to the traditional business procedure of checking the market and the competition and trying to devise a strategy to find a weakness and exploit it.

> What is the purpose of business? Most people will answer "profits." If you continue to look outside yourself, then you can only conclude that the answer must be based on some set of *external criteria*—the financial bottom line, environmental impact, discrimination, diversity management, women's rights—all worthwhile *effects* of a spiritual concern. But they are not *causes* of spirit in business. If your criteria are *internal*, then internal profits is the individual realization of the direct experience of God.
>
> **Larry Leigon**

"In the past, I was only concerned about finding a defensible position in the marketplace, and maintaining it against predator competition. This put me in the position of a small animal at an African watering hole, waiting for a larger animal to come and eat me."

## HUNTERS, GATHERERS, FARMERS, BUILDERS, STEWARDS

Not unlike the burrowing of earthworms that improves the soil by allowing more air and water to reach deeper into the ground, our spiritual longings create deeper responses to our environment—including our business and financial environment. The global restlessness described in the First Insight is both a symptom of the transition that is taking place and a force that is drawing us together, personally and professionally, to work for world unity. Business is at once the steward of change and at the effect of change. The striving for technological development and the struggle to keep up with our creations is still a powerful and volatile mix because we are trying to stay "in control" of it from an external viewpoint. We truly have a tiger by the tail. We haven't asked ourselves, Why do I want to keep holding on to the tail? The question of why is the internal viewpoint.

### OH, JUST FOR FUN

Imagine yourself getting out of bed in the morning and saying, "Hey, I'm a spiritual being!" Would that make you laugh or cry? Imagine yourself entering your office, briefcase in hand, cellular phone ringing, waving to your workmates and saying, "Good morning, you spiritual beings!" Imagine yourself hanging up angrily from a phone call, but suddenly recalling you had just been talking to a spiritual being—and you still were one, too!

This no doubt sounds ludicrous to you, but the Tenth Insight is a level of awareness in everyday situations that could make a difference in the quality of your life, right now. No waiting. You don't have to do anything overt like making a fool of yourself "being all spiritual." Listen and act from heart-centered intention. Begin to look for those souls with whom you vibrate, and strengthen your ties to them. Remember that your time on earth was carefully chosen so that you could work quietly in concert with other groups of souls participating in the planetary developments. Notice how others work. Is the emphasis on building a personal empire, or is the work done in the spirit of inclusiveness and generosity? Make no judgments about anyone, and let them continue on their path. Align yourself with those with whom you have a flash of recognition or a deep sense of resonance. Your receptivity to meeting others on a spiritual path will attract them to you, and your quota of consciousness telepathically helps to achieve humanitarian aims on a global scale, even though you may feel frustrated in your own office!

### AS YOU THINK, SO SHALL YOU REAP

Commerce, bartering, trade, business—the cornerstone of civilized communities—have evolved in line with our values and beliefs. The underlying Western capitalistic values such as independence and hard work have devolved into fierce takeovers, ruthless competition, and workaholism. Other countries are panting to join us in the dysfunction. Efficiency, self-sufficiency, and technological prowess have gradually devolved into ultimately self-defeating obsessions such as planned obsolescence, "bigger is better," "looking out for number one," and placating the stockholders. However, all of these seeming "negative" energy trends serve to awaken us from complacency, and, oddly, stimulate the higher knowing of humanity. Intense materialism is but one stage in a continuum of perspectives and has been a necessary step in the evolution toward the unification of the two spheres.

> James Rouse, called by *Time* magazine "America's Master Builder," is one of a number of individuals who are working to give control over resources back to local communities. . . . "Profit is not the legitimate purpose of business," he says. "Its purpose is to provide a service needed by society. If you do that well and efficiently, you earn a profit." **Corinne McLaughlin and Gordon Davidson, *Spiritual Politics***

### THE INTERCONNECTED, SPIRAL MODEL OF BUSINESS

It's true that many of us may not yet be able to see these ideas fulfilled in our immediate workplace. However, changes are happening so rapidly that in a few years, the table on page 225 may seem quite oldfashioned. One response to changing some of the hierarchical energy in business is to use a deep ecology model. What that means is that every decision and action we make affects everything else. While this is a more enlightened model for business than a predator/prey model because its goal is to work for sustainable growth instead of raping our resources, it still places the focus on external conditions. The ecology model is a *result* of the internal focus on spiritual attunement, not the *cause* of spirit in business. If we follow our intuition, if we listen to our hearts, we will make certain choices. The energy created by those choices will flow through a network, developing with the cooperation of other systems. Changes will come as we adapt intuitively to feedback. Feedback will prompt new questions, and we'll tune in again to our spiritual knowing, tuning into the long-range needs of the whole organism of humanity.

As the Ninth Insight suggested, we are at a critical place in history where we will demand that business develop broader goals beyond simply making money for a few individuals. One of the higher purposes of business is to synthesize, to influence the entire breadth of the human family. Businesspeople are continually reaching out, networking, creating alliances, synergistically creating new forms.

As we change our visual picture of business from a linear, money-making machine to a living system whose purpose is to bring us closer to God, business will take on new forms. There is, for example, a huge movement in home-based businesses as people grow more and more dissatisfied with the quality of life in large, impersonal, hierarchical organizations that treat employees as resources to be used up. More people are beginning to carve out niches for themselves, either out of necessity from having been laid off, or by trusting their instincts and hearts to lead them to a livelihood that makes getting up in the morning pleasurable. This trend promotes the archetypal elements of adaptability and diversification (so important in the ecological model for sustainability). Spreading out into connected units, people are instituting, in their own intuitive way, the nonhierarchical unification and democratization of humanity. You can see that a higher purpose is served by people deciding on their own what feels right for themselves, and what looks like a business decision may be a telepathic response to a universal movement. We are not suggesting that everyone should quit their job or change their occupation, because each individual serves a need in each situation until he/she is called to make a change. But is it a coincidence that such technology as telephones, personal computers, faxes, copiers, and delivery services have come at a time when many of us are desiring autonomy—within a supportive network?

> Money . . . is only crystallized energy or vitality. . . . It is a concretization of etheric force. It is therefore vital energy externalized, and this form of energy is under the direction of the financial group. They are the latest group [of souls] in point of date, and their work (it should be borne in mind) is most definitely planned by the [Spiritual] Hierarchy. [The financial soul groups] are bringing about effects upon the earth which are most far reaching. **Alice A. Bailey, *A Treatise on White Magic or The Way of the Disciple***

## SPIRITUAL "PROFITS": TRUST, SERVICE, SELF-ESTEEM, ENTHUSIASM, EFFORTLESSNESS, PROSPERITY, AND JOY

Karen Burns Thiessen, a marketing consultant in Sausalito, California, was laid off when her department in a large corporation was downsized. She told us, "Until last year, I had always worked for somebody else. When I got laid off after ten years, I decided I wanted to go out on my own. The day I started my business [Kalena Associates, Marketing Creative Minds] a big corporation called and offered me a job with everything I would have wanted—money, car, vacation, everything. I knew this had to be a test!" Instead of going back to the old life, Karen moved forward even though she was not at all certain of what would happen. "I gave myself a year to get established, and began experimenting. I started meditating and reading everything. My intuition just kept leading me to the right books. People would give me advice, or tell me something wouldn't work, but I kept trusting that my creativity was leading me somewhere. Something shifted at the beginning of 1996 when I wrote a six-month 'wants list.' In one month I have achieved everything I had on that list—including the income level I wanted and the kind of clients I want to work with."

Karen encourages her clients to trust their intuition and take risks, and works to help them find balance in their personal and professional lives. As she explained, "When you are a small business owner, your business is your life. You have to recognize the activities that bring you pleasure, whether it's sailing, being outdoors, whatever you enjoy, and integrate pleasure into your business."

Karen also reminds business entrepreneurs that emotional blocks drain energy and may inhibit the flow of finances. "If your money flow is not happening," she says, "ask yourself, 'What unresolved personal issues are draining my energy?' I also tell people that it's okay to let go of your clients from Hell. If your energies are not in sync, let them go. It makes room for the people that you really like doing business with to come into your life!"

These comments from Mark Bryant, Larry Leigon, and Karen Burns Thiessen exemplify a new attitude emerging from within the old hierarchical, combat-oriented business model which all too often produces disenchanted, burned-out people.

### FAILURES OF THE HEART

In the Montreal lecture mentioned above, Dr. Borysenko asked people to raise their hands if they knew someone who had had a heart attack in the last few months. Out of about seven hundred people, approximately one hundred hands went up!

According to statistics, most heart attacks occur on Monday morning. Why? Dr. Larry Dossey, one of the most brilliant thinkers about the new paradigm, summed up the worst of the Monday-morning blues when he coined the term "joyless striving." How endemic is this attitude in our culture—working without attention to a purpose greater than ourselves?

Defining criteria for health in the four areas of life, Dr. Borysenko rates "*resiliency* in responding to challenges" highest for the physical plane. In the rat studies we mentioned earlier, the rats who had some control over their shock stress actually thrived, or performed better than, rats who had not been stressed at all. Stress can actually stimulate greater creativity in us as long as we feel we have some degree of control over what happens to us. This is not to say, however, that we must be "in control." Borysenko quotes studies conducted by researcher Suzanne Kobasa (SUNY). Consulting with a company undergoing divestiture, she saw people who were under severe stress. The ones who were really falling apart said they felt helpless and *saw change as a crisis*. They had trouble with their families, couldn't sleep, abused alcohol and drugs, and generally felt out of control. They seemingly fit the mode of joyless striving.

## CHANGE AS OPPORTUNITY

On the other hand, other people in the same scenario saw the changes as a challenge and felt as if they were being given a great opportunity. People who see change as an opportunity are what Kobasa calls "psychologically hardy." They have a good sense of control in spite of what's going on. They understand that to be in control sometimes means *letting go of control*. They also had a sense of commitment— commitment to an ideal, to their community, to their family, to a greater purpose—which is opposite to the idea of joyless striving.

Borysenko believes that along with resiliency in physical behavior, emotional *maturity* is necessary for optimal health. What is emotional maturity? He believes that we must all do a healing on the immature subselves we created as a child to maintain the love connection to our parents. His description of the various subselves resonates very closely to the four Celestine control dramas, which were also developed as a survival response.

Intellectual health stems, says Borysenko, from *curiosity* about the world, a curiosity that is all too often stifled in institutional life. The fourth criterion for spiritual health, he believes, is *spiritual optimism*— exactly what the Tenth Insight advocates for holding a positive worldview!

The mystery of our life *wants* to unfold, and it does unfold when we listen to our intuition and allow order to blossom despite seeming chaos—even in business. Again we have a choice of whether to view the world as a work in progress—complete with contradictions, uncertainties, *and* incredible opportunities—or as a collapsing, out-of-control planetary failure.

## BUSINESS IS AN INSIDE-OUT JOB, DISMANTLING THE *WALLS* OF THE BOARDROOM

Business is well known for its cyclical nature. In the old mechanistic viewpoint we talked about getting plugged in, implementing, measuring, quality control, remeasuring, calibrating, setting policy (but "not in concrete"), and reengineering (even people). The only result that counted was an increase in revenue. No measurements were taken about the cost to human spirit, the damage to the environment, the legacy to our children. When business is approached from a spiritual viewpoint, people begin to consider the long-range implications of their choices. They start with the commitment to do what matters to them, to stay in alignment with integrity, and to try—as best as possible—to serve others as they would like to be served.

Margaret Wheatley speaks eloquently about learning from the "emergent creativity" of nature. She speaks about living in the world with the purpose of "exploring what's possible, finding new combinations—not struggling to survive, but playing, tinkering, to find what's possible." When we change the way we view "the problem," we change the nature of how we work with that situation. If we give ourselves permission to be "messy," which is the soul's preference, then we experience the richness of life, and out of that, order will come. She writes, "Scientists say it takes a lot of messes to finally discover what works. But underneath is the realization that all of those messes are tending toward the discovery of a form of organization that will work for multiple species. Life uses messes, but the direction is always toward organization; it's always toward order."[2] This is not the linear, goal-setting mode most of us have valued (even though most of us have never, ever had a five-year plan). Tuning into our values and aligning with a positive force, we will be more energized and alert to the "opportunities" life sends us. Boardroom meetings, with awareness at the level of the Tenth Insight, become places where common goals, intentions, and intuitions can be explored in order to find the higher order or to express the deeper values of the situation. The metaphor for the boardroom will be the circle, not the ladder; the cradle and the crucible, not the prison or the emperor's court.

## RENAISSANCE CYCLE

Social researcher Paul H. Ray speculates that we are currently experiencing a change in the dominant cultural pattern, a revitalization that happens perhaps only once or twice in a millennium. Our inner restlessness is a sign that neither the nostalgic conservative element *nor* the techno-modern (whose motto is "Technology rules!") views of life provide adequate physical or spiritual nourishment. His study reveals the opportunity for an emergence of what he calls the Integral Culture. Not a by-product of a system, but rather a heart-centered demand for personal integrity, this new culture is changing the old forms of cities, jobs, workplaces, markets, businesses, universities, and governments. Prompted by their internal need to feel congruent with their beliefs, people are reading the small print on product labeling, asking questions about the origin of products, gathering together with like-minded people to discuss health, healing, ecology, human rights, children's issues, and all manner of topics. "The cultural revitalization response is to invent a new way of seeing ourselves, and to use old ideas and technologies in new ways," writes Ray. "It is a hopeful and creative period in the life of a culture, usually following a period of defeat and despair."[3] Ray is also careful to caution us that this emerging transformation of culture will not shift the dominant paradigm unless we *maintain* a strong intention for positive change and an optimistic outlook.

We seem to be in between stories, and on a personal level, we may not be quite sure what is going to work. However, at a planetary level, preparations for this time in history have been in progress for hundreds of years through the work of many spiritually attuned people who serve quietly and selflessly with no worldly ambitions.

## BREATHING IN AND BREATHING OUT

Talking about breathing when we're discussing business? The simplest ideas are often the ones we overlook in our rush to control our lives and speak from our "expertise." Let's ask ourselves how we can be related to our work and busyness with a more enlightened attitude.

## BUSINESS BELIEFS CREATE REALITY

| Old Beliefs About Business | Result In: | New Ways of Thinking | Result In: |
|---|---|---|---|
| Business is a machine | Rigidity | Business as another way to experience God | Flexibility, joy, trust, optimism, creativity |
| Unlimited growth | Greed, ultimate failure | Purposeful action, sustainable growth | Harmony, physical prosperity |
| Hierarchical | Fear, rigidity, high turnover | Self-organizing around a mission | Bringing out the best for all |
| Competition is healthy, necessary, and desirable | Fear, scarcity, inefficient use of resources | Right livelihood and right action | Mutual benefit, trust, creativity efficiency |
| Rugged individualism | Greed, rampant downsizing | Democratic leadership partnerships | Synergistic solutions |
| Success as financial bottom line only | Short-term gains, limited vision | Thriving financially, emotionally, physically, and spiritually | Stable community, at-onement |
| Be all business—leave out the personal | Fragmentation breeds disloyalty, unrealistic view of life | Congruent work, sense of authentic connection, whole self at work | Actualized brotherhood of human beings |
| Management of objective | Rigidity, blind to synchronicity, less adaptive | Setting intention, following intuition, accountability, trusting that everything happens for a purpose | Right action, increased creativity, universal support, miracles |

If business sometimes sets us up to die of stress (as it does in such workaholic countries as America and Japan) and joyless striving, what can we do to take back our lives? If spiritual optimism and purpose are the new paradigm for health, what can we do in practical terms to work within the new paradigm? Dr. Borysenko and other stress experts remind us of our inborn "relaxation response," the opposite reaction to the flight-or-fight response. He says, "If you want to get some control over your life, learn to breathe from your diaphragm. This automatically puts you into the relaxation response. When you induce the relaxation response, heart rate and blood pressure decrease, as well as serum cholesterol and blood lactate. You decrease pain, allergic reactions, and chance of infection. You literally increase the flow of blood to the brain and the periphery [the biological analogue of being "in the flow"!]. You are more tuned in, more aware, and more alert in a quiet kind of way. This is the perfect condition for self-examination. You facilitate coping through this response because you are decreasing anxiety, forestalling depression, and you generate a positive self-statement that provides the platform for effecting change. You are able to *decondition* yourself and *recondition* yourself. That's what the paradigm shift means."

## A New Light on "Teamwork"—Soul Groups in the Spiritual Dimension

In *The Tenth Insight*, the characters reach a higher level of energy that allows them to become aware of their original Birth Vision. In this higher vibration, they become aware of the presence of groups of souls in the Afterlife that send them energy. One by one, they realize that each one has his or her own group—a group that has been with them perhaps for centuries. These groups hold the memories of the Birth Vision and assist the person on Earth by sending energy when requested. The characters begin to recognize that they have chosen various occupational categories through which to manifest their original Visions.

Admittedly, businesspeople may find the idea of an otherworldly group of souls assisting them in their daily life at the office something of a fantasy. But what if? What if we were to take what we know about spiritual teachings and *really* apply it to our life—knowing that every action, every arena of life, is an opportunity to experience God? If we are at the level of the Tenth Insight in our understanding, we would already be tuning into our intuition, following our hunches, and recognizing that the synchronicities that occur are "no accident." This is the effect of, often unnoticed or not attributed to, the intelligence of the universal field. By meditating, we raise our vibration closer to the soul group level, but most of us are unable to recognize the telepathic connection that we may have. We may not relate inspirations and creativity to a higher connection or notice any other worldly dimension when we experience the magic of inspired teamwork. However, according to esoteric teaching, we are greatly assisted by beings in a higher dimension if we are working in alignment with planetary purpose and our own Birth Vision. If we are not in attunement with higher purpose, no judgment is made against us, as the law of cause and effect creates our own consequences.

## CLEARING NEGATIVE FEELINGS BEFORE DOING WORK TOGETHER

The group of seven in *The Tenth Insight* knew that they were close to finding the secret of why they had been drawn together in the valley. But certain interpersonal reactions among them seemed to cause their energy to fluctuate, also causing their contact with the Afterlife to be sporadic. They had begun to glimpse that they had been together in other lifetimes with other purposes to achieve as a group, and failed.

"Charlene's smile told me she had remembered.

" 'We've remembered most of what happened,' I said. 'But so far we haven't been able to recall how we planned to do it differently this time. Can you remember?'

"Charlene shook her head. 'Only parts of it. I know we have to identify our unconscious feelings toward one another before we can go on.' She looked into my eyes and paused. 'This is all part

Everyone—including businessmen—needs time to pause, to stop. Perhaps businessmen could practice telephone meditation. Every time the telephone rings, they breathe in and out in order to establish peace within, using the telephone ring like a signal to come back to themselves.

If the person who called has something very important to tell you, she will not hang up after the first two rings. When it rings for the third time, you can pick up the telephone. And now you are much more calm, and that is not only good for you but also good for the person who is calling. That is just one way to practice peace. **Thich Nhat Hanh, *Inquiring Mind***

of the Tenth Insight . . . only it hasn't been written down anywhere yet. It's coming in intuitively.' . . .

" 'Part of the Tenth is an extension of the Eighth. Only a group that's operating fully in the Eighth Insight can accomplish this kind of higher clearing.' "[4]

The Eighth Insight in *The Celestine Prophecy* emphasizes that we have the power to uplift others by seeing them with love, creating the loving vibration that releases their higher wisdom. Many of us have found that we can do this quite well with some people. However, in other situations, we are not able to sustain, or perhaps not even achieve, loving energy with someone. This often happens in precisely those situations that are most important, such as working with people to do a project whether it is rolling out a new product, building a freeway, or rewriting a policy manual. Why?

The evidence from many research studies on the subject of reincarnation seems to show that we tend to reincarnate with the same souls over and over again. It may very well be that you are working with one or more people with whom you have had a previous lifetime. Sound wild? Think about any especially memorable past business dealings or projects. Do you remember any strange occurrences? Did you meet in a synchronistic way? Was there an immediate feeling of pleasure or animosity? Did you learn a big lesson from the experience?

Each of us chooses various things to accomplish in our lifetime— for example, increasing our capacity for patience, independence, or trust. Those people who are interested in evolving certain occupational fields to another level will incarnate and gravitate to one another to further their chosen field. However, souls also may have chosen to pay back a debt owed to someone from previous lifetimes. In a work-related group, there may be people with whom we

> Whatever you are doing, talk about how you've been doing it. That is, put aside for a time the talk about solutions and talk instead about how it is that you have been trying to reach a solution. If meetings on the problem are getting you nowhere, talk about what your meetings are like. If you've been unsuccessful in being creative, talk about how you've been going about being creative. If you aren't communicating well, talk about how you typically communicate with each other. Dolphins talk a lot to each other *about* the process and as their reward often discover the solution *in the process*, where it was all the time. **Dudley Lynch and Paul L. Kordis, Strategy of the Dolphin**

resonate in common purpose, and some with whom we have unconscious issues. We have been attracted to a particular situation in order to work through these issues. Negative issues *will* make themselves known as conflicts, strong attractions, or strong repulsions. Therefore, sending these people loving energy may be harder, and we may feel stuck. Even though we may be angry or frustrated with our situation, the very financial exigencies that keep us there may *compel* us to deal with someone we would rather just ignore.

The group of seven in *The Tenth Insight* comes to the realization through Maya that in order to function at the highest level of resonance needed to accomplish their goal, they must bring the negative emotions among them to conscious awareness and be willing to talk it through, no matter how long it takes. Maya says, "The key is to acknowledge the emotion, to become fully conscious of the feeling, and then to share it honestly, no matter how awkward our attempts. This brings the emotion fully into present awareness and ultimately allows it to be relegated to the past, where it belongs. That's why going through the sometimes long process of saying it, discussing it, putting it on the table, clears us, so that we're able to return to a state of love, which is the highest emotion."[5]

## ACTIVE LISTENING

At this point in the novel, all the characters speak out as to how they feel about each other, checking their gut feelings to see if there is any resentment. One by one, they state their feelings as best as they can in the moment, without blame. In one instance, our intrepid adventurer becomes defensive about Charlene's comment that he was "so practical and detached," which, of course, has been the recurrent aloofness that we have seen him use as a control drama throughout *The Celestine Prophecy*. Maya comments that whenever we come back with a defensive statement to someone, the other person doesn't feel he or she has been heard. "The emotion she harbors then lingers in her mind because she continues to think of ways to make you understand, to convince you. Or it goes unconscious and then there's ill feeling that dulls the energy between you two. Either way the emotion remains a problem, getting in the way."[6] So the character admits that his being overly practical and detached had prevented him from trying to help her. Becoming honest about his less than adequate response helps him to take responsibility about these old wounds and clears the air between them. Since Charlene feels that her message has been honestly received, she no longer needs to carry around the desire to deliver it to him.

## WE ARE ALL SOULS IN GROWTH

We may judge another person at work as "difficult," "selfish," "pig-headed," or worse. What do we do? It's probably unrealistic to expect that you will say to your pigheaded boss, "You know, Frank, I have a real problem with your stubbornness, but I think that's because you were my father in a past lifetime and you never let me leave the family and marry the girl from the donkey seller's tribe in Egypt." Even if it's true!

Only you, in the present moment, can know what your heart is murmuring to you—even at your place of work. Only you can find or intuit the right action that the situation seems to require. If it doesn't work, you listen again. Trust and learning to take in the lesson of an experience or mistake is how we learned to walk, run, and dance as a child. All too often, we try to maintain a *position* in the face of over-whelming conflict (it's called covering your you-know-what). Out of fear or helplessness, when we're stuck, we will re-create more of what we don't want. Under stress we use our old methods—intimidating others, trying to make *them* wrong (Interrogator style), being aloof, or crying "poor me!"

## REACHING GROUP POTENTIAL

Please remember that we are talking here about an evolutionary proc-ess. If you rush ahead to accomplish all your clearings when your heart and mind are not fully engaged, you may feel frustrated or feel like giving up. Be gentle with yourself. If you come up against brick walls with people, let go of trying to make anything happen, but keep your ideal in mind. Relax. Remember the main points of what you are working on as you expand your consciousness: (1) realize there is a deeper level to all interactions; (2) instead of blaming yourself or oth-ers, try to look at what reasons or greater purpose brought you into this situation; (3) listen to the messages the situation is bringing you; (4) ask for help from the universal intelligence in working through differences; (5) visualize yourself being in telepathic communication with your soul group; (6) watch for synchronicities that seem to offer an unexpected direction; (7) keep your energy stabilized; and (8) visualize yourself and the other person remembering your Birth Visions.

In the novel, the light energy of the soul groups began to flicker around the group of seven, amplifying their energy. The human souls began to receive a flow of intuitive information. This is when your group is really working at an inspired level. Many work teams or collaborators have felt this synchronization, but may not have associated it with divine support!

Maya explains that relationships will not find their full flower until we consciously find a higher-self expression in everyone we meet. It's an ongoing process, and one that we may not be adept at every time, but the growth for each of us is in the commitment to keep holding our ideal. Even if we don't always feel we are making headway, we are still contributing to the critical mass needed to shift consciousness in all aspects of culture. Maya reminds us, "All great teachers have always sent this kind of energy toward their students. . . . But the effect is even greater with groups who interact this way with every member, because as each person sends the others energy, all of the members rise to a new level of wisdom which has more energy at its disposal, and this greater energy is then sent back to everyone else in what becomes an amplification effect."[7]

## BIRTH VISION

In the novel, Curtis realizes that his original Birth Vision involved working to transform the way business is done. He had chosen to be born when the technological field is moving in full force toward its destined planetary purpose—the first step of which is to unify the consciousness of humanity to recognize its brother-and-sisterhood, and its unity with the One Force of God. Curtis was part of a soul group that wanted to shift the tunnel vision of commercial growth that exploits natural resources for short-term gain. His Vision included being part of a more aware and concerned citizenry that would *take responsibility* for the protection of wildlife and resources, rather than fighting pro or con for the role of government. Think about the leaders and ordinary businesspeople who have already been able to make major differences in corporate policy. True democratic process, the foundation of spirituality, gives all of us the opportunity to make our voices heard wherever life has stationed us.

## ANOTHER FORM OF POLARIZATION

Interestingly, political scientist, Benjamin R. Barber, a Rutgers University professor, writes about the threat he sees to the democratic process in the current polarization between religious positioning and commercial colonialism. In his book *Jihad vs. McWorld*, Barber describes the forces of fundamentalist, retro-thinking, tribal provincialism (jihad) intersecting with "onrushing economic, technological, and ecological forces that demand integration and uniformity and that mesmerize peoples everywhere with fast music, fast computers, and fast food—pressing nations into one homogenous global theme park, tied together by communications, information, entertainment, and commerce." Barber raises the concern that at both extremes of the polarization is the indifference to and suspension of civil liberty. The rush to erode national borders to create markets creates a new global culture of transnational banks, trade associations, news services, and lobbies and bypasses the actual people whose lives are affected by these decisions which have eliminated the democratic process.

"Markets are not designed to do the things democratic communities can do. They allow us as

> True Democracy is as yet unknown; it awaits the time when an educated and enlightened public opinion will bring it to power; towards that spiritual event, mankind is hastening." Alice A. Bailey, *The Rays and the Initiation*

> Even though history may be on the side of the cynics, and their wounds are real, they can choose to have faith in the face of that experience. This is the invitation we make to them. We need to affirm their version of history and support them in their doubts. We replace coercion and persuasion with invitation.
>
> At the same time we need to affirm the choice we have made. We choose stewardship and strive for political reform in the face of our own wounds filled with our own doubts. We say to the cynics, "I understand what you say. The doubts and perhaps bitterness you express I, in some ways, share. I, though, have decided to have faith that this time we can do something here that will matter, and I hope you will make the same choice and join in the effort." This will not be persuasive, it will not change their position. What it does is neutralize the power they have over the community. They have a right to their own stance, they do not have a right to hold back others from investing. Peter Block, *Stewardship: Choosing Service Over Self-Interest*

consumers to tell producers what we want, but prevent us from speaking about the social consequences of our choices. As a consumer, I may want a car that goes 130 mph, but as a citizen I may vote for a reasonable speed limit that will conserve gasoline and secure safe streets. As a consumer I may pay to see violence-saturated Hollywood thrillers and listen to misogynist, woman-hating rap lyrics, but as a citizen I may demand warning-labels that help us and our children make prudent moral judgments. The point is markets preclude 'We' thinking and 'We' action. Markets are also contractual rather than communitarian. They offer durable goods and fleeting dreams but not a common identity or a collective membership, and so they can open the way to more savage and undemocratic forms of identity, like tribalism [jihad in all its forms]. If we cannot secure democratic communities to express our need for belonging, undemocratic communities will quickly offer themselves to us."[8]

So we see that these two poles exist in dynamic tension, each in some sense creating the need for the other. Conservative jihad mentality seeks to preserve tribal identity no matter the cost in a time when commercial globalization is putting corporate identities such as Nike on feet around the globe and KFC in stomachs across the planet. Neither position makes room for what Barber calls a "civil voice," the voice of the democratic process. Outside of our national duties of voting and paying taxes, and beyond our working life, we also attend church or synagogue, perform community service, participate in the PTA, and become involved in other social movements that are needed to give expression to our spirit. When we lie awake contemplating our future, wondering which way the world might go, we must remember that it is still our heart, mind, and soul—our civil voice—that more than likely expresses our individual Birth Vision and creates the World Vision. Traditional business asks us to check this voice at our office door—to split off those values that are "personal," that make us who we are—and to buckle our seat belt of compliance.

## DOWNLOADING THE INFORMATION AGE

In *The Tenth Insight*, Maya asks a question many of us might ask, "What about all the displaced workers who are losing their jobs as more of the economy is automated? How can they survive?"[9] Curtis, working with the group energy, brings through some ideas about this from his soul group. He reminds us that we live in an information age.

As we each tune into our intuition, and live more synchronistically, we will get the information we need at just the right time. This is why it will be very important to have learned to work through our Fear, to hold to the positive World Vision so that we can live with the inevitable uncertainty of these changing times. He informs us that we must learn to self-educate in a niche that suits our talents and interests, so that we can be in the right place at the right time to give service or advice. Choosing a field that you are naturally interested in raises your vibration, of course, and opens up the flow of energy to your doorstep. Meditation is our link to higher mind and wisdom.

The Tenth Insight also reminds us that the more quickly the world changes, the more we need information from just the right person arriving in our lives at just the right time.

### The Natural Step Checklist

Dr. Robèrt notes that none of us has the capacity, in making daily decisions on everyday issues, to take in their implications for the whole living system. We therefore need a checklist, which he calls "four non-negotiable system conditions" necessary to sustain life.

1. Nature cannot "take" (i.e., withstand) a systematic buildup of dispersed matter mined from the earth's crust (e.g., minerals, oil, etc.).
2. Nature cannot take a systematic buildup of persistent compounds made by man (e.g., PCBs, etc.).
3. Nature cannot take a systematic deterioration of its capacity for renewal (e.g., harvesting fish faster than they can replenish, converting fertile land to desert or asphalt, etc.).
4. Therefore, if we want life to go on, we must be (a) efficient in our use of resources and (b) just—in the sense of promoting justice—because ignoring poverty will lead the poor, for short-term survival, to destroy resources that we all need for long-term survival (e.g., the rainforests). Walt Hays, "The Natural Step: What One Person Can Do," in *Timeline*, Foundation for Global Community

In order to create the World Vision that we originally wanted, the purposes of business will shift as individuals shift, one by one, moving toward critical mass (15 percent?). Instead of asking, What can I do to make the most money? our new questions will be along the lines of: Is what I'm doing going to add to my life and make the world a better place? Am I going to heal or wound with this new choice? Is there a better way to do this that will be in alignment with right use of resources, honest profit, and the good of the whole?

## THE NATURAL STEP

The foregoing questions must have prompted the inspiration of Dr. Karl-Henrik Robèrt of Sweden. Walt Hays reports on an exciting new development in *Timeline*, the newsletter for the Foundation for Global Community. In an article entitled "The Natural Step: What One Person Can Do," the Foundation cosponsored an "interactive public event" with Dr. Robèrt, founder of *Det Naturliga Steget* (The Natural Step) in Sweden. In 1988, Dr. Robèrt was head of the leading cancer research institute in Sweden. "Working on a daily basis with human cells, he took in two basic facts at the gut level—that the conditions for life in cells are 'nonnegotiable' and that in virtually all respects the cells of plants, animals, and humans are identical."[10] Reflecting with a good deal of frustration on how scientists tended to quibble about the peripheral issues of how the environment is being destroyed, Dr. Robèrt began to look at how the larger issues of life mirrored the conditions of a cell. He began to "daydream" for several months about sidestepping the walls of complexity and seeking fundamental areas of agreement. "Finally, determined to take some action even if it meant 'dashing his head against a wall,' he wrote a paper on the basic conditions for a sustainable human society." After soliciting comments from colleagues (through twenty-one drafts), his dream was to send this paper to every household and school in Sweden.

After a long series of meetings with educational groups, politicians, and media and corporate leaders, he came up with a checklist, a series of simple guidelines, which he calls "the four system conditions." These, he explains in presentations to corporations, are nonnegotiable for sustaining life.

His initiative has so far established seventeen networks of various professionals for the envi-

### Questions to Ask

1. Does your organization systematically decrease its economic dependence on underground metals, fuels, and other minerals?
2. Does your organization systematically decrease its economic dependence on persistent unnatural substances?
3. Does your organization systematically decrease its economic dependence on activities that encroach on productive parts of nature, e.g., overfishing?
4. Does your organization systematically decrease its economic dependence on using an unnecessarily large amount of resources in relation to added human value?

*natstep@2nature.org*

ronment comprising 8,000 people, and has sponsored an interactive television broadcast to 150,000 youth. Leading industries have begun to implement his four conditions of sustainability and are educating their employees. Obviously, here is a man who "daydreamed" his Vision, who went to the heart of the matter with new information that cuts through "the impossible."

How did he do it? First he had a vision and he followed through with the search for the nonnegotiable conditions. He asked for support from like-minded people and kept holding his ideal of disseminating the information to the largest possible group. He attracted others with his enthusiasm and clarity. He used the language of business in helping companies understand the benefit to them if they made changes that ultimately affected their environmental impact. Instead of a plea to save the environment, he asked them to look at such issues as efficiency, resource use, productivity, and long-range gain. Consultants for the Natural Step process talk about "investing for the future." Instead of telling people how to run their businesses with these new guidelines, they affirm that "the company leaders know best how to apply them to their businesses."[11] They trust that the intuition and creativity needed for the specific situation will come through the higher wisdom of those concerned. The model focuses on the main conditions of sustainability without which the company will surely be at risk over time, so the model uses enlightened self-interest as a motivator instead of blame, regulation, or penalty.

Secondly, in the face of strong opposition, the Natural Step consultants don't fight it. Instead they ask for advice on how to make their statement clearer and more to the point. "According to Dr. Robèrt, that request almost always leads to a constructive contribution and a better product—either because the proposed draft was wrong and needed to be corrected; or it was correct but unclear and therefore misunderstood; or . . . in some cases, it was opposed because the *input of a particular person had not been sought*" (emphasis added). In about 10 percent of the cases, the opponent remains opposed, and in those cases Dr. Robèrt advises moving on, since *scientists agree that only 15 percent of a population need to be convinced to achieve a paradigm shift*" (emphasis added).

A branch of the Natural Step has just been opened in Sausalito, California. We spoke with education director Steve Goldfinger, who said that requests from businesses for training are already exceeding their capacity. According to Goldfinger, "Business is responding because they can see that this program ultimately helps reduce risk for them in certain areas that ultimately are good for the environment. We don't try to tell them how to run their businesses, but it's amazing how the amount of creativity goes way beyond what we might expect. The Natural Step seems to have struck a chord."

Dr. Robèrt's impact on corporations shows us how a new code of ethics can actually contribute to a healthier bottom line—as well as be the right thing to do. Ultimately, with enough information about what the consequences of their present choices are, companies would be foolish not to anticipate the future. Even though the choice to make changes may not stem from pure altruism, a new vision can nevertheless come about. Interestingly, Dr. Robèrt is a cancer special-ist, not a businessman, and yet he came up with this crucial and prac-tical vision for helping business self-monitor for environmental damage. This new business ethic echoes the Tenth Insight's message that "we have to come awake wherever we are and ask, 'What are we creating and does it consciously serve the overall purpose for which technology was invented in the first place: to make everyday subsis-tence easier, so that the prevailing orientation of life can shift from mere survival and comfort to the interchange of pure spiritual infor-mation?' "12

## LOWERING PRICES

According to the Tenth Insight, another part of the new business ethic will be based on lowering prices a specified percentage as a conscious statement of where we want the economy to go. This would be the business equivalent of engaging in the Ninth Insight force of tithing.

If these ideas seem pie-in-the-sky, remember that this new ethic may not make sense at the present level of consciousness for many businesspeople. Tithing does not arise out of a greed mentality. Enough people have to grasp the Ninth and Tenth Insights, under-standing that life is a spiritual evolution, with spiritual responsibili-ties. In the present mode of increasing profits by every possible cost-cutting measure, reducing prices voluntarily so that all may benefit will be a challenge. But if Dr. Robèrt can convince corporations that it is in their best interest to switch from using toxic chemicals, who knows how the new ethic will come about? Some inspired daydreamer will, no doubt, bring it through!

"If we operate our economic life in the flow of the overall plan, we synchronistically meet all the other people who are doing the same thing, and suddenly prosperity opens up for us." If we open up and follow our intuitions and coincidences, "we'll remember more about our Birth Visions and it will become clear that we intended to make a certain contribution to the world." If we don't, we feel less magic, less alive, and "eventually we may have to look at our actions in an After-life Review."[13]

## CREATING FROM OUR WHOLE SELF

In the new worldview, we will value each person's unique qualities and be more open to seeing him or her as a soul in growth just like ourselves. By the same token, we must be willing to accept ourselves in that way, bringing our authenticity, our intuitive and rational skills, and our heartfelt values into the workplace. We must be willing to stop asking, How can I live my spiritual values in the workplace? Asking how puts us into looking for external answers, when the real answer is waiting within, the silent promise that we came to fulfill.

> For us as individuals, our purpose gets deflected from what matters to what works. The intensity of the question "How?" [to implement empowerment and participation] is an expression of our having surrendered some part of ourselves, our own struggle with purpose and destiny, by constantly kneeling at the altar of expedience.
>
> If we took responsibility for our freedom, committed ourselves to service, and had faith that our security lay within . . . we could stop asking the question "How?" We would see that we have the answer. In every case the answer to the question "How?" is "Yes." It places the location of the solution in the right place. With the questioner. **Peter Block**, *Stewardship*

## THE NEW BOTTOM LINE IS HIGHER PURPOSE

Living our purpose is more than identifying ourselves by occupation, educational class, or worldly achievements. For most of us, living our purpose means living in alignment with our head and heart, making a living joyfully by expressing our abilities and talents that help the common good. We feel rewarded by the intrinsic value of what we are doing. When we take this attitude to the workplace, we have a greater chance of feeling more centered, more creative, and more fulfilled.

## INDIVIDUAL STUDY

### Visualizing Success

When was the last time you felt really "in sync" with a group of friends or colleagues? Have you ever been involved in a humanitarian project that just flowed? How would you explain what made your project so successful or satisfying? Close your eyes and re-create the feeling you had when you felt really good about something you achieved. Immerse yourself in the sounds or smells or taste or touch of that empowering moment.

### Give It to the Unconscious

Are you working on something now that you want to bring to fruition? Think about your goal or write out the best possible outcome. Close your eyes and immerse yourself in a very specific scene in which you can taste, smell, see, and feel the success, recognition, self-esteem, and abundance that you desire. Notice as many details as you can and re-create this scene once or twice a day, preferably before going to sleep and upon awakening. Focus on it for only five minutes at the most and then let it go with the silent affirmation "This or something better." Remember, your inner world is creating your external circumstances, and you are a self-organizing being connected to universal intelligence.

### Check-In

How excited are you about your occupation? If money were no object, what kind of work would you bound out of bed in the morning to do?

### Bird in the Cage

Write a few sentences about how you see yourself as a bird in a cage with an open door. What is keeping you in your cage? Why? Where would you fly if you left the cage? Is your cage okay for now? How have you already tried to enlarge your cage? Do you need to rethink the whole idea of your cage?

### Learned Helplessness

Over the next few days, notice your language and self-talk. What expressions are you using that subtly give your power away, downplay your qualities, or indicate a perceived lack of freedom? ("I'm not good at managing." "I just want to hold on to this job until retirement." "I'd move in a second, but I've got too much seniority." "It's easy for people with degrees to talk about freedom. I have to take whatever work there is.")

### Write It Out

Notice when you get anxious and frustrated at work. Write out your feelings about the situation before or after work for twenty minutes, for five days in a row. Answer for yourself the question "What do I want?" and write it out. Then forget about it.

## GROUP STUDY

### Topics for Discussion

Any of these topics can be written about for a few minutes and then shared in the group dialogue.

- "Bird in the cage" (see writing exercise above)—discuss how you see your bird.
- Self-imposed limitations
- "If I could have it any way I want it at work, or in my business"
- Write a really great scenario of the perfect life—what you do for a living, where you live, whom you work with, how much you make, and what service or product you provide. Then work backward in time to the present moment, writing down what you would be doing just before the end goal, and then what you would be doing before that, and before that. For example, let's say your goal was to raise organic vegetables and fruits in Florida and win awards for your produce. Just before getting the award, you would have harvested some outstanding tomatoes that were growing in your greenhouse. Just before that you would have planted the tomatoes, just before that you would have selected the seeds, just before that you would have built the greenhouse, just before that you would have designed the greenhouse, just before that you would have bought

the property, just before that you would have signed the papers for the property, just before that you would have looked for property with your real estate agent, just before that you would have looked around Florida for a spot that appealed to you, just before that you would have got in your car, just before that you would have landed at the airport in Florida, just before that you would have bought your tickets in your hometown, just before that you would have decided to take a fact-finding trip, just before that you would have talked about your ideas with friends, and just before that you would be writing down your perfect life in your group where you are now. Now, life may not be that linear, but anytime you start a process you put yourself in the path of opportunity. Try this exercise with the support of the group, and have fun sharing your dreams and hearing other people's! (For more on this backward planning process, refer to *Wishcraft*, by Barbara Sher.)

- Write a list of all the jobs you have ever worked. What services, inventions, and products have you brought to the world? What has been the most important work activity in your life, including volunteer work? Don't be modest! What has been the funniest thing you ever did for money? What was the worst? Let your friends know what you have been about so far. This may work best in groups of three or four rather than a large group, but see what feels comfortable. The purpose of this topic is to simply listen and give energy to others, letting your unconscious pick up whatever is relevant. Something that is said may trigger a feeling or a thought or a possibility in you that was waiting to come forward.

- What three factors are absolutely critical for your happiness at work? Why? What three values are most important to you in your work? Why?

# CHAPTER 11

# Tenth Insight Group Action

"Do you see what's happening?" Charlene asked. "We're seeing each other as we really are, at our highest level, without the emotional projections of old fears."

THE TENTH INSIGHT:
HOLDING THE VISION[1]

WOLF
PATHFINDER

## LIKE MINDS CREATE ENERGY

Remember when Christ said, "Where two or more are gathered together, there I will be"? When we meet with even one or two or three people who are like-minded, we feel a mysterious connection. That current of energy is the divine spirit. As the Celestine Insights predicted, independent, spiritually oriented people are finding each other, maybe even for an afternoon or a few days, and are spontaneously getting together informally across the planet. We meet in conferences, workshops, playgrounds, and living rooms. We gather, and disperse, maintaining a telepathic connection through our common purpose. We read each other's newsletters, articles, and books. We are cohorts.

## WORLD SERVERS

Throughout history we have felt the impact of great minds, people of genius, and groups such as the brilliant, deeply spiritual, and esoterically educated founders of the United States, who have shifted the entire course of destiny for millions. Working with purposeful anonymity alongside these well-known figures have been other planetary workers who integrate, guide, and maintain the World Vision. One of the requirements for souls who choose to work for the upliftment of mankind is that each be able to follow his or her own spiritual mission *independently*, to be able to follow the inner wisdom and the inner personal bond to spirit without needing an external authority or organization to set the course. These people seek out teachers at times, read books, train themselves in various methods and skills, but retain a focus on world unity and simple truths rather than separatism and dogma. Spiritual beings in the Afterlife are aware of the efforts and contribution of these world servers, although the people themselves do not seek outer recognition. You know them, too, although perhaps not consciously, and have been attracted to this path yourself; otherwise you would not be reading books like this one.

Alice A. Bailey, discussing planetary evolution in the 1940s, wrote, "They [world servers] are being gathered out of every nation, but are gathered and chosen, not by the watching Hierarchy or by a Master, *but by the power of their response to the spiritual opportunity* [emphasis added] . . . they are emerging out of every group and church and party, and will therefore be truly representative. This they do, not from the pull of their own ambition and prideful schemes, but through the very selflessness of their service. They are finding their way to the top in every department of human knowledge, not because of the clamor they make about their own ideas, discoveries and theories, but because they are so inclusive in their outlook and so wide in their interpretation of truth that they see the hand of God in all happenings. . . . Their characteristics are synthesis, inclusiveness, intellectuality and fine mental development. They own to no creed, save the creed of Brotherhood, based on the one Life. They recognize no authority, save that of their own souls, and no Master

> As you become attuned to your Higher Self, you also become aware of the dimensions your Higher Self exists in. You can consciously join with the higher community of beings your Higher Self is already a part of.
>
> Part of the higher purpose of the community of higher beings is to work with the Universal Mind and Higher Will to assist life in evolving. They work continually to assist people in the awakening. . . . Every call for help is always heard. . . . Every resource is made available and nothing is spared when you ask for assistance.
>
> There is no feeling of separateness in the higher realms. All beings contribute wherever they can create the most good, just as you work together with each other to create important things in your reality. **Sanaya Roman, *Spiritual Growth***

save the group they seek to serve, and humanity whom they deeply love. They have no barriers set up around themselves, but are governed by a wide tolerance, and a sane mentality and sense of proportion. They recognize their peers and equals, and know each other when they meet and stand shoulder to shoulder with their fellow workers in the work of salvaging humanity. . . . They see their group members in all fields—political, scientific, religious, and economic—and give to them the sign of recognition and the hand of a brother."[2]

As soon as we grasp that we are not alone,

> Jung described the ideal setting of soul-work as an alchemical *vas*, a glass vessel in which all the stuff of the soul could be contained. Friendship is one such vessel, keeping the soul stuff together where it can go through its operations and processes.
>
> In times of emotional struggle, our first recourse might be to talk with friends, for we know that our most difficult material is safe with a friend, and that the friendship can hold our thoughts and feelings, no matter how painful or unusual, as we sift through them and watch them unfold.
> **Thomas Moore, *Soul Mates: Honoring the Mysteries of Love and Relationship***

and that we *do* seem to be moving toward our birth purpose, we are united to universal intelligence. What do we mean by universal intelligence? The concept of a universal mind sounds abstract until you understand that it is the underlying current of our lives. We experience divine mind directly through inner intuitions, coincidences, and usually *through the messages of other people*. At that point, says the Seventh Insight, we are in the flow. Knowing that there are cycles of "progress" and cycles of integration (plateaus) gives us support when things get tough or slow. It's all part of the flow.

### INSPIRED BY PURPOSE

Imagine that all of a sudden you knew exactly what your original intention for being born was. How would you feel? Probably, you would be excitedly envisioning where this purpose would take you, whom you would meet, what kinds of help you would need to fill in some of the blanks. *Perception at the level of the Tenth Insight is sharpened by the filter of our sense of purpose.* Inspired, we begin "to follow [our] synchronistic path into exactly the right positions within [our] culture."[3] We know when we're on the right track. Nobody has to tell us.

Have you ever gone to a fortune-teller who predicted, "You are going to meet a mysterious stranger"? Skepticism aside, of course, didn't you secretly feel a tiny bit intrigued, hoping that there *would* be a mysterious stranger, someone who would open the doors to your destiny? As much as we laugh at the fortune-teller's prediction, we actually do meet strangers, on the street, sitting next to us at a café, in the bank, on the park bench, at a rock concert, on a steamer bound for the Seychelles, and at the shoe store. Sometimes we see these mysterious world servers, even talk to them, and then they vanish.

## LINKED THROUGH COMMON PURPOSE

Linked through common purpose and telepathic communication, we will not always be in formal groups with our fellows. For example, in one of the Mount Shasta workshops Carol Adrienne co-led with therapist Donna Hale, a middle-aged woman whom we'll call Janice shared an experience. She had driven up the mountain with a friend and had stopped at one of the parking lots at a vista site. The area was deserted at that time of the year, but when she turned to look out her car window, a man was approaching. Feeling no fear or trepidation at talking with a stranger in an isolated area, Janice began listening to what the stranger was telling her. "He began to tell me that I was here with a purpose, and that I would soon be going in a different direction than what I was doing now. He told me things like how important it was not to have fear, to keep my heart open, and that certain people were probably going to move on in my life. For some reason, I thought all this was very natural, but I was amazed that he seemed to know so much about me!" Fascinating us with her story, Janice continued, "Well, my friend just sat silently at the steering wheel during this conversation. I was vaguely aware of her looking out at the view, but she said nothing until I looked back at my window, and the man had vanished into thin air. There were no bushes or cover for him to hide behind. He had simply vanished. I had tears streaming down my face, remembering the loving way he talked to me." We

> The soul requires many varieties of vessels and many kinds of spaces in order to work day by day with the raw material life serves up. Friendship is one of the most effective and precious of those containers. **Thomas Moore, Soul Mates: Honoring the Mysteries of Love and Relationship**

never know when or how our lives will be touched by miracles, but they often come through others.

## What Is a Tenth Insight Group?

When we speak of Tenth Insight groups, we are speaking about a *process* rather than a form. Many people, after reading *The Celestine Prophecy*, started study groups. However, the idea of a Tenth Insight group is not about studying the Celestine principles, although some people may want to do that. As we have mentioned, groups of souls have been born into the same time period in order *to do work together*. That work might be something large-scale such as building a health center, conserving the environment, promoting a new vision within politics or an occupational field. Or a group may form for one express purpose, such as coming together to study books, support self-help efforts, or brainstorm new solutions.

> . . . true greatness is not expressed through such activities as those of Alexander the Great, Julius Caesar, Napoleon or Hitler, but by those who see life, humanity and the world as one united whole, interrelated, cooperative and harmonized. Those who struggle for this world unity, and who educate the race in the Principles of Harmony and of right human relations, will some day be recognized as the true heroes. **Alice A. Bailey,** *The Rays and the Initiations*

The second concept behind Tenth Insight groups is that in order to accomplish their mission, these people will have to be willing and able to function more *consciously* when together and more *telepathically* when dispersed. People must be willing to educate themselves and speak the truth as they experience it, trusting that each contribution will further integrate into the World Vision. Each person will begin to naturally crave more reflection, quiet time, and meditation (the uplink to universal intelligence), since receiving insights will become more fun than some of the habits we used to pursue!

## Inspired Networking

We believe that much of the change that will occur over the next few decades will be the result of people working together, rather than isolated individuals forging ahead on their own. Have you had a desire to start a healing center? Learn Japanese? Work with children? Are you burning to get into something useful, but don't know what it is or where to start?

For practical methods to help you discover your life purpose, or start a supportive group, you might want to read Julia Cameron and Mark Bryan's book *The Artist's Way: A Spiritual Path to Higher Creativity* (which we also referenced in *The Celestine Prophecy: An Experiential Guide*) or one or more of the books by Barbara Sher. Sher's first two books, coauthored with Annie Gottlieb, *Wishcraft: How to Get What You Really Want* and *Teamworks! Building Support Groups That Guarantee Success*, and her latest book, *Live the Life You Love in Ten Easy Step-by-Step Lessons*, detail how to form your own groups to help you discover and implement your heart's desire. Their methods, designed to make networking the honest and enlivening exchange of energy and talent that it was meant to be, break down the barriers between strangers. The process of the group gets you to be precise in asking for what you want out of life and gives energetic support to move ahead on specific plans. A group acts as a feedback and accountability factor, encouraging you to follow through on what you are trying to accomplish.

> Whenever you make a phone call, run into a friend, have coffee with a colleague, tell him about your dream. Ask for ideas. **Barbara Sher and Annie Gottlieb, *Teamworks!***

These books abound with success stories of ordinary people accomplishing their dreams, publishing books, discovering latent talents, moving to foreign countries, starting new businesses, and building a community of friends. Cameron's, Bryan's, and Sher's methods raise energy, stimulate creative juices (some of the best solutions come out of the most unlikely brainstorming suggestions), and open people to flow and synchronicity.

One example in *Teamworks!* shows the power of intention and how it attracts synchronistic solutions. "The director of publicity for a university press was taking her summer vacation in Yugoslavia. She wanted to take along a Serbo-Croatian phrase book, so she could say good morning to people in their own language. A search of several bookstores and the local library turned up nothing. As a last resort, she mentioned the problem to her colleagues in the office, doubting that anyone would know where to find such a book. Within a few days, not one but two different Serbo-Croatian phrase books were on her desk.

"You may think you don't know anyone with the special knowledge you need, but you'll be amazed at what the most unlikely people come up with so: Ask everyone. Don't only ask people you think will know. Remember, experts are sometimes experts on what can't be done."[4]

Another example of how a project would never have been completed without networking came from a woman named Andrea who said, "The main thing I found was talking—just talking non-stop about the project, whenever I got a chance—people would overhear me and say, 'Oh yeah!' . . . and the most unexpected people know things. . . . I tried to make our first brochure . . . and I just couldn't do it. . . . So this friend suddenly appeared out of the woodwork and helped me with the logo . . . a directory of nursing homes was suggested by someone where I work, [someone in accounting] gave me a list of nursing homes in Florida . . . I went to the Foundation Center where you research grants, and found it really intimidating. I was sitting there with my head in my hands and books piled up around me, and someone came up who I hadn't seen in five years, who's now working as a specialist in getting grants for the arts! *That* kind of weird thing . . . it just kept happening the whole time. And I found that people really like it when you ask for their advice. Often nobody has asked them before. They're very flattered."[5]

## SERVICE AND SUPPORT

If the idea of working with others for a common purpose appeals to you but you feel confused about which activity is right for you, make an intention to be on a path of *discovery*. Ask for inspirations and examples to come to you through newspaper articles, newsletter reports, National Public Radio, or other sources. Thousands of people have seen a need and moved to address it. More often

Dolphins confer just beneath the surface before taking group action. Underwater researchers say each pod member chirps some input. **L. M. Boyd, *The Grab Bag***

than not, change is initiated from outspoken community concern, not legislative decree.

When an issue touches your everyday life, you are more likely to take action. Dr. Beverly Rubik, interviewed in *Towards a New World View*, brings to our attention one example of how an informed general public can influence governmental and scientific authorities. She cites the example of Robert Becker's research in the 1970s which demonstrated profound biological effects from weak electromagnetic fields. Becker was concerned about the risks of living near high-voltage power lines, but he could get no governmental funding, and a lot of the research was silenced by the military. Rubik says, "So he wrote several popular books on the subject that activated and aroused the general public. People began openly expressing their concerns about the increased risk of cancer to their congressmen, and research monies became available soon thereafter. When consumer groups start clamoring and making noise, then change happens. I think that's a good strategy for making a paradigm shift today," she says, "whether it's in medicine or in new energy technology."[6]

> There is a spiritual community of many high beings who work together on the inner planes.
>
> If anyone is working on a project, it is everyone's concern. There is no feeling that one must do it all alone. Sanaya Roman, *Spiritual Growth*

Another recent example of mobilized concern by consumers is the drastic change in the Rhine River, which for decades was considered the "sewer of Europe," already considered dead in 1970. A near catastrophe in 1986 killed tons of marine life and prompted a drinking water alert for 50 million people. Only then did the environment become a hot political issue. "Companies realized they had to change their behavior or face consumer boycotts that would destroy profits. . . . Recognizing that protecting the environment improves their stature with consumers, chemical companies all along the Rhine . . . donated hundreds of millions of dollars to university research centers that are pursuing new methods to protect the river. 'They all want to be considered good guys now,' says Gobillon [director of the Rhine-Meuse water agency]. 'It's quite a change from the days when companies were trying to cut costs by cheating on the environment.' "[7] These changes came about through group awareness, but not necessarily from a formalized group structure.

## LEAPS AND BOUNDS

Informal group activity is soaring. According to a recent article in the *Noetic Sciences Review*, a tremendous network of people exists around personal, local, and global concerns. The Institute of Noetic Sciences lists some 275 groups, triple in number from two years ago. "Robert Wuthnow of Princeton University suggests that four out of every ten adult Americans participate in voluntary small groups. This represents approximately 75 million people and some 3 million small groups, including Bible study groups, 12-step programs, self-help groups, and [others]. Like other commentators on the necessity for the civic voice, Wuthnow notes, 'The large number of people who are involved in small groups, the depth of their involvement, the extent of their caring for each other and the degree to which they reach out to others in the wider community . . . are a significant feature of what holds our society together.' "[8]

We called Carrie Timberlake, a registered nurse with a private practice in Jin Shin Jyutsu, in Mill Valley, California. Timberlake has been facilitating an informal group for the last four years that explores such diverse topics as Feng Shui, Eastern healing techniques, spiritual principles, earth changes, pagan sites, and dream work. She said, "One of my favorite phenomena that happen in a group is that the strength of each individual can come out. When you have a group, you almost have a separate entity. Even though we welcome the challenge of different points of view, we often have more agreement than disagreement. Being in the group helps me to affirm my own progress, and I learn so much more than I would have on my own."

> Revelations provide you with information about the greater reality you are a part of, the higher plan for humanity, and your higher purpose. Through a series of insights, you will gradually learn more about your path, your mission, and your next steps.
>
> Revelations will show you why things are happening from a higher, wiser perspective. . . . You will gradually discover the meaning of life, the purpose of the universe, and the "why" behind the "what." Each revelation will lift the veils between your dimension and the higher ones and give you more pieces of the bigger picture.
> Sanaya Roman, *Spiritual Growth*

Timberlake's group is advertised along with other community groups in the bulletin of the Institute of Noetic Sciences, a nonprofit organization founded in 1973 by astronaut Edgar Mitchell to expand knowledge of the nature and potentials of the mind and spirit and to apply that knowledge to advance health and well-being for humanity and the planet. The word "noetic" derives from the Greek word *nous* and has to do with ways of knowing. Membership has grown from 2,000 people in 1984 to over 50,000 throughout the world. If you are interested in joining with like-minded souls, see our reference at the end of the book. It's energizing just to read the personal entries of the members in the directory. Timberlake said, "The synchronicity of who shows up for which meeting is pretty amazing. Someone might come for just one meeting to see what's going on, but they will come when we have a speaker or topic that is exactly what they needed, or *they* will add something special to that meeting."

## SELF-ORGANIZING

At the heart of groups who function at the level of the Eighth and Tenth Insights is the principle of self-organization. When people come together out of genuine self-interest, willing to share their strengths and to create a shared vision, magic happens. Synchronicities abound, and doors open. Life naturally evolves out of the chaotic and disorderly, to a higher level of organization. No leader is needed when people are following their own vision and are drawn together in common interests. The vision, the intention, takes everyone where they need to go. Groups might appeal to us just at the time we need to germinate the seeds of a new intention.

> Every time you rehearse in your mind what you will say to people, you are sending energy into your future interaction with them. Often you rehearse so that you may come from a deeper and more compassionate level in your actual communication. If you can make this the goal of mental rehearsal you will find your relationships clearing up.
>
> If you you are rehearsing to protect or justify yourself or get something from another person, you will find yourself uncomfortable when you are speaking to him or her. You will have an incomplete communication, one which will lead to further energy expenditure and perhaps further struggle. **Sanaya Roman, *Personal Power Through Awareness***

According to Dee Hock, the founder of VISA International, the most powerful and creative form of social organization in today's world is what he calls the "chaordic" system, which has characteristics of both order and chaos. These types of groups, like Eighth Insight groups, are flexible and nonhierarchical. Margaret Wheatley, author of *Leadership and the New Science*, says, "A lot of great community organizing begins in informal groups. In a self-organizing world, we need to be thinking much more about localized connections among people and about letting them create solutions that stay with them. All we need to do is create the conditions so they can connect, so they can form a sense of self, a sense of purpose. Then they do the work that's right for them."[9]

Peter Senge, author of *The Fifth Discipline: The Art and Practice of the Learning Organization*, talks about the aspects of leadership beyond what we normally understand as vision, deep conviction, and commitment: ". . . the real leadership that matters is actually the leadership of groups. I believe this very strongly. The day of the 'individual' hero-leader is past, an artifact of a certain time and place. We don't need better heroes now.

> The question is how a Success Team can handle . . . issues without getting bogged down in confessions and obsessions—or straying into risky regions that require professional skill . . . empathy here gets expressed as strategy. So you listen for a few minutes, and then you ask three questions: "What do you want to do?" "What's stopping you?" and "How can we help?"
> **Barbara Sher and Annie Gottlieb, *Teamworks! Building Support Groups That Guarantee Success***

We need groups of people who can lead, groups of people who can walk ahead. That being the case, there is another aspect of leadership and that's the ability to tap and harness collective intelligence, where it's not just my insight and my vision that matters—it's our insight and our vision. It's not just my conviction that matters, it's our conviction."[10]

## STUDY CIRCLES

"Two years ago we had study circles in four cities," said Molly Barrett, project coordinator and assistant editor for the Study Circles Resource Center. "Today there are Circles in eighty cities." Established by Paul Aicher, an engineer and businessman ("We call him a visionary philanthropist," said Barrett), Study Circles are broad-based communitywide discussion groups that promote what they describe as "deliberative democracy." "We're observing that even though Study Circles don't require a consensus, people are coming to that point voluntarily. They are finding common ground even in divisive issues such as race relations. They are building community."

Barrett said that about two years ago, the mayor in Lima, Ohio, knew he had a problem—a racial problem. Even the clergy weren't talking to one another. By using the Study Circles format, the city was able to pair up congregations and involve about fifteen hundred people in dialogue. The changes that evolved from the groups were so fundamentally positive that the city went on to expand their coalition to include the police force. The Study Circles have their origin in the early Chautauqua movement when the country was trying to inform and educate a largely rural, and often illiterate, population. "In the Study Circles every voice is equal," said Barrett, "and the discussion starts out where each person is in their own life with that particular issue. For example, if the topic is educational reform, we'll suggest people talk about their own education and what they liked, or what they would have changed. You get a very diverse group of people, all ages and professions. You have a chance to hear other people's values and how they think." Interestingly, because people are coming voluntarily to these circles, there doesn't seem to be a great deal of polarization about issues as a rule. About 150 Study Circles were organized in Los Angeles after the O.J. Simpson trial to ease the tension. Since people recognized that the hour-and-a-half sessions were not enough time to address these community issues, an ongoing program is being designed. According to Barrett, the entire Ohio Department of Human Services is now doing Study Circles, and they have a two-year plan to involve everyone in brown-bag-lunch sessions. "Everyone does it a little differently," says Barrett. "It takes a little time to build trust, but some amazing things

> You will also become more aware of the effect people have on you by looking at your thoughts. Be aware of what issues you begin thinking of when you are around various people.
>
> When you are with one person you may find yourself constantly thinking of love, transformation and the beauty of the universe. When you are with another, you may find yourself thinking how hard things are, how difficult your life is, how much work you have ahead of you.
>
> Monitor your thinking when you are with people and when you spend time alone. Unless you know how you think when you are alone, you will not be able to recognize the effect other people have on your thoughts. **Sanaya Roman,** *Personal Power Through Awareness*

have happened. For example, people in Utica, New York, did a round of circles on race relations, and we weren't even really aware of what they were doing. But one day they called us to thank us for the Study Circles. They had already involved hundreds of people in the topic of race relations, and when a really difficult racial incident occurred, they knew what to do. They had already been talking to one another, and they got together with the mayor and about five hundred people, and instead of a confrontation, they had a healing."

## WHAT MAKES A CONSCIOUS GROUP SUCCESSFUL?

Have you had the experience of being in a project-oriented group and eventually dropping out because you were frustrated for one reason or another? Perhaps the problem was a person who drained the rest of the group by talking too much, being too needy, or being obstructive. Perhaps the group lacked direction and focus, and every issue was talked to death and nothing ever happened. Reasonably you might ask, If we are living our spiritual principles, how can we create a group that works harmoniously and effectively? What do we need to do, or look for?

### COMPELLING SELF-INTEREST

Being "spiritual" in a group means letting your spirit be present. The key to feeling committed to a group is your own inner *need* to be there. Unless you have a compelling enough interest, your conscious mind will begin to look for other ways to spend your time. We do what we are compelled to do—or be. For example, Francine, a publisher's rep, whose twin sister had a child with learning disabilities, created an after-school tutoring group with other children and their parents. She says, "Watching the faces of those kids when they read to me or giggle about the

> . . . I believe there is a way to imagine common ownership as a way of fostering soul. If our city leaders, for instance, lived under this vow, they would do their best to preserve public places such as parks, riverways, and lakefronts. They would know that it isn't enough to ensure people's survival, but that such simple pleasures of communal living are also essential. **Thomas Moore, Soul Mates: Honoring the Mysteries of Love and Relationship**

stories is worth every minute I put into the group. Knowing that I can help these parents, who are often tired and overwhelmed, makes me feel good about myself." Although her actions are obviously altruistic, Francine said, "I have always loved books, and ideas, and I didn't want my niece to miss anything here. I just love being immersed in problem solving." More than anything, Francine's innate drive to work with language, reading, and teaching, coupled with her love for her sister and her little niece, created her commitment to the group.

Our inborn drives show us what we are "about"—or what business it is that we are in. Look to what it is that *you* are compelled to do, whether it's gardening, remodeling, organizing, recycling, hiking, performing, making jokes, shooting baskets, talking about spiritual ideas, singing gospel songs, or shopping for bargains. Within your interest is your Birth Vision—and service waiting to be shared.

### OPEN ATTITUDE, GIVING ENERGY, AND WILLINGNESS
### TO LISTEN, LEARN, OR LEAD

In *The Tenth Insight*, the characters try to attain the attitude of complete openness and honesty. They strive to remember their own intention to serve in the world—their Birth Visions—and *they focus on what*

---

We were a strange group as we moved down the block to a small park—three white women, two white men, a black woman and 15 black boys. "What do you do about violence?" the psychologist asked me as we walked in front of 15 boys, aged eight to 18, careening down the street yelling, punching and kicking at each other. . . .

When we entered the park, I saw . . . a sprinkler watering an area of grass. Suddenly, I ran through the spray of the lawn sprinkler toward a grassy area . . . I purposely fell down; [the boys] hurled themselves on top of me. We launched ourselves at and over each other like tumblers in a circus act. In the midst of our loud play were moments of silent rest when our bodies would lie across each other like strands of spaghetti.

To my delight their house mother laughed heartily and bowled me over just like the boys. We were delighted in her laughter and energy. Then from underneath a pile of boys I motioned to Marian and Liz to join us. They crawled right in. The boys loved it. They were very physical, yet there were no punches or kicks. And they knew how to blend their play with each of the adults. **O. Fred Donaldson, Ph.D.**, *Playing by Heart: The Vision & Practice of Belonging*

---

*the Birth Vision is for each other.* They concentrate on seeing Maya in her glory—knowing who she really is—and imagine her fulfilling what she came to do. Filled with universal energy, Maya suggests that her friends "feel as if the atoms in your body are vibrating at a higher level." With the help of the positive group energy she receives, her mission becomes even clearer. Now, of course, this example comes from a novel, but the idea is still applicable in any group in which we work with others. Appreciating the progress people have made, rooting for them without feeling a need to fix them, sending them loving energy to use for their highest good are all practical ways of "being spiritual."

Tenth Insight groups will exhibit no sense of exclusivity or group ambition. They will be attuned to beauty, democratic sharing, friendliness, and cooperation. They will have no desire to impress each other or desire to recruit large numbers of members. They will meet to increase their own understanding and investigate new methods and ideas. They will familiarize themselves with each other's fields and ways of knowing. They will respond to community needs and look for ways of benefiting others without being intrusive or anti this or against that. They will seek common ground, knowing that each person is learning at his or her own pace.

Michael Chamberlain, minister of a Presbyterian church in Vincennes, Indiana, facilitates a community group that concentrates on healing. "I know that some people would rather quit a group than express their feelings if they felt another person would override their feelings," he said, "but in attitudinal healing, one of the most important things you can do is to learn to express your feelings to others, and so being able to practice that in the group is a real gift." Chamberlain feels that people come to his group because "they want to feel connected with like-minded people. People say they felt like they were lost to their family, but had found their real family in the group."

## CONSCIOUS GROUP INTERACTION

Being in a conscious group should not feel like "putting in time." You either want to be there or not. Usually, you will be looking forward to getting to the group, will make every effort to get there on time, and will feel energized and connected when you leave. Beyond being really present, no effort is made to make the group "work" or flow smoothly.

When we are on purpose—that is, doing something that feeds our soul—we are most likely in touch with our soul groups. This blending with each other initiates a kind of "entrainment" or connection with universal energy. When this happened in *The Tenth Insight*, our character cries out, "This is it! . . . We're reaching the next step; we're seeing a more complete vision of human history." At that point, they begin to see nothing less than the history of the universe. Feeling part of a much larger picture energizes us and allows us to be brilliant, selfless, and innovative, as in the stories we hear from people in extraordinary circumstances.

Michael Murphy and Rhea A. White report in their book *In the Zone: Transcendent Experiences in Sports* many examples of seemingly mystical states achieved in individual and team sports. For example, back in 1951 the New York Giants "came from behind in the closing weeks of the season to win the National League. . . . Over that period of time, many extraordinary plays were made by the team, and these were climaxed by Bobby Thompson's famous home run . . . Thomas Kiernan wrote a book about it called *The Miracle at Coogan's Bluff* . . . and throughout his book, Kiernan questions the members of the team, trying to search out the 'Question'—namely, whether or not 'some kind of extraterrestrial energy . . . took over the club and made it perform feats that were beyond its ordinary human capabilities.' "[11]

In another example of intention and focus, Murphy and White report John Brodie of the San Francisco 49ers saying, "[There are] times when an entire team will leap up a few notches. Then you feel that tremendous rush of energy across the field. . . . When you have eleven men who know each other very well and have every ounce of their attention—and intention—focused on a common goal, and all their energy flowing in the same direction, this creates a very special concentration of power. Everyone feels it. The people in the stands always feel and respond to it, whether they have a name for it or not."[12]

Nowhere is the presence of energy more felt than at events featuring people who have committed their lives to excelling. Murphy and White cite the example of Joan Benoit, who set a new American record when she ran a marathon in 2:26:11. "She felt she did not do it alone. 'I felt the energy being passed to me from the fans . . . I had to respond when I felt their collective emotion rise.' "[13] And "Boulderer John Gill hypothesized that the friendship that develops in a roped team 'may be a manufacturer as well as a transmitter of psychic energy.' "[14]

## MERGING WITH THE POWER OF SOUL GROUPS IN THE AFTERLIFE

When we are able to understand life at the level of the Tenth Insight, "we remember our Birth Visions and integrate them together as a group, [and] we *merge* the power of our relative soul groups in the other dimension, which helps us remember even more, so we finally get to the overall vision of the world."[15]

Can we do this now? You are approaching this level if you are aware that you are more than your physical body. If you have had an ecstatic communion, you are beginning to interact at more than the physical level of reality. You may be merging with your soul group in the dream state, even though you are unaware of your adventures in waking life. According to the researchers in metaphysical and paranormal fields, many of us are leaving our bodies in the sleeping state and performing work and service in other dimensions.

Telepathic messages are received instantaneously . . . I cannot tell you how to be aware of your telepathic reception of higher guidance, for it occurs outside of awareness.

Suddenly you have a new way of handling a problem, or a change in your consciousness, which is the first indication most of you have that you have received the broadcast . . . you soon find that old situations no longer trigger the emotional response they used to. . . . You begin communicating ideas to others in new and different ways. **Sanaya Roman, *Personal Power Through Awareness***

Interestingly, Ruth Montgomery, who had done so much to reveal the communications from souls in the Afterlife, seems to have been chosen precisely because she was a journalist. In her book *A Search for Truth*, she writes, "One morning, as the mysterious typing [automatic writing] continued its preachments, I dared again to ask the Guides who they were. Rather reproachfully they replied: 'This question which interests you so much is truly not important. The most that we want of you is cooperation in helping others. We were writers, and that is why we want to work through you, who are of our calling. The interest between us is such that we can work well through you if you will give this regular time each day to the joint enterprise. . . . As writers we were fantastic successes in the worldly sense, yet what we failed to do was help other people. We were too busy pouring out our torrents of words and enjoying public acclaim. We should not have been so concerned for fleeting earthly fame, but for the survival of the souls of all of us. . . . Let us impress upon you that we are all of one progression. We are as you will be, and you are as we once were—and not so long ago, at that. There is nothing which separates us now except the thin barrier of the mind. We see you as you are, but you do not yet possess the ability to see us as we are now. . . . We are eager for you to learn by our mistakes in that life; *for by aiding you we can progress*, just as you will progress by helping others in your own life. The most important thing that you will ever learn is this: *To live for self alone is to destroy one's self*."[16]

According to the Tenth Insight, our positive intentions and actions in the here and now help not only human society but the culture in the Afterlife as well. As we work together, each of our soul groups comes into closer vibration with us on Earth and we with them. We have the advantage of being able to create in the physical dimension through time, space, and mass, and the spiritual workers have the advantage of greater wisdom, prescience, and timelessness.

With Tenth Insight awareness, we intuit that humanity is coming to the point of being able to transcend the barriers between physical life and the Afterlife, which is esoterically called "lifting the veil." If consciousness is evolving in the direction of a higher frequency, we may be creating access to the whole realm of nonphysical forces and entities. Communication is already increasing, as the two dimensions open to each other. We have been getting a tremendous amount of firsthand reports of unexplainable phenomena, such as the appearance and intervention of angelic presences, near-death reports, UFO sightings or abductions, and after-death communication. In time we may be able to develop our inner capacity to become more aware of our soul groups in the nonphysical world, and pick up on their knowledge and memories.

> This is the spirit of adventure . . . leaving the bounded world in which you have been brought up . . . going beyond all that anybody knows . . . into domains of transcendence . . . and then acquiring what is missing and coming back with the boon. **Joseph Campbell**

Many of us are already aware that shamans, healers, and psychically developed people tap into metanormal realities or converse with the spiritual dimension. If a few of us can do this now, it seems logical to speculate that when enough people accept these possibilities as realities, the unified field will shift. In a few decades or tens of decades these abilities may be as accepted now as is our ability to travel in space. The Tenth Insight, therefore, suggests that when we connect to the soul groups, in the Afterlife "the groups themselves come closer into resonance with each other. That's why the Earth is the primary focus of the souls in Heaven. They can't unite on their own. Over there, many soul groups remain fragmented and out of resonance with each other because they live in an imaginary world of ideas that manifests instantly and disappears just as quickly, so reality is always arbitrary. There is no natural world, no atomic structure, as we have here, that serves as a stable platform, a background stage, that is common to all of us. We affect what happens on this stage, but ideas manifest much more slowly. . . ." Our world is built from *consensus*, and humanity must reach some *agreement* on what we want to happen in the future. ". . . this agreement, this consensus, this unity of vision on the Earth . . . also pulls the soul groups together in the Afterlife dimension. That's why the Earth dimension is deemed so important. The physical dimension is where the true unification of souls is taking place!"[17] The First Insight tells us that a critical mass of people is waking up to its spiritual destiny. The Tenth Insight says that not only are we awakening to that destiny, but that we are *still connected* to the spiritual dimension where those destinies were first born.

## INDIVIDUAL STUDY

### Go Where the Energy Is

You are already on your path, and you have the awareness and interest that will lead you to exactly the information, experience, or assistance that you need at this time. Trust that your excitement in a field of interest will attract like-minded people, books, and teachers that will open your consciousness. Your job is to spend some time each day quietly with yourself, and go where the energy is.

### Your SoulMate Cluster

Just for fun draw a big circle on a piece of paper. Around the circle, or in it, write the names of people you feel most connected to. Write down a couple of words that describe how you feel about them or what they bring to your life. You might want to even write down the year you met them. Do you see any pattern?

---
## GROUP STUDY
---

### Knowing Consciously What You're Going For

From time to time in a group, you may wish to talk about what drew you together. You might start by talking about your own reasons for being there.

- What is the *absolute best result* I could wish to have happen in this group? (Be bold.)
- If I could wave a magic wand, what would I like to accomplish with this group?
- What talent, interest, ability, feeling, can I give to this group that is unique to me?
- What is the one feeling that will keep me coming back to this group?

Be aware that there are unconscious reasons for being in the group, which may be revealed to you over time. We don't always know all the reasons that bring us together.

### Define Your Purpose—Consensually

Condense individual purposes into one sentence that expresses the unique purposes of this particular group dynamic. This may seem tricky to do in one sentence, but keep working on the group consensus about *each word*, until it feels like there is a shift in energy—more laughter, more agreement, and a sense of excitement about the words chosen to express the purpose. Try to avoid technical-sounding language and jargon that sounds like bureaucratese, such as, "The mission of our group is to participate in the spiritual evolution of our souls and manifest abundance and complete balance in every area of life." That may be what you want to do, but it's a long and ponderous statement!

The ideal is something short and full of feeling. Some groups who came together to study the nine Insights of *The Celestine Prophecy* came up with such purpose statements as: "We want to live the Mystery!" "We want to flow and go!" "We want to experience the magic of purposeful direction."

## Let Everyone Speak

- In the beginning of a meeting, let everyone have a turn to express his/her ideas and opinions without any response from the rest of the group. People who tend to be shy will appreciate knowing that they will have a turn to speak without having to compete with more dominant personalities.
- Always speak simply and from your heart—from your feelings. If you are used to quoting facts and figures and arguing points, try to refrain from using abstract concepts about what others are doing and stay with how issues affect you personally.
- Give each speaker your full attention and consciously try to see the beauty of the soul behind the person.
- Look for the truth, or the merit, in each idea that you have or that others suggest. Build on the positive germ you can find, rather than looking to tear down others' ideas. For example, if Jack says, "I think we need to rip out all the old buildings on the property and start fresh," you might respond by saying, "I like the idea of getting rid of everything we don't need anymore, *and* we might save one or two structures if they turn out to be worth renovating." This allows Jack to feel that his idea was heard, without you having to agree to tear everything down until other options have been considered. The point is to use the Seventh Insight about giving people energy so their higher-self wisdom can emerge.

## Stay Tuned with the Flow of Energy

Let the energy of your group guide your decisions large or small. For example, be willing to speak up if you feel the group energy is low and may need a short break. On larger issues, notice if the energy "gets stuck" when one person is dominating the group with overtalking, blaming, or being needy. Be willing to state your perceptions and ask for what the group feels is the next step.

## Birth Vision Practice

Some of you may have already been drawn to form a group to study the nine Insights. You may want to include the following meditation on your Birth Visions in your study. You may devote the whole meeting to this meditation exercise or do one or two individuals per meeting. The purpose of this exercise is to come together, raise your vibration as a group, and tune into one person at a time to see what information you might bring through about that person's Birth Vision.

This exercise can be done for each person one or more times over a period of weeks or months. Even though some people in your group may be relatively unknown to you, you will still be able to pick up images and intuitions about them that may indicate talents, interests, or future directions.

It's a good idea before doing the meditation the first time to have your group write a short statement of purpose to be read at the beginning of each person's Vision "quest." For example, your purpose statement might be something like, "We are now coming together in the circle to love and honor Julie. We ask that our higher selves be present with the higher self of Julie, that we may come to know and understand her greater purpose and Birth Vision for this lifetime. We ask that only positive energy helpful to her growth come through. Let the meditation begin."

Realize, too, that the entire plan for any one life is probably unknowable.

### Birth Vision Meditation

- Everyone should have paper and pen.
- Sit in a circle. Circles are the traditional symbol of shared energy and wholeness.
- Create a sacred feeling by dimming lights, using incense, and putting natural objects representing earth, air, fire, and water in the center of your circle.
- Use a special sound to signify the beginning of the meditation, such as a drum, Tibetan bells, or a few minutes of meditation music. Ritual helps signal the unconscious to open.
- One of your members will read the statement of purpose for this meditation (see above).
- Decide how many minutes of silence you wish to focus on the person, and assign someone to watch the time and quietly alert the group when the time is up.
- One person volunteers to be "it," and sits with eyes closed or open (whichever is more comfortable), feet flat on the floor, and hands resting on knees or in lap (but not crossed).
- Everyone focuses in silence on the person. Feel loving energy coming through you and filling the space between you and the person.

- Imagine raising the vibration of your cells to a higher level. Stabilize that loving feeling for a few seconds.
- Notice any images that arise in your mind. Begin to jot down anything and everything that comes into your mind about the person. Focus as much as you can on the *positive qualities* you see in the person, any scenes that you see, and write them all down without judging the "accuracy" of what you are getting. If you don't get visual images, write down the kinds of feelings you get from the person. Single words or phrases are fine.
- When the time is up, everyone can then take turns going around the circle and reading or talking about the information they received.
- (Optional) After the silent meditation, you may want to have a period of two or three minutes when everyone calls out spontaneously all the positive qualities they see in the person, letting someone write down everything that is said. After this, people can take turns reading or talking about what they also received in the silent focus.
- When everyone has had a chance to contribute, the person who is "it" gives his or her feedback about what she/he received and thanks the group.
- Continue around the group until the energy feels like it is time to stop.
- Decide how you would like to close the exercise—with a short period of silence, a prayer of thanks for what has been received, and the closing sound of a drum, bell, or group clap.

### Brainstorming Party for Getting Started on Goals or Solving Problems

This exercise is adapted from *Teamworks! Building Support Groups That Guarantee Success*, by Barbara Sher. We suggest you get the book to take full advantage of her work.

Invite as many imaginative and resourceful people as you can fit into your living room, and ask people to bring their friends. Sher suggests not to invite any experts in the field of your goals or problems because they will be prone to offer suggestions based on their experience, and may not be able to offer the unlimited thinking of people who have no fixed opinions about whether something will work or not. Weekend evenings or Sunday afternoons are good times to meet.

Ask people to bring food to share, as this makes everyone equal and gets people involved in a safe way. Give everyone pencils and paper and find out who wants to put out a goal or problem for brain-storming. Decide on a time limit per person and then go for it. Ask someone (not the brainstormer) to write down every idea that people come up with, no matter how "dumb" or "crazy." Go back over all the ideas and find something useful in every idea, no matter how off-the-wall it appears at first glance. Usually, if someone has been prompted to offer an idea, there is a kernel of truth in it. You can turn your brainstorming people into a weekly or biweekly group if people want to continue meeting to support each other and report progress.

Sher suggests that these parties might become a regular part of your social life. As you meet new people and gain a wide circle of acquaintances, you will have formed a talent pool of contacts that will be useful to all members.

---

### SOUL GROUPS

- The World Vision is the unification of the physical and spiritual dimension. This Vision has been the abiding thrust behind humanity's long historical journey on Earth.

- Soul groups in the Afterlife preserve the World Vision, through the millennia of Earthly evolution, resonating with those on Earth devoted to ceaseless praying.

- Unification can only be accomplished if individuals, one at a time, remember that they are here to build a critical mass of consciousness in alignment with the frequency of the spiritual dimension. If we are without attachment to egoistic ambition, we receive energy and inspiration from our soul groups.

- Certain unfoldments had to take place on Earth—such as the development of critical thinking *along with* the intuitive trust in the mystery of life.

- A spiritual awakening is currently happening all over the planet, in spite of outward appearances.

- Each of us has a piece of the complete Vision.

- When we share what we know and unify our soul groups, we're ready to bring the whole picture into consciousness.

- The time now is critical for the completion of the work.

### CLEARING

If someone's behavior is causing a problem in the group, you may find that this is an opportunity to learn something about yourself. Clearing must come out of a deep sense of commitment to each other's well-being, and not be an excuse to bash someone. If someone has been courageous enough to call the behavior out into the open, you may decide to ask everyone to do some writing individually on the following questions. Decide the best, and most compassionate, way to handle your dialogue or discussion. Ask yourself, how might a council of wise beings handle this situation?

- What do I want for myself in this situation?
- What traits or behaviors in this person do I recognize in myself?
- What images or intuitions am I receiving about my relationship to this person?
- What feelings do I have in my body about this person?
- How could things be better for me in this group?
- Am I willing to say how I feel when the other person is "disturbing me" or the group?
- What might be the higher purpose that this person is trying to express in his or her life?
- What might be the lesson that this person is teaching the whole group?
- Can I feel the love behind the fear or anger in this situation?

As in any venture, one has to show up, be present, tell the truth from the heart, and let go of trying to control what happens next.

# CHAPTER 12

# New Visions for Occupational Groups

BEAVER
COMMUNITY

The result of the projected energy would be an unprecedented wave of awakening and remembrance and co-operation and personal involvement, and a virtual explosion of newly inspired individuals, all of whom would begin to fully recall their Birth Visions and follow their synchronistic path into exactly the right positions within their culture.

THE TENTH INSIGHT:
HOLDING THE VISION[1]

## MOVING TOWARD IDEAL EXPRESSION AND DESTINY

One by one each of you is waking up to the fact that the *restlessness or conflict* you may be experiencing is the *discrepancy between what matters to you and what you experience externally.* As we were writing this chapter, a friend, A.T., called one morning. "I just had to stop what I would doing at the computer and call you!" she said. Earlier in the week, we had been discussing how she was expanding her consulting practice. Suddenly, A.T. was having some "inspirations" that just couldn't wait. "You know, I've been beating myself up because the phone hasn't been ringing much this month. I'm doing really great over at X, but nothing is coming out of Y! I've been so frustrated, and I keep thinking I'm doing something wrong. This one company who is supposed to be booking clients for me is not sending me anybody. The other one is going great guns." We talked briefly, and then she said, "You know, this is really about vision, not about me. Company Y is very limited in the way they think. They don't really get what I'm all about, and so they're not promoting the service. The people at X, though, are giving me a whole page in their brochure."

During this time of transition, people who are operating from the new worldview will inevitably have to be creative and flexible as they initiate new projects in the face of old ways of thinking. In the last few years, A.T., like many of you, has been struggling, at the external level, to establish her new business and at the same time educating people about its value. At the internal level, she has been meditating more, exploring spiritual ideas with friends, and exercising in order to give herself some balance and time alone. She has also been choosing to stay in a small community for the sake of her children, instead of living in a large city which might have given her more access to clients. She feels it's important to spend as much time as she can outside, at the park with the kids, or taking them to the ocean.

A high-energy person with creative ideas flooding through her at three in the morning, she says, "There's so much information coming in! There's so much I feel out of control about that sometimes the only thing that saves my sanity is knowing that there's a purpose somewhere in all of this, and I just try to find it. When I let go, I see the messages. *Everything that is coming in to me is information. It's just all messages.*" A.T. finished our conversation by realizing that she was going to have to let go of her association with Company Y because it felt fruitless to continue if they were not on her same wavelength in terms of service. "I've been hanging on, thinking that I needed the little bit they give me. But you know, I've always known that when you let go of what's not working, you make room for the next thing."

A.T. was unaware that her "interruption" that morning to our writing schedule provided a good example of the issues in this chapter. She represents a sentiment that many of us have voiced and that is important to recognize as we participate in the changing forms of various occupational fields.

Both the Ninth and Tenth Insights have indicated that as people awaken to their spiritual destinies, they can't help but change the way things are done in the world. We might imagine that all occupational fields are a sea of energy, each field being a particular matrix of human intention. The evolution of occupational groups happens through three levels: the personal, the professional, and the cosmic level.

## PERSONAL LEVEL

The search for a better way to work is an innate drive for those people who are natural leaders, inventors, and pioneers. Self-motivated and enthusiastic, they are natural revolutionaries and reformers. Ultimately, every change comes from a person following his or her intuitive hunch and taking the risk to be different.

The search for meaning is becoming so prevalent in our culture that even market researchers are picking it up as *the* trend for the 1990s. The connection to what matters to us—whether it's a new way of treating drug addiction, improving vaccination for children, preserving indigenous cultures and spiritual practices, reducing herbicides in public parks, zero population growth, or any other cause that benefits the whole of humanity—is revitalizing every field. It's a personal thing. Nobody makes us do it. True, there are more regulations about public issues than ever before, but the primary thrust for change comes from a concerned and dedicated human being.

Very closely allied to the intuition is the faculty of imagination . . . our power of forming mental images upon which we dwell . . . form a nucleus which, on its own plane, calls into action the universal Law of Attraction, thus giving rise to the principle of Growth.

The relation of the intuition to the imagination is that the intuition grasps an idea from the Great Universal Mind, in which all things subsist as potentials, and presents it to the imagination in its essence rather than in a definite form, and then our image-building faculty gives it a clear and definite form which it presents before the mental vision, and which we then vivify by letting our thought dwell upon it, thus infusing our own personality into it, and so providing that personal element through which the specific action of the universal law relative to the particular individual always takes place. T. Troward, *The Edinburgh Lectures on Mental Science*

What if your child went to a school where she learned to garden and experience the cycles of life from seed to table? What if she learned math and science by participating in the restoration of an environmentally damaged creek? If she came home from school feeling that she was an important part of her family and her community, that she had been truly heard, she would feel that she had done something today that mattered. She would wake up full of energy each day, excited about learning, and knowing that she belonged in the world and had an important part to play. That she had a future. Your daughter would be a very different person at the age of twenty-one than if she had been raised on synthetic food and television, required to put in "seat time" in a concrete building surrounded by asphalt from eight to three, five days a week, worse yet warehoused on city streets with other idle friends during her important years of individuation.

New forms of education, to name only one occupational field, are already beginning to arise to meet the challenges of providing these kinds of growing experiences for healthy, active, open minds. The truly exciting part of the Tenth Insight is that these ideas are becoming realities by people who have a vision—not of utopia, but of what is possible. But, in each case, the ideas come from inside out.

## PROFESSIONAL LEVEL

What if each occupational group began to consciously shift its customary practice toward one that consciously considered its *relation to the rest of life* and its *impact on future resources* and fostered *mutual learning between practitioners and clients*?

What if your lawyer was able to represent you during your divorce or dispute *and* help catalyze a deeper understanding of the circumstances that resulted in the divorce or dispute and help you heal that?

What if your medical team's approach included an examination of some of the mental, emotional, and economic conditions that surround your state of dis-ease, and was flexible enough to provide appropriate care from a *range* of allopathic and complementary health practitioners from acupuncturists to psychic and spiritual healers?

You may be snorting with disbelief and hooting with hilarity at the absurdity that any of these ideas might actually happen, but they *are* already coming alive through the efforts of small groups of people in many far-flung places, too numerous to name here.

In each instance, the practitioner or organizer is a *person* who has a strong belief in helping others and who brings a larger perspective to the problems. She is persevering not because it's trendy or easy or even hugely rewarding financially, but because it feels right. It matters to her to express her principles in life. The personal motivation to serve is an integral part of the worldview—*is* the transformation of consciousness. Our worldview is changed by people who want to make a difference, and get *intrinsic* satisfaction from what they do, even though they may go to bed tired, frustrated, and very discouraged at times. A shift toward *recognizing* and *remembering* the spiritual foundation of life will never be accomplished by someone *enforcing* a new code of ethics.

## COSMIC PLAN

Occupational groups are not haphazard. According to esoteric teaching, there are seven groups whose mission it is to develop specific states of consciousness in humanity. In the past four hundred years, humanity has had to develop a strong mental quality to balance the earlier, more instinct-based and sentimentally based qualities of perception. Scientific inquiry brought method, structure, and integration, and strengthened the investigative channels. It gave us a greater understanding of the world of form, humanity's part of the task in the unification of both dimensions.

Along with new information about the structure of life, we "identified" (or created?) a variety of enemies and perils. Vicariously, through radio, TV, magazines, and newspapers, we psychically share and almost physically take part in the realities of other people's calamities. In response to all these "facts," we developed whole industries for managing fear: weapons, drug companies, mega-entertainment companies, insurance companies, security and advertising companies. We divided up the world and decided what we liked and what we didn't like.

### INTEGRATION AND SYNTHESIS

Until now, forward thinkers have been, almost inadvertently, shaping the emerging worldview in whatever group they have chosen. Many of us have been working without realizing the greater purpose for our work. Only in the last couple of decades have we been able to see the network that connects us to other world servers. The next step, now, is to become aware of our interrelatedness and consciously dialogue about putting some of our work together.

*We are now moving into place to make our evolution more conscious. We have already begun to understand the power we have in using intuition and focused intention. These ideas are flowing*

> . . . we must remember that development is always by perfectly natural growth and is not brought about by unduly straining any portion of the system.
>
> . . . the intuition works most freely in that direction in which we most habitually concentrate our thought; and in practice it will be found that the best way to cultivate the intuition . . . is to meditate upon the abstract principles of that particular class of subjects rather than only to consider particular cases.
>
> . . . you will find that the clear grasp of abstract principles in any direction has a wonderfully quickening effect upon the intuition in that particular direction. T. Troward, *The Edinburgh Lectures on Mental Science*

effortlessly around the globe throughout the collective mind/body. It's interesting that our language now reflects this weaving idea in such words as flow, networking, holism, synergy, alliances, partnerships, circles and centers, and the World Wide Web.

What soul group do you think you belong to? What type of *activity* have you been furthering?

Cultural

*Developing* relationships
*Socializing* and *civilizing*
*Providing* humanitarian relief
*Inspiring* humanity through art, music, dance, poetry, and literature
*Expanding* through education, photography, film
*Disseminating* through media, travel, and communication
*Regulating* through laws and advocacy

Philosophical

*Theorizing* about the nature of reality
*Separating* and *comparing* ideas, cultures, history, and the future

Political

*Revolutionizing* and *reforming* nations
*Building* and *stabilizing*
*Separating* and *defending* cultures and borders
*Expanding* intercommunications
*Mobilizing* resources
*Elevating* issues (pro and con) of human rights to public awareness

Religious

*Preserving* the mystery
*Structuring* the mystery
*Converting* and *protesting*
*Providing* community
*Separating* community
*Anchoring* the spirit
*Providing* support and cohesion in times of turmoil
*Creating* times of turmoil
Ceaseless *praying*

Scientific

*Developing* external expertise
*Promoting* mass communication and interrelatedness
*Creating* analysis and standards
*Correlating* and *synthesizing*

> *Exploring* the limits of everything, including objectivity
>
> *Enforcing* military agendas

Psychological   *Developing* internal expertise
*Completing* past issues
*Freeing* blockages
*Enhancing* the quality of life
*Promoting* communication and sensitivity
*Understanding* and *modifying* behavior

Financial   *Controlling* and *ordering* commercial intercourse
*Expanding* and *implementing*
*Building* and *connecting*
*Consuming* resources and *providing* goods and services
*Creating* international alliances and bridges

## Conducting a Symphony of Lemons and Light Beings

Each group, of course, is capable of producing from the positive or negative *extremes* of its area of influence. In what way have you been negatively affected by one of the seven soul groups? How have you or the culture at large been impacted so far by two or more of these groups combining information, talents, and influence?

In the old order of thinking, these groups tended to work in an individualist, separatist, isolated mode. In the new way of thinking, each group must now come together in a sort of "united disciplines" metaphor to integrate their advances for the benefit of the whole of humanity. Each group has a piece of the truth. Without neglecting any parts, nations, cultures, languages, species, or religions, the work of these groups will be to *support*

> The real problem of the Third World is ignorance . . . the people . . . have to be educated. And it has to be done energetically, without any sentimental reticence. It's an immediate necessity, it's an emergency. They have to be told, despite all the misunderstandings it may involve: you're on the wrong track, your demographic growth is much too large, it's leading you to even more terrible poverty. . . . We have to fight this growing gap. That ought to be our goal. Bringing the two worlds close enough to make them comparable, and if possible equal. Yes, that should be our goal. **The Dalai Lama in** *Violence and Compassion,* **by Jean-Claude Carrière**

*each part to contribute its necessary influence to the whole.* The goal now is to harvest the inherent values of each part to nourish the whole. How do we harmonize our bands of influence and lessen the ambition for further separation and the creation of further structures? What would cause or force us to do that?

Well, what about concern for the environment, fear of nuclear holocaust, worldwide famine, overpopulation, disease, concern for human rights, natural disasters, and self-interest? These powerful forces in the world whose impact is considered horrible, unthinkable, unpleasant, bothersome, and *time-related* can either polarize us or unite us to begin to bridge the gap created by greed and fear. Maybe we are at the lemonade-stand level of worldview—if all you've got is lemons, make lemonade. If what we face seems out of control, let's work with the foundation that says, we all have to pull together this time. The unification of the world spheres—material and spiritual—is the same thing as unifying our world by compassion, love, friendship, tolerance, and holding out a hand to someone who needs our help. If people like Dr. Robèrt, working on cancer cell research in his lab in Sweden, can come up with a plan that helps businessmen all over the world reverse their impact on the environment, what else can humanity come up with?

### Résumé Requirements for Holders of the Vision

What's it take to qualify for a world server, a holder of the Vision? First on the list would be the ability to love, compassion, tolerance, and a strong desire to serve. Remember that these qualities are not abstractions that you take out of your closet and hang on yourself in order to be "spiritually correct." These are givens at the level of Tenth Insight awareness. You already have these qualities—you only need to remember to leave people in a better place than when you met them, and enjoy the flow that comes back to you.

Some of the other qualifications are:

- Desire to work intuitively
- Able to assess the truth and the messages in synchronicities and hunches, unegotistically
- Ability to think about the impact on the whole when making decisions large and small
- Highly attuned mentally, emotionally sensitive and mature, spiritually developed

- Sense of humor, and ability to laugh at oneself
- Knows that prayer works
- Prays and meditates
- Recognizes the gifts in others, and ability to uplift and inspire every-one he/she meets
- Detached from the ambitions of the ego personality
- A well-rounded individual with a variety of experiences, interests, and talents
- Physically and mentally flexible
- Good grasp of financial common sense
- Ability to turn obstacles into opportunities
- Ability to listen with more than the ears
- Inclusive, curious, and generous about sharing knowledge
- Eschews partisanship and formal affiliations
- Ability to speak the truth without a desire to control, convert, or "fix" others
- Ability to be spontaneous *and* able to work for a long time with no immediate results
- Ability to travel out of the body or tune into psychic information and discriminate about the quality of information received
- Makes decisions based on what feels congruent inside and what "matters most"

## DUTIES AND RESPONSIBILITIES FOR HOLDERS OF THE VISION

How will the holder of the Vision interact with others in order to maintain purpose? Certainly, it would be helpful to notice who starts showing up in your life now. As soon as you make the shift toward selfless action, desire to serve, and work toward the World Vision, a connection is made with the soul groups who watch over the Earthly plane. Your energy will go to a higher vibration, so you may start attracting, or being attracted to, those who are working along similar lines of intent. Spend more time with people who energize you with their ideas, and allow relationships to evolve as they will without try-ing to force or hold on to anyone. Work for what you believe in, but don't waste your time in attacking others or in showy forms of rheto-ric and arguments. We must be careful not to impose our ideas on anyone. Judging the "level of development" in others indicates a lack of understanding about the wide range of lessons for human souls. It's important to avoid being critical of others, even when you think their ideas are working against your own. It's more important to work toward finding common ground with people and *being* the type of person you would like to know yourself.

Part of the work now is to start gathering together the people you resonate with and introducing them to others and fostering community support and sharing of ideas. Slow down in your life, so that you have more time for reflection away from your occupation. Begin to ask for new ideas to come to you about how you might start doing something different in your work that would be an upgrade in terms of efficiency; positive human connections; fun; studying new ideas; looking at an old problem from a different viewpoint (ask a child how to do it!).

## IF YOU DON'T LIKE THE JOB YOU HAVE

If you don't like the job that you have now, step up your intention to understand the purpose of being here. Put more love and attention into the job and people you work with, *while you are there*. You may find that you naturally exit the job just as you were beginning to get recharged about it! This has happened to many people we know.

## EXPANDING YOUR CONTACTS

If you want to expand your contacts with people, or if you are just starting out in a new business, don't be a loner! Organize a monthly brainstorming group if that appeals to you. Ask three friends every week for suggestions about new organizations, books, lectures, and workshops. Classes in every kind of new field of knowledge are available in community colleges and programs such as the Learning Annex in San Francisco, Los Angeles, San Diego, New York City, and Toronto. Omega Institute in New York, Interface in Boston, and Esalen Institute are just three of the many established centers that have been holding the Vision for many years. These accessible "universities" represent the democratic and "attractive" nature of the emerging spiritual consciousness.

Keep asking the universe to open up the best direction for you. Be clear on how you want to serve other people in your work. Give something away. Always look for ways to help others, and listen to their needs and concerns at the *heart level*. They may say they want something for a lesser price, for example, but what they may really want is contact with a real person with *real* concern for their needs. Talk to them about *their* purpose in life, *their* dreams.

There is no need to feel you must recruit people or colleagues to your way of thinking. Everyone who is in the occupational groups to serve the World Vision are already in it. They know what they came to do. If you sense you know someone who really wants to work at a higher or deeper level than he or she currently is, just share your enthusiasm for your own work in a friendly, open way. There is no one to impress, no one to change. As we have said before, keep your attention on the ideal state toward which you desire to move.

---

### Applying the Law of Least Effort

Today I will accept people, situations, circumstances, and events as they occur. I will know that this moment is as it should be.

Having accepted things as they are, I will take *Responsibility* for my situation and for all those events I see as problems.

I will relinquish the need to defend my point of view. I will remain open to all points of view and not be rigidly attached to any one of them. **Deepak Chopra, M.D.,** *The Seven Spiritual Laws of Success*

---

## MODELS OF THINKING HELP US SEE THE BIG PICTURE

We are going to cover four occupational categories below. Whether or not you agree with the description, we would encourage you to use it as a springboard to reflect on the progression you see in your own field since 1965 or 1985.

In the Health section, we present four paradigms that show the progression of thinking in that one field.

In the Law section, we are describing a process that favors inclusivity, networking, and probing beneath the obvious conditions on the surface, which you might apply in some way to your own field. How? That's up to you.

In the Educational section, we describe some new formats for education that require creativity and breaking out of boundaries, more than the allocation of millions of dollars.

In the Art section, we wish to remind ourselves of the life-giving qualities of aesthetic perception that make us unique among the species. Unless dolphins have art galleries in the Bermuda Triangle!

## HEALTH

Pain and illness get our attention like nothing else. There is nowhere to run when you are not feeling well.

Patients and health-care practitioners are dancing each other toward the new field of psychospiritual/bioenergetic healing. Increasingly, an educated public is demanding guidance and support to maintain good health. The healers both lead and follow the demand.

In the past, Westerners tended to be interested in the body only when it had "broken down." With our dependence on the scientific framework, it seemed to make sense that our bodies must "work" like machines, with parts that needed repairing every now and then. With typical ingenuity, we got very good at fixing the parts, and excel at technical medicine which is absolutely essential for many of the traumas and overindulgences to which we subject ourselves.

Other hearts and minds, however, asked different questions, and found different answers, and now we have a more complete view of the visible and invisible energy states that create and maintain what we call our body, but for which we really have no adequate name. We speak now of our body/mind/spirit energy matrix—still pretty technical-sounding for the great spiritual being that we are!

The "holistic" approach is to ask, What's happening in your life? Are you eating fresh foods? How much exercise do you get every week? What's your family history? Are you happy with your work? Are you lonely? Angry? How do you feel about your parents? What happened to you when you were three? Have you recently lost a loved one? What kinds of plans are you making for the next

> The people who succeed best at any endeavor are generally following a pattern of handling their desires without undue struggle with their environment—they are in the flow . . . they allow the solution to present itself, trusting their own abilities to cope with difficult challenges. **Deepak Chopra, M.D.,** *Ageless Body, Timeless Mind*

few years? How do you feel about life? Do you meditate or pray? Do you believe in something greater than yourself? Do you paint? Dance? What kinds of community work do you do? Do you have enough vacation time every year? Are you having fun?

Through the work of millions of inspired and risk-taking individuals we have more ability to heal ourselves—physically, emotionally, financially, and spiritually—than at any other time in history. How did we get here? We got here because we were curious. We couldn't help it. The more we learned and listened to people *with all kinds of experiences, needs, and ideas,* we began to realize that our physical body is the outpicturing of our spiritual core and karmic purpose. The old mechanical view of the body didn't go far enough. It wasn't set up to include the invisible, but vital, *generative* spiritual matrix upon which our body grows. Advocates for mind/body healing such as Deepak Chopra, Larry Dossey, Christine Northrup, Bernie Siegel, Leonard Laskow, and Richard Gerber, to mention only a famous few, are part of the pioneering group that is bringing to life the new medicine and healing methods for the twenty-first century. By acknowledging and using the gifts of technology *and* of psychospiritual healing, we have enormously exciting possibilities in the field of wellness and aging. It even seems that in the not too distant future, we may even go beyond the prevention and management of disease, into a proactive exploration of how to develop superhealth, or metanormal capacities.

Interesting, isn't it, that the advent of managed care, with its financial strictures about what and how physicians, nurses, and technicians can provide services, has arisen just now? We might well ask ourselves, What could be the higher purpose behind the introduction of this contracting force of financial limitations? We are in a transitional stage

> An intention is a signal sent from you to the field, *and the result you get back from the field is the highest fulfillment that can be delivered to your particular nervous system.* **Deepak Chopra, M.D.,** *Ageless Body, Timeless Mind*

that is exploring our boundaries of what is and is not possible and/or desirable. Many people will be attracted to work out new answers in these complex arenas.

Psychology and psychiatry will also be profoundly reoriented to include knowledge of the possible energetic disruptions to the psychospiritual/bioenergetic matrix of the etheric body. Robert Monroe, the late businessman, author, and astral-naut who traveled out of body for thirty years, postulated that perhaps what we now call psychosis may be a *barrier leak* between the spiritual and physical dimensions. Frozen states of energy such as catatonia and autism, he speculated, may be a form of dissociation between the physical and second bodies.

On a macro level, exploring the intersection of our physical and nonphysical states may create whole new fields of scientific inquiry. On a micro level, thanks to the work of scientific researchers such as Candace Pert, former director of the brain biochemistry division of the National Institute of Mental Health, there may be a biological parallel of the "unified field" of consciousness. In a much-referred-to study, Dr. Pert discovered that there is a molecule in the body called a neuropeptide so small it can travel anywhere in the body, reaching every cell. Pert's question was, "What are these molecules doing?" What she found was that every cell in the body has receptors for these little neuropeptide visitors. Formerly, it was thought that these molecules were limited to the central nervous system. However, her studies show that not only can all cells of the body *receive* the messengers, they can *make* them as well. The ability of cells to communicate with each other seems to suggest that the *mind* exists in the whole body, not just in the brain. Since every emotion has a certain kind of neuropeptide profile, every time we get angry or fall in love it's reflected in our internal bodily secretions. Remember rat 2, Mr. Learned Helplessness, in Chapter 10? Neuropeptides probably carried the word around that this rat was a Poor Me!

The big questions, however, is how the body gets the information from its etheric energy body *outside* the physical body. How do we pick up psychic influences from other people across the planet? When you walk in the woods, what makes you feel that you are in sacred space? Perhaps scientists of the future will discover that the neuropeptides or similar molecules are the link between the energetic fields and the physiology of the body. Forward thinkers are now, however, coming to the conclusion that the body is more a network of information than a matter of flesh and blood.

### Form Follows Thought

Richard B. Miles, executive coordinator of the Integral Health Professional Network, has been tracking the frontiers of the health-care field since the early 1970s, promoting new thinkers and designing "integral" health-care curricula. Miles began a new career in the medical field just at the time that the cultural soul groups (hippies, flower children, peaceniks, and potheads, as they were not so affectionately called) were instigating social change. "Back in 1967 Peter Drucker wrote *Managing in the Age of Discontinuity*." Miles told us, "He was already seeing that leading thinkers in all the major disciplines were questioning the assumptions on which the disciplines were built. I had just quit a job in marketing, and after a year or so of research with my partner Jack Drach, we concluded Drucker was right. The whole playing ground was being reworked.

"The most important book at that time was *The Phenomenon of Man*, by Teilhard de Chardin. His view was that what moved life forward in biological form was not the survival of the fittest. His theory was that each exterior form has an interior form, and the organizing principle was consciousness. As life moved forward, biological life moved forward and became more complex. As it became more complex, it became more self-aware—proving that consciousness had been there all along. The more complex an organism became, the more capable it became. According to his theory, biological forms changed through consciousness, and so consciousness is designing its own future. In the scientific paradigm," said Miles, "that is an extremely radical idea.

"My partner and I became aware, through de Chardin's ideas, that all around us, the cultural consciousness was organizing itself to a different order. All disciplines were reinventing themselves." What has been the evolution of thinking in the health-care field? we asked.

"There are four paradigms for how we look at health and disease," said Miles, who has been teaching these ideas at JFK University and the California Institute of Integral Studies in San Francisco. "The first one was in operation until only about a hundred years ago. This is the *authority paradigm*, which has two subsets: (1) 'God is punishing me [by this disease]'; and (2) 'I'm possessed by evil spirits and demons.' You can still see some of this thinking in the current response to the AIDS epidemic.

> With even the slightest change of awareness, energy and information move in new patterns. The reason old habits are so destructive is that new patterns aren't allowed to spring into existence—conditioned awareness is therefore synonymous with slow dying. **Deepak Chopra, M.D., *Ageless Body, Timeless Mind***

"The second model is the *war*, or *conflict, paradigm*. This grew out of our belief in things we couldn't see. People used to talk about these unseen forces as 'miasmas.' Then with microscopes we could see the miasmas as specific organisms. That's when the disease became an enemy, and science became the hero. Our goal was to find the enemy, kill it, and solve the problem. That's been our outlook for the past eighty years or so. Actually, that model ceased being effective in 1922 because the greatest positive effect on public health was cleaning up the water, killing mosquitoes, putting food in refrigerators, and replacing kerosene lamps with electric lights. By 1944, when we started developing effective treatments through antibiotics, infectious diseases had long been on the wane.

"The third paradigm for thinking about health and disease is *pattern recognition*. This is the idea of looking at the whole pattern of the person's lifestyle and how it affects her health. It's not looking for the enemy, but at the process that's leading to the problem—like substance abuse or a stressful family system. One of the major improvements in heart disease has come about through educating people about improving their nutrition and exercising, instead of *attacking* something. That idea came up to consciousness because we shifted our focus from infectious diseases to chronic degenerative disorders. In chronic ill health, there is no enemy to kill, although you still hear people talking about the 'war on cancer' or the 'battle with diabetes' or 'the war on AIDS.' Crucial to the 'pattern' for good health, besides physical and emotional wellness, is the perception that one has a purpose for being alive, a will to live, and a perception of some degree of control over one's choices.

"The fourth paradigm is still emerging, but it is the idea of *the universe as a metaphor*. Therefore we are starting to ask ourselves, What's the *message* for me in this illness or injury? What do I need to pay attention to here?" Miles cautions, along with other medical writers such as Larry Dossey and Bernie Siegel, that it is not helpful to tell people that their disease is "their fault," or to imply that they are lacking in spirituality because they have fallen ill. While disease may stem from deeply rooted unconscious processes, or karma, according to Eastern philosophy, suggesting that someone has deliberately caused his or her illness is counterproductive and unloving.

Disease and pain *do* get our attention. We may not be too alert to our inner messages, but changes in our health stop us in our tracks. Why me? Why now? we ask fretfully. Many people have made major transformations in their worldview and values during and after an illness. "In the metaphoric universe," says Miles, "clarify your questions and the universe will answer."

The emerging beliefs about health are part of one organizing energy in the evolution of the Great Plan. Do you see a parallel between the war model and your field? Do you see changes in the way people think in your field? Is the pattern of your occupational field shifting to be more inclusive or isolationist (i.e., are there turf wars?)?

---

## WORLDVIEW FILTERS

| Health and Disease Model | Worldview |
| --- | --- |
| Authority Paradigm: Evil Spirits/ Demons | The universe is hostile. |
| War, Conflict Paradigm | The universe is random. The only thing you can do is win the war. |
| Pattern Recognition | The universe is friendly. If you can see the pattern, you can learn something. |
| Disease as metaphor. There is a purpose for everything. | The universe is integral. It's not only friendly, but it is unfolding purposefully. |

---

### NEW WORLD VISION IN THE LEGAL PROFESSION

"Every profession is evolving," says Bill Van Zyverden, the Vermont attorney who founded the International Alliance of Holistic Lawyers, with a membership of over five hundred, in forty-three states and seven countries. "If you could take a pulse of society's dissatisfaction with the legal profession and the profession's dissatisfaction with itself, you would find that it is absolutely boiling. The frequency of its vibration is *boiling*," said Van Zyverden, director of the Holistic Justice Center in Middlebury, Vermont. "As frequency increases, so does the coming of enlightenment. So I see that law is evolving toward its own enlightenment. We don't have to know what that looks like, but the existence of the International Alliance of Holistic Lawyers is a milestone that tells you the path we're on."

In the holistic medical field, the belief is that true healing only happens when we look at the roots and cause of an illness in light of the per-

I entered the cupola and told the technicians . . . that I wanted to see Saturn and a number of the galaxies. It was a great pleasure to observe with my own eyes and with the utmost clarity all the details I had only seen on photographs before.

As I looked at all that, I realized that the room had begun to fill with people, and one by one they too peeked into the telescope. I was told that these were astronomers attached to the observatory, but they had never before had the opportunity of looking directly at the objects of their investigations. **Victor Weisskopf, *The Joy of Insight***

son's whole life. Practicing law from a similar holistic standpoint makes the same kind of sense to holistic lawyers. "It's no longer enough to deal only with the legal aspects of a person's dispute," says Van Zyverden. "I believe that we have to help our clients look at the inner conflicts which have become externalized in their disputes." The new perspectives in holistic lawyering foster healing through whatever difficulty has presented itself, very much like the illness process.

### The Roots of Conflict and Personal Responsibility

Holistic lawyers try to help clients focus on what is really important to them, while dealing with all the current pain and frustrations of their situation. The philosophy that nothing has happened to us that we didn't invite for our own higher learning is, to say the least, revolutionary in the legal profession. For example, if someone is arrested for driving under the influence, the holistic lawyer not only looks at the legal consequences but may also help the person face the cause of abusive drinking and the effect that it has on himself and his work, friends, and family. Justice is more truly served, says this broad-thinking lawyer, when the person doesn't try to dodge the charges through loopholes or suppression of evidence. In the case of drunk driving, it's in the person's best interest, over the long term, to take responsibility, accept the consequences, and get counseling to help develop new behavior. The holistic approach helps the person to work out the causes and resolutions of the conflict on every level—the spiritual, mental, emotional, and financial. Holistic justice is the awareness of the past behavior, the responsible acceptance of consequences, and the personal commitment to change.

### Empathy and Civility to Adversaries

A holistic approach also acknowledges the humanity of the other person. "One of my traditional colleagues once asked me," said Van Zyverden, " 'What are you practicing, wimpy law?' and obviously there was a confrontational tone to the way he put the question. I said no, I'm 'practicing law from my heart.' I wasn't implying that other lawyers don't do that, but the traditional practice of law seems to have no emotional empathy. A dispute doesn't feel good to either side, and demonizing one's 'opponent' only creates more suffering for everybody." The holistic lawyer helps a client look for a greater healing, for his own well-being, rather than buying into the desire for revenge. "I can be passionate about someone's case," says Van Zyverden, "but I won't carry their anger."

### Client Participation and Partnership

Another shift in attitude in holistic law is that the attorney is a guide and counselor, but not an all-knowing authoritarian figure to which we give our power. A person is much more likely to be empowered when she is a participant in the legal process. Self-awareness and the opportunity to look at why she got into the conflict in the first place is much more likely to occur if, for example, she carries out the investigation and gathering of data, interviews witnesses, and reviews the options of the case. Van Zyverden feels that the idea of partnership with the client also aids the *lawyer* tremendously. "If lawyers cease to see themselves as mouthpieces, hired guns, and alter egos, they can free themselves from the painful adversary system, including stress, alcoholism, drug abuse, and suicides." The holistic approach decreases the gap between people. It fosters truer consequences and puts responsibility where it belongs—on the individual.

### Referral to Related Disciplines

Nowhere than in legal matters is it more important to look at the whole situation. We no longer can turn to the criminal justice system and penitentiaries as the only answer to serious offenses. At all levels from divorce to murder to terrorism, the new World Vision requires that we have integrative approaches to problems that affect, not just the people immediately involved, but all of us. A new vision of law will encourage a person to get help from professionals in other fields as needed, for example, arbitrators, psychiatrists and psychologists, social workers, integrated medical services, or accoun-

---

In a museum I saw a display of several sea shells that could conceivably have been the successive homes of the same animal over the course of its life. When these creatures outgrow one shell, they crawl out and spin a new one.

We, too, spin shells. They are called "belief systems." When I was ten years old, I believed that the purpose of life was to have a great collection of baseball cards . . . years later rock 'n' roll had become the purpose of life in the universe . . . later, when the *Doors* movie came out, I surprised myself by not even going to see it. I had moved into a bigger shell. **Alan Cohen, *I Had It All the Time***

tants and educators. The ideal situation will include collaborative family and community support services that provide the counseling and education to help a person become independent and productive once again.

Those people in political, cultural, and financial occupational groups will be drawn to create rehabilitative and preventive resources and solutions, instead of allocating money solely for punitive measures.

## Appropriate Dispute Resolution

In the old model of competitive win-or-lose thinking, outcomes are everything. At the soul level, outcomes are not necessarily as important as the lesson or purpose behind the whole experience.

Van Zyverden says, "I'm in favor of using whatever method is required to resolve a conflict, and sometimes that's court, sometimes not." He prefers the term "appropriate" dispute resolution to "alternative" dispute resolution because the latter gives the impression that the court is the only place to resolve disputes. "I think problems have their own unique resolution method and only the person involved knows what that method is. Sometimes all they need is an apology from the other party. Our current system places an unfair expectation on the courts as the place for ultimate resolution. Courts are just a place that imposes an end to the quarrel because the parties are unwilling to look at their own responsibility."[2]

Mariza Vazquez, founder of the Florida chapter for the International Alliance of Holistic Lawyers, says, "One of the most important things that people want is *to feel that somebody heard them*. One of Bill Van Zyverden's clients was sure she wanted to go to trial. She didn't have a very strong case, so Bill set up a mock trial for her so that she could do a run-through on her presentation. The mock jury listened to her story but they found against her. The jurors explained the weaknesses of her case to her, and she decided not to go to trial. But she came away from that experience feeling complete, because what she liked was that *she had been thoroughly heard*."

## Collaborative Law

Even though 98 percent of civil cases filed are settled prior to trial, are the parties' dispute or relationship really healed, or have the parties merely "settled" for something that still leaves rancor? In the cases where a technical interpretation of the law resolves an issue that carries little emotional attachment, judgment by a third party usually gives closure to both sides. But in most cases, there are strong emotional attachments to the issues that are not addressed by legal rulings.

Van Zyverden believes that neither the judiciary system nor traditional lawyers who channel their clients through the system is as effective at creating true resolution as are the parties themselves. In that case, the holistic lawyer needs to guide his or her clients toward self-introspection — examining their beliefs and

---

This is the path of working where you find yourself, with what is found here and now. This, then, really is it . . . this place, this relationship, this dilemma, this job.

The challenge of mindfulness is to work with the very circumstances that you find yourself in—no matter how unpleasant, how discouraging, how limited, how unending and stuck they may appear to be—and to make sure that you have done everything in your power to use their energies to transform yourself before you decide to cut your losses and move on. It is right here that the real work needs to happen. **Jon Kabat-Zinn,** *Wherever You Go There You Are*

---

expectations. "What I have found," he says, "is that the root of the problem usually lies less with the action of other people or outside events than with the clients themselves. For example, in the case of one prenuptial agreement, we talked about the pros and cons of the document . . . but it wasn't until the stories of their childhoods came up that each discovered that the dispute between them was a result of personal inner conflict spawned by the material fears of their parents. Resolution of the dispute came about, in part, by putting the views of their parents in perspective and not between them."[3] Most of the time when we have an internal conflict, we are quick to blame outside events or people.

Van Zyverden's approach was to suggest that the man and woman talk about what each brings to the marriage. Instead of coming from the negative idea of "what would happen in a divorce," he had this couple consider what each wanted to "keep forever," and why that was so important. "I saw this as an opportunity," said Bill, "for each person to get in touch with his or her fears and how these fears create a feeling of possessiveness."[4]

While arbitration has become an increasingly popular and more cost-effective method, it still operates from a polarized view of the opposing parties and does not attempt to look, as a group, to the root causes of the conflict. Collaborative law, on the other hand, is a new integrative approach that is a cooperative effort by opposing parties and their counsel to freely and openly explore the nature of the dispute between them. Without name-calling and blame, the group investigates why and how the relationship evolved the way it did. This type of group, which attempts to come to a greater understanding and resolution, is a good example of the Tenth Insight point of view. According to Van Zyverden, "This approach upholds standards of integrity and . . . does not take advantage of inconsistencies and miscalculations but rather seeks to have them corrected. The method focuses on the future rather than on the past, and on problem solving rather than on assigning blame."[5]

## An Opportunity to Grow in Consciousness

We asked Van Zyverdan how he would handle two angry partners arguing over their assets. "First of all, I have to let go of the idea that I have the answer. It's usually obvious to me that the pain between them is more about the relationship than the things they are arguing over, but usually you can't just tell that to people. They can't hear it when they're upset.

"I start by taking them through an experiential process. We discuss what they want, what they're upset about and so on, but I don't let them just give me an answer and stop there. I keep going deeper. 'What does it look like? What color is it? Does it feel like gravel or water?' Oddly enough, these questions seem very relevant as people start to *experience* whatever the issue is. When you don't have a word for something, you don't have an answer. I don't try to analyze their answers, because the intellect is not the only way to understand something."

Vazquez adds, "When a client comes in, a part of his life is not working, and I want to look at him as a whole human being instead of just taking care of the paperwork. The person is facing a disruption in his life, and he wants to get back to peace. The barrier to that peace is usually his anger. I talk to people about how suing somebody doesn't usually lead to the goal of peace. I also talk about the pain and expense of this route, and that their expectation that they are going to be completely vindicated is probably not going to happen the way they think it will. I know that for some people they *do* have to learn to stand up for themselves, and then litigation may be the right answer."

## Holding the Vision

How easy is it to be a holistic lawyer? Bill responds, "A lot of our members were very drawn to the word 'holistic,' but we have had quite a bit of controversy among ourselves about maybe using another word like 'cooperative' to soften the message. We finally came to the conclusion that we couldn't worry about what others were going to think about our name or our methods.

"Many of us are struggling with how to practice law without competing when we're faced with another lawyer who takes a completely adversarial approach," says Vazquez. "When I talk to attorneys who are struggling with the ideas of holistic practice, I tell them to go back to the essay they wrote when they started law school. Over 50 percent of these essays show that they started out in law for humanitarian reasons. Somewhere along the line, a lot of us got lost. We are reawakening to the idea of why we went into this profession."

> Following your spirit requires trust in God. You must have faith that there is a bigger plan than meets the eye, deeper principles running the universe than the rules dictated by society, and a grander destiny than your past conditioning.
>
> It means that the thinking mind is not the sole or final arbiter of what will serve the highest good.
>
> It means extricating your behavior from the expectations of others, and transferring authority from outer demands to inner knowingness.
>
> It means launching out as a pioneer of freedom in a world where imprisonment has become the norm. . . . It means being *you* and living as what *you* are without apology or explanation. **Alan Cohen,** *I Had It All the Time*

When Mariza Vazquez started calling lawyers in her area who were interested in practicing holistically, she said, "I was struggling to be on a spiritual path and still maintain a practice in law. There were eight of us within driving distance of each other who had all found the national organization by coincidence. The word 'holistic' drew us all together, but we also had challenges about what that means for law and began to meet monthly to discuss these issues. I think about it from the two roots of *whole* and *holy*. In medicine and healing we're finding that the body operates as a whole, and I think that applies to all other professions."

Working to better society in a holistic way is more than altruism. *We* are transformed in the doing, and we find many more blessings to *ourselves* even than to those to whom we have reached out. Van Zyverden says, "I have realized that I chose to become a lawyer so I can learn certain things that no other occupation could have taught me. That's why it attracted me. The law attracted me in order that I could be of service to it. . . . There hasn't been a client who has come into my office that hasn't shown me a similar problem or issue within myself." We see in Bill Van Zyverden and Mariza Vazquez the type of world server whose desire for more personal satisfaction drew them to gather together others who shared their vision. The work happens through the law of attraction, rather than through promotion.

Vazquez shared with us a particularly revealing encounter on a recent trip to the Middle East. She had a glimpse of another culture's spiritual approach to accident and tragedy. Vazquez' tour guide enlisted her to help interpret for a very young, very scared Italian tourist. A three-year-old girl had darted in front of his car and was now in the hospital while he faced the questioning of local police. "I knew that this was some kind of coincidence," she said, "so I tried my best to use a little Spanish and English to talk to the police and the Italian. It seemed it was clearly an unfortunate accident, and after explaining his side to the police as well as I could, I asked them to tell me what the next procedures would be for the young man.

"They told me that under the law, the parents or a family representative has to come to the police and decide whether they want to pursue charges or *forgive* him. That's the word they used, forgive. If they forgave him, the story ended there. As I was explaining this to the young man, an old man, clearly the grandfather of the little girl, came in. After only a brief conversation with the old man, the police threw up their hands. I asked them what was going on. They said that without even hearing the facts, the grandfather was telling them that he forgave the tourist! The young man was obviously overwhelmingly relieved.

"The highlight of this story for me came from my tour guide, who explained to our group that in their culture, it is understood that we draw into our lives certain experiences and lessons. The grandfather had obviously felt that the little girl had created this drama in her life for a deeper purpose. He was very aware of the limited role that the tourist

Reformers and those who bring major changes to society often have had a personal problem themselves that was similar or related to one in the larger society. In working through their own problems, they discovered a useful resolution to the social problem. **Corinne McLaughlin and Gordon Davidson, *Spiritual Politics: Changing the World from the Inside Out***

played in the drama. Allah would decide the fate of the child, and the family was not going to change the energy and create another scenario. I was very impressed by this philosophy. It really changes the idea of victimization."

Practicing holistically is going beyond just what the law allows in ethics. It's answering to a higher calling, something else that is telling us what feels right and what feels wrong. Vazquez says, "Everybody likes to bash lawyers. But we have these kinds of lawyers because all of us have created the current legal system out of our own need to get something from others no matter what the cost. What responsibility are we each willing to take for the way the law is practiced?"

## EDUCATION

Fourth-grade teacher Laurette Rogers and her class had been discussing the plight of endangered species. One boy raised his hand. "But, Mrs. Rogers, what can *we* do to help endangered species?" From that question grew an amazing experience that forever changed the lives of the students, teachers, and the fate of a nearly extinct species of freshwater shrimp and its degenerating habitat.

### Ranchers, Shrimps, and Willows

Driven by a sincere desire to make a difference in their environment, these children and their remarkable teachers and a risk-taking principal began a journey of discovery that eventually involved parents, ranchers, businesspeople, biologists, journalists, and county and state representatives. Within six months the California Freshwater Shrimp Project at Brookside School in San Anselmo, California, had received local and national recognition, including the grand prize of $32,500 from the Anheuser-Busch Theme Parks Environmental Awards program. The intangible rewards, however, proved to be even more important.

> The planetary environmental crisis looks hopeless when viewed only from the physical, or form, level. But when seen from the inner side, things look quite different. Nature is not a blind force, but a conscious one that works through inner essences and energy fields. The inner forces of nature play a key role and can be of major assistance if we can learn to cooperate with them consciously. **Corinne McLaughlin and Gordon Davidson, *Spiritual Politics: Changing the World from the Inside Out***

## Learning in the Flow

In her recent publication describing the project, Laurette Rogers gives the reader a thrilling look at a new vision for education. She writes, "The kids' motivation and enthusiasm were phenomenal! Their eyes twinkled. They talked fast. They were serious with the gravity of their tasks. . . . Alexander said, 'I don't feel like I'm going to school anymore, I feel like I'm going to work!' "[6] Rogers describes a class that can't wait to get to school, who devote time on the weekends to their "Shrimp Work." "Suddenly," she says, " 'school work' lapped over the boundaries of the classroom, spilled over the boundaries of the school day. Everyone was learning."[7]

Project-based teaching methods are supported by research in brain-based theory that says the brain is a pattern seeker. Rote learning (e.g., multiplication tables, spelling, history dates) requires memory and repetition, but the brain has a smaller capacity for that type of activity. One the other hand, the brain seems to have an infinite capacity for remembering patterns because you fit new ideas into what you have already learned—it fits into your life. Ecosystems teach us that networks learn faster than hierarchies. Therefore, a child will learn best when she *participates* in the discovery, integration, and use of information. Instead of sitting and listening to the teacher at the head of the class (hierarchy), she will learn faster when she can share her own ideas with others in a safe, friendly, give-and-take environment.

The Center for Ecoliteracy, founded by physicist and author Fritjof Capra in Berkeley, California, has begun to develop a revolutionary curriculum for elementary education based on the concepts found in living ecosystems: interdependence, cycles, partnerships, energy flow, flexibility, diversity, coevolution, and sustainability.

## Let the Kids Do It

Using these principles, Rogers and colleague Ruth Hicks created a democratic environment which allowed children to direct their own learning. In the process they experienced and understood the interconnectedness of all things on the Earth and created a foundation for what they can hope to accom-

---

Work like God. No task too humble. No scheme too grand. **Roy Doughty, poet and project evaluator for the Center for Ecoliteracy**

---

plish in the future. Nine-year-old Adam says, " 'I thought that this project really changed my point of view because I thought that teachers would make the path and the students would follow, but really in this case, students make the path and the teachers follow.' "[8]

This project is an example of

1. All the elements—ranchers, teachers, kids, shrimps, trees, fences, money, community support—organizing themselves effortlessly (even though hard work was involved, it was not *effort*) once everyone followed their feelings about how they wanted to participate. Teachers didn't have to fight discipline problems because nobody had time to pick fights and get in trouble. They were too busy having fun and being in the service of something larger than themselves.
2. The joy that comes from being in nature and being a part of nature
3. Regaining a sense of control (instead of despair) over one's environment, which research has shown to be one of the keys to good health. This was not simulated learning within the walls of a classroom. Everyone, not just the children, experienced the bona fide satisfaction of making a difference in what matters—our home and the home of tiny little organisms that keep the stream bed healthy.

These fourth graders achieved meaningful results, not only for themselves but for their community and other species. For example, the children had to contact local ranchers who were weary and suspicious of "citified people" coming in to blame them for creek side damage. But one of the rules of the project, and a lesson in tolerance, was that good manners and diplomacy *must* be used at all times. Teachers asked children to consider how they would feel if someone came into their bedroom and started telling them what to do and what not to touch. The children's sincerity about the gravity of their work, and their willingness to be open and respectful of everyone, allowed them to gain support from ranchers, journalists, government officials, and funding agencies.

### Primary Experience of the Mystery of Life

Learning in context, children participated by writing reports and press releases, analyzing scientific data, researching other endangered species, calling reporters, designing and selling T-shirts, choreographing a Shrimp Dance, planting willow saplings, designing and building fences, and visiting other sites. In every aspect they were having a *primary experience* of learning, not the usual secondhand knowledge of book learning without consequences or feedback.

Cooperation, tolerance, respect, and responsibility develop organically, without the authoritarian heavy-handedness that wastes so much energy in traditional classrooms oriented to keeping the child in her seat. Rogers believes, "If the students themselves take control of the 'what,' 'when,' and 'how' of teaching, they will become experienced decision-makers, questioning and responsive citizens, gentle and effective teachers."[9]

The key principle here is that the new way has nothing at all to do with the old way. There is no linear connection; quantum physics did not evolve as an extension of Newtonian principles. Just as the new title implies, there was a quantum shift between what was, and what is. We had to look at the game from an entirely different angle to see more of what is happening. We are playing in a new ball park with a brand new set of rules. **Alan Cohen,** *I Had It All the Time*

### Reflection and Response

The essential ingredient to positive changes in any occupation area is conversations between forward-thinking individuals with a common goal to take their work to a deeper level. Zenobia Barlow, executive director of the Center for Ecoliteracy, told us, "Teachers are under such time pressures that in a lot of cases they don't even know each other. The fragmentation of the curriculum makes them almost like independent contractors that sublet rooms in the school building. They've rarely been on a retreat together, for example, to reflect deeply on what they are doing or to design collaborative projects.

"It's been interesting to watch the Shrimp Project because all of a sudden the classroom has been expanded out to include the district, the watershed, and the ranches. If we want to see more of this kind of integrated teaching, we need to give teachers time to get to know one another and envision, or daydream, the evolution of their field."

### The Edible Schoolyard Project

Another example of one citizen's response to her immediate environment that has changed and invigorated a school in Berkeley, California, is the Edible Schoolyard project. Alice Waters, the innovative chef and owner of Chez Panisse (and supporter of other programs such as Share Our Wealth), had to look at the lifeless grounds of Martin Luther King Middle School every day on her way home from her restaurant. She also observed that lunchtime for the students consisted of a snack bar selling microwaved pizzas, burgers, chips, and sodas. When she voiced her concerns to the principal, he challenged her to suggest an alternative. Thus was born the Edible Schoolyard project, whose vision includes a revitalized campus, an organic garden, an outdoor bread oven, a commercial bakery, groves of olive, fig, and citrus trees, herb and vegetable beds.

## Food and Community

The vision is to see the school within the garden. Waters sees food as a central civilizing ingredient in our lives, not only as nourishment for bodies. In a letter to President Clinton and Vice President Gore, she says, ". . . how can we reasonably expect people to know how to begin to [build community] when so many of them believe that nothing they do will make any difference? . . . Our project, called the Edible Schoolyard, plans to create and sustain an organic garden and landscape that is wholly integrated into the school's curriculum and lunch program. Students will be involved in all aspects of farming the garden—as well as in preparing, serving, and eating the food they grow. The purpose of this is to awaken their senses and teach the values of community responsibility, good nourishment, and good stewardship of the land. I am delighted that Delaine Eastin, the California State Superintendent of Education, has decided that a school garden should be an integral part of each demonstration school that is participating in the United States Department of Agriculture's Team Nutrition program for improving school lunches."[10]

> What else might I be doing besides harvesting tomatoes, running water over their skins, cutting their tops and slicing them into a giant pot on the stove to heat and stew so I can grind them in the food mill for puree? The abundance in my life at this moment is tomatoes, and my creative act is to make tomato sauce. **Arlene Bernstein, *Growing Season: A Healing Journey into the Heart of Nature***

## True Ownership Means Caring for the Land

Synchronistically, an article appeared in the newspaper on the day this chapter was being written, about another grammar school class in Northern California that has adopted the last remaining salt marsh in Marin County. These elementary school youngsters began to feel protective of the garbage-ridden, stagnated marsh that used to cover about half of the developed area. The idea is to involve the children from the neighborhood in the restoration of the wetland area for the next ten years. "There was almost instantaneous ownership by these kids," said Maureen Parton, aide to Marin County Supervisor Annette Rose, who created the restoration project.[11]

## Everything in Its Time

If the aim of education for young children is to connect with their natural love of learning, methods must resonate with their natural development capacities. While currently priorities in educational reform tend to center on buying computers, a trend enjoyed by the computer industry, some researchers caution that too early use of computers actually reduces the contextual learning that is critical to the early childhood years. In a recent article, Fritjof Capra says, "Recent research indicates strongly that the use of computers is simply inappropriate at early ages (grades K–3) and needs to be carefully monitored at all ages in order to avoid harmful interference with the child's cognitive and neural development."[12] Technology, while useful in freeing people to pursue their creative and spiritual interests, does not replace the natural conditions that produce creativity.

> Grapevines grow in place, They send their roots deep into the earth and draw up its nourishment, which sustains them for decades, sometimes as long as a century.
>
> Each has to grow from its own connection to the source, alone, and only when its growth is firmly established do the graceful new shoots reach far enough to entwine another's. **Arlene Bernstein, Growing Season: A Healing Journey into the Heart of Nature**

## Dig and Grow Rich

New or old ideas? Alice Waters cites educator James Ralph Jewel, who in 1909 wrote a booklet entitled "Suggestions for Garden Work in California Schools" that said, "School gardens teach, among other things, private care for public property, economy, honesty, application, concentration, justice, the dignity of labor, and love for the beauties of nature." Are these not the very values that *both* liberals and conservatives consider worthwhile? Every aspect of what we fruit-lessly attempt to mandate by exhortation and law—respect for prop-erty, honesty, justice, meaningful employment, and the conservation of our environment—can be nourished and accomplished by educat-ing our greatest living resource: the consciousness of our children.

## New World Pattern

A new worldview is a new world pattern of creative energy. Within our problems, the answer is found. If our children are dying in the street, in the home, from their own despair and lack of hope for the future, let them come forth to take back the reins. They have been born with a vision, and it's up to us adults to give them space to let that vision—the vision that will be the future—flourish. We must do everything in our power to nourish children, and encourage them, even at a young age, to delve into their own creativity and intuition. With fresh eyes and enthusiastic little hearts, they just might give us the keys we so desperately seek from the old paradigm that created the problems! In the great scheme of life, the nurturing of our species starts with mother's milk and continues with meaningful education that unleashes new hearts and minds, eager for the tasks before them.

### ART AND BEAUTY

Art and music are the dreams and depths of the human spirit. Beauty inspires, energizes, and heals us. Art keeps us in touch with what it means to be human, to have imagination, and to be civilized. Painting

---

Full of rapturous colors and yielding surfaces, [Georgia O'Keeffe's work] fur-nishes a sense of astonishing discovery: the heart of the flower lies as a dark, mysterious core at the charged center of these paintings. Though the work is explicitly feminine, it is convincingly and triumphantly powerful, a combination that had not before existed.

The great flowers echo O'Keeffe's childhood fascination with the miniature world of the dollhouse. It was there that she had learned of the magical trans-formation that occurred with a shift of focus.

"When you take a flower in your hand and really look at it, it's your world for the moment. I wanted to give that world to someone else." **Roxana Robinson, *Georgia O'Keeffe: A Life***

---

and sculpture force us to ask questions about life that often get lost in everyday concerns.

New York painter Robert Zakanitch has strong feelings about the higher purpose of painting and sculpture. He told us in an interview, "The role of art up till now has been a reflector of society. I think technology has changed that. Television does a much better job of that, and it does it instantly. I believe that now the artist's role is to become a director of society—directing our attention toward healing energies rather than sending out more destructive images. Art plants seeds very deeply. It makes statements that slowly get into the psyche of the society. Art speaks to your soul. We don't know what the soul is, but without it we don't exist." According to Zakanitch, whose huge canvases pulse and drip with vivid organic patterns and mysteriously ambiguous objects that you might find in a cosmic thrift store, every society has a specific look, character, and attitude, and that all comes about through its art. We are such a part of the expression, but we are scarcely aware of it. "Art is almost like magic," he says. "Images are so powerful you run out of words to describe them. When cubism and impressionism and Jackson Pollock hit the scene, there were no words to describe their new view of the world."

### Flowers and Oil Derricks

Zakanitch is clear that his intention is to speak to the eternal, healthy, loving parts of us. "My themes in the past twenty years have been on evoking the parts of ourselves that care, nurture, and feel joy. My latest series [Big Bungalow Suite] is about the domesticity and comfort we can surround ourselves with and give to each other. All of this is in the minute acts of caring that we do. Flowers are so wonderful when you're living next to oil derricks, and there is a sparkle to life even in the small decorative items my mother used to have in the kitchen and dining room. I have another series of adornments, which I think are a very positive thing because they represent a spark of joy when we wear them or give them to somebody we love. My work is about reinforcing the delicate things in us. My question when I paint is always how I can talk about the elation of the human spirit—about rebirth. If you can give that to people in your work it's magical."

In our explorations of where our new World Vision is taking us, and the new dimensions of spiritual life toward which the Tenth Insight suggests we are moving, it's important not to lose sight of our Earthly nature. Awakening all of our senses, including the intuitive one, is the goal. Too often we shut down in reaction to our surround-ings, out of fear and avoidance of pain, poverty, or ugliness. How can we then open up to people who may have messages for us, to the power of nature, or to let in symbolic messages?

## *Refreshing the Soul*

James Hillman, archetypal psychologist and author, points out that in our society we anesthetize ourselves by blocking awareness with pills and drugs or loud music, and overstimulate with kicks and highs. We con-ceptualize through sci-ence and theologies in place of experiencing. Art's job is to lure us back into our senses and to reengage the world. He says, "The artist's eye is for the sake of refresh-ing the soul rather than curing society or sharp-ening the wit or pointing out social injustice, all of which can be very worthy things. But they depend on an awakened soul. So refresh the soul, then something else will happen. And the soul is refreshed by beauty, by love and by remembrance of death."[13]

> Back at the kitchen table, reading the Help Wanteds, infused with the desire to change her life on every level, in every way—to get moving, forward—she idly lifted a bottle of nail polish and, with a forlorn look on her face and a gap-ing, heavy hole in her chest, spent the next half hour slowly tipping the bottle back and forth, watching the swaths cut in the polish by the sil-ver stir beads, the silvery etchings in crimson.
> **Anne Lamott, *Rosie***

The desire to uplift people is applicable to any kind of creative work we do. If our inner intention is to value the best in each other, and to bring that to the surface, then we are holding the World Vision.

## INDIVIDUAL STUDY

### Résumé Review

Make a list of all the occupations you have had in your life. Reflect on how you might have been guided to get into your occupational group(s). In what ways, large or small, have you made an impact on that field? Have you maintained it, clarified its purpose, advanced its cause, expanded its influence, brought innovations to it, reformed it, or interconnected it to some other field?

Who is your mentor or hero?
What would you like to do now?
What is stopping you?
What do you need?
What one new step can you take?

If you worked on one project to benefit the planet or your community, what would it be?

Seek out others who resonate to that goal and support each other to take action.

### Job Interview

Read over the list of requirements for the new world server on pages 274–275. Circle the characteristics that you think you already possess even if it's minimal. Which missing characteristic would you like to develop? How might you do that? If you *strongly* want to bring that quality into your life, even if you cannot see a way to develop it now, set an intention to be shown how to accomplish it. (You have to really want it! Just thinking it would be nice isn't usually strong enough to manifest it.)

## GROUP STUDY

### Then and Now

Begin your session by writing down any changes you see in your own field of interest, say in the last fifty years, ten years, or five years. What trends do you see? Then let people discuss the changes they see. This could bring some interesting information that no one bothered to notice before. It doesn't matter if you are all involved in different fields or not. In fact, the more diverse, the more interesting this discussion should be.

### Group Development

Some of you may feel an urge to gather together with people from your occupational network and kick around ideas for a new vision for this work. Rather than seeing each other as competitors, come together to brainstorm about a common problem or issue in your personal experience of your profession.

In your meeting, concentrate on feeling the common bonds that attracted each of you to your occupation. Once you feel in resonance, as was discussed in the Eighth Insight, people can begin to talk about the feelings they have about specific questions (e.g., new regulations, lack of public acceptance, new developments and how they affect your work). You may want to first throw out imaginative speculations about where the field is headed. Later, you might silently visualize the higher vision for your occupational group and share your intuitive impressions.

## Expanders, Maintainers, Pioneers, and Builders

- Just for fun, separate into small groups according to the predominant role you tend to take. Are you an expander, a maintainer, a pioneer, or a builder? Make up your own subsets, but get together with people in the same subset (all the expanders sit together and all the maintainers, etc.).
- Get together and talk for five minutes each about what you did in that role.
- What did you like about it?
- What didn't you like?
- What would you do differently today in the role or job?
- Knowing what you know now, what would you have liked to see happen?
- Now reorganize yourself with a new group where there are expanders, maintainers, builders, and pioneers all together. Listen to each other's stories about what you did.
- Don't worry if you feel you are a combination of these roles/activities. Just pick the one you'd most like to be today!
- How would you organize taking a group of young people to work at something that would be of service to a village in a Third World country (with their permission and invitation, of course)?

TO EFFECT CHANGE

- Take your desire for accomplishment seriously.
- Don't dismiss it because it seems impossible or because others think it's too "pie-in-the-sky."

- You wouldn't have strong aspirations if there were not something to be achieved on that path. Dreams get us started down a certain path, but the outcome may be something you would otherwise never even have imagined or attempted.

- Visualize your field at its highest level of service. How does it benefit others?

- Improve your ability to hold your intuitive vision and *let it show you how it wants to manifest*, rather than imposing your goals on *it*.

- Commit to something that excites you, not just because it seems like "a good idea." Ability to hold the vision increases when you are really jazzed.

- Stay sensitive to your gut feelings. Trust them at least as much as your rational mind.

- Keep your focus on the whole. If the vision doesn't happen the way you expect, look for the higher purpose in the experience.

- Look for subtle signs that your guides and soul group are working through you. You might notice an increase of energy or clarity, or a willingness to do something entirely new. A chance phone call, finding a book, or an unexpected meeting could be a sign that your soul group is assisting your development.

- Replace your "confusion about what I'm supposed to be doing" with one small concrete step or action in the service of another.

## PART SIX

# Full Circle

# CHAPTER 13

# The World Vision

Suddenly our focus shifted to the Afterlife dimension, and here we could see with great clarity that our intention all along was not merely to create a New Earth, but a New Heaven as well.

THE TENTH INSIGHT:
HOLDING THE VISION[1]

HAWK
MESSENGER

## THE UNIFICATION OF THE DIMENSIONS

"As above, so below." Elementary truths do not change. Our problem is to stay in touch with them and remember that we are carrying the spirit into everyday life.

As each of us grasps the reality of themes of the Tenth Insight *for ourselves*—the existence of the Afterlife; reincarnation; understanding we are part of a soul group; holding the images of our intuitive guidance; giving service; clearing our fears and our unwanted conditioning—we rise to another field of potentiality. In effect, our consciousness is spiritualizing the material dimension through our expanded thought patterns.

What is the spiritual message beyond the racial or cultural drama of one particular lifetime? Each lifetime has the potential for contributing to the evolution of the whole. From a Tenth Insight perspective, looking around at the life we have, we realize that we were born into a particular area or culture to learn a specific lesson. The time has come to increase our awareness of how each of us is ultimately serving the planetary family. Are we increasing the emphasis on materiality, consumption, and separation? Or are we increasing the emphasis on uplifting the whole?

Alice A. Bailey, writing in the 1940s, believed that the clashing of religious and national ideologies served the purpose of starting people thinking in every culture. She said, "In past centuries, it was only those who had benefited by education and those in the 'upper brackets' who thought and planned. This tendency to thought indicates the coming into activity of a new and better civilization, and this is preparatory to spiritual events of major importance. . . . The spirit of [mankind], usually unconsciously, is driving onwards towards a more spiritual civilization and culture. . . . But the mentality of [man] is daily developing and his [or her] ability to grasp world affairs is growing. That is one of the greatest of spiritual events and is the foundational fact which makes the life of the soul and the growth of intuitive perception possible on a large scale. This is a by-product of the clash of the ideologies, but is the true and beautiful result of the universal educational system which—faulty though it may be and is—has made it possible for all [people] to read, to write and to communicate with each other."[2]

## TREASURING THE MEDLEY

Imagine what life would be like if we stopped judging people and started asking, What piece of the puzzle do they have? What was *their* Birth Vision? What can I learn from them? A critical mass of people holding the big picture would allow global unity to *happen through ordinary people,* rather than as a result of political national regulations. From this awakened perspective, we would treasure the diversity of cultures and religions, not try to make everybody blandly the same (even if that were possible!). Like curious and enthusiastic students of chemistry experiments, we would discuss, compare, and honor everybody's different destinies. Realizing that each quiet act of service or assistance that we gave to others would truly be a gift *to ourselves,* we would look for ways to nourish and benefit each person we met.

---

I would like to remind you here that the spiritual Hierarchy of our planet cares not whether a man is a democrat, a socialist or a communist, or whether he is a Catholic, a Buddhist, or an unbeliever of any kind. It cares only that humanity—as a whole—avail itself of spiritual opportunity. It is an opportunity which is present today in a more compelling way than ever before. Alice A. Bailey, *The Rays and the Initiations*

---

## THE NEW EXPLORERS OF INTERDIMENSIONAL
## TRAVEL—PIERCING THE BARRIER

The Tenth Insight suggests that as certain individuals and groups reach levels of consciousness approaching that of the Afterlife dimension, they would go back and forth, as out-of-body researcher Robert Monroe and others have already done.

Monroe, along with other researchers in the spiritual and parapsychological field, believed that most of humanity, if not all, has what he calls the Second Body—a nonphysical body that travels to other dimensions in the Afterlife. He believed that most of us travel out-of-body at night in the sleep state without retaining a conscious memory of it. In one of his extraordinary excursions in his Second Body, Monroe visits a friend. While in the Second Body he physically pinches the person, who expresses a moment of pain. Some days later, the very real physical pain of that pinch is corroborated by the person in a meeting with Monroe. By this experiment, Monroe demonstrated that a person operating in the Second Body can have both a physical and an emotional effect on others.

His findings prompted him to consider the ethics involved in such power. If a certain percentage of people are at the evolutionary point of being able to consciously "pierce the veil" between dimensions, are we at risk for the misuse of this power? He speculated that up to now we may have been protected by such barriers as: (1) not knowing we had this power; (2) superstitious fears about contacting spirits; (3) suspicion of transcendent experiences by organized religions; (4) scientific disdain which resists exploring the spiritual plane as a valid area of research. Monroe also includes the possibility that "use of such power may be under the control and direction of animate, intelligent, or impersonal regulators, and may preclude non-constructive interference"[3]—suggesting that perhaps groups of souls are keeping us from destroying ourselves through ignorance or malice.

What would happen, Monroe asks, if humanity accepts the existence of the spiritual dimension and learns the technique of entering the higher vibration at will? One of the most important shifts for human consciousness will be the shift from *belief* to *knowledge*. Most important, we will have unequivocal *knowledge* of our relationship to God and our place in the universe. With a *personally experienced knowledge of the divine,* we would be very close to eliminating a great deal of Fear (which is ultimately fear of death) and perhaps many of the lower emotions. Like those who have gone through a near-death experience, we would *know* that death was a transition into another dimension of our eternal life, and that we *are* more than our physical body.

As the Ninth Insight reveals, the collective rise in energy would promote expanded knowledge in all spheres, creating a matrix within which solutions would naturally appear as people followed their intuition. Religious conflict would be impossible as each religion would remember that its individual message had a necessary place in the overall vision. As Monroe says, "Each will rationalize by saying 'That's what we've been trying to tell you all along.' "[4]

## HELLO FROM HEAVEN

According to Bill and Judy Guggenheim, after-death communications happen in a variety of modes. Sorting through over 3,300 cases, they presented a range of accounts from people who experienced a full visual appearance, hearing a voice, feeling a touch, smelling a fragrance, in the dream state, and even as part of an out-of-body experience. For example, a nurse in Wisconsin had a mystical encounter with her five-month-old baby girl who had died of a heart defect: "About three or four weeks after Amanda died, I was lying in bed, but I wasn't asleep. All of a sudden, I felt myself being pulled out of my body. I felt I was higher up in the bedroom, near the ceiling, looking out the window. The entire window became filled with the brightest golden light that I could ever imagine! It was like someone coming at you in a car with their high beams on. I felt absorbed by the light, and I felt the presence of my daughter.

"Then I saw Amanda! I saw her spirit in that light! And I heard her—it was a telepathic communication. She said, 'Thank you very much for all that you gave me. I love you very much.' Suddenly, I felt a very, very powerful presence—the presence of God. I felt the most incredible sense of love and understanding that I've ever experienced in my life. And at that moment, I understood everything!"[5]

In another account, a real estate broker in North Carolina named Richard saw and touched his father, who had died of a stroke at age sixty-six. "Three days after his burial, someone woke me up. I sat up to see who it was, and it was my father! Street lights coming through the window behind me were shining on his face. I could see him very well—there was no question it was him.

"He said, 'Richard.' I knew my father's voice, and I raised up from the bed. He shook hands with me immediately, and his hand was very familiar and warm. Then he said, 'I'm so glad to see you, Richard. Don't worry about anything. I love you.' I heard this externally, directly from his lips. His voice sounded clearer than ever. I couldn't take my eyes off his face. He looked better than I'd ever seen him look in my whole life . . . he appeared contented and happy, like there was something much better than I could ever dream of. And then he left.

"I was greatly astonished and thrilled. I had been in deep bereavement, and that experience gave me assurance that there is life after death. It was real—there is no question in my mind, no question."[6]

## NEW HEAVEN, NEW EARTH

The Tenth Insight states that "our intention all along was not merely to create a New Earth, but a New Heaven as well." As the World Vision is remembered, it transforms the Afterlife. As individuals and groups vibrate high enough to reach the spiritual dimension, so, too, do soul groups in the Afterlife achieve the ability to enter the physical dimension, completing the transfer of energy into both realms. The Afterlife, our eternal home, has been the dimension in which our souls hold

> Our errand on this planet is informed by a decision to partake in the building of the Earth's cosmic origin, and to promote awareness of our celestial identity to others who are less evolved. Our elders taught that some of the universe's inhabitants were as much in need of help as others had the need to help them. This Earth was one of the many places where those who craved to help could find this desire easily satisfied, and where those who needed help could easily become recipients of it. **Malidoma Patrice Somé, Of Water and the Spirit**

the Vision and the memories. The physical plane is the dimension in which we bring the Vision into material existence.

The Insight continues, "Then, as consciousness on Earth progressed and the population increased, the balance of energy and responsibility had slowly shifted toward the physical dimension, until, at this point in history, when enough energy had shifted and the World Vision was being remembered, the full power and responsibility for believing and creating the intended future would be shifting from the Afterlife to the souls on Earth, to the newly forming groups, to us!"[7] With the increase in contact with souls in spiritual existence, human consciousness is forced to confront the reality of this dimension. As a critical mass of acceptance lowers the barriers between worlds, *while raising the vibration on the physical plane,* the spiritual realm will be able to interpenetrate more easily.

## FUTURE TRENDS FOR THE EARTHLY PLANE

To imagine is to design. To dream is to enter the fourth dimension. We already know that what was science fiction last year is being telemarketed next month. As the human race plunges ahead, we wonder where in the world, or nonworld, are we going. What's up? What is it going to be like if we lift the veil between the hierarchies of consciousness? What light switch are we carrying around in our DNA that hasn't been turned on yet? Scientific pioneers such as Hank Wesselman, paleoenvironmentalist and author of *Spiritwalker,* the tale of a shamanic trek into the future five thousand years from now, believes that we all have within us a dormant "software program" that allows us to enter the fourth dimension at will. Michael Murphy, who presents an enormous body of work on extraordinary human functioning in his book *The Future of the Body,* says that "exceptional abilities develop most fully in cultures that prize them . . . conversely, such abilities are often distorted or inhibited by social conditioning. Some athletes, for example, exhibit a sensitive self-control that suggests they might be accomplished yogis if they lived in Hindu culture. . . ."[8]

Culture has a hand in shaping our capacities, and even mystical revelations are filtered through the social matrix, though they spring from the universal energy of God. Evolution, then, seems to be not merely an automatic process, but is the long field of creativity, shaped in part by our intentional, emotional, and spiritual bodies. Evolution is shaping us and we are consciously participating in the design, although we have no complete picture of the plan.

Since we are dropping our old-model literalness, we can also drop the literal interpretation of scriptural prophecies of physical destruction. We don't have to buy into the picture of floods, fire, and apocalypse. With the knowledge and experience of how we create our world through intention and desire, co-creating with divine mind, we can reinterpret the scriptural messages as a metaphorical description of these transitional times.

Penney Peirce, an internationally recognized clairvoyant based in Marin County, California, has developed a description of future trends from intuitions, dreams, and visions that resonates very closely with the principles of the Tenth Insight. In a lecture at Unity Church, Walnut Creek, California, recently, she spoke about her predictions. We have presented some of the primary aspects of her vision of evolutionary psychological and spiritual events in the not too distant future. Perhaps these speculations will stimulate your own visionary abilities.

## FATHER SKY AND MOTHER EARTH—UNIFICATION OF THE DIMENSIONS AND MASCULINE AND FEMININE ARCHETYPAL ENERGIES

Peirce sees a unification of the dimensions as the coming together of Heaven and Earth, represented metaphorically by the sacred marriage of the descending masculine (sky) energy and the ascending feminine (earth) energy. This celestial merger will be expressed in "real life" by men consciously cultivating and integrating their ability to receive, listen, empathize, and cooperate/nurture (feminine energies), and by women consciously cultivating and integrating their ability to lead, define, and produce (masculine energies). According to Peirce, in the future, relationships will be more fluid, allowing each partner to work with whole brain creativity with a natural exchange of roles—each partner being sometimes more dynamic, sometimes more receptive. A balance of male and female energies will occur in both interpersonal dynamics and in the right and left brain connection. The archetypal

> The masculine, differentiating approach . . . between the human being and the world has reached a point of crisis. Yet, we also see now, in many ways, the potential for great transformation and healing, a coming into wholeness by the tremendous resurgence of the feminine archetype . . . not just the obvious ones of feminism . . . and the new openness on the part of men to feminine values.
>
> It is also visible in a whole different approach to life—our scientific theories of the human psyche, the new sensibility of how human beings relate to nature and other forms of life on the planet—all of these reflect the emergence of the feminine archetype on the collective scale of the culture which is manifesting as a new sense of connection with the whole . . . the coming together of the human being and nature . . . intellect and soul. . . . It's an extremely multileveled, complex transformative process we're involved in right now. **Richard Tarnas in *Towards a New World View*, by Russell E. DiCarlo**

tendency for *uniting* might even result in more soulmates finding each other, especially since more and more souls are incarnating in groups to work together.

The unification of the dimensions and the masculine and feminine energies is also represented by specific new areas of social, spiritual, and scientific study. For example, we are already noticing an increased interest in mental and spiritual phenomena such as angels, extraterrestrials, near-death experiences, and interest in sacred geometry, all signs of the higher mental and spiritual nature of the archetypal descending masculine energy. Likewise, archetypal ascending feminine energy is already birthing an increase in Earth-based spirituality such as shamanism, crystals, herbs, and interest in all natural systems.

In earlier agrarian-based cultures the matriarchy developed our ability to merge and blend. In the more recent technology-based culture, the patriarchy has given us the ability to differentiate ideas (a masculine, linear, rational mode) and make things happen in the outer world (science, commerce, control, and war). With wholeness of perception, there will be both an appreciation of our *inner* process (feminine intelligence) and the confidence to explore new ways of doing things (masculine intelligence).

## CHANGES IN PERCEPTION

In the new worldview, an integrated mind/body/spirit perception is replacing linear perception. At this stage of consciousness we will be able to handle *paradox*, which means that we will be able to think in terms of both/and, not just either/or. Instead of drawing lines about *concepts* (such as more government vs. less government), we will be able to see the greater context and come up with actual solutions that work for everyone.

Because we are able to stay in touch with our energy flow (the Third Celestine Insight), we will be quick to recog-

The full synchrony of planetary harmony can't really be understood by the intellect alone; it is more of an intuitive experience. The intellect can talk of it, but to experience it directly and live it in our daily lives requires a deeper and more direct approach. This is one area where the meditative experience, in which we naturally and spontaneously experience this unity awareness, is a most effective way to imbibe this consciousness. *Meditation in this context is not a luxury, but a necessity for global survival.* Gabriel Cousins, M.D., *Sevenfold Peace: World Peace Through Body, Mind, Family, Community, Culture, Ecology, God*

nize the difference between feeling heavy and light. We will understand that when we are separated from wholeness (forgetting the big picture of our spiritual purpose), we experience a drop in energy and feel alone. This feeling of being drained and alone will be a trigger, reminding us that our thinking has become cloudy. Then we can remember to ask for intuitive guidance for returning back to our center.

### HIGHER ATTITUDES AND EMOTIONS

With an ability to see more than simple black and white choices, we will increase in energy and creativity. Feeling filled with purpose, everyone will naturally desire to fulfill themselves by taking more responsibility because that will be in our own self-interest. *We will be serving our own need to give and receive energy.* Once we know that *we are our soul,* we immediately connect with universal intelligence, and things start flowing again. Feeling our connection to our spiritual purpose raises our vibration and the vibration of any interaction we have with soul awareness. With energy flowing between people, compassion and tolerance naturally follow.

### SHIFTS IN THE LEVEL OF UNCONSCIOUS ENERGY

According to Peirce, a change in attitudes and perceptions will also affect the level at which we bury the collective shadow. She feels that a higher collective consciousness will pop more of our rejected subconscious material up to the surface. She envisions a transitional period of turmoil, national and international dramas, and recurrences of old fears or regression to negative patterns, which is a natural first step to clearing collective fear in the world. What used to be subconscious will have been raised to a conscious level, as we are seeing even now with the popularity of television talk shows that expose every human crisis, trauma, and weakness imaginable.

### THE 6 O'CLOCK NEWS

Seeing chaos in the news is nothing new. Peirce makes the analogy between the seeming increase in bombings and explosions and the eruption of our collective suppressed rage, fear, and frustration. Terrorist acts trigger our deepest fears of vulnerability. Without a spiritual perspective, however, we have only partial understanding of these global events, and fear, containment, and retaliation appear to offer

---

The Maya knew what their purpose was. They knew when their demise would be, just as the Tibetans foresaw the invasion of their country. . . . Because the Maya were Keepers of Time, they were able to evacuate Earth, knowing that their purpose was done.

This is one of the deepest secrets of the Maya—they knew the date and the time . . . from their point of view, they were transported to another physical dimension. . . . And they knew that one day their knowledge, their keys, would be uncovered and discovered by the Family of Light—by you. We suggest that there are some people who have discovered these keys already. **Barbara Marciniak, Earth: Pleiadian Keys to the Living Library**

---

the only rational response. Often our first response is to go back to what worked before—which would be seen as a conservative backlash. Other evidence of shifts in the collective shadow might be more national scandals or a reexamination of old taboos (again we see this happening on TV talk shows). We might also begin to hear more about alien abductions, which force us to reconsider the limits of our belief system.

### OPTIONS—FIGHT OR FLIGHT OR . . . ?

Instinctive responses to threat (world turmoil) are fight-or-flight (suppression and denial). Without knowledge of the World Vision, we have been trying to suppress and control the people we deem as our enemies. The *flight* or denial syndrome also includes finding (voting for) a powerful parental figure to take care of us. Peirce predicts that there will be a temporary resurgence of charlatans and dictators as we seek security.

Think about yourself as one cell in the cosmic body. Instead of thinking about humanity as the web of life, begin to understand humanity as one strand in the cosmic web of life. **Gabriel Cousens, M.D., Sevenfold Peace**

If we allow the second response of *fight*—we will return to dualistic thinking. "I'm going to try to get rid of you through violence and war." There will be a battle of ideas and the polarized positions we have already discussed. Part of the fight response—gangs, splinter groups, fierce bipartisan politics, and racism—will continue to create dominators and victims.

## PSYCHOLOGICAL AND PHYSICAL REACTIONS

In Peirce's model, the aftermath of using old paradigm habitual responses such as fight-or-flight inevitably results in disillusionment. All of the polarization we see today is a denial of the chaos that seems to be just around the corner. However, chaos is an important phase of our development if we look at it as the letting go of old values and old behaviors that are inappropriate for the next millennium. At a personal level, Peirce predicts an increase in moroseness or resignation in the population. We have already seen an increase in teen suicides, and suicides in displaced people, as well as an increase in the use of mood stabilizers such as Prozac. We may also see an increase in such diseases as chronic fatigue syndrome, panic attacks, environmental allergies, and addictions.

During times of chaos there tend to be fuzzy boundaries and fear of being invaded. Illegal immigration is already a controversial issue in the United States. Shifts in world economies and environments raise the need for a redefinition of who belongs where. On a community scale, homelessness is another sign of people not being centered in their own self-worth (not "at home") and symbolizes, in a very real way, a lack of identity and belonging. Lacking the self-organizing boundaries of tribal areas that tended to keep population balanced, we face overpopulation (uncontrolled growth) on a macro level, while at the micro level we battle diseases of wild growth like cancer. Even the lower fertility rate in men and women may be a micro response to world chaos.

> The flesh-food industry accounts for over fifty percent of our water usage, eighty-five percent of soil loss, and twenty times more land usage than required for a vegan diet. A vegan diet saves one acre of trees per year. **Gabriel Cousens, M.D., *Sevenfold Peace***

## RECENTERING—LEVEL ONE

After being overwhelmed by all this chaos, Peirce envisions a time of recentering, the first level of which is a reactionary reentering of the ego. Our first step will be taking our power back from cultural influences such as consumer programming and the affiliation with traditional political parties. People will say, "I deserve some respect, and I'm not going to take it anymore."

Signs of an increase in the desire for individuality may perhaps even be seen in the current rise of coffee bars—revving up the adrenaline—and the use of personal computers, telecommuting, and using psychotherapy in order to become a more developed person. Globally, the desire for individuality will be seen as a rise in nationalism and patriotism.

## RECENTERING—LEVEL TWO

After our initial growth spurts toward a higher level of individuation, we arrive at a deeper level of authenticity. At this stage we realize, "I'm here. I have always been myself. I'm connected to something much larger than I thought." We start to relax and feel the universal laws operating inside (the Seventh Celestine Insight). We also realize that every other person is part of the same energy as we are (the Eighth Insight). At this stage of consciousness we are in the new paradigm. Echoing the First Insight, Peirce sees that one by one people will have their own experience and revelations of insights about the worldview, affecting the unified field. As we take the next step of using this new energy positively, we will have new forms of education, health care, law, social nurturing, architecture, and government.

## HEALING AND INTEGRATION

The last step in Peirce's model is healing personal and global suffering as a critical mass of people realize that we are all interrelated. A critical mass of people will begin to choose not to add pain to the world, but to live, as the Buddhists say, skillfully. As situations arise that look scary to us, we will be better equipped to make positive choices because we have the big picture (the ideal) in mind. We will prefer to work in fellowship. Instead of think tanks, Peirce says there will be meditation tanks where people learn to merge into one loving, healing frequency to effect change. New skills and new problem-solving methods will come out of these cross-disciplinary meditation groups. She sees more satellite conferencing. The increase in fellowship will foster an appreciation for those people who have abilities that we lack, and a new field of diversity management will develop.

She feels strongly that the dualistic and linear concept of opposition will be turned into the paradox of *both/and*. Hierarchies based on high vs. low will transform into circles and councils where all are related equally. We will automatically look for the higher unifying factor or the third alternative in solving problems. For example, instead of struggling with men's issues and women's issues, we'll look at the *human* issue. People will demand that politics shift away from the two-party oppositional system to a both/and search for what works for the greatest good.

> We think that we living beings are different from inanimate objects, but according to the principle of interbeing, living beings are comprised of non-living-being elements. . . . Why discriminate against what we call inanimate?
>
> To protect living beings, we must protect the stones, the soil, and the oceans. Before the atomic bomb was dropped on Hiroshima, there were many beautiful stone benches in the parks. As the Japanese were rebuilding their city, they discovered that these stones were dead, so they carried them away and buried them. Then they brought in live stones.
>
> Do not think these things are not alive. Atoms are always moving . . . these atoms and stones are consciousness itself. **Thich Nhat Hanh, *Love in Action***

The hospice and right-to-die movements will grow as people become more aware that death is a transition to the spiritual level of existence. As people desire to retain consciousness and knowledge of their purpose and lessons learned on Earth, we will see more research and technology in death and dying. There will be a balance between saving a person's life and allowing the death process to progress naturally without undue resistance or fear.

Tuning into global energy patterns, analogous to our own elevated ability to tune into energy, weather patterns will be seen as signs of the state of the collective emotional body, and currency fluctuations will be read as signs of shifts in value systems.

## NEW SOUL GROUPS

Peirce also sees, along with other spiritual teachers and educators, that a new group of souls is coming into the Earth plane. They may be souls who have not incarnated for a long time and are more adept in the higher frequencies of the mental/spiritual plane. Since about 1970, there seems to be an increase in children who are described as hyperactive, allergic to certain environmental compounds, or learning impaired. Far from being unintelligent, these souls are often brilliant, but have trouble fitting into the existing structures of family and school. Peirce suggests that they might be vibrating at a different level than what we consider "normal." They may be having trouble adjusting their frequency for the density of the Earth plane. However, they may also be part of the transformation of the planet, accelerating the frequency of consciousness. A higher frequency of brain activity may attract them to such technology as video games, computers, and virtual reality. Their challenge will be to keep themselves balanced, so they may need more help with their emotional development, or more physical contact and touching. Without physical grounding or stilling the mind with meditation, they may have trouble staying connected to Earth energy. Research studies already show that hyperactive kids slow down with beta waves, unlike "normal" people, who slow down with alpha and theta frequencies.

It all started when I asked them what they felt at the beginning of the school year. Regardless of background, they didn't want to come back, saying, "I feel restless." One little girl said, "My spirit can't sit still."

That struck a chord with me. I knew we were talking about spirit. They loved anything that had the words spirit, mystery, or anything unknown that somehow governs us. They also like hearing that they are in charge of their spirit.

When I read, "Mana is the life force coming from a great universal source—a higher power—and the journey on earth is a spiritual journey," all the children said, "Ah." **Shirley Richardson, Co-founder, Summit Intermediate School**

Since many more children in general are being born into single-parent homes, Peirce believes we will develop a new kind of school. She envisions this new environment as a cross between a school and a foster home, with lots of activities that develop the children's intuitive skills and ability to work collectively with a diverse group of people. Parents, as well, would receive training in parenting or therapy while their children were going to school.

These souls may be so used to functioning as a group in the spiritual dimension that they have difficulty functioning without a similar group in the physical plane. Working with their special needs may help us to develop methods to access group mind, creating one huge brain that might be able to bring in technology that is totally unlike anything we know today. Perhaps we will find children patenting new devices and learning to produce things themselves.

## BAND OF LIGHT SOULS

Peirce also reports a vision she had that resonates clearly to the Tenth Insight concept of supportive soul groups holding our Birth Vision in the Afterlife. In her vision a great band of souls was watching the Earth, moving closer and closer to our plane of existence. She also saw humans lifting their eyes to the heavens, intuiting these invisible souls. She saw the band of light around the earth grow brighter and saw the souls in spirit move closer to the souls on Earth. Eventually, an overlapping meeting zone was created where the incarnate and discarnate souls could telepathically exchange knowledge.

According to the future trends outlined by Peirce, the polarizing pull of consciousness at this time will cause some people to get clearer and feel more connected to each other, and others will get denser and feel more isolated. Those who are further toward the pole of negativity will feel drained and hopeless from the lack of energy. As the polarization reaches critical mass point, an energetic bifurcation will occur. Those with denser consciousness will die off because they will be unable to exist at the higher frequency of the physical plane. When they reincarnate, they will come back to the old level they remember and not sense anything unusual has happened. Souls who have more light in their energy bodies will create an Earth dimension for themselves that is light-filled, and their bodies will be translucent. The different vibrations will live in parallel worlds, which seems to fit the model of quantum physics. Quantum physics tells us that light is both a particle and a wave. On a human scale of that concept, we can imagine ourselves as oscillating between knowing ourselves as individual consciousness and intuiting our existence as the field of consciousness as well.

> . . . every twenty-five hundred years—the Kumaras release a greatly-increased outpouring of Cosmic Love, Wisdom, and Energy. This Blazing Light and Transcendent Radiance flooding the earth and its inhabitants, interpenetrating all, is a tremendous lifting process, and gives a forward impulse to the growth of the entire earth, as well as its humanity.
>
> Just preceding each of these Great Outpourings, extraordinary physical disturbances occur, and general unrest is felt throughout by the people. Such disturbance is due to the discord that has accumulated during the last of the preceding period. . . . such inharmony is due, always, to the wandering away from the fundamental "Principle of Life." **Godfré Ray King, *Unveiled Mysteries***

To hold the World Vision, then, we must keep moving toward people and fields of interest that vibrate at the level we wish to attain or exist within. We must keep the *ideal* of what we are striving to achieve ever in our heart.

## ANDEAN PROPHECIES

According to Andean prophecies, between 1990 and 1993, the world underwent a *Pachakuti,* an event that is considered a "cosmic transmutation through which the preparation is made for the coming of a new era of cosmic reordering." Elizabeth Jenkins, director of the Wiraqocha Foundation for the Preservation of Indigenous Wisdom, has been working in the Andean mystic tradition since 1987. Since 1990 she has been collaborating with Peruvian anthropologist Juan Nuñez del Prado, who himself has been studying with the Q'ero Indians of Peru for more than thirty years.

Jenkins told us, "The prophets of the Andes, the holy men and women who are the seers and visionaries of their people, say that the current time period, 1993–2012, is a 'critical period' in the evolution of human consciousness. We have entered the time they call the *Taripay Pacha,* the 'Age of Meeting Ourselves Again.' Until recently, these prophecies were not discussed openly. Now, however, the Andean people say "it is time to put away *fear* and come together for the common good."

The Andeans believe that the new era will be ushered in when a leader emerges with perfect healing powers. This will indicate that the unified field of consciousness has created the conditions whereby individuals will be working less on individual karma than on the collective karma of the planet. The prophecies also predict that now many people are making a transition in their psychospiritual development, from what is called the third level of awareness to the fourth level. At the third level of awareness, there is still widespread fear, conflict, and a sense of separateness. At the fourth level, which resonates with the changes that the Tenth Insight also addresses, we learn to make friends or allies with fear and with the forces of nature. Being able to integrate the collective shadow, the place where the Fear resides, people begin to contribute to the collective evolutionary shift. The fourth level is the place where we also learn to communicate directly with the energies of nature—mountains, rivers, trees, sky, and Earth as discussed in the Third Insight of *The Celestine Prophecy.*

The challenge is to cleanse the collective energy from fear and third-level consciousness, and draw down enough spiritual energy to pass collectively into the fourth level. These ancient prophecies are clear, however, that the shift will not happen if we cannot overcome the Fear.

By gathering human psychic energy, the Andean priests believe that we *seed* the future evolution. All human powers of the body, the mind, and the spirit will then be enhanced, as has been discussed in the Ninth Insight. According to Andean mysticism, the conditions are right—that the developmental stage has arrived—to shift the consciousness of humanity.

Ironically, as our problems become more complex and seemingly intractable, there seems to be less and less the average citizen feels he or she can do. But this is in fact precisely the signal that citizen involvement and community engagement is indispensable and required. Until we recognize and act upon this fundamental truth, we won't be able to significantly change the social conditions we face. **Bill Shore, *Share Our Strengths***

---

WORLD VISION 101

- There is more to life on earth than what the five senses can tell us.

- Until now, we have had only partial information about the world.

- There are many layers of intelligent existence (higher and lower).

- These layers exist in nature (outside us) and inside our own consciousness.

- The other planes of existence are beginning to be known by us through near-death experiences, out-of-body experiences, after-death communications, interventions through saints and angels (and perhaps even extraterrestrial abductions).

- Our fixation on the material plane was purposeful, but is now crumbling.

- Extraordinary experiences that don't fit into our beliefs about reality are forcing us to grow intellectually, emotionally, and physically. This is the paradigm shift.

- Everything happens for a purpose. There is a World Vision of which we can only imagine.

- A critical mass of souls has incarnated in order to hold the World Vision.

- Part of the World Vision is to lift the veil between the dimensions.

- The veil is lifting.

## INDIVIDUAL STUDY

Can you remember the last time you were at a gathering—a picnic, a barbecue, a school play, a vacation spot, a wedding, a baptism, a sacred site—and you wished the day would not end because you felt happy, loved, and connected? At these times you exist in the continuum of energy that has infinite capacity for refinement and joy.

Close your eyes for a moment and re-create a feeling of great joy that you have experienced in the past. Breathe energy and light into the feeling. Now take it even higher.

# CHAPTER 14

# Holding the Vision

BUFFALO
ABUNDANCE

. . . when we pray in the correct fashion, we are not asking God to do something. God is inspiring us to act in his place to enact his will on the Earth. As divine emissaries, we create the physical domain. Every thought, every expectation—all of what we visualize happening in the future—is a prayer, and tends to create that very future. But no thought or desire or fear is as strong as a vision that is in alignment with the divine.

THE TENTH INSIGHT:
HOLDING THE VISION[1]

## TALKING TO THE SPIRIT OF THE RIVER

"Once you've experienced the impossible, your definition of reality is broken open. At that point, you just don't know what's going to happen when the collective energy starts moving through you to open up your life path." Elizabeth Jenkins, the woman who has been studying with the priests of Peru, had called at the *exact moment* this chapter was about to be rewritten. She had just returned from a trip to New York. Before she left, she had called to chat about the trip and was unclear about whether the timing was right. Her intuitive guidance kept saying, "Go now!"

"It turned out that it was absolutely essential that I went," said Jenkins. A writing project had apparently been stalled, and the trip enabled Jenkins to resolve the difficulties in a way that would not have been possible any other way. "The more I trust in these feelings, and follow my heart, the more I am amazed at the coincidences that keep piling up, one after another. I just have to be open to the divine wind blowing in my ear and leading me to the next new thought, the next new sign."

Jenkins has been on her amazing journey for the past eight years, after her initial, synchronistic introduction to the nature mysticism of the Andean tradition. Her nonordinary experiences have already changed the way she sees "reality," and her work of bridging these ancient, powerful practices with "business-as-usual" life is instructive to all of us who are working to serve during the transition. What advice did she want to pass along? we asked.

"Well, I've been very aware of how our filters stop us from taking in a new piece. For example, when I talk about some of my experiences with the Andean priests, I've noticed it's been hard for my more traditional friends to take in what I'm saying—about power objects, for one example. The information about another culture might be vaguely interesting, but it doesn't fit into their life. So, in some cases, I won't dwell on the importance of a *symbol,* but talk about the meaning behind it. If someone is getting stuck on the literal, try to get to the essence of what the information is about. For example, if I were to say to a friend, 'Oh, this object is reputed to have such and such powers,' that picture of a 'magical object' gets stuck in her brain, and the rational part of her has to start arguing with me about whether or not an object can have those powers. That's not really the point. If I want to make our conversation move again, and make it flow, I'll say something like, 'Look, it doesn't matter if we call this a stone or the Holy Grail. The important thing is how it led me to meet so-and-so.' *The importance of an object or an idea is the movement it gives me.* The energetic movements that followed from my having this object may or may not have come from the object itself. The object, per se, is not the point.

"This is how I received messages and kept going forward," said Jenkins. "I was following symbols that had energy for me. That led me to the next point in my story. I then knew what I had to do. I was able

> If we take seriously what . . . contemporary thinkers and explores say . . . then we must be open to the possibility that people like Indian yogis, Tibetan lamas, and some monks on Mount Athos may be in contact with realities inaccessible to ordinary people, who are focused on and attached to the preoccupations of daily living within the gross material world. Given these considerations the wise alternative is not to dismiss a priori the stories that the monks on Mount Athos tell us about miraculous happenings as nothing more than delusions or hallucinations. Rather we should just listen.
>
> Kyriacos C. Markides, *Riding with the Lion*

to go to the next people I had to meet. The literal meaning of something doesn't matter as much as seeing the signs and symbols as messages. You flow with the energy pattern. The form is unimportant and shouldn't take precedence over the energy flow.

"When you go through these encounters with the spiritual, and then back out into the world, I'm finding that my ego expands and contracts. One day you might feel like Jesus Christ. Then the next day you feel like you're nothing, just a little worm learning about life. I think it's just part of the process. We have to get through that part— just not get attached to the fluctuations of the ego. Amazing synchronicities might happen that blow our mind, but then we have to be able to continue even when everything seems boring again."

It was wonderful to hear Elizabeth Jenkins put a voice to some of our own feelings, and to articulate for all of you reading this book one person's experience of what it's like to be on the path. On what path? you ask. Yours! We can't tell you what to look for, or what you are looking for. It wouldn't be a mystery, then, would it? Just be assured that you are one of the bridge-builders. Whatever you can do to wake up to the power in yourself, the clarity within your being of what it is that matters most to you, will pull you across all the thresholds you need to cross. Let's return for a moment to the revelations Elizabeth had on her trip to New York.

"The Pachamama [spirit of the Earth] in New York City is very, very, very powerful," she told us quietly. "People think New York is a place of big buildings, but the *land* of New York City is incredibly powerful [exactly what Joseph Campbell said, by the way]. This is why it has attracted such a mass of creative human energy. I was staying with my friend Linda Michaels, and I went out the door on Saturday morning, thinking that I was going to go to the Metropolitan Museum of Art. I started walking toward the museum. All of a sudden, I hear the voice of the [Hudson] river talking to me. I heard her say in my mind, 'Excuse me! You haven't come and given me an offering. You haven't come and greeted me and said hello.'

"I had no idea where I was," said Elizabeth. "I could have been in the middle of anywhere, because I didn't know where the river was. I got a map at a kiosk. The river was two blocks away from me. I went straight to her and made an offering. She was a big, beautiful, powerful spirit, and she told me everything I needed to know for my meeting with my editor. She also told me, 'Human beings are a part of nature, and you might as well admit it. Human beings keep trying to dominate nature, but show me one human being that can resist the power of a volcano, or resist a tornado, or stop an earthquake. Why not join with nature? Admit her power, and work with her. If you work with me,' the river said, 'you have access to all this power.'

"I was standing in New York City two blocks from Central Park," Elizabeth said softly, "and I could *feel* the power of nature *like a huge force*, and that the city was just a little scab on this force of nature. The city wasn't totally insignificant, but relatively insignificant.

"The rest of that weekend, I had a completely different experience of the city than usual. I had a great time. I usually hate cities, and think that I like to be in nature. But what I realized is that *wherever* I am, I'm in nature. Where can you go that you're not on the Earth?" She was quiet a moment on the telephone before she continued.

"Father Maxime, do you know of a gerontas [teacher] by the name of Vasilios?" I asked as he sat next to me. He smiled and remained silent for a few moments. "Well?" I persisted. "Father Vasilios is my gerontas. I work with him." It was one of those coincidences that make you wonder whether they are in fact coincidences or the result of some ineffable cause hidden from ordinary consciousness. . . . Mt. Athos is a Byzantine survival, a part of an earlier civilization where they believe in miracles. There, gentle, almost invisible miracles actually happen, strings of coincidences that no statistician would believe. Sometimes these sequences follow one out into the world and change one's life. Kyriacos C. Markides, *Riding with the Lion*

"I had just come from Brazil, where I had been studying with my teacher, Don Manuel. We were at the Rio Negro, not far from the Amazon. We walked down to the river, and he began to tell me what the spirit of the river was saying. He was teaching my 'energy bubble' to communicate with the river spirit. So this was exactly the experience I was going to need when I went to New York. The energy of any river has a consciousness, and if you learn to connect to it you can receive information or even get a healing. By the way, I had had a stomachache when I walked down to the Hudson River, and when I left it was gone."

## BEING THE VISION

Holding the World Vision means *being* the World Vision. Holding the Vision is *living it* for yourself and projecting the intention of highest good into the future. In the last chapter of *The Tenth Insight,* David says, "The key aspect of this Vision is not the mere experience of it, although that's hard enough. It's how we *project* this Vision of the future, how we *hold it* for the rest of humanity. That's what the Tenth Insight is really all about."[2]

Hold the Vision by knowing you are here for a purpose. Learn to talk to the Earth spirits. Learn to smell the wind. Listen for the sound that comes out of the crowd. Discipline your mind to take in new information, turning it around and around in your belief system until you see what fits for you at this time in your life. Follow the track that synchronicity lays down, sniffing, listening, standing still like a deer, watching, waiting—then leaping like Pegasus, the winged horse, leaping, leaping across the ravine.

Remember, too, that timing will play a definite part in your plans. Imagine that you are sitting in the center of a cave that has been carved out of yellow-ocher sandstone. The walls, dramatically striated from a million years of river flow, are black. One small piece of the cave wall, however, is illuminated. Seventy-five feet above your head is an opening in the cave that drops a shaft of yellow sunlight on that piece of the wall. You move closer to examine the markings on this clearly lit face of the cave. You see symbols there, and realize that the symbols represent *you* at this exact moment in your life. Until the sun moves in its orbit, you will not be able to see the symbols for your future. Everything has been perfectly timed according to your awakening.

#### BUILDING THE BRIDGE SO THAT WE CAN REACH EACH OTHER

In *The Tenth Insight,* near the end of the story, the group has been struggling to become cohesive enough in their concentration to stop the experiment in the valley. As hard as they try, they cannot hold the vision. There is a flaw. The flaw was in their seeing Feyman, the man who was trying to develop energy technology at any cost, as their enemy—someone to be fought against and defeated. They were giving him energy by focusing on him and empowering him. This is the pitfall that awaits us when we stay in adversarial, "anti-" energy. The group realizes that a more effective action would be to visualize Feyman remembering *why* he was working with energy technology, thus sending energy to his original, positive Birth Vision.

### 1. *Release the Power Struggle and "Get on the Same Side"*

Three principles emerge from this example that will be helpful in your work as a Holder of the Vision. First, treating others as if they are enemies strengthens them *because our "enmity" gives them something to fight against.* This does not mean that we agree with them, but that we try to understand what it is that they are trying to achieve from a positive point of view. What's their ultimate intention? What is the positive force behind their intention? In sending energy to *them* to remember what their original purpose was, we are not trying to "fix" or change them.

Our main thrust should be to keep our attention on our ideal, and work in cooperative ways that advance humanity. It is not helpful to the work you are doing, nor efficient, to get stuck on people and personalities and feeding the polarization of viewpoints. Working solely on outer effects keeps us in the problem. Working on the inner planes, on our own development and openness, helps create the telepathic channels that will attract the support and information we seek. Making use of prayer and visualization to focus our intention is the most powerful co-creative dynamic of the universe. Understanding the fears or diverse points of views that other people carry helps us intuit how we might build a bridge to them.

## 2. No Them There

The second point in the story was that the group learned that everyone must be included in the Vision. Their struggle with Feyman reminded them that we are all interdependent. No longer can we afford to think in terms of "us" and "them." There is no them. There is only us. What one person does, what one group accomplishes, what one country develops—*each thought*—affects every one of us no matter how far away the person, group, or country may physically be. Consciousness, the foundation and interconnecting element of all life, is everywhere.

---

Memory is not a term used by physicists, and yet it is easy to find it in the quantum world—particles that are separated by immense distances of space-time know what one another are doing. When an electron jumps into a new orbit on the outside of an atom, the anti-electron (or positron) paired with it must react, no matter where it lives in the cosmos. In fact, the entire universe is knitted together by this kind of memory network. Deepak Chopra, M.D., *Quantum Healing: Exploring the Frontiers of Mind/Body Medicine*

---

### 3. Ensouling and Making Whole

The third lesson the group taught us was that healing and remembering have much in common energetically. In changing the world, our model might be one of healing—making whole—that which we want to change. Rather than using a model to "fight" crime, poverty, war, and ecological destruction, we might be better equipped when we come from the idea of adding what is missing—loving and nurturing that which is fractured and suffering. Until now, our stage of consciousness has tried to solve things in a confrontational way that all too often winds up in conflict or struggle. Like we saw in the war or conflict paradigm in the health field, we seem now to be ready to move into a pattern-recognition mode which gives us more breadth and depth. By working with the pattern of what we are trying to achieve, we can waste less energy in the conflict, and redirect the energy toward building the positive outcome.

Remembering that each of us is a piece of God (or All-That-Is or Allah), listening to people, respecting their point of view, and letting them know you hear them, increases the vibration of the whole of humanity. In the novel, Wil remarks, "When the five of you increased your energy, and consciously remembered most of the World Vision, you lifted this whole valley into a higher vibratory pattern. It rose closer to the vibratory level of the Afterlife, which means that I now appear clearer to you, as you appear clearer to me. Even the soul groups will become more readily visible in this valley now."[3]

### WALKING YOUR TALK

Remember when you've been in the supermarket and a clerk calls out, "Check stand three is open. No waiting"? You can, no doubt, recall that minor rush of relief that your frustration is at an end, and you can complete your business in the store and move on. Imagine that check stand three is open. There is no waiting. It's time now to practice what you have been reflecting on and reading about. You are in exactly the place you are supposed to be, and there will be no lack of opportunities to meet others. Explore chance encounters. Keep your heart open and your mind alert for where you can do the most good.

The way you handle the next telephone solicitor, the way you lovingly guide a child, the quiet perseverance in handling your work, are all your part of the World Vision. Love and kindness strengthen every soul in his or her purpose.

The benefit is not how much you do, but that you do something, and you do it from your heart. Take the holistic view, which sees a "problem" as only one piece of a larger picture. We have an ability to intervene in the *cycles* of poverty, crime, violence, and unemployment when we reach out to one person at a time. Keep the feeling of love flowing between you and others. Stay connected to the *passion* of why you are doing something. This passion is your connection to the spirit. If you lose your connection to that *value,* you will quickly burn out in your zeal to serve others. Or you will start getting attached to success and fame instead of why you started doing what you're doing. Don't try to save the world and lose yourself. The trick is to work from enlightened self-interest, which means you get a kick out of helping humanity!

> Driving a car you can [practice peace]. Practice breathing and smiling. Walking from your office to the bus stop, you might like to practice what we call walking meditation, not thinking of anything at all, just enjoying walking on this beautiful planet. If you walk like that for three or five minutes, you will recover yourself, and bring serenity back into yourself. That is what we call the practice of meditation in daily life. **Thich Nhat Hanh, interviewed by We the People and Jerry Brown**

Realizing that each obstacle can teach us something valuable that we needed to know helps prevent burnout. Usually we want to remove an obstacle as fast as possible. Reflect on what the obstacle is telling you. What isn't working? What am I not seeing? What does this obstacle have to teach me that I am not aware of right now? Remember A.T.'s words, "It's all messages."

### BLAMING OR SERVICE

Breaking ourselves of the tendency to give in to fear and look for the worst, we stop blaming the external world or "authorities" for the way things are. Instead, we notice what paths open up for us to do something ourselves.

Begin to become aware of other people who are developing, even in small ways, methods to reduce suffering. Is there some organization you feel drawn to? Is there a new way to think about something you feel needs addressing?

Zen Roshi, Bernard Tetsugen Glassman, moved to Yonkers, New York, to start a Zen community. His vision has produced projects and businesses that create affordable housing for homeless people, housing and services for people with AIDS, job training programs, and a Zen center. In an interview for *Inquiring Mind*, Glassman says, "The real teachings of a teacher is his or her life, and students are attracted to a particular teacher because of that teacher's interests and concerns. . . . I do a lot of what I call street retreats or 'bearing witness' work, and some people come here to do those retreats with me, while others come to work at our various projects in Yonkers."

Glassman's approach is to have people raise money from friends, so they can feel what it's like to ask for money and being looked at askance. After the money is raised, it goes to the shelter project, and the person begins to prepare for living on the street for a week. Glassman says, "When you try to panhandle from people, you almost always see their eyes moving away. It's a feeling of rejection that we middle-class people are not used to, and nobody who has been with me on the streets can ever be the same with a street person again. When you're out on the street, pretty soon you start to smell, and nobody wants to look at you, and they don't want you in their restaurants where you would normally go for a cup of coffee. It's a very profound experience."[4]

---

A woman I know sat in a quiet room in her house every day and looked out at the frozen lake and thoughtfully put down what she thought and what was happening day after day—what her little girl said, her husband, the small events of their lives together.

She typewrote this out on yellow sheets of paper and put them away—a big, accumulating pile in a drawer and did not read them again—for nearly a year.

The queer thing was that as she sat there writing and looking at the lake she thought of herself as a pleasant, middle-aged woman with a quiet, ordinary, comfortable, rather uninteresting life.

But a year later when she looked at what she had written—when it had become cold and separate from her, like the writing of a stranger—she was utterly astounded. In the first place she could hardly believe it because it was so good!

"Why—it is very good—startling, remarkable!" she wrote to me. . . . "And I find that instead of having a quiet, pleasant, ordinary life, I have the most violent, extraordinary, terrific life. . . . And the picture of my little girl stands out like a painting by Goya." Brenda Ueland, *If You Want to Write: A Book About Art, Independence and Spirit*

---

Whether we are conscious of it or not, we are all guided by inner intuitions to help. Courage is the natural outcome of 100 percent intention. We have selected a few stories about the actions and programs of ordinary people, whose courage has made an extraordinary difference.

## VISION—IN THIS WORLD

### SAVING THE KIDS

In 1993 Joseph Marshall, Jr., a San Francisco math teacher and cofounder of the Omega Boys Club, spoke before a joint congressional committee consisting of Christopher Dodd's Senate Subcommittee on Families, Drugs and Alcoholism and the House Committee on Children, Youth, and Families. He writes about the experience in his book, coauthored with Lonnie Wheeler, *Street Soldier: One Man's Struggle to Save a Generation—One Life at a Time.* " 'It's funny,' I said on the Senate floor . . . 'but this is not unlike going into a prison or going onto a street corner, where I have to convince the [homeboys] to stop doing what they're doing—to stop dealing drugs, stop gangbanging, stop shooting people. And the key to the whole thing is to get them to believe that it's possible. . . . You need to know that it's possible. And it is. I gotta say that in the beginning. It is.' "[5]

As Lonnie Wheeler says, "Where we see numbers, Marshall sees kids. He sees intelligence, talent, sensitivity, and ambition. Where we see wantonness, he sees potential. Where we see hopelessness, he sees college."[6] Without a whole lot of courage and conviction the numbers look like hopelessness. What are the numbers?[7]

- In 1990, there were 22 handgun deaths in Great Britain, 68 in Canada, 87 in Japan, and 10,567 in the United States.
- Every four hours, an American black child is killed by a gun.
- Of the black men between ages twenty-five and thirty-four who have dropped out of high school, 75 percent are in prison or on parole or probation.
- Although blacks make up only 12.4 percent of the general population of the United States, they constitute more than 50 percent of the inmate population.

And the statistics go on. Joseph Marshall, Jr., and Jack Jacqua see these numbers as evidence of a disease that has infected the country. Over the last twenty-five years, there have been *three times* as many Americans killed in suicide or homicide than Americans killed in all the foreign wars of the twentieth century. Marshall and Jacqua take the view that this infection of violence stems out of conditions and beliefs that can be changed.

In an interview with *San Francisco Chronicle* reporter Catherine Bowman, Marshall says, "I grew up in South-Central Los Angeles. And when I was a kid, I always had a job . . . those kind of jobs don't exist for kids like they did when I was growing up. Right outside their doorstep now there's an illegal way, and a lot of kids get into that at 8 or 9 years old, and never get out of it.

"The second big change [from when I was young] is the proliferation of weapons. . . . these kids have access to Uzis, AK-47s, 9mm weapons of war on the streets of America . . . and I think the biggest thing, certainly the most devastating . . . is the presence of crack. I think it's the worst crime to hit black America since slavery."[8] Marshall relates the story of one nine-year-old whose mother started to neglect him when she became a crack addict. "People were dying in his house, cooking up drugs in the kitchen, blowing crack smoke in his face. His friends told him to smoke dope and drink alcohol. They told him to get a gun and kill the people who had done things to his mother."[9] Eventually, this boy ended up shooting a police officer and was given a seven-year sentence. While he was in the Youth Authority, he met one of the members of the Omega Boys Club and is now on his way to getting his GED with a 3.75 grade point average and is looking forward to going to college this fall.

> There's a fall chill in the air. The north wind is flapping and clanging the loose tin on the barn roof, announcing that the season is changing. The oak trees let go of their leaves, and the wind blows them across the house roof with a crinkling sound. The autumn reds and yellows of the grapevine leaves are at their height. . . . One killing frost will turn the leaves crisp and brown, and they, too, will fall. Arlene Bernstein, *Growing Season: A Healing Journey into the Heart of Nature*

Marshall sees himself as "just the adult down the street looking after kids just like the adults down the street looked out for me." In his case, however, through the work of the Omega club, he has helped send more than one hundred youths to college. The true measure of success for the boys in this program, he says, is that they remain alive and free. College is the icing on the cake.

What Marshall and his partner found by looking at the milieu of violence, watching films, reading books, and using kids as their research base is that there are certain things that constantly happen in violent incidents. "What we tried to do is get a tangible list of things that if you avoided you would decrease the risk of violence. Even if you grew up in a violent neighborhood . . . you could still decrease the risk of something further happening."[10] Their program works with a prescription that promises to significantly increase the chance that these boys will stay alive and out of jail.

Out of their experience, what works with kids are four "rules for living" that replace the negative street codes that get people killed. First, says Marshall, "our definition of a friend is someone who would never lead you to danger." Second, since getting respect is such a big part of street dynamics, he says, "We tell them respect comes from within. You can't get it from anybody else." Third, "we have to talk to them about change. If you want things to change, you have to change yourself." Finally, "the first rule of life is that there's nothing more precious than a person's life."[11]

The two men started the Omega Boys Club "without a dime" and are now funded through foundations, and private and corporate donors. Marshall says proudly, "It costs about $40,000 a year to put one kid in the Youth Authority. I can send 10 kids to college for $40,000— and we're doing it."[12]

## PEOPLE ARE COUNTING ON US

When we can stop dehumanizing people by making them stereotypes and statistics, or by viewing them as either victims or perpetrators, we regain our feelings. In getting in touch with what we have in common with each other, we no longer can sit by and take suffering for granted. The greatest spiritual work we can do is to reduce the gap between "us" and "them," whether it's in a neighborhood, the office, or politics. We do that inside ourselves, by changing our perception and being willing to see their experience.

We, like Joseph Marshall, Jr., and Jack Jacqua, and others in our soul groups, can begin to recognize that people are counting on us for help. For those involved in life that has some grit in it, apathy and denial are replaced by an unexpected smile, a child taking our hand, or somebody that we can call in the middle of the night. We can work like a beaver, shed our skins like a snake, work as tirelessly as the ant, sound the signal like the crow, or fly like the birds.

Once we taste a little success in small actions, there's no going back. That's what spiritual awakening is: no going back. Our intuition will naturally give us direction and strength to "take the time to intervene in conflicts at every level of human culture."[13] The Tenth Insight reminds us that we will act more courageously because we know we will have to face the inevitable Afterlife review "in which we must watch the tragic consequence of our timidity [or failures to intervene]." It reminds us also that taking any position that does not promote inclusiveness is counterproductive.

In the novel, Wil says, "We can learn to intervene spiritually! And that means helping to bring the whole process into consciousness, as these souls here [in the Afterlife] are doing for those caught in the illusions [habitual, destructive mental constructions]. We know that no matter how undesirable the behavior of others is, we have to grasp that they are just souls attempting to wake up, like us."[14]

## GIVING BACK

At age twenty-one Palena Dorsey looked in the mirror and saw a skeleton. "Somewhere I knew that I had two choices," she said. "Either I had to change and walk a different path, or I would *be* that skeleton." Over twenty-two years later she has helped more than 112 troubled young people onto that different path that she herself chose. A single mother with two children of her own, Palena has opened wide the doors to her house to foster children of all races and ages. "The youngest was a nine-year-old prostitute who was put out on the street to support her father's drug habit. Most of my kids have had drug habits, histories of abuse, and run-ins with the law." At one point, Palena, who also held down a full-time job, had twenty-two kids in her eight-bedroom house. Her philosophy is that no child wants to be a prostitute or drug addict.

"The one thing that kids need to know is that

To build a school in northern Baltistan [northern Pakistan] is not an easy endeavor. The area is so rugged and remote that an 85 meter bridge first had to be built over the Braldu river to carry the construction supplies to the school site. Today the bridge is complete, the foundations are laid for the first school, qualified local teachers have been recruited, and a second school is in the works for the village a day's walk from Korphe. . . . it is fitting that the name of the project is Lam Bela—tomorrow's pathway.
*American Himalayan Foundation Newsletter,*
**summer 1996**

you believe in them and trust them," she said. "They need to know that you're for real. I've shared my whole history with them, and they know that I believe they can change, too. Once they feel that you believe in them, they look at themselves in a new light and their whole attitude shifts. If they were in gangs because they needed that group identity, they'll shift away from that street attitude. They don't need to hide behind the gang anymore."

How did she get started? "Well, in 1978, my pastor called me to see if I'd foster a girl who was going to the juvenile home. I agreed to do it because I felt like I wanted to give back since I had overcome so much myself. It wasn't easy in the beginning. I learned what worked and what didn't work. I believe that the most important thing you can do is to listen to kids. Most people talk *at* children, not with them. So I learned to talk with them and to listen to them. I let them know that I trusted them, and expected certain things from them.

"We have certain rules in our house that are nonnegotiable. If they break the rules, they're out and they know that. We also have a big chart with everybody's name and their list of chores. There's a house captain, and if someone doesn't do their chores, the house captain has to do it, even if it takes till midnight. There's also a bowl of consequences—like missing treats for a month or doing more chores. We have two daily meetings, one in the morning before we go off to work, and one after dinner. I don't have any structure to the meeting. I just ask, 'Does anybody have an issue?' "

One of Palena's rules was that each child had to earn the money to buy his or her own bed or bedroom furniture and bring it back to the house on his or her own. "I don't make it easy for them, but once they have achieved something, that experience is theirs to keep." Her goal is always to teach the child to have self-esteem, stimulating their growth with lots of love as well as expectations of responsibility.

"The scariest thing for me, in the beginning, was feeling that I might have been jeopardizing my own children by having them around kids who were talking about their drug highs. But, luckily, they turned out great, and I even have two grandchildren now." Besides the continuing support of the pastor of her church,

It is notable that Dr. Hoerni, one of the grandfather's of the microchip industry, has decided to help children still writing in the dirt. *American Himalayan Foundation Newsletter*, summer 1996

Palena has also received many tangible gifts from the community to help her clothe and feed her brood. She is still in contact with sixty or seventy of the children, now adults, that she fostered. "There's always some percentage of failure, but most of my kids have stayed on their new path, and some of them are now helping other street kids."

What advice does she have for anyone wanting to work with troubled kids? "I believe that there is a reason for everything, and that if there is a wrong, there must be a way to make it right. All my kids were the most important thing in my life, even beyond the fear that I might lose my job if my own past was known. You have to be willing to listen to the kids and let them know you really trust them to do the right thing. They have to have the freedom to speak their mind. Also you need to have patience. You either have patience or you don't, and I don't think you can learn it. I've seen too many people who shouldn't work with kids, but they do and then they wonder why nothing turns out right." What other advice does she have?

"When you go to the foster home, instead of taking the best kid there, take the worst one. The kids that really need you are the ones that nobody else wants."

People like Palena Dorsey, Joseph Marshall, and Jack Jacqua are living examples of the Tenth Insight's prediction that "volunteers working as 'big brothers,' 'big sisters,' and tutors . . . all guided by their inner intuitions to help, [would remember] their intention to make a difference with one family, one child."[15]

---

. . . the villages of western Nepal . . . are so poor that desperate families often sell their young daughters into brothels in India. Five to seven thousand Nepali girls are forced into prostitution each year this way. Many contract AIDS, and most never see their homes again, their young lives cut brutally short.

A safehouse has been established where girls who have been rescued or are in danger can find shelter; if they have nowhere else to go, they also find a home and education . . . a small stipend can help the girl stay in school. The longer they are in school, the less likely it is they will be sold into prostitution.

This approach was piloted with 56 girls in the village of Syangja and was so successful that, with AHF support, it will expand this year to a second village. It is amazing that so little money [$100 per girl/year] makes such a dramatic difference. *American Himalayan Foundation Newsletter,* summer 1996

## SEEDS SPROUT IN DARK PLACES

Recently, the *San Francisco Chronicle* highlighted the work of the Delancey Street Foundation, considered the nation's leading self-help residential education center for former substance abusers and ex-convicts. Although the average resident is functionally illiterate and unskilled when entering Delancey Street, all residents receive a high school equivalency and are trained in three different marketable skills before graduation. During that time, residents learn not only academic and vocational skills but also the interpersonal, social survival skills, along with the attitudes, values, the sense of responsibility, and self-reliance necessary to live in mainstream society drug-free, successfully, and legitimately. One of the unique features of Delancey Street is that this "extended family" has not cost the taxpayer one dime.

The foundation supports itself primarily through a number of training schools such as a restaurant, catering service, moving company, and print shop, which provide vocational skills to all the residents. Under the principle "each one teach one" everyone works.

After twenty-five years of rehabilitating convicts, drug addicts, and prostitutes, the organization has become an accredited satellite campus of Golden Gate University.[16] Engraved in their logo are the words "*Vertere Vertute*," meaning "to transform through courage." Shirley LaMarr, who typifies the type of transformation that Delancey Street has become famous for,

> And all carrying the contagion of the Insights and the crucial message that no matter how tough the situation, or how entrenched the self-defeating habits, each of us can wake up to a memory of mission and purpose.
> *The Tenth Insight: Holding the Vision*

at the age of forty was a drug addict and prostitute with four children and a long line of arrests. Her next stop was prison, but through a deal with police and prosecutors, she chose Delancey Street instead. For her, transformation came in very small pieces. Over time, simple, small things—"like telling the truth, and admitting you messed up, and asking what do I do to fix that"—began to make a difference in her attitude toward what might be possible. "The Delancey Street philosophy is basic," LaMarr said. "There is nothing mystical. It's being responsible, it's learning integrity, to have character, not compromising. It's treating people how you want to be treated, and it's discipline. Good, strong, hard discipline. It ain't soft-stroked. It's tough, hard love." Asked what legacy she'd like to leave, she suggests the words from the new logo, *Vertere Vertute*. "I'm happy with that," she said. "That's what it's all about." This outstanding organization is a tribute to the principle that ordinary people can transform extraordinary—even impossible—dreams into reality by pooling their resources, supporting one another, and living lives of purpose and integrity.

## PRISON MISSION

Our character in *The Tenth Insight* reminds us that transition happens as an evolutionary process. For example, he grasps (in the World Vision) that "in the short run, there would be a need for new prisons and detention facilities, as the traditional truth was recognized that returning offenders to the community too soon, or leniently letting perpetrators go in order to give them another chance, reinforced the behavior. Yet, at the same time, we saw an integration of the Insights into the actual operation of these facilities, introducing a wave of private involvement with those incarcerated, shifting the crime culture and initiating the only rehabilitation that works: the contagion of remembering."[17]

Traditional solutions that focus only on punishment no longer meet the needs of our culture. Warehousing social offenders without any kind of education, training, or psychological rehabilitation will never help society at large.

According to Peter Breen, executive director of Centerforce, a service network concerned with children and families of the incarcerated, "55 percent of children of incarcerated parents are going to end up in prison." In the belief that these already-at-risk children can be diverted from the paths their parents have taken, Centerforce's mission is to help these children heal the wounds that separate them from their mainstream brothers and sisters. In California alone there are now over 350,000 children who have one or both parents in state prisons, and this does not include the children with parents in county and local jails. The number of children with incarcerated parents is expected to nearly double within the next two years. At the present time, nationally, there are an estimated 2.5 million children who have one or both parents in prison.

Centerforce started in 1975 by simply providing basic transportation and child-care services to families visiting inmates at San Quentin. Today it has grown to a network of twenty-seven centers serving thirty state prisons.

Programs such as these are going to be an important aspect of a new World Vision as we shift our culture away from the fear-based denial about crime and *its affect on the whole society*. Holistically, it makes ultimate sense, morally and financially, to help these damaged families who are ostracized and condemned, snubbed by friends, classmates, and community, along with the inmate. Incarcerated parents and spouses often have not had parenting themselves, and lack the skills to deal with their children. Spouses, too, suffer tremendously from economic and emotional pressures. The well-being of these families is an integral part of our own future. The best chance the prisoner has of returning to normal life is to stay connected to hope and love. He needs to be able to watch his kids grow, talk to his wife, and gain insight into himself and his choices, and develop skills that will support him and his family when he returns to the community. In our technical sophistication, we may tend to overlook the necessity for basic tutoring in reading and math and the teaching of discipline, delayed gratification, personal responsibility—and loving forgiveness.

Crow is the omen of change. The Ancient Chiefs tell us that Crow sees simultaneously the three fates—past, present and future. If Crow medicine appears in your [life], you see the laws of the Great Spirit in relation to the laws of humanity.

Crow medicine signifies a firsthand knowledge of a higher order of right and wrong than that indicated by the laws created in human culture. With Crow medicine, you speak in a powerful voice when addressing issues that for you seem out of harmony, out of balance, out of whack, or unjust. **Jamie Sams and David Carson, Medicine Cards**

Four years ago San Quentin instituted a new program, Boot Camp, an alternative sentencing regime for first-time, nonviolent offenders. This unique pilot program, modeled after one in New York, combines military-style drills and early morning exercises with community work details, education, and intensive counseling. In a recent article in the *San Francisco Chronicle,* Erika Zak Bencich, staff psychologist for the program, said that for many inmates, "It's the first time they've had any discipline in their lives, any positive role models. We're teaching them how to live in the first place."[18] So far none of the inmates who have completed the full program—from boot camp through parole—has returned to prison. These kinds of programs depend in large measure on community support and volunteers. Are you called to offer tutoring, counseling, transportation, or child care? Are you in a position to meet with a group of women inmates once a month just to share feelings, hopes, or good books?

## ENVIRONMENTAL MISSION

Pollution happens because of tacit compliance, ignorance, and apathy. We see garbage in the creeks. We cough behind someone's billowing exhaust pipe. We also keep on driving, turning our attention back to our own concerns. With a shift in perspective from our "learned tolerance," one person *can* make a difference.

Like the "inspired witnesses" mentioned in the World Vision, the people in the stories below saw what was needed and took action.

### FOREST GUARDIANS

An environmental organization in New Mexico called Forest Guardians has acquired over 2,500 acres of land in order to protect endangered streamside woodlands from cattle grazing. John Horning, the director of conservation for the organization, interviewed by Salle

---

There is a lovely road that runs from Ixopo into the hills. These hills are grass-covered and rolling, and they are lovely beyond any singing about it . . . the grass is rich and matted, you cannot see the soil. But the rich green hills break down. They fall to the valley below, and falling, change their nature. For they grow red and bare; they cannot hold the rain and mist, and the streams are dry in the kloofs. . . . It is not kept, or guarded, or cared for, it no longer keeps men, guards men, cares for men. The titihoya does not cry here any more.

The great red hills stand desolate, and the earth has torn away like flesh. The lightning flashes over them, the clouds pour down upon them, the dead streams come to life, full of the red blood of the earth. Down in the valleys women scratch the soil that is left, and the maize hardly reaches the height of a man. They are valleys of old men and old women, of mothers and children. The men are away, the young men and the girls are away. The soil cannot keep them any more. **Alan Paton, *Cry, the Beloved Country***

---

Merrill Redfield in *The Celestine Journal*, said, "We were born out of controversy. Back in 1989 the Forest Service proposed to cut the last old-growth forest in the Santa Fe National Forest. Sam Hitt, the founder of the organization, thought the timber sale was not in the public interest and so the organization was founded out of the desire to preserve the old-growth forest. We ultimately prevailed and to this day the unique forest still stands."[19] More recently, Forest Guardians has worked to prevent damage to stream sides caused by cattle stripping away vegetation and polluting the water. "In taking on the cowboy/ranching icon, we realized it would be a very difficult and sensitive issue. So we felt the free market was a way to make the issue as noncontroversial as possible. This was the way we chose to pursue our objective of protecting endangered streamside woodlands without relying on appeals and lawsuits—not that we haven't met with some resistance. The irony in it all is that the ranching community, despite being icons of rugged individualism, has called upon state, county and even the federal government to prevent environmentalists from using the free market." The organization has acquired over 2,500 acres of land, at about fifty cents per acre per year.

Here is a circumstance where the old way of life—ranching—has to give way to a higher vision to serve the land. According to Horning and the Forest Guardians group, there are many areas where livestock grazing is not in the public interest. In addition to the damage being done to public lands, tax dollars—as much as $70 million—are being spent to subsidize the devastation.

Other advocacy efforts to reduce Forest Service cutting have helped, but there is still more work to be done to protect the remnants of the old-growth forest from multinational logging corporations. Unbelievably, the Forest Service may refuse to sell timber rights to the Northwest Ecosystem Alliance, the highest bidder, because they plan to

---

### Wolves—Guardianship, Ritual, Loyalty, and Spirit

Wolves are the epitome of the wild spirit . . . the true spirit of the free and unspoiled wilderness. The wolf has an extreme intelligence . . . a sense of smell [that] endows it with great discrimination . . . and excellent hearing sensitivity.

[The wolf] is a reminder to listen to inner thoughts and words. The wolf has a capacity for making quick and firm emotional attachments. Learning to trust your own insights and to secure your attachments accordingly is part of what wolf medicine teaches. **Ted Andrews,** *Animal-Speak*

---

do no logging. Horning says, "I think it is indicative of the fact that the Forest Service is in bed with the multinational timber companies. . . . the reason we are even in this predicament is that Congress and President Clinton passed a law that suspended all environmental laws on national forests under the guise that somehow logging will help the health of the ecosystem. It is an excuse to go in and cut the last of the ancient forests. We are really trying to foster a connection between people and place. To the extent that we can foster that connection, people will be fiercely passionate about defending the places they know and care about."[20]

At the level of consciousness represented by the Tenth Insight, we can expect new coalitions such as between "old-view hunters and nostalgic history buffs and those who perceived the natural sites as sacred portals" which would help save natural resources such as virgin forests and rain forests. Part of this change in perception will come as intuition and awareness and remembering expand, and developed cultures integrate the mystical knowledge of native peoples.

### AWARD-WINNING ENVIRONMENTAL HEROES

Four 1996 recipients of the Goldman Environmental Prize characterize the kind of awareness, will, and courage in the face of great personal risk that is leading the forefront of the World Vision.

### Jaguars, Wolves, Parrots, and People

Surviving three attempts on his life in drug-trafficking violence, Edwin Bustillos, thirty-one, founded a human rights and environmental organization in 1992 called CASMAC (Advisory Council of the Sierra Madre). The plan is to create a 5-million-acre biosphere reserve

---

[The woodpecker] is a bird connected to the heartbeat of the Earth itself . . . it may also reflect a need to drum some new changes and rhythms into your life.

[The woodpecker] flies in a manner and rhythm unique to itself. All of this serves to emphasize the fact that it will become increasingly important for you to follow your own unique rhythms and flight. Do what works for you in the manner best for you. When woodpecker comes into your life, it indicates that the foundation is there. It is now safe to follow your own rhythms.
**Ted Andrews, *Animal-Speak***

---

in the Sierra Madre Occidental in northern Mexico to protect the highly endangered ecosystems and the four different native cultures that have lived in the mountains for two thousand years. Home to the Tarahumara Indians, whose long-distance running ability is legendary, as well as jaguars, Mexican gray wolves, thick-billed parrots, and hundreds of species of pine and oak, the land has recently been under the domination of militant drug growers. The core indigenous community, surrounded by an old-growth forest, has been officially sanctioned as a reserve recently as a result of the sustained lobbying efforts of Butillos and his tiny organization. Bustillos believes that "amongst dense forests and deep canyons, amongst the noise of birds and falling waters, and amongst an abundance of plant and animal species nothing more is necessary to live. For that reason those who live in harmony with their surroundings live with intelligence."[21]

## Courage in Amazonia

Marina Silva, thirty-eight, spent her childhood making rubber, hunting, and fishing to help her father support their large family. Born in the heart of the Brazilian Amazon, she moved to the city at age sixteen. Although illiterate and suffering an illness, she studied at night and quickly earned a university degree. In the 1980s she returned to the state of Acre and with rubber tapper leader Chico Mendes helped develop the peaceful demonstrations of forest-dwelling rubber tappers against deforestation and the expulsion of communities from their land. Following Mendes' assassination in 1988, Silva continued to work for the creation of sustainable extractive reserves. Today there are 2 million hectares of forest, producing rubber and nuts and managed by indigenous communities. Despite health problems, Silva has become the first rubber tapper to be elected to Brazil's federal Senate. She says, "Our best alternative today is to prolong our days on this planet. All

> The Parrot is a wonderful teacher of the power of light and colors. Some parrots have been taught to mimic humans. Because of this ability, the parrot has been considered a link between the human kingdom and the bird kingdom. Parrots, in this sense, could be likened to ambassadors, diplomats, and interpreters for the bird realm. They have a magic that will enable you to understand others more effectively. They can help you awaken a sense of diplomacy.
> **Ted Andrews,** *Animal-Speak*

of our technical and scientific capacity will have to be used to revert the process of destruction we have created. That is why I am proud to be from Amazonia where we still have a chance to start a sustainable history."[22]

## "I Am Just for the Environment at All Times"

In 1984 Mahesh Chander Mehta, forty-nine, now one of the foremost public interest attorneys in the world, visited the Taj Mahal. He saw that the marble had turned yellow and was pitted as a result of the pollutants from local industries. He filed his first environmental case in the Supreme Court of India, followed by a second on behalf of the seriously polluted Ganges River, which caught fire from industrial effluents. Since that time, every Friday a courtroom has been set aside just for Mehta's cases.

In 1993, after ten years of court battles, the Supreme Court ordered 212 small factories surrounding the Taj Mahal to close because they had not installed pollution control devices. Another 300 factories were put on notice to do the same. Working mostly on his own, Mehta personally investigated the sites and filed cases in response to the suffering he saw. As a result, he has single-handedly won about forty landmark environmental judgments. Mehta is responsible for regulations requiring 5,000 factories to install pollution control devices, and 250 towns to set up sewage treatment plants. He petitioned the Supreme Court to order the federal government to make lead-free gasoline available in the country's four largest cities, and ordered 9,000 pollution industries to be relocated to areas outside of New Delhi. His efforts have also resulted in mandatory environmental education in schools and public gathering places. He cofounded the Indian Council for Enviro-Legal Action, a nonprofit organization of lawyers, scientists, and medical

Elephants embody strength and power. They were seen as symbols of clouds, and many believed that elephants created the clouds . . . they are symbols of the mist that separates the formed worlds from the unformed.

The elephant . . . relies upon its sense of smell. Those with an elephant totem should pay attention to what smells good and what smells bad. Are you not discriminating as you should? Are others? Does something smell funny? Are you not responding, even though things don't smell right? Ted Andrews, *Animal-Speak*

doctors that promotes environmental awareness and strives to get other lawyers involved in public interest environmental litigation. He says, "I am not against anyone at any time, as I am often perceived to be. I am just for the environment at all times. Those whom I oppose in court will realize themselves, one day, that they and their children, too, have been the beneficiaries of environmental protection."[23]

### Show-and-Tell

Amooti Ndyakira, a journalist with *New Vision*, one of the independent newspapers in Africa, has worked relentlessly to raise the public's consciousness about environmental issues. He says, "Only when people are informed will they be aware. Only when they are aware will they take action, and only when they take action will species and the environment be saved."[24] His exposé of the poaching of mountain gorillas and illegal tree-cutting led to stronger protection. Putting himself at great personal risk, Amooti helped in a sting operation to catch a wildlife smuggling ring. He also helped pressure the government into signing an international treaty on endangered species.

## REVOLUTION AT THE HEART OF HUNGER

There are thousands of organizations and groups who are tirelessly working to bring food and shelter to people. One innovative group, Share Our Strength, provides not only food for the stomach, but a whole new model of community service. At a time when most of us are discouraged that neither governmental policy nor charitable organizations can provide sufficient resources for those in true need, there is a new vision of creating community wealth that has already demonstrated that we can reimagine inspired solutions for entrenched problems.

After spending many years in politics as an aide to Senators Gary Hart and Bob Kerry, Bill Shore came to a crossroads. His experience working in government had not only given him valuable skills for organizing and connecting with people but also shown him what government could and could not be expected to do. Around 1987, he made the decision to invest his experience and energy in designing a new model for addressing hunger and poverty. Along with his sister, Debbie Shore, he founded the organization Share Our Strength, which has grown in ten years to a $30-million grant-giving entity that takes none of its funding from the government. In his book *Revolution of the Heart: A New Strategy for Creating Wealth and Meaningful Change*, Shore gives us a powerful blueprint for reinventing the whole idea of the nonprofit organization. The first part of his plan is to change the nonprofit sector from being supported by donations and grants that rely on leftover funds from already strained budgets, to being self-sustaining, entrepreneurial businesses. Secondly, his strategy takes into account our personal need to contribute in meaningful ways—to contribute not just a few dollars here and there, but to give of what we do best.

If we drew up a list of high-priority needs in the world, certainly feeding ourselves and our young would be at the top next to birth control and peaceful co-existence. Children who are undernourished are not only more susceptible to disease, but if they do not receive adequate nutrition when a certain organ needs to be growing—like the brain, for example—the damage can be incalculable and irreversible. These children will have shorter attention spans, less ability to concentrate, and less curiosity. The long-term implications of these deficiencies should be obvious. While hunger in other parts of the world may stem from war or famine, the hunger in the United States stems not only from economic poverty but from a poverty of vision about what's possible to heal it.

> No other animal, except for perhaps the wolf, epitomizes the idea of community more than the prairie dog. A prairie dog community is always filled with activity. The entire town is divided into coteries or individual communities in which the members depend on each other.
>
> They are very sociable . . . greet each other by kissing and hugging. . . . With mouth open, they touch their teeth together. They love to show affection.
>
> Examine your sense of community . . . are you participating fully? **Ted Andrews, *Animal-Speak***

"Before Share Our Strength was an organization it was an idea. And before that, it was an emotion, a reflex, a response," writes Bill Shore. "I've always thought of the impulse that gave birth to SOS as my response to the horrors of the Ethiopian famine, but I can see now that it was a response to that and more. It was also a response to a decade's toil in the trenches of congressional policy making—the triumphs and the disappointments, a response to the superficiality of presidential politics, a response to a childhood made comfortable by caring and compassionate parents. It was the turning of a corner from a place where I'd always seen government or business or other institution as having the principal responsibility for solving social problems to a place where I'd come to see the responsibility, and the promise, that I and others like me held."[25]

Initially, SOS organized a series of national food and wine events called Taste of the Nation in which chefs, restaurateurs, wine merchants, and coffee and liquor companies contributed their talents, time, and resources. Since then, SOS has developed the concept of what they call a Creative Wealth Enterprise—an entrepreneurial hybrid that "provides a product or service for people who want to buy for reasons independent of their charitable intentions."[26]

Shore and his colleagues found that people preferred to give nonmonetary contributions of time and skill. For example, well-known writers such as Anne Tyler wrote stories that were published, with the fees going to SOS. Authors also raise money through readings of their work and publishing anthologies. "SOS now has over 100,000 contributors. A groundbreaking partnership with American Express has more than doubled the size of the organization and helped build other partnerships with Northwest Airlines, Universal Studios, Seagram's, Fetzer Vineyards, Barnes and Noble, Starbucks Coffee, Calphalon Cookware, Gallo Wines, and many more. In 1996 Share Our Strength will raise and spend more than $16 million to support community-based efforts aimed at both relieving and preventing hunger. None of this money comes from the government, nor will it come from other foundations or direct mail. Instead, new wealth will be generated and new dollars will be brought to the effort so that all groups fighting hunger and poverty can benefit."[27]

One of the practical suggestions listed in *Revolution of the Heart* is to select an item in your business whose purchase will benefit whatever

> If everyone in the world took five or ten minutes daily to stop and think, it would help us all to go about God's work, because we need reflection, we need to ask God for His blessing daily, and we need to bring Him into our lives so we can give Him to others. When we have God in our lives it brings meaning into them, it makes everything worthwhile and fruitful, too. The absence of God usually accompanies the less-than-perfect things in our world. **Lucinda Vardey,** *Mother Teresa: A Simple Path*

cause is closest to your heart. Shore says, "It not only raises money and awareness of important community issues but gives your customers an opportunity to make choices that are socially responsible as well."[28]

Patronize Community Wealth Enterprises such as Newman's Own (Paul Newman's food company donates 100 percent of after-tax profits to a wide range of charitable and educational causes), Working Assets, Timberland, American Express, House of Seagram's, and FILA.

Use your skill or teach it. Find a school, community center, or nonprofit organization where you can teach or volunteer your skill or creative passion. If you are attracted to this kind of approach, read Bill Shore's book or call the office of Share Our Strength listed in our Resource Directory in the appendix.

When we focus on blaming others, whether it be an inefficient government or multinational corporations, we unwittingly fall into dehumanizing people and feeding the polarization of good and bad. When we look for higher solutions—like sharing what we do best— and personally take responsibility, we are holding the Vision. We feel good about ourselves, our energy stays full, and people are helped. We are connected to our original intention.

## CONTINUING TO AWAKEN

In *The Tenth Insight*, Wil brings us an important message: "These same experiences are occurring to people all over the planet. After we grasp the first nine Insights, each of us is left at the same place— trying to live this reality day-to-day, in the face of what seems to be a growing pessimism and divisiveness all around us. But at the same time, we are continuing to gain a greater perspective and clarity about our spiri-

> The challenges of the last decade before the millennium can be successfully met once we realize the necessity to truly reorder our world, based on higher principles and not just tinker with current systems. **Corinne McLaughlin and Gordon Davidson, *Spiritual Politics: Changing the World from the Inside Out***

tual situation, about who we really are. We know we are awakening to a much larger plan for planet Earth."[29] It happens one step at a time.

## PLANTING AND HARVESTING TOGETHER

Janine Echabarne, a single mother and artisan, has lived in Central California for twenty years. She and her two adolescent boys live in a tiny but cozy old house set in the middle of almond orchards. Janine's story illustrates how a burden for her was a gift of life for someone who had lost not only family and friends but identity and a homeland.

"I have a large garden," she told us. "After being away from it for a year, I found myself in June standing in waist-high weeds. To me a garden is the center of a home, and I wanted the garden to bloom again. I had asked my neighbors if they would like to revive it with me, but they weren't interested.

"One day a thought popped into my head that I could ask a Hmong family to come and share the garden with me. There is a large community of Hmong who have settled here in Merced county when they were forced to flee their homeland after the Vietnam War. I had noticed some of their own wonderful gardens in the area.

"I called Lao Family Community, Inc., an agency that helps Southeast Asians to adapt to American culture. They put my name on cable access TV, and the very next day I got a call from twelve-year-old, May Der, who said her mom was interested because her garden had just been ruined by neighbor kids.

"After I hung up the phone, I started thinking a little, and I got scared. There are some Asian gangs around here now as a result of the breakdown of their original family structures in the relocation. I started thinking, 'Uh-oh, what am I inviting in here?' Then I remembered that this fear has been with me before whenever I've taken a new step. It seems to be a natural reaction of opening the heart. As soon as my heart opens it also allows fear to enter. So I moved through it. The next day Gee Vang and her daughter came over, and we talked about the terms of our sharing. Foremost in my concerns was that no poisons or chemical fertilizers be used. Otherwise, we'd just begin and see what happened.

"Within a month the garden looked like it had always been there. Everything Gee puts into the ground grows like magic. She has taught me so many things! Fresh food is very important for the Hmong people. Even if they live in an apartment, they will use every scrap of ground. I have gotten to know the whole family,

. . . we try not to store the things that we need, and just to manage with whatever comes as it comes. I think in this way we will continue to receive God's blessings, especially if we don't become extravagant and if we don't get caught up in living for the future, instead of right now in the present. **Lucinda Vardey, Mother Teresa: A Simple Path**

and sometimes I tutor the kids. I also help with language problems with insurance and so forth. Getting to know the community of Hmong through Gee I realized how much personal suffering they have all endured. Most have lost families in the escape from Laos. Here they experience a feeling of soul loss and culture loss, but I think in their beautiful gardens they retain much of their spirit and connection to their culture. Gee has seeds that originated in Laos and have been propagated in many seasons of growing in America. I am very honored that she shares them with me, and that I can be helpful to her once in a while.

"I'm enjoying the friendship with Gee, her husband, Chue, their nine children, and their vast extended family. She and I eat together, shop together, and I often go to school functions with all our kids.

"Gee says, 'We share ideas like a mother and daughter. I can trust Janine and she can trust me. And everything I don't know she tries to explain to me, and tells me what to do. The information is very important to keep in my mind forever.'"

This story reveals how one person acted in spite of her fear. Her action is a bridge to those who have been harshly uprooted through no fault of their own, and a role model for the rest of the community.

---

Mary, a volunteer for Missionaries of Charity, works in a soup kitchen and says, "I've found that practical help can actually put people down unless it's done with love. . . . making contact comes in stages . . . it's best to try not to get too busy with giving out the food and clearing up the plates but to try to make a point of talking to somebody while you're there, or sitting down beside somebody—trying to make one-to-one contact." **Lucinda Vardey,** *Mother Teresa: A Simple Path*

---

There is no recipe for action. Just notice what you are experiencing and ask for guidance as to what first step you might take. Notice what shows up for *you.*

### GOING TO GRANDMOTHER'S HOUSE—A NEW STORY

Kim Burroughs of Toronto also acted on intuitive guidance. One day she decided to accomplish one small project that had been a kind of "nagging idea" for a long time. Kim said, "I kept thinking what a waste it was to have all these seniors living in nursing homes who still had a bright mind and lots of energy, but not the ability to get out on their own. And I thought how great it would be if they could spend time with children, who also need that kind of one-on-one attention that is so rare in families today. Most of us don't spend a lot of time with grandparents and they are such a link to our sense of heritage. I was determined to see if I could accomplish some kind of connection between the two.

> They are hungry not only for food, they are hungry to be recognized as human beings. They are hungry for dignity and to be treated as we are treated. They are hungry for our love.
> **Lucinda Vardey, *Mother Teresa: A Simple Path***

"I first looked in the phone book to get addresses of nursing homes and elementary schools. I drove around on a Saturday with a friend. By the afternoon we had found just what I was looking for—a school and a nursing home that were literally across the street from each other.

"I called up the principal at the school, met with her and some teachers, and told them my idea, and we looked at what would have to happen to make it work. I then talked to the coordinators at the nursing home, and we all got together to work out the details. No one knew if it would work out or not, but we decided to give it a try.

"It was pretty exciting to see those kids come bouncing into the home the first afternoon. I had told the seniors, 'Just listen to the kids. You don't have to correct them or anything, but just let them read to you or you read to them. Just see them as special and bright little kids.' I purposefully did not tell the seniors anything about the kids, like whether they were considered shy, or troublemakers, or slow or gifted or anything. I didn't want anybody labeled.

"I encouraged the seniors to tell the kids about what Toronto was like in their day, and the kids were fascinated by the changes from then to now. Sometimes, they even just played bingo together. Well, after four months of these weekly visits we were all amazed. The principal was blown away by the positive changes in these kids. One boy in particular had been very aggressive in class, and he totally calmed down and was more attentive in class, but all the kids expressed some kind of improvement. We did a little graduation ceremony, and I asked the children to write a short statement about what they had experienced with the seniors and then read it to everybody. It was so great—they said things like, 'Old people aren't boring.' 'I had a really neat time.' 'I liked hearing about the old days.' The staff in the nursing home were also impressed at the changes in attitudes in the seniors who participated in this program. We're definitely going to do it again next year.

"There was one woman, Margaret, who had never had children of her own. She always came early to the sessions, and had all her books ready. On the day of the graduation she stayed up in her room

---

Once I was playing the piano and a musician, overhearing it, said to me: "It isn't *going* anywhere. You must always play to *someone*—it may be to the river, or God, or to someone who is dead, or to someone in the room, but it must go somewhere." **Brenda Ueland, *If You Want to Write: A Book About Art, Independence and Spirit***

---

because she didn't want to see the program come to an end. Two of the kids went upstairs and read their statement to her and said, 'You are our best friend,' and gave her a big hug."

## Ceaseless Praying

Most of this book has been oriented to describing how ordinary people open up to their spiritual guidance in order to serve the greater good of humanity *in the secular world*. Some souls are born to work for the benefit of the World Vision in complete anonymity and seclusion. Hermits and sacred orders of monks and nuns have retreated from the mainstream of life, and dedicated their energies to direct and ceaseless communication with divine spirit. The literature is filled with legends of miracles and healings from mystics who have, through many lifetimes of perseverance, been able to achieve nonordinary states and perform materialization, teleportation, miraculous rescues, and much more.

Any reputable spiritual adept, however, will deny any such powers! The way to these powers, ironically, is to reach a state "where one does not have any personal desires, when one becomes pure, clean of any egotistical yearnings, [and] then what one asks is given because his will becomes one with the will of God. What the saint desires is exactly what God desires, therefore it is given. This is the purpose of *askesis* [the ascetic way of life]."[30] Markides goes on to say that the person who pursues this very focused way of life overcomes any fixation on personal passion and desire in order that the Holy Spirit may have a clear channel, emptied of egotism, through which to flow. Markides was given an esoteric text by an Orthodox Finn, Tito Collianter.

In this book, *The Way of the Ascetics,* he reads, " 'For him who has no individual, passionate desires, all things go in the direction that he desires them to go. . . . His will converges with the will of God and anything that he may ask in prayer is given.' It is for this reason, I was led to understand, that when gerontes or staretzs like Father Vasilios pray for the welfare of the world their prayers are extremely important. And it is for this reason that they ceaselessly pray."[31]

We each have a place on the planes of consciousness. "And you must know that if those who pray disappear then that would bring the end of the World."[32]

## You Are a Great and Powerful Being of Light

Take a moment now to close your eyes and return to the cave in which you saw the symbols of your life. Go inside and sit in the very middle of the cave, inside the shaft of light that is streaming down from the opening high above your head. Sit in the shaft of light and notice that you are becoming translucent as the golden light washes over you.

Your translucency splashes against the striated ocher walls of the cave, illuminating the cave in all directions. You are at one with the light.

# Directory of Resources

Center for Ecoliteracy
2522 San Pablo Avenue
Berkeley, CA 94702
tel:510-845-4595
fax:510-845-1439

> The Elmwood Institute's Ecoliteracy project fosters ecological literacy in schools by helping design an ecologically oriented K-12 curriculum and by transforming schools into collaborative learning communities.

Foundation for Global Community
222 High Street
Palo Alto, CA 94301
tel:415-328-7756
fax:415-328-7785

> Publishes *Timeline,* a six-issue-per-year journal dedicated to discovering, living, and communicating what is needed to build a world that functions for the benefit of all life.

Institute of Noetic Sciences
475 Gate Road, suite 300
Sausalito, CA 94965
http://www.noetic.org

> Provides research grants for leading-edge science and scholarship, organizes lectures and conferences, and publishes the *Noetic Sciences Review,* a quarterly journal.

Integral Health Professional Network
Richard B. Miles, executive coordinator
6876 Pinehaven Road
Oakland, CA 94611
rbmihpn@aol.com
tel:510-655-9951
fax:510-654-6699

> Publishes a six-times-a-year newsletter, *New Health Catalyst,* exploring the frontiers of integral health.

International Alliance of Holistic Lawyers
William Van Zyverden
P.O. Box 26
Middlebury, VT 05753
tel:802-388-7478

> Dedicated to promoting long-range problem-solving rather than short-term litigation as a means of resolving disputes.

Religious Science International
P.O. Box 2152
Spokane, WA 99210
tel:509-624-7000
fax:509-624-9322

> Dedicated to fostering new thought principles in spiritual practice.

Summit Intermediate School
Shirley Richardson
5523 Santa Cruz
El Cerrito, CA 94804

> Dedicated to emphasizing the enjoyment of academic learning, to foster respect for the individual and for our society, and to promote a sense of higher purpose for our lives.

The Natural Step
4000 Bridgeway #102
Sausalito, CA 94965
tel:415-332-9394
fax:415-332-9395
natstep@2nature.org

>  Dedicated to discovering and implementing ecologically sustainable methods of business and manufacture.

The Spirit of Health!
114 Washington Avenue
Point Richmond, CA 94801
khnow@aol.com
tel:510-236-2075
fax:510-236-1979

>  Publishes the *Work and Spirituality Guide,* a comprehensive directory of resources to help managers improve performance by addressing worker's spiritual concerns.

Unity School of Christianity
1901 NW Blue Parkway
Unity Village, MO 64065-0001
tel:816-251-3535
fax:816-251-3550

>  A beacon of spiritual light to the world community.

Universal Foundation for Better Living
11901 South Ashland Avenue
Chicago, IL 60643

>  A Christian foundation that seeks to model the principles of new thought.

# Notes

## CHAPTER 1

1. James Redfield, *The Tenth Insight: Holding the Vision* (New York: Warner Books, 1996), p. 8.
2. Paul H. Ray, "The Rise of Integral Culture," *Noetic Sciences Review* 37 (spring 1996), p. 11.
3. Ibid., p. 8.
4. Ibid.
5. Daniel Goleman, *Emotional Intelligence: Why It Can Matter More Than IQ*, p. xii.
6. Patricia Hurley, letter, *The Celestine Journal,* January 1996, p. 7.
7. Marla Cukor, letter, *The Celestine Journal,* January 1996, p. 7.
8. Kyriacos C. Markides, *Riding with the Lion: In Search of Mystical Christianity* (New York: Penguin, 1995), p. 337.

## CHAPTER 2

1. James Redfield, *The Tenth Insight: Holding the Vision* (New York: Warner Books, 1996), p. 14.
2. Ibid., p. 2.
3. Alvin Stenzel, M.D., *The Celestine Journal* 2, no. 12 (December 1995), p. 7.
4. Caroline Myss, "Why People Don't Heal: How You Can Overcome the Hidden Blocks to Wellness," Sounds True Studios, Boulder, CO 1994.
5. Michael McCabe, "A Decade of Opportunity," *San Francisco Chronicle,* March 8, 1996, p. A4.
6. Larry Dossey, M.D., *Healing Words: The Power of Prayer and the Practice of Medicine* (HarperSanFrancisco, 1993), pp. 86–87.
7. Jack Kornfield, *A Path with Heart: A Guide Through the Perils and Promises of Spiritual Life* (New York: Bantam Books, 1993), p. 162.
8. Pat Brady Waslenko, letter, *The Celestine Journal* 2, no. 2 (February 1995), p. 6.

## CHAPTER 3

1. James Redfield, *The Tenth Insight: Holding the Vision* (New York: Warner Books, 1996), p. 3.

2. Ibid., p. 23.
3. Sandra Fry, letter, *The Celestine Journal* 2, no. 3 (March 1995), p. 7.
4. Redfield, *Tenth Insight,* p. 71.
5. Sam Whiting, "A Friend for Life," *San Francisco Chronicle Datebook,* April 7, 1996, p. 35.
6. Allan Ishac, letter, *The Celestine Journal* 2, no. 6 (June 1995), p. 7.
7. Redfield, *Tenth Insight,* p. 73.
8. Marilyn Allan, letter, *The Celestine Journal* 2, no. 11 (November 1995), p. 7.
9. Redfield, *Tenth Insight,* p. 82.
10. Marie-Louise Von Franz, *On Divination and Synchronicity: The Psychology of Meaningful Chance* (Toronto: Inner City Books, 1980), p. 81.
11. Redfield, *Tenth Insight,* p. 220.
12. Ibid., p. 77.
13. Ted Andrews, *Animal-Speak: The Spiritual & Magical Powers of Creatures Great & Small* (St. Paul: Llewellyn Publications, 1994), p. ix.
14. Ibid., p. x.
15. Ibid.
16. Ibid., p. 13.
17. Redfield, *Tenth Insight,* p. 219.
18. Dan Miller, letter, *The Celestine Journal* 2, no. 11 (November 1995) p. 7.
19. Jean Houston, *The Possible Human* (Los Angeles: Jeremy P. Tarcher, 1982), pp. 98–100.
20. Ibid., p. 221.
21. R. L. Wing, *The I Ching Workbook* (New York: Doubleday, 1979), p. 9.
22. Nancy Vittum, letter, *The Celestine Journal* 2, no. 6 (June 1995), p. 7.
23. James A. Swan, *Sacred Places: How the Living Earth Seeks Our Friendship* (Santa Fe, NM: Bear & Co., Inc., 1990), p. 33.

## CHAPTER 4

1. James Redfield, *The Tenth Insight: Holding the Vision* (New York: Warner Books, 1996), p. 156.
2. Caroline Myss, "Why People Don't Heal: How You Can Overcome the Hidden Blocks to Wellness," Sounds True Audio, Boulder, CO 1994.
3. Ibid.
4. Russell E. DiCarlo, *Towards a New World View: Conversations at the Leading Edge* (Erie, PA: Epic Publishing, 1996), p. 148.
5. Ibid, p. 150.
6. Ibid.
7. Redfield, *Tenth Insight,* p. 177.
8. Hans TenDam, *Exploring Reincarnation* (London: Penguin Books, 1990), p. 106.
9. Redfield, *Tenth Insight,* p. 175.
10. Brian L. Weiss, M.D., *Many Lives, Many Masters* (New York: Simon & Schuster, 1988), p. 69.
11. Ibid., pp. 176–77.

## CHAPTER 5

1. James Redfield, *The Tenth Insight: Holding the Vision* (New York: Warner Books, 1996), p. 57.
2. Ibid., p. 168.
3. Larry Dossey, M.D., *Healing Words: The Power of Prayer and the Practice of Medicine* (HarperSanFrancisco, 1993), p. 49.
4. Ibid., pp. 109–10.
5. Rosemary Altea, *The Eagle and the Rose* (New York: Warner Books, 1995), pp. 210–11.
6. Redfield, *Tenth Insight*, p. 67.
7. George Leonard and Michael Murphy, *The Life We Were Given: A Long-Term Program for Realizing the Potential of Body, Mind, Heart, and Soul* (New York: Jeremy P. Tarcher/Putnam Books, 1995), p. xv.
8. Ibid., p. 20.
9. Ibid., p. 22.
10. Ibid., p. 29.
11. Henry Dreher, "The Healing Power of Confession," *Natural Health*, July/August 1992.
12. Redfield, *Tenth Insight*, p. 64.
13. *San Francisco Chronicle*, April 1996.
14. "Who Says There Are No Heroes Anymore?" *San Francisco Chronicle*, May 4, 1995, p. C14.


## CHAPTER 6

1. James Redfield, *The Tenth Insight: Holding the Vision* (New York: Warner Books, 1996), p. 24.
2. Robert Monroe, *Journeys Out of the Body* (New York: Doubleday, 1971), p. 74.
3. Ibid., p. 75.
4. Ibid.
5. Raymond L. Moody, Jr., M.D., *Life After Life* (New York: Bantam Books, 1988), p. 120.
6. Ruth Montgomery, *A Search for Truth* (New York: Ballantine Books, 1966), p. 177.
7. Ibid., p. 178.
8. Ibid., p. 86.
9. Kenneth Ring, Ph.D., *Heading Toward Omega: In Search of the Meaning of the Near-Death Experience* (New York: William Morrow, 1985), pp. 39–40.
10. Moody, *Life After Life*, p. 68.
11. Hans TenDam, *Exploring Reincarnation* (London: Penguin Books, 1990), p. 179.
12. Brian Weiss, *Only Love Is Real: A Story of Soul Mates Reunited* (New York: Warner Books, 1996), pp. 54–55.

13. Ibid., p. 85.
14. Bill Guggenheim and Judy Guggenheim, *Hello from Heaven!: A New Field of Research Confirms That Life and Love Are Eternal* (New York: Bantam Books, 1995), p. 20.
15. Moody, *Life After Life*, p. 135.
16. Ibid.
17. TenDam, *Exploring Reincarnation*, p. 217.
18. Redfield, *Tenth Insight*, pp. 81–82.
19. Guggenheim and Guggenheim, *Hello from Heaven*, p. 342.
20. TenDam, *Exploring Reincarnation*, p. 149.
21. Moody, *Life After Life*, p. 24.
22. Raymond A. Moody, Jr., M.D., *Reflections on Life After Life* (New York: Bantam Books, 1977), p. 23.
23. Ibid., p. 26.
24. Kenneth Ring, *Heading Toward Omega: In Search of the Meaning of the Near-Death Experience* (New York: William Morrow, 1985), p. 111.
25. Ibid., pp. 111–12.
26. Ibid.
27. Ibid., p. 114.
28. Ruth Montgomery, *A World Beyond* (New York: Ballantine Books, 1971), pp. 65–66.
29. Ibid., p. 70.
30. Weiss, *Only Love Is Real*, pp. 168–69.
31. TenDam, *Reincarnation*, p. 343.
32. Ibid., p. 219.
33. Malidoma Patrice Somé, *Of Water and the Spirit: Ritual, Magic, and Initiation in the Life of an African Shaman* (New York: Penguin Books, 1995), pp. 18–19.

## CHAPTER 7

1. James Redfield, *The Tenth Insight: Holding the Vision* (New York: Warner Books, 1996), p. 81.
2. Thomas Moore, *Soul Mates: Honoring the Mysteries of Love and Relationship* (New York: HarperPerennial, 1994), p. viii.
3. Redfield, *Tenth Insight*, pp. 113–14.
4. Ibid., p. 114.
5. Ibid., p. 78.
6. Hans TenDam, *Exploring Reincarnation* (London: Penguin Books, 1990), p. 149.
7. Ibid., pp. 244–45.
8. Redfield, *Tenth Insight*, p. 80.
9. Ibid., p. 120.
10. Ibid., p. 121.
11. TenDam, *Exploring Reincarnation*, pp. 149–50.
12. Ibid., p. 150.
13. Redfield, *Tenth Insight*, p. 113.

14. Ruth Montgomery, *A Search for Truth* (New York: Ballantine Books, 1996), p. 100.
15. Glenn Williston and Judith Johnstone, *Discovering Your Past Lives: Spiritual Growth Through a Knowledge of Past Lifetimes* (Wellingborough, England: Aquarian Press, 1983), p. 207.
16. Ibid., p. 208.
17. Montgomery, *Search for Truth,* p. 95.
18. Albert Savedra, *San Francisco Chronicle,* February 1996.
19. Ross Sondergaard Rasmussen, ibid.
20. Brownie McGhee, ibid.
21. Eleanor Clark, ibid.
22. Rosalie E. Taylor, ibid.
23. Eligio Panti, ibid.
24. Page Smith and Eloise Smith, ibid.
25. Benny Ong, ibid.

## CHAPTER 8

1. James Redfield, *The Tenth Insight: Holding the Vision* (New York: Warner Books, 1996), p. 143–44.
2. Robert Monroe, *Journeys Out of the Body* (New York: Doubleday, 1971), p. 78.
3. Glenn Williston and Judith Johnstone, *Discovering Your Past Lives* (Wellingborough, England: Aquarian Press, 1983), p. 210.
4. Robert Monroe, *The Ultimate Journey* (New York: Doubleday, 1994), p. 113.
5. Ibid., p. 123.
6. Redfield, *Tenth Insight,* p. 134.

## CHAPTER 9

1. James Redfield, *The Tenth Insight: Holding the Vision* (New York: Warner Books, 1996), p. 26.
2. Andrew Bard Schmooker, in *Meeting the Shadow,* edited by Connie Zweig and Jeremiah Abrams (New York: Jeremy P. Tarcher, 1991), p. 190.
3. Robert Bly, *A Little Book on the Human Shadow* (San Francisco: Harper & Row, 1988), pp. 26–27.
4. Redfield, *Tenth Insight,* p. 97.
5. Ibid., p. 106.
6. The Dalai Lama and Jean-Claude Carrière, *Violence and Compassion,* (New York: Doubleday, 1996), pp. 7–11.
7. Ibid., p. 23.
8. Ramon G. McLeod, "U.S. Population Expected to Be Half Minorities by 2050," *San Francisco Chronicle,* March 15, 1996.
9. Fran Peavey, with Myrna Levy and Charles Varon, "Us and Them," in *Meeting the Shadow: Hidden Power of the Dark Side of Human Nature,*

edited by Connie Zweig and Jeremiah Abrams (New York: Jeremy P. Tarcher, 1991), pp. 206–207.
10. Ibid.
11. Ibid.
12. Ibid.
13. Ibid.
14. Robert Monroe, *The Ultimate Journey* (New York: Doubleday, 1994), p. 149.
15. Ibid., p. 150.

## CHAPTER 10

1. James Redfield, *The Tenth Insight: Holding the Vision* (New York: Warner Books, 1996), p. 209.
2. Margaret Wheatley, "The Unplanned Organization: Learning from Nature's Emergent Creativity," *Noetic Sciences Review*, spring 1996, p. 19.
3. Paul H. Ray, Ph.D., "The Rise of Integral Culture," *Noetic Sciences Review*, spring 1996, p. 13.
4. Redfield, *Tenth Insight*, p. 173.
5. Ibid., p. 175.
6. Ibid., p. 176.
7. Ibid., p. 178.
8. Benjamin Barber, "The Global Culture of McWorld," *The Commonwealth*, February 26, 1996, p. 12.
9. Redfield, *Tenth Insight*, p. 181.
10. Walt Hays, "The Natural Step: What One Person Can Do: The Story of Karl-Henrik Robèrt," *Timeline*, The Foundation for Global Community, Palo Alto, CA, March/April, 1995, p. 2.
11. Ibid., p. 5.
12. Redfield, *Tenth Insight*, p. 182.
13. Ibid., pp. 183–84.

## CHAPTER 11

1. James Redfield, *The Tenth Insight: Holding the Vision* (New York: Warner Books, 1996), p. 199.
2. Alice A. Bailey, *A Treatise on White Magic or The Way of the Disciple* (New York: Lucis Publishing Company, 1980), p. 400.
3. Redfield, *Tenth Insight*, p. 205.
4. Barbara Sher and Annie Gottlieb, *Teamworks!: Building Support Groups That Guarantee Success* (New York: Warner Books, 1989), p. 44.
5. Ibid., p. 46.
6. Russell E. DiCarlo, interview with Dr. Beverly Rubik, *Towards a New World View: Conversations at the Leading Edge* (Erie, PA: Epic Publishing, 1996), p. 50.

7. William Drozdiak, *Washington Post*, "Onetime 'Sewer of Europe,' The Rhine Is Reborn," printed in *The San Francisco Chronicle*, April 1, 1996, p. A9.
8. Tom Hurley, "Community Groups," *Noetic Sciences Bulletin*, spring 1996, Institute of Noetic Sciences, Sausalito, CA, p. 2.
9. Ibid., p. 3.
10. Russell E. DiCarlo, interview with Peter Senge, Ibid., p. 217.
11. Michael H. Murphy and Rhea A. White, *In the Zone: Transcendent Experiences in Sports* (New York: Penguin Books, 1995), p. 75.
12. Ibid., p. 76.
13. Ibid.
14. Ibid.
15. Redfield, *Tenth Insight*, p. 186.
16. Ruth Montgomery, *A Search for Truth* (New York: Ballantine Books, 1966), p. 95.
17. Redfield, *Tenth Insight*, p. 188.

## CHAPTER 12

1. James Redfield, *The Tenth Insight: Holding the Vision* (New York: Warner Books, 1996), p. 205.
2. William Van Zyverden, "Holistic Lawyering," *Legal Reformer*, January/March 1994, p. 5.
3. William Van Zyverden, "Collaborative Law—Moving Settlement Toward Resolution," *Vermont Bar Journal & Law Digest*, February 1994, p. 35.
4. Ibid., p. 36.
5. Ibid.
6. Laurette Rogers, *The California Freshwater Shrimp Project: An Example of Environmental Project-Based Learning*, (Berkeley: Heyday Books, 1996), p. 3.
7. Ibid., p. 3.
8. Ibid., p. 35.
9. Ibid., p. 14.
10. Alice Waters, "Dear Mr. President . . . ," monograph, The Center for Ecoliteracy, Berkeley, CA, 1995.
11. Torri Minton, "Schoolkids Help Save Marin Salt Marsh," *San Francisco Chronicle*, May 4, 1996, p. A13.
12. Fritjof Capra, "Hyping Computers in Education," *San Francisco Chronicle*, March 12, 1996, editorial page.
13. James Hillman, interview, *Sculpture*, March/April 1992, p. 16.

## CHAPTER 13

1. James Redfield, *The Tenth Insight: Holding the Vision* (New York: Warner Books, 1996), p. 212.

2. Alice A. Bailey, *The Rays and the Initiations,* vol. 5, *A Treatise on the Seven Rays* (New York: Lucis Publishing Company, 1960), p. 749.
3. Robert Monroe, *Journeys out of the Body* (New York: Doubleday, 1971), p. 267.
4. Ibid.
5. Bill Guggenheim and Judy Guggenheim, *Hello from Heaven!* (New York: Bantam Books, 1995), p. 146.
6. Ibid., p. 94.
7. Redfield, *Tenth Insight,* p. 213.
8. Michael Murphy, *The Future of the Body: Explorations into the Further Evolution of Human Nature* (Los Angeles: Jeremy P. Tarcher, 1992), p. 160.

## CHAPTER 14

1. James Redfield, *The Tenth Insight: Holding the Vision* (New York: Warner Books, 1996), p. 223.
2. Ibid., p. 217.
3. Ibid., p. 234.
4. Barbara Gates and Wes Nisker, "Street-Wise Zen: An Interview with Bernard Tetsugen Glassman," *Inquiring Mind* (Berkeley, 1996), p. 11.
5. Joseph Marshall, Jr., and Lonnie Wheeler, *Street Soldier: One Man's Struggle to Save a Generation—One Life at a Time* (New York: Delacorte Press, 1996), p. xxv.
6. Ibid., p. xiv.
7. Ibid., pp. xiii–xiv.
8. Catherine Bowman, "A Man Malcolm Could be Proud of," *San Francisco Chronicle,* Sunday Section, April 28, 1996, p. 5.
9. Ibid.
10. Ibid.
11. Ibid.
12. Ibid.
13. Ibid., p. 6.
14. Redfield, *Tenth Insight,* p. 149.
15. Ibid., p. 205.
16. George Raine, "25 Years of Tough Love at Delancey," *San Francisco Chronicle,* March 17, 1996, p. B1, B3.
17. Redfield, *Tenth Insight,* p. 206.
18. Donna Horowitz, "Out of San Quentin by Their Bootstraps," *San Francisco Chronicle,* May 5, 1996, pp. A1, A6.
19. Salle Merrill Redfield, "Visionaries at Work: An Interview with John Horning," *The Celestine Journal* 3, no. 4 (April 1996), p. 4.
20. Ibid., p. 7.
21. Press Release, Goldman Environmental Foundation, San Francisco, CA, 1996.
22. Ibid., p. 4.
23. Ibid.

24. Ibid.
25. Bill Shore, *Revolution of the Heart: A New Strategy for Creating Wealth and Meaningful Change* (New York: Riverhead Books, 1995), p. 66.
26. Ibid., p. 83.
27. Ibid., pp. 72–73.
28. Ibid., p. 130.
29. Redfield, *Tenth Insight,* p. 234.
30. Kyriacos C. Markides, *Riding with the Lion* (New York: Penguin Books, 1995), p. 282.
31. Ibid., pp. 282–83.
32. Ibid., p. 304.

# About the Authors

JAMES REDFIELD lives with his wife, Salle, in Alabama. He is the author of *The Celestine Prophecy* and *The Tenth Insight: Holding the Vision*.

For information or subscriptions to *The Celestine Journal,* a monthly newsletter, call 1-800-814-6462 9 A.M. to 5 P.M. CST (Alabama). International orders: 1-205-620-9972.

CAROL ADRIENNE, M.A., is the co-author with James Redfield of *The Celestine Prophecy: An Experiential Guide.* She is also the author of *The Numerology Kit* and *Your Child's Destiny.* Ms. Adrienne has been an intuitive counselor, teacher, and lecturer since 1976.

For a free copy of *The Spiritual Path: Tips and Tales from the Spiritual Adventure* (a quarterly newsletter to which readers may contribute), send your name, address, and telephone number to Carol Adrienne, M.A., 12400 San Pablo Avenue, Suite 110, Richmond, CA 94805. Fax:510-235-6727 or tel:415-553-2535.

Twenty-five page personal Numerological Life Charts are also available at the above address.

THE TENTH INSIGHT
by James Redfield

**The journey continues in this eagerly awaited sequel to *The Celestine Prophecy*.**

*The Celestine Prophecy* and its companion *The Celestine Prophecy: An Experiential Guide* have taken the world by storm – capturing the spiritual moment and focusing on the quest for knowledge and enlightenment.

With *The Tenth Insight*, James Redfield continues the compelling spiritual adventure that began in *The Celestine Prophecy* and carries his readers further into a new spiritual understanding that is emerging in human culture throughout the world. As he travels beyond the here and now, he explores what might be called the Fourth Spatial Dimension, or the Afterlife Dimension, where Near Death Experiences occur. It is through the insights we gain on such spiritual journeys that we can reach a greater understanding of the way we live our lives and about the path of evolution as it relates to us today.

A Bantam Paperback
0 553 50440 1

**The phenomenal international bestseller**

**THE CELESTINE PROPHECY**
**An Adventure**
by James Redfield

*In the rain forests of Peru, an ancient manuscript has been discovered. Within its pages are nine insights into life itself – insights each human being is predicted to grasp sequentially, one insight then another, as we move toward a completely spiritual culture on Earth.*

*The Celestine Prophecy* contains secrets that are currently changing our world. Drawing on the ancient wisdom found in a Peruvian manuscript, it tells you how to make connections between the events happening in your own life right now . . . and lets you see what is going to happen to you in the years to come.

A book that has been passed from hand to hand, from friend to friend, since it first appeared in small bookshops across America, *The Celestine Prophecy* is a work that has come to light at a time when the world deeply needs to read its words. The story it tells is a gripping one of adventure and discovery, but it is also a guidebook that has the power to crystalize your perceptions of why you are where you are in life . . . and to direct your steps with a new energy and optimism as you head into tomorrow.

**A book that comes along just once in a lifetime to change lives forever**

'A fabulous book about experiencing life . . . I couldn't put it down'
*Elisabeth Kübler-Ross, M.D.*

A Bantam Paperback
0 553 40902 6

**The Celestine Prophecy:**
**AN EXPERIENTIAL GUIDE**
by James Redfield and Carol Adrienne

WHY ARE YOU HERE? WHO WILL YOU MEET? WHERE ARE YOU GOING? A GUIDE TO YOUR OWN PERSONAL ADVENTURE AS REVEALED BY **THE CELESTINE PROPHECY**

James Redfield's *The Celestine Prophecy* is an extraordinary, life-changing book. Perhaps you, like hundreds of thousands of readers, have discovered in its pages a new vision of coincidences in your own life, the energies involved in communicating with others, and the purposes behind human history.

Now this companion volume to that moving work helps you intensify and expand the exciting knowledge contained in each of the 9 insights of *The Celestine Prophecy*. Through detailed explanations and carefully designed exercises, you can uncover further revelations about your family and partners, and the ways your past has been a preparation for the special contribution you can make to the world. Most exciting of all, you can explore a deeper connection with your own personal energy and divine source.

Already in use by study groups all over America, *THE CELESTINE PROPHECY: AN EXPERIENTIAL GUIDE* fosters your spiritual growth by putting you in touch with the evidence of your own experience. From the First Insight to the Ninth, it clarifies ideas and directs your application of the Prophecy's message, empowering you to make an essential difference in the lives of the people you care about and the planet you cherish.

A Bantam Paperback
0 553 50370 7

**The Celestine Prophecy:**
**A POCKET GUIDE TO THE NINE INSIGHTS**
by James Redfield

Now the essence of *The Celestine Prophecy* can be with you always.

In this special pocket edition based on one of the most beloved spiritual guides ever published, author James Redfield defines, and concisely explains, each of the Nine Insights of *The Celestine Prophecy*.

A little book that you can carry everywhere and study at your convenience, it is a perfect way to keep in touch with our changing world and your unfolding adventure.

'[*The Celestine Prophecy*] **homes in on the deepest, most urgent search of our times, the search for meaning . . . This is a book like no other'** *Daily Telegraph*

Available from Bantam Books
0 553 50551 3